Treating Attachment Pathology

Treating Attachment Pathology

Jon Mills

𝒜

JASON ARONSON
Lanham • Boulder • New York • Toronto • Oxford

Published in the United States of America
by Jason Aronson
An imprint of Rowman & Littlefield Publishers, Inc.

A wholly owned subsidiary of
The Rowman & Littlefield Publishing Group, Inc.
4501 Forbes Boulevard, Suite 200, Lanham, Maryland 20706
www.rowmanlittlefield.com

PO Box 317
Oxford
OX2 9RU, UK

British Library Cataloguing in Publication Information Available

Library of Congress Cataloging-in-Publication Data

Mills, Jon, 1964–
    Treating attachment pathology / Jon Mills.
        p. cm.
    Includes bibliographical references and index.
    ISBN 0-7657-0130-8 (cloth : alk. paper) — ISBN 0-7657-0132-4 (pbk. : alk. paper)
    1. Attachment behavior—Case studies. 2. Attachment disorder in children—
Complications. 3. Psychology, Pathological—Treatment. 4. Psychoanalysis. I.
Title.

    RC455.4.A84M555 2005
    155.4'18—dc22   2004020771

Printed in the United States of America

∞™ The paper used in this publication meets the minimum requirements of
American National Standard for Information Sciences—Permanence of Paper
for Printed Library Materials, ANSI/NISO Z39.48-1992.

To my daughter Chloe
—*amor magnus doctor est*

It remains the first aim of the treatment to attach to it and to the person of the doctor. To ensure this, nothing need be done but to give him time. If one exhibits a serious interest in him, carefully clears away the resistances that crop up at the beginning and avoids making certain mistakes, he will of himself form such an attachment and link the doctor up with one of the imagos of the people by whom he was accustomed to be treated with affection.

—Freud

Contents

Preface

This book attempts to broach a comprehensive framework for conceptualizing and treating attachment pathology in a wide scope of clinical populations and diagnostic groups from a psychoanalytic perspective. I use the term *attachment pathology* to characterize the breadth of attachment-related disturbances that inform abnormal development, clinical symptomatology, and disorders of the self. While the term *pathology* has fallen into disfavor among certain psychoanalytic audiences, I believe we need to return to a discourse of pathology that appropriately eschews the divide between normativity and abnormality while instead emphasizing a distinction in functional and dysfunctional modes of being. Just as the Greek notion *pathos* (πάθος) signifies the enduring process of disease, pathology was first the study of human suffering. *Pathos* displaces the pejorative meaning the term has acquired in modern times by obfuscating the antipodes of normalcy and aberration within a more holistic ontology of human experience. For the Greeks, to be human is to suffer. Despite the fact that we are attempting to address the underlying dynamics of human experience that inform and explain dysfunctional attachments, attachment processes by nature are forged through forays into discomfort and psychic pain; hence our emphasis on pathology does not betray our humanistic commitments.

I should warn the reader up front that this project is not about the assessment and treatment of children, although I do rely on select case examples to illustrate various theoretical and diagnostic considerations; but rather this book is offered as one of the few existing clinically oriented contemporary works that examine attachment disorders in adults and adolescents. Attachment theory has garnered a great deal of burgeoning support from within the contemporary fields of academic developmental psychology, child psychiatry, pediatric medicine, psychophysiology, cognitive psychology, social work, and psychoanalysis with mounting empirical evidence to legitimize and substantiate its conceptual vitality and clinical utility. Concomitant with profuse findings from infant research and neuroscience—from the investigation of face-to-face regulatory dyadic interactions to dissociation and dreams—the interdependency of attachment studies, neurobiology, and cognitive science has lent substantial credibility to psychoanalytic viewpoints. Here I wish to reiterate the claim, following Bowlby, that the notion of attachment may be viewed as a general psychological theory that is substantially fortified by psychoanalytic interpretations of mind, parent–child relations, developmental, cognitive, and social maturation, and the intersubjective forces that govern normativity and psychopathology. Understanding attachment pathology in nonchildhood clinical populations becomes a much needed corrective. It is my overall expressed hope that this work will be received as a fresh paradigm for conceiving of and treating disorders of the self.

Interest and investigation in attachment processes were prepared by early object relations theorists, the British middle school, ego psychology, and the American interpersonal movement that flourished almost concurrently with early developmental research on attachment. After Bowlby and Ainsworth's time, attachment theory took a backseat until more recent behavioral scientists brought it out of hiding. Now it appears that attachment theory is very much in vogue, at least for the time being. Currently, the cornucopia of attachment research lends empirical credibility to psychoanalytic theories on object relations, the mother–infant interpersonal matrix, the primacy of relationality, and intersubjective dyadic systems approaches to understanding child development. Despite shifting currents in theory and practice, it becomes important for proponents of both attachment theory and psychoanalysis to respect theoretical differences and nuances without jeopardizing the possibility of seeing fruitful parallels and convergences with each respective discourse, methods of scientific inquiry, and technical interventions that guide the clinical process. Purists and loyalists may heckle at attempts to promote a comparative integration between these divergent schools on the grounds that it waters down their procedural considerations and preferred mode of colloquy, while others may view it as a welcome addition to clinical explication and theoretical diversity. Equally, there is an obscene amount of infighting among various advocates of psychoanalytic thought who may view complementarity and synthesis as an unwelcome trespass. If I can reach some type of middle ground, I will consider myself successful.

This book is intended to be of interest to the specialist and beginner alike. As a result, I have endeavored to navigate between more formal theoretical scholarship and technical principles to more relaxed monologue that may appear spontaneously in informal settings or communications among students and colleagues when discussing case studies. Admittedly, some of the text is dense and esoteric, while case presentations tend to be more "down to earth" and "real," grounded in the immediacy of the analytic process. Because this work is concentrated on clinical treatment, I have relied on dozens of case studies gathered from my many years of clinical experience and practice. The therapeutic dialogues presented here are authentic and not manufactured for aesthetic ingestion; thus, I have largely reproduced them in unedited form, and mainly from extensive process notes and tape recordings of actual sessions. In this way, the reader is afforded a genuine look into the parameters of intersubjective exchange that inform the treatment process. Appropriate attempts have been made to disguise all pertinent confidential information that could potentially breach a patient's privacy.

Throughout each chapter, I refer to *therapist*, *clinician*, and *analyst* interchangeably; they are meant to be viewed synonymously, whereby the clinician is under the direction of psychoanalytically informed principles guiding dynamic conceptualization and technique. While one may easily object to such convergences as a blurring of boundaries, I make them for the sake of parsimony with the hope that this work may appeal to a wide audience of readers who are not necessarily bound by psychoanalytic doctrine. Just as Merton Gill (1954) dismissed the necessity of the frequency of visits, duration of treatment, and the irrelevant nature of whether one lies on a couch or sits in a chair as appropriate criteria for conducting psychoanalysis—as did Jung, Ferenczi, and Fairbairn before him—the main issue in determining whether a therapy or formal psychoanalysis is analytic or not is whether the clinician follows a defensible protocol guided by psychoanalytic sensibility.[1] While therapists from any theoretical persuasion or training background may likely find this book of interest, it is within the spirit of psychoanalysis—literally the analysis of the human psyche—that I offer this contribution.

All references to Freud's texts will be to *The Standard Edition of the Complete Psychological Works of Sigmund Freud*, trans. and ed. James Strachey in collaboration with Anna Freud, assisted by Alix Strachey and Alan Tyson, 24 vols. (London: Hogarth Press, 1966–1995); however, I have relied on Freud's original German monographs compiled in his *Gesammelte Werke, Chronologisch Geordnet*, ed. Anna Freud, Edward Bibring, Willi Hoffer, Ernst Kris, and Otto Isakower, in collaboration with Marie Bonaparte, 18 vols. (London: Imago Publishing Co., 1940–1952). I have compared Strachey's translation to the *Gesammelte Werke* and provide my own in places that warrant changes. Attempts have been made to use gender-neutral referents; however, for the sake of euphony, and to avoid awkward locutions such as *s/he*, I have used the traditional masculine form and alternate between genders to equally signify both sexes.

Throughout this work, I have produced with permission revised portions from various articles that have appeared in previous forms: "Countertransference Revisited," *Psychoanalytic Review* 91, no. 4 (2004): 467–515; "Structuralization, Borderlineopathy, and Schizoid Phenomena," *Psychoanalytic Psychology* 21, no. 2 (2004): 319–26; "Structuralization, Trauma, and Attachment," *Psychoanalytic Psychology* 21, no. 1 (2004): 154–60; "Ameliorating Suicidality," *Psychologist-Psychoanalyst* 23, no. 4 (2003): 68–70; "Lacan on Paranoiac Knowledge," *Psychoanalytic Psychology* 20, no. 1 (2003): 30–51; "Deciphering the 'Genesis Problem': On the Dialectical Origins of Psychic Reality," *Psychoanalytic Review* 89, no. 6 (2002): 763–809; "Hegel on Projective Identification: Implications for Klein, Bion, and Beyond," *Psychoanalytic Review* 87, no. 6 (2000): 841–74; "Dialectical Psychoanalysis: Toward Process Psychology," *Psychoanalysis and Contemporary Thought* 23, no. 3 (2000): 20–54; and "Unconscious Subjectivity," *Contemporary Psychoanalysis* 35, no. 2 (1999): 342–47. I wish to thank the publishers for their courtesy.

I owe a debt of gratitude to my close friend and colleague John Perrin. His inspiration and talent as a clinician helped to plant the seed from which this project took growth. I also wish to extend my greatest appreciation to Andrew MacRae and the Research Institute at Lakeridge Health for providing me with a research grant with regard to this book. I am further grateful to Jason Aronson, who has enthusiastically supported and nurtured the production of this text. Equally, Sonya Kolba from Rowman & Littlefield has been a wonderful managing editor to work with, and I extend my profound thanks to her and her production staff.

NOTE

1. It should be noted that Freud originally conducted much shorter analyses—anywhere from a few weeks to a few months—especially in the early days of establishing psychoanalysis as a science (Grosskurth 1991; Jones 1955), and later preferred longer treatments, even taking his patients on his family vacations as a means to maintain his income (Roazen 1995). Alexander and French (1946) recommended decreasing the frequency of analytic sessions in order to manage the intensity of the transference and to promote less dependency (also see Alexander 1948), as did Jacobson (1971) with manic-depressive patients because they could not tolerate the closeness associated with daily sessions. Perhaps Fairbairn (1958) is most noted for sitting face to face while conducting analysis, although this has become a standard practice for many clinicians, including Jungians and self psychologists, as well as contemporary relational analysts. Other analysts have argued for shorter session times and duration of treatment, including Lacan (1973), who introduced variable-length sessions (*seances scandées*), while others have concluded that pragmatics, finances, expediency, and the amount of productivity seem to determine the time and length of an analysis (Thomä and Kächele 1987). As Gill (1984) put it, "One cannot simply assume that more is better. The optimal frequency may differ from patient to patient" (174). Hartocollis (2003) has recently pointed out that "the average analytic patient can hardly afford to pay as much per hour as

a one- or two-hours-per-week psychotherapy patient pays" (944n2). Although psychoanalysis is still popular in cosmopolitan Britain, bourgeois Europe, and Argentina's psy culture (Plotkin 2001), it is a common observation that in North America the demand for psychoanalysis has shrunk among the general public, which is more concerned about fast symptom relief for the least amount of money, a most unfortunate social phenomenon. But as Freud (1913) aptly reminds us, "Nothing in life is so expensive as illness—and stupidity" (133).

Introduction

Attachment theory and psychoanalysis have not shared a harmonious past. There have been decades of bitter feuds between these respective fields, resulting in a polarization of each discipline from the other. Much of the attachment research conducted today is largely extricated from psychoanalysis because of its emphasis on experimental methods, laboratory observation and measurement, and the dominance of scientifically informed principles dictated by quantification, parsimonious explanation, and reduction, not to mention its abhorrence for speculative theory. This group of attachment researchers is informed by the demands of empirical psychology and is radically different in terms of its education, training, and academic orientation in juxtaposition to psychoanalytic theoreticians and clinical practitioners, who rely on data culled from individual case studies, the phenomenology of self-reports and qualitative descriptions, and the primacy of inferential theory as an orienting and explanatory device that guides conceptualization and treatment considerations.

Peter Fonagy (2001) provides a brilliant exposition of the historical precursors informing tensions between attachment theory and psychoanalysis, as well as current controversies, points of contact, divergences, disagreements, and turf wars that continue to preside over each camp, thus potentially leading to incompatible theoretical projects, methodologies, case conceptualizations, and epistemologies governing each discipline. He argues that, due in part to Bowlby's ethological-scientific favoritism and his tendentious distortions of developmental psychoanalytic theory, the study of attachment became isolated from mainstream psychoanalysis for rigidly endorsing academic psychology over a creative synthesis and partnership between the two schools. In retaliation, psychoanalysis saw Bowlby as a rogue, and he was subsequently cut out. In the words of Jeremy Holmes (1995), he was "airbrushed out of the psychoanalytic record" (20). This was unfortunate yet understandable on many accounts, but contemporary attachment researchers and the psychoanalytic community are now beginning to see the value of mutual recognition.

We do not have to accept everything from attachment theory or psychoanalytic doctrine, which is neither possible nor desirable, in order to appreciate fruitful semblances in dynamic formulation, methods of inquiry, and their implications for clinical practice. Fonagy does not stress a complete convergence, but he succeeds admirably in showing the complex relationship and areas of overlap between the two fields, which do not share a coherent or unified set of propositions governing their respective discourses to begin with. While I do not wish to duplicate his important work here, Fonagy provides us, as do others before him, with a basic appreciation of how attachment dynamics have direct utility for the consulting room.

Throughout the psychological literature, attachment is typically associated with research in child development, pediatrics, early education, and psychosocial adjustment, with an emphasis on the biological, behavioral, and cognitive sequelae that accompany family, school, and peer relations. Rather than focusing on childhood populations, this book aims to be a unique contribution to understanding and treating attachment disturbances in adults and adolescents with a broad range of pathologies. It is here that I hope to persuade the reader to view attachment as a central ontological process informing the development of personality organization and unconscious structure. Attachment is the most fundamental organizing principle of the nascent psyche, and it concomitantly influences subsequent psychic development. It becomes necessary to view attachment as a broad theoretical construct potentially explaining myriad forms of normative and pathological processes for the simple fact that early attachment experiences become the bedrock of the emergent self, which furthermore conditions unconscious organization, ego development, object relations, adaptation and defense, fantasy formation, the experiential processes of identification, internalization, and representation, self-identity, and the overall evolution of personality structure. We should not assume that attachment begins and ends in childhood; rather, it is a contiguous developmental trajectory that informs adolescent and adult relations throughout the life cycle. This is why so many patients who present with complex and variegated clinical profiles, adjustment difficulties, and symptomatology have fundamental deficits in the capacity to form and sustain healthy relationships with others. Therefore, attachment-related pathologies constitute a disorder of the self in response to deficient, faulty, or failed attachments with significant caregivers early in life. Attachment pathology is a disorder of the self by virtue of the fact that personality structure is replete with developmental deficits and intrapsychic lacunae that continue to go unabated and hence spill over into sundry forms of clinical disorders and syndromes and the intersubjective milieu that defines psychosocial life. In this sense, attachment pathology is fundamentally rooted in early disturbances in object relations within the parent–child interpersonal matrix, which lead to structural deficits that constitute disorders of personality realized on a continuum of functional health and maladjustment.

Disruptions in early attachment security have been associated with a number of childhood difficulties and disorders, including moodiness and sadness (Kobak 1999); overstimulation, restlessness, and short attention span (Sroufe 1983); poor frustration tolerance and aggressiveness (Goldberg, Gotowiec, and Simmons 1995; Lyons-Ruth, Easterbrooks, and Cibelli 1997); oppositional defiance, poor peer relations, impulsivity, and problems in self-control (Carlson and Sroufe 1995); phobias and underachievement (Brisch 2002); conduct disorders (Shaw et al. 1996); anxiety and depression (Weinfield et al. 1999); chronic grief, mourning, and complicated bereavement (Fraley, Shaver, and Greenberg 1999); and gender identity disorder (Goldberg 1997), which can be seen as reliable predictor variables for anticipating maladaptive behavior and psychiatric conditions in adolescence and adulthood (Greenberg 1999; Jacobovitz and Hazen 1999). Attachment pathology in infancy has been correlated with anxiety (Warren et al. 1997), dissociation (Hesse and Main 2000; Ogawa et al. 1997), and severe psychopathology (Rosenstein and Horowitz 1996) in adolescents (including substance abuse, affective disorders, obsessive-compulsiveness, and character pathology); and linked to negative affect style (Diamond and Doane 1994), alexithymia (Troisi et al. 2001), eating disorders and addictions (Allen et al. 1996; Brisch 2002), mood and anxiety disorders (Armsden and Greenberg 1987; Blatt and Bers 1993), agoraphobia (Bowlby 1973), psychosomatic illness (Eagle 1999; Hazan and Shaver 1990), unresolved trauma (Allen et al. 1996), personality disorders (Gunderson 1996), suicide (Holmes 1996), authoritarianism (Hesse 1999), and relationship violence (Owen and Cox 1997) in adulthood.

Research in psychophysiology and neurobiology also offers evidence that attachment disturbances and early relational trauma affect neurological development (Barnett et al. 1999), right hemisphere brain lateralization (Siegel 1999), affect regulation (Taylor, Bagby, and Parker 1997), and trauma-induced impairments of the regulatory system in the orbitofrontal cortex, which may predispose the child to posttraumatic stress and dissociative disorders later in life (Schore 2001). These findings have led to a plethora of studies that conclude that disturbed and unresolved attachment processes condition parents to act in deficient and abusive ways toward their offspring (Cassidy and Shaver 1999; Fonagy 2001; Solomon and George 1999), thus ensuring that the transgenerational transmission of attachment pathology is likely to become an endemic, socially systemic epidemic. Although the relationship between attachment insecurity and psychiatric morbidity does not support the simple equation of a causal model (Fonagy et al. 1996), one would be hard-pressed to ignore the substantive correlations between early attachment disruptions and the development of psychopathology.

This book is organized into three main divisions: (I) Theoretical and Diagnostic Considerations; (II) Treatment Perspectives; and (III) Extended Case Studies. In the first part I am preoccupied with examining the scope, range, and qualitative degree of attachment-related phenomena in relation to the development of personality formation, object relations, unconscious self-structure, and psychopathology of the self. Chapter 1 is largely devoted to a historical overview of the attachment research field, beginning with classical theory and continuing through current classification systems and psychoanalytic constructs related to attachment, motivation, identification, and contemporary relational approaches. By situating attachment paradigms within the broader domain of psychoanalytic thought, we may gain advances in bridging the gulf between the often dichotomized fields of scientific psychology, phenomenology, inferential theory, and clinical practice.

Chapter 2 specifically considers attachment pathology as a disorder of the self. By drawing on clinical, developmental, and philosophical traditions in my conceptualization of the self, I argue for an integrative model of the self that incorporates drive theory and defense, schools of object relations, self psychology, and intersubjectivity within contemporary infant and developmental research. I further address the process of representation and fantasy in the neurobiology of interpersonal experience and show how attachment deficits lead to a disordered self plagued by object relations pathology that informs its instantiation.

Chapter 3 comprehensively explores the relationship between attachment, trauma, and character structure. Here I am particularly interested in advancing the thesis that attachment pathology is largely organized on borderline levels of functioning that derive from disorganized self-states resulting from developmental trauma. Attachment pathology results in deficient unconscious organizational processes within self-structure and predisposes patients toward developing character disorders with many overdetermined, polysymptomatic profiles. The effect of developmental trauma on attachment capacities and corresponding emergent structuralization processes is intimately associated with a broad array of clinical presentations that are largely organized on borderline levels of functioning. After highlighting the polysymptomatic spectrum of borderline conditions, I provide several case studies of children, adolescents, and adults and show how attachment deficits mediated by trauma lead to specific forms of structural pathology in personality organization. I conclude this part by offering my own classification system on structuralization and character development.

In part II, I am interested in exploring the basic parameters as well as advanced technical principles of conducting therapy with attachment disordered patients. Chapter 4 is a practical introduction to beginning the treatment and concentrates on the initial consultation. I argue for a relational philosophy of treatment as both an orienting technical posture and a means of ameliorating attachment deficits. Here I consider conceptual and procedural issues for assessment and intervention within the initial phase of therapy, focus on engendering mutual collaboration, and address the pragmatics of conducting business practices. In the next chapter I turn to the nature of establishing a therapeutic alliance through empathic responsiveness, recognition, and incremental intimacy with this difficult population group. Through extensive case material I give specific attention to the clinical phenomena of benign resistance, premature termination, malignant transference, and alliance disruptions.

Chapter 6 outlines a dialectical approach to working with primitive defenses. Beginning with the dynamics of denial, paranoiac knowledge, and the avoidant need for flight from emotional pain, I then trace the phenomenology of the erotic transference, therapeutic impasse, mitigation of suicidality, containment of psychotic anxieties, and de-escalation of potential violence in vulnerably attached patients.

The question, nature, and meaning of countertransference continues to be a contested theoretical and clinical phenomenon. In chapter 7, I examine classical through contemporary perspectives and argue that countertransference is best understood within an emergent dialectical framework of intersubjective relations. I then make an appeal for us to face countertransference honestly, within ourselves and within our profession, as a human subjective process that must be embraced rather than repudiated under the illusion of transcendence. After offering a comprehensive spectrum of various countertransference reactions that often beset the analyst, including those specific to attachment disorders, I then turn our attention to the role of projective identification as unconscious communication and offer general strategies for transmuting countertransference.

In chapter 8, I address the therapeutic efficacy of reaching the affect and working through conflicted emotional resonance states that continue to nourish and sustain structural pathology. Following a theoretical inquiry into the psychoanalytic theory of emotions; the relationship between affect, trauma, and attachment; the emotional tie to the clinician; reservations around the disclosure of feelings; and the vulnerability of abreaction, I elaborate the process of working through within the context of attachment disordered affect styles.

In the final part, I provide detailed case histories, including course of treatment and extended dynamic formulations of working with three highly traumatized, attachment disordered patients. Taken together, this work constitutes a treatise on the psychic processes of attachment governing self-organization, adaptation, and conflicted interpersonal dynamics, and on the intervening relational parameters in treating their emergent clinical pathologies. Whether this project yields a fruitful contribution to our understanding of attachment-related disturbances will be up to others to decide, but my hope is that this venture will at least generate increased appreciation for the value and potential harmonies between attachment perspectives and psychoanalytic practice.

I

THEORETICAL AND DIAGNOSTIC CONSIDERATIONS

1

ꙮ

Conceptualizing
Attachment Pathology

Arguably one of the most important realizations of twentieth-century health care was the necessary and inextricable connection between psychological development and an infant's attachment to its mother. By contemporary standards, an infant's being deprived of sufficient attachment potentially constitutes child abuse and is grounds for the legal apprehension of that child in order to ensure that it receives basic legislative rights as deemed humane by most civilized societies. The promulgation of child welfare is such an entrenched social value that it becomes unfathomable in industrialized countries to question this basic tenet. Psychoanalysis teaches us that what goes on during infantile development largely conditions how a child will become later in life—to the degree that causal inference becomes a presupposition underlying the notion of psychic determinism.[1]

Since John Bowlby's and Mary Ainsworth's groundbreaking observational research on childhood attachment patterns, there is no longer any doubt that early relational experiences with parents substantially determine the course of personality development and adjustment.[2] The relational primacy of the parent–child attachment is so elemental and influential on the formative stages of psychic organization that without such rudimentary bonds, the self could hardly emerge nor thrive. It is widely accepted among developmental, clinical, and psychoanalytic paradigms that the mode and style of parental relatedness—especially from the maternal object—leaves lasting impressions on the child's burgeoning self-structure and related ego capacities. Developmental psychoanalysts, from Klein to Winnicott, Sandler, Mahler, Brody, Kohut, Emde, and Stern, among others, have long since alerted us to how early parental responsiveness patterns can build, hinder, facilitate, and/or delay childhood psychic development. Whether this parental response takes the form of a general failure in relational attunement and responsiveness from an optimal holding environment (Winnicott 1965), or the inability to contain projected internal disruptions, fears, and anxieties (Klein 1946; Bion 1962a), which thereby leads to further ruptures in role-responsive solicitations (Sandler 1976), and/or the delivery of vital selfobject needs (Kohut 1971, 1977),[3] such as empathic understanding, validation, and affirmation of the self—the unequivocal evidence that early parental interaction affects the process of human attachment becomes an irrefutable empirical fact.

The aim of this book is to give attention to a much neglected area in the conceptualization and treatment of attachment disorders. The interface between attachment, psychic structure, and character pathology has been largely ignored in the clinical literature until recent years, and, when discussed, it has been generally relegated to the domain of child psychopathology. Because human attachment is such a basic aspect of motivation and adjustment, attachment disruptions in childhood color psychic development and often leave deep and enduring deficits in personality and adaptive functioning. Most of the literature on attachment disorders is based on developmental, empirical-observational research in children (Atkinson and Zucker 1997; Hughes 1997; Solomon and George 1999). As a result, there are few works on the application of childhood attachment theory to adult populations (see Simpson and Rholes 1998; Sperling and Berman 1994), and there is virtually nothing on the understanding and treatment of attachment pathology in adolescents.

Throughout this project, it will become important for us to repeatedly focus on how attachment-related deficiencies negatively affect character development, adaptation, and interpersonal functioning, thus leading to a cornucopia of concurrent, comorbid, and superimposed mental disorders that typically accompany this population group. Rather than emphasize the treatment of childhood attachment disorders, a subject the literature is already replete with discussions of, I will be more concerned with addressing attachment theory in the clinical context of treating character pathology manifested in adolescence and in adult populations across the lifespan. In order to orient ourselves toward conceptualizing the nature of attachment pathology, we will first need to focus on theoretical considerations primarily derived from the developmental and psychoanalytic literature. Then we will turn our attention toward diagnostic and treatment approaches with a wide variety of psychiatric populations with diverse and overdetermined psychological profiles; our exploration will be grounded in extensive individual case studies garnered from my clinical practice and experience as a psychologist and psychoanalyst.

Among the broad spectrum of attachment pathology typically viewed in the literature, there is an overwhelming emphasis on impairment in early parent–infant interactions, which leads to developmental ruptures throughout childhood that are by and large quite predictable. For example, from a phenomenological standpoint, when a small child is removed from his biological parents due to neglect, abuse, or abandonment and then placed into an unfamiliar foster home environment, that child more often than not suffers further adjustment problems based on the simple fact that he was removed from his primary attachment figures. Most of the research has concentrated on the psychological and physiological correlates of attachment disorders in infancy and the resulting social and cognitive sequelae of maladjustment exhibited in family, school, and peer relations (Jacobvitz and Hazen 1999; Moss, St-Laurent, and Parent 1999). Yet the long-term impact of early attachment deficits on character structure (and subsequent psychosocial adaptation) has been barely addressed in the context of clinical intervention, despite the burgeoning prevalence of interpersonally based conflicts curtailing capacities for healthy relatedness, intimacy, and individual adjustment. What is especially germane is how qualitative deficiencies in early object relationships deleteriously affect personality development and the rudiments of psychic structure. As a result, attachment disordered patients tend to present with differential forms of character pathology accompanied by diverse complaints and multiply determined clinical symptoms. Therefore, it is understandable why many clinicians are often confused and even lost when attempting to conceptualize or diagnose patients who present with sundry psychiatric profiles. Based upon my work as an applied clinician, I will attempt to show that those with attachment deficiencies and associated characterological vulnerabilities have fundamental structural deficits in personality organization that lie at the heart of our current understanding of disorders of the self.

ATTACHMENT PATHOLOGY AS DISORDER OF THE SELF

A central thesis I will continually emphasize throughout this book is that attachment pathology is a disorder of the self. Although the conceptualization of the self and its related clinical manifestations will be thoroughly addressed in our next chapter, it becomes important to highlight the notion that the basic organizing principles of psychic functioning are fundamentally contingent on a relational-intersubjective system of mutually regulating dyadic attachments. The earliest maternal bond and the resulting interactions (viz., biological-anaclitic-affective-communicative) that fuel and fortify object relatedness become foundational structures of subjectivity that predispose the self toward a developmental trajectory of seeking human affiliation. Therefore, incipient psychic structure is forged through attachment processes from the beginning of life, and these processes inform both mental health and illness.

Attachment theorists identify the first seven months of life as the primary formative period in developing capacities for human relatedness, including the introjection of maternal responsiveness and selfobject functions necessary for building and regulating a cohesive sense of self. While it is often thought that attachment disorganization—here used to denote the disorganization of the self—is associated with extreme forms of developmental arrest such as autism, it is also associated with less severe but, arguably, equally troubling clinical conditions. Attachment difficulties are both (1) *structurally* manifested, that is, in terms of their penetrable impact on the unconscious ontology of psychic organization, and (2) *phenomenologically* realized, hence marked by their qualitative, behavioral, epistemological, and experiential valences that saturate conscious subjective existence.

Attachment pathology largely results in structural deficits of the self due to the incorporation, amalgamation, and buildup over time of toxic introjects, negatively internalized objects, and resultant disturbances in self-representation that are unconsciously organized and form in direct response to developmental failures in parental attachment. Such attachment disruptions impinge on self-integrity and the formation of secure object relationships, thereby leaving uncohesive self-states and unabated unconscious conflicts that perpetuate structural disfiguration. Various defenses are mobilized during attachment disturbances and often lead to dissociated inner experiences that become encoded and organized on somatic and subsymbolic levels of representation dominated by emotional schemas and unconscious fantasy systems that are recalcitrant to linguistic mediation or transmogrification. Because attachment pathology materializes out of myriad and profound developmental traumas, self-structure is constantly assailed by disruptions in affect regulation that often lead to deficits in self-reflexivity and in functional capacities for developing an observing ego, thereby generally predisposing patients toward borderline levels of adaptation.

Attachment pathology is a disorder of the self based on the simple deduction that personality development is predicated on human relatedness, without which the self would not exist.[4] And just as the self cannot exist in isolation from otherness, the disordered self always stands in juxtaposition to disturbances in interpersonal functioning. As I will argue, disruptions in acquiring healthy capacities for attachment and self-regulation are often due to real or perceived *developmental traumas*. Whether discrete, acute, or cumulative, such traumas may be as overt as surviving early childhood sexual molestation, abandonment, tenuous foster care placements, parental neglect in caregiving abilities, and split or blended home environments, or they may be moderate forms of prolonged emotional abuse or repeated rejection, invalidation, and failed responsiveness from a parent. Furthermore, and perhaps equally insidious, developmental trauma is often *cryptic* and *secretive*—confined to the privatization of lived subjective reality—such as the experiential presence of relational privation, absence, and lack. Developmental traumas leave an affective aftermath that often escapes linguistic mediation and conceptual understanding; because the child is particularly susceptible during preverbal experience prior to the formal acquisition of language, these traumas are translinguistic and ontologically imprinted on the deep structural configurations of the psyche. As a result, they largely persist as unconscious emotional resonance states, affective schemas, fantasy systems, and representations of embodiment that vacillate between moments of unrecognizable conflict, which affect mood and coping strategies, and internal somatic disruptions that cannot be consciously accessed or articulated by the subject. Such traumas are typically ineffable and tarry through pronounced fixations to psychic pain.

Developmental trauma is largely informed by *toxic introjects*, which are highly selected and specified experiences of psychic reality that are emotionally charged, mnemonically encoded, unconsciously organized, and dominated by the fixed presentation of negativity in the mind that sullies self and object representation. Toxic introjects are taken in at a very early age and form the cumulative bedrock of self-structure under the constant press of unconsciously enlisted variants. Because an infant or small toddler is highly susceptible to the malignant effects of toxic introjects that transpire during the sensory-motor and preoperational stages of cognitive development, these introjects are likely to be registered and organized through sensory-somatic processes or bodily representations that cluster into affective schemas that typically occur before the acquisition of language and are therefore largely segregated from linguistic intervention. Because toxic introjects are incorporated during the emotional immediacy of interpersonal conflict or fear, they acquire an affective significance or prereflective semiotic meaning that is imbued within the introject itself as it is related to self-representation. In fact, these introjects fall under the spell of chaos and negative contagion ruled by unconscious fantasy systems that inform structuralization processes. Moreover, the content of such introjects is often naively, concretely, and uncritically absorbed as unadulterated truth and is thus callow and vulnerably registered as inexpressible, preformulated trauma that is not acknowledged as such because it becomes sensuously dissociated, affectively filtered, and somatically converted on unconscious symbolic levels subjected to fantasy formations that are foreclosed from linguistically intervening semantic processes. Developmental traumas are therefore pathognomonic occasions delivered by the hands of attachment figures that are often not subject to self-reflective, self-conscious awareness at the time of their occurrence because they are early formative acquisitions. As a result, they tarry in agitated unconscious self-states of inarticulate and unarticulated trauma imbued with emotional significance, manipulated by fantasy, and sequestered from conscious awareness, for they linger as unformulated unconscious experience yet materialize through various forms of psychopathology.

If attachment breaches occur within the primary relational dyad—such as with the unabated internalization of negative introjects, or pervasive threatening, critical, judgmental, shameful, and/or devaluing experiences that retard the cultivation of psychic cohesion—then we may reliably predict future impairment in psychological adaptation. More specifically, because attachment evokes, kindles, and bolsters psychic structure, core capacities for affect tolerance, anxiety regulation, reality testing, and executive ego functioning are fundamentally informed by the archaic primacy of early internalized representations influencing self-organization. While it may be argued that early attachment experiences largely inform the trajectory of developmental sequelae and predispose the self toward future patterns of relatedness, this does not necessarily mean, with qualifications, that attachment capacities are predetermined or fixed, only that degrees of enactment and qualitative modes of freedom are mediated by archaic pressures. It is often the case, however, that when attachment pathology is present in childhood, we may later observe truncated adjustment and psychic lacunae in adolescent and adult character structures. From a clinical standpoint, this is an uncontested certainty: I have never encountered a patient who has not suffered from some form of self-deficiency, an observation that may extend to us all.[5]

The term *attachment* elicits connotations associated with the field of ethology and, more specifically, the biological interactions and regulating components of maternal-infant bonding, nurturance, and organismic thriving derived from our animal evolutionary past. Yet this common assumption is both insufficient and imprecise. Not only is attachment biologically mediated, but it is also ontically conditioned and socially derived from reciprocal (albeit asymmetrical) dyadic interactions predicated on intersubjective processes; thus, attachment is the groundwork of psychic development. But the word *attachment* also carries a more basic meaning: namely, to fasten onto, affix, or conjoin [OFr. *attachier*, > ME *attachen*]. Attachment is a *process of connection*, a binding to another based on a need—biological, affective, interpersonal—for human relatedness and affectional fulfillment. Therefore, as I will argue, the nature of attachment is not merely a biological mechanism; rather, it is largely an *emotional process* based upon affective ties, relational longings, and primary identifications with love objects.

Attachment motivations are informed by instinctual, innate pressures—hence constitutional processes inherent to our embodiment—and normatively instantiated in every human culture, yet they are neither fixed or static behavioral tropisms nor merely determined by behavioral genetics. Instead, they are unconsciously informed organizing principles within a relational ontology directing intrapsychic activity from the most primordial impulses to the higher constellations of reflective self-conscious life. I concur with Mary Main (1999) that attachment involves a unique or special form of affectional bond to a select few identified caregivers, who are usually parents, and should not be viewed as affectional feelings in general, such as a child's developing bond to peers or others who may be viewed among a whole host of significant relationships, such as a relative or the family dog. Nor do we wish to equate the mother's bonding to the infant shortly after birth with attachment. Attachment is a developmental achievement having evolutionary, biological, and regulatory interactional elements elaborated within a socially constructed matrix with overdetermined motivations for procuring protection and safety via parental proximity, thereby regulating fear, anxiety, and affect; this accomplishment leads to an increased emotional dependency on an identified attachment figure.

It may be useful to distinguish between what we mean by (a) attachment disorders, (b) attachment deficits, and (c) attachment vulnerability, for there is potentially a great deal of overlap and specificity depending on how we define our terms. Attachment disorders, as I conceptualize them, largely denote a delineated range of clinical symptomatology due to compromised object relations development resulting in structural pathology of the self. Attachment deficits refer to structural limitations or deficiencies within personality formation that interfere with actualizing various attachment-related capacities instantiated on a continuum of functional health and maladjustment. Finally, attachment vulnerabilities are typically normative processes that all people possess, yet they may inform structural deficits of the self. In turn, deficits in self-structure always prefigure attachment pathology.

There is a far-reaching spectrum of attachment-related disorders—from the pervasive developmental disorders, to the residual impact of trauma, abuse, neglect, loss, and/or complicated grief, which further induces characterological and dissociative disruptions in the self, often leading to intolerable abandonment, psychotic, and annihilation anxieties. Whereas personality structure bulwarks early attachment experiences via defensive constellations, thus serving to facilitate or encumber adaptation due to these developmental encounters, psychic organizational resources (along with capacities to enact and attach to objects) emerge on an intrapsychic *continuum* and are therefore interpersonally realized *contextually* based upon one's experiential contingencies. As I will outline later, the formation of the self is fundamentally organized around the equiprimordial function of modifying internal impulses and subjective affective resonance states—hence unconsciously derived processes—and internalizing object (and part-object) presentations based upon the available resources the self has to initiate and draw from its continuum of attachment

need to

capacities. This is why it becomes an important task for us to understand the development of the attachment disordered self in relation to character structure and specifically illuminate the nature of intrapsychic deficits that manifest themselves in intersubjective clinical contexts.

The clinical literature is preoccupied with attachment disorders in childhood on the one hand, and character pathology in adulthood on the other, primarily focusing on borderline, narcissistic, and antisocial manifestations. Here a comment about adolescent attachment pathology is warranted. Adolescent psychic development is normatively inconsistent and fluctuational at best (Blos 1962), and tumultuous at worst (Erikson 1950), dominated by emotional and cognitive transformations in parental, family, and peer relationships (Allen and Land 1999). Given the pervasive social pressures and tribulations that influence adolescent adjustment in our increasingly multicultural and geopolitical environments, we are hard-pressed to see those unaffected by the conflicts that absorb North American culture, including violence, racism, addiction, trauma, crime, domestic abuse, ethnocentrism, and religious fanaticism, just to name a few. Adding to these challenges, when psychic organization is besieged by dysfunctional attachment experiences, it is no wonder that we are encountering an epidemic of personality disorders among our youth.

Adolescent character pathology is an important topic to address, and generally the literature has either admonished us not to pass diagnostic labels or has ruled out the possibility of making definitive judgments regarding adolescent personality disorders to begin with. This argument, put laconically, is that personality formation in adolescence is still developing and open to multiple influences; hence, it is not as permanent or enduring as adult character structure; and, therefore, we should be prudent in our clinical formulations of attributing character pathology to adolescent development, which is subject to a fluidity of changing factors. We must be respectful of and sensitive to this caveat; however, this argument assumes that character pathology may only be attributed to a self-structure that is stable and enduring over time, when in fact the self is a temporal *process* of transforming and mediating experience, punctuated by competing desires, defenses, and social-environmental interactions. Here it becomes important to note that when I refer to psychic structure, I am referring to *unconsciously mediated processes* that provide temporal (momentary) unification and synthetic adaptation to the myriad forces that besiege and populate mental life. Psychic structure is never fixed, static, stagnant, or reified as immutable properties or attributes inhering in the mind. Mind is pure *activity*, the process of its own becoming (Mills 1996). Therefore, structural organization refers to how intrapsychic processes operate to form invariances that are relatively stable over time yet are transmutable within their own contingencies and contexts. It is for descriptive purposes that I refer to psychic structure as enduring, for it signifies the deeper ontological configurations that inform unconscious organizing principles and their mental derivatives. The self, both structurally and phenomenologically, is constantly in a process of becoming marked by the transmogrification of subjective human experience in relation to the world. From this standpoint, adult character is no more fixed or complete than adolescent personality simply because the psyche is always dialectically evolving (Mills 2002a). As a result of this oversight, many important insights on adolescent character formation are glossed over or omitted altogether, especially insights on the precarious and transient nature of attachments, the inner diffusion of cohesive self-states, the dissociability of the psyche, and the fragmentary and depressive anxieties that plague normative development, let alone their clinical counterparts. When these factors are compounded by early attachment disturbances affecting psychic structure and ego regulatory functions, more severe forms of character pathology, including psychotic, schizoid, borderline, sociopathic, and narcissistic organizations, serve to *bind the threat* of psychic fracturing and compensate (albeit maladaptively) for failed or faulty attachments. Put another way, character pathology is a compensatory defense as compromise formation against the impending threat of a disintegrating self due to defective attachments and chronically deficient selfobject experiences.

Before we address the concept and function of attachment theory in treating disorders of the self, it becomes necessary to survey the literature on infant and childhood development in order to understand the force and loci of early attachments in the process of psychic formation. Since Bowlby's and Ainsworth's studies of securely and insecurely attached children during laboratory conditions of separation and reunion with their mothers, attachment research has centered on providing more descriptive explanations of attachment-related stress and illness. As with any field of inquiry, points of disagreement and controversy exist among researchers and clinicians on methodological and definitional considerations, on how to interpret observational data, and on generating viable new hypotheses and conceptual models on the nature and function of attachment. What proves especially relevant is how various inferences can be drawn about the preverbal child and his or her inner representational world, dynamic conflicts, defensive constellations, and the structural organizations of the psyche. Because the attachment literature is highly dominated by developmental and empirically driven observational research, relatively little has been said about attachment processes in the clinical encounter. While attachment researchers have proffered classification approaches and clinical annotations derived from observation, they have preferred ethobiological, psychosocial, and systemic models of explanation rather than those that are more psychoanalytically informed. With the exception of Bowlby (1973, 1980), who examines the role of inner representation and defense, and Daniel Stern (1985), who attempts to provide a speculative developmental narrative on the internal subjective experience of the infant, the attachment field has virtually ignored the ontological rudiments and unconscious reverberations of attachment-related phenomena and their impact on self-experience. I am specifically concerned with understanding the psychodynamics of attachment pathology within the relational matrix, its intrapsychic impact on character formation and adjustment, and its clinical and therapeutic consequences.

CLASSICAL ATTACHMENT THEORY

Bowlby's three-volume magnum opus, *Attachment* (1969), *Separation* (1973), and *Loss* (1980), represents the foundation of classical attachment theory. While psychoanalysis since Freud has emphasized the ubiquity of psychogenic childhood conflict within adult personality functioning, Bowlby was one of the first developmental theorists to apply empirical-observational methods to aid in clinical speculations on the emerging inner world of the naive infant. More specifically, he systematically drew attention to the mother's role and impact on the child's developing psyche, and, as a corollary, the predictive influences she later has on psychological adjustment.[6] Bowlby has not always found support among psychoanalysts, primarily for deviating from classical theory with his own competing theory of motivation; however, his approach is largely compatible with psychodynamic paradigms.

For Bowlby, attachment is a universal social instinct influenced by the contingencies of the maternal environment.[7] Bowlby's (1969) conception of attachment largely draws on an ethological framework of behavior based on Darwinian biology, control systems theory, evolutionary psychology, object relations theory, and cognitive information processing models; he thus produces a grand theory of personality development that extends across the lifespan. It may be said that Bowlby's model rests on the interrelatedness of three main constructs: (1) activation of the attachment behavioral system; (2) the role of self and object representations; and (3) strategies of defensive exclusion. According to Bowlby, the attachment system constitutes a constellation of internal goal-directed behaviors and intentions aimed at promoting and procuring proximity to an identified attachment figure, usually the mother. Under variable perceptual and cue-related circumstances, the attachment system (viz., the child's subjective agency) becomes activated to seek satisfaction from the attachment figure via close proximity and protection from encroaching threats that may disrupt desired levels of security. A vast range of conditions, both internal and extrinsic to the infant or child, may affect the attachment system, including strange situations, the presence of others, perceived alterations in the environment, fatigue or illness, the awareness of being alone, and the caregiver's physical absence. When the environment is experienced as nonthreatening, the child is more likely to engage in other goal-directed activities such as play or exploration, although monitoring the environment for possible sources of threat continues to be an adaptive behavioral habit.

Bowlby envisioned the attachment system as a dynamic tension, evident from birth onward, between the mother's and infant's individual needs and actions, activities that both promote and hinder dyadic proximity, and behaviors that promote the child's autonomous exploration and mastery of the environment. Bowlby stressed how perceptual experiences, affective states, and emotional appraisals are associated with activation levels of needs for attachment. Generally, low activation levels are correlated with positive internal states and feelings of safety, while high activation levels are mobilized during the presence of intense negative affect, anxiety, alarm, fear, or dread. When the attachment figure is perceived as being unavailable or inconsistent, anger and sadness are typical accompanying emotional reactions.

In concurrence with many object relations paradigms, Bowlby (1973) proposed that during late infancy the child's attachment patterns become increasingly organized at the representational and behavioral levels. Representational models or schemas of self and others, primarily the mother, are constructed and serve to facilitate internal cohesion of the self; to judge the accessibility and willingness of the attachment figure to provide functions of protection, warmth, and care; and to guide future appraisals and goal-directed behavior. Bowlby (1980) argued that self and object representational models are fairly aligned when child-rearing practices foster feelings of lovability and security in the child; but when the attachment figure is perceived as inconsistent, unreliable, rejecting, and/or unresponsive, the child struggles with integrating these contradictory and incompatible experiences. As a result, the child fights to avoid negative appraisals of self and others that might bring about emotional pain and trepidation if she were to accept such appraisals as real or accurate.

Following homeostasis theory, Bowlby envisioned attachment as a system motivated to maintain a balanced state in the service of the organism's overall functioning. The caregiver is the child's instinctive line of defense against physiological, environmental, and psychological stress of all kinds. Once a bond has been formed to the maternal figure, any threat of the actual or perceived loss of the mother, as well as the mother's love and protection, must be negated or minimized through defensive strategies that exclude these painful realizations from conscious awareness. When persistent attempts—calling, searching, pleading, banging objects, and/or crying—fail to regain the mother during separation, denial, thought blocking, suppression, and repression are common defensive maneuvers.

Bowlby defined two qualitatively distinct forms of defensive exclusion, namely, *deactivation* and *disconnection*: the child is able to stifle object-seeking affects and appraisals or detach altogether, thereby barring such processes from entering consciousness. When the child's subjective experience of defensive exclusion is chronic and austere, activation levels of attachment remain heightened but unfulfilled. This situation often leads to more profound attacks on the attachment system, whereby the child's affective, behavioral, and representational appraisals deteriorate. Under these prolonged conditions of assault on the attachment system, various capacities for information processing and psychic regulation are "segregated" from attachment motivations; this segregation potentially leads to pathological forms of exclusion and distance from the maternal object.

Bowlby's observations of prolonged child–mother separation, experiences of loss, and disciplinary actions taken against the child for displaying attachment-seeking behavior led him to conclude that segregated systems were attempts to preserve positive self and object representations and stave off disabling anxiety that overwhelms ego functioning. Under certain circumstances, sometimes quite idiosyncratic ones, unconscious processes are evoked by attachment-relevant cues that serve to breach repressed material. But when inhibitory or segregating processes are circumvented, attachment patterns may appear quite dysfunctional, chaotic, and unpredictable, thus leading to: (1) a pronounced absence of attachment-soliciting activity in situations where it is warranted or expected; (2) out-of-context or out-of-control behaviors, affects, and cognitive disruptions; and/or (3) a vacillation between these ambitendent states (Solomon and George 1999).

EARLY ATTACHMENT CLASSIFICATION

Bowlby's (1969) theory was derived from an extensive body of detailed observational research on children who had experienced major separations from their mothers or an identified attachment figure when placed in an unfamiliar environment such as a hospital or residential nursery. Bowlby (1973) noted that when separation from the mother was strained and protracted, often the child's behavior upon the mother's return was considered to be anxious, ambivalent, or detached. Robertson and Bowlby (1952) first presented their findings based on observations of toddlers separated from their parents, which led to a series of controlled experiments by Heinicke and Westheimer (1966). These studies showed that toddlers separated from their parents, placed in unfamiliar surroundings, and provided with no subsidiary caregivers underwent three stages of response to separation, namely, (1) *protest*, (2) *despair*, and (3) *detachment*.

≫ During the initial period after separation, children's preoccupations with the missing parent were quite salient: they would typically display signs of protest through verbal solicitation, crying, and hopeful anticipation of their mother's return. Within a few days, however, toddlers entered into anguished states of despair characterized by helplessness, weak and hopeless periods of crying, and visible withdrawal from the environment, including interactions with others. In the final stage, children began to "settle in" their new environment and attended to immediate interactions and experiential activities with nurses and other children. However, children who reached this stage of detachment actively avoided, ignored, and even, in some cases, failed to recognize the attachment figure upon her return. What is particularly interesting is that secondary attachment figures, such as the father, relatives, or neighbors, were instantly recognized and greeted by the detached children. This points to the power of repressive forces rather than the simple failure of memory (see Main 2000),[8] which further led Bowlby to develop a defense hypothesis as part of his attachment theory. From today's standpoint, such defensive exclusions can be readily interpreted as acts of dissociation. It is not surprising that children's reactions to these forms of parental abandonment parallel conflicted experiences of adult depression, chronic grief, failed or complicated mourning and loss, object relations pathology, and structural deficiencies of the self that accompany characterological disorders.

Bowlby's research influenced Mary Ainsworth and her colleagues to develop a classification system of dysfunctional attachment patterns in child populations based on their responses when exposed to encounters with strangers (Ainsworth et al. 1978). From her extensive naturalistic-observational research in Kampala, Uganda, and Baltimore, Maryland, involving direct mother–infant interactions in their home environments, Ainsworth developed a laboratory-based procedure she called the *strange situation*. From her research, Ainsworth identified three main behavioral classifications: (1) *secure*, (2) *avoidant*, and (3) *resistant/ambivalent* manifestations. In the strange situation, infants are likely to exhibit a range of behaviors upon the reunion with the mother, including gaze aversion, physical distancing, redirecting of their attention to the physical environment, and other approach–avoidance demonstrations; however, within two minutes these children are usually prone to initiate interaction with their mothers when separation under supportive conditions has been favorable (Main 1981; Robertson and Robertson 1989). Regardless of the infant's reaction to the strange situation (customarily ranked as A, B, or C classifications), immediate "cutoff" behavior following the mother's reappearance after separation is nearly a universal feature.

Ainsworth found that secure organizations were promoted by mothers who were sensitive to their infants' distress signals and cue-related communications, while detached-avoidant, resistant, and ambivalent organizations were related to maternal unpredictability and overt rejection. She further observed that unfavorable reunion responses were exhibited by twelve-month-old infants from nonseparated environments, a phenomenon typically observed in older toddlers (Main 2000). This observation in all likelihood may be the result of cumulative strain due to chronic maternal unresponsiveness, unpredictability, and/or deficiency (Kris 1956; Sandler 1967).

It may be postulated that reorienting attentional faculties to the surround or engaging in displacement activities, such as manipulating physical objects, is a defensive means of warding off conflict by modulating behavioral arousal. Avoidant behaviors allow the child to temporarily resolve such conflicts and prepare the way for reconnection. Those classified as secure or ambivalent, however, are more likely to show immediate signs of attachment-seeking behavior or displays of anger directed toward the mother. When separation from primary caregivers is protracted for several weeks, it is not surprising that severe adjustment disturbance is noted upon reunion, including profound disorientation to the current environment, confusion, affect suppression, behavioral withdrawal from the mother, detachment, extreme passivity, and many variations of these conditions (Bowlby 1973).

CONTEMPORARY PERSPECTIVES ON DISORGANIZED ATTACHMENT

There are a number of contemporary developmental researchers who have greatly advanced our understanding of attachment-related disorders, including Mary Main, Erik Hesse, Carol George, Judith Solomon, Nancy Kaplan, Patricia Crittenden, Peter Fonagy, Mary Target, Karlen Lyons-Ruth, Jeremy Holmes, Karl Heinz Brisch, Otto Weininger, Morris Eagle, and many others who are important to include among this abbreviated list. Focusing mainly on childhood populations, their work proves invaluable for understanding attachment pathology. Main and Solomon (1990) have recently advanced the attachment classification system to include a fourth subgroup of behavioral responses called *disorganized/ disoriented* attachment (referred to as the D classification), which they argue may explain Bowlby's segregated systems hypothesis, Ainsworth's observations of resistant and avoidant attachment aversions, and those behavioral indicators that are unclassifiable under previous criteria. Indices of disorganization and disorientation include

a. sequential display of contradictory behavioral patterns, such as displays of attachment gestures or anger followed abruptly by avoidance or dazed responsiveness;

b. simultaneous display of contradictory behavior, such as proximity-seeking yet contact-resisting enactments;

c. undirected, misdirected, incomplete, and interrupted movements and expressions;

d. stereotypies, asymmetrical movements, mistimed movements, and anomalous posturing;

e. freezing, stilling, and slowed movements and expressions; and

f. parental apprehension.

Main and Hesse (1990) claim that disorganized attachment is due to the child's perception of the caregiver as frightening and/or frightened, which causes contradictory reactions of approach-avoidance due to the agitated level of attachment motivations. It is often the case statistically that attachment disordered children come from developmental backgrounds in which their parents have various forms of attachment pathology. It is not surprising that mothers who themselves suffered from attachment disruptions or developmental trauma are likely to provide conflicted signals, fail to adopt adequate role-responsive strategies with their children, and thus contribute to the formation of hostile and/or helpless interactional styles (Lyons-Ruth, Bronfman, and Atwood 1999). Tragically, the transgenerational transmission of attachment deficits continues to perpetuate and sustain them as children who suffer from attachment disorganizations grow into adolescents and adults; these deficits thereby continue to beget developmental pathologies in generations to come. Although a contributing factor to this dysfunctional cycle is parents' own unresolved responses to trauma (Hesse and Main 2000), the cycle furthermore points to how attachment- and developmentally related trauma leave organizational deficiencies in personality structure and predispose those affected to chronic and enduring object relations pathology.

Cassidy, Marvin, and the MacArthur Working Group have devised a five-category attachment classification system for preschool- and kindergarten-age children that identifies "disorganized/controlling" behavioral patterns, which are conceptualized as outgrowths of the Main and Solomon criteria in infancy (Cassidy and Marvin 1992; Cassidy, Marvin, et al. 1987). The Cassidy-Marvin system identifies the major attachment groupings of (1) *secure* children (group B), with three subclassifications: (i) *secure-reserved*, (ii) *secure-comfortable*, and (iii) *secure-reactive*, each determined by the degree of separation protest and proximity-seeking behavior toward the parent; (2) *insecure-avoidant* (group A), marked by parental avoidance and blunted communication typically accompanied by little if any protest or distress upon separation; (3) *insecure-ambivalent* (group C), typically showing a mixture of babyish, coy behavior with subtle signs of resistance and/or anger directed toward the caregiver; (4) *disorganized* or *controlling* (group D), with three subclassifications: (i) *controlling-caregiving*, marked by overly solicitous, nurturing behavior directed toward the parent, thus demonstrating a reversal in role responsiveness; (ii) *controlling-punitive*, characterized by overt hostility directed toward the mother designed to humiliate, reject, and/or punish; and (iii) *controlling-general*, which is typically controlling behavior that is neither nurturing nor punitive but may contain elements of both; and (5) *insecure-other* (group IO), which is observed behavior that does not easily fit into any of the other categories but may have components of fearful, depressive, and/or sexualized behavior.

Crittenden's (1992, 1995) Preschool Assessment of Attachment (PAA) protocol provides further subclassifications of behavior that overlap with the Cassidy-Marvin system while delineating other indices of insecurity and disorganization. In addition to the secure, disorganized, and insecure-other classifications, Crittenden identifies a *defended* attachment pattern, which corresponds to the insecure-avoidant criteria (group A). The defended group is based on behavioral strategies that function to allow access to the parent without the child's having to become emotionally involved or reliant, while also avoiding confrontation. There are three identified subcategories of defended children, including: (i) *inhibited*, where there is an overcontrolled comportment of negative affect, avoidance of interpersonal contact or closeness, and a strong focus on external factors such as playing with toys as a means of deflecting attention from the relationship; (ii) *compulsively caregiving*, characterized by excessive nurturing and cheerful behavior directed toward the parent; and (iii) *compulsively compliant*, signaled by excessive fear, tension, and hypervigilance around the mother, gaze aversion, and alertness to her facial expressions, body posturing, and so forth. A *coercive* attachment category (group C), corresponding to the insecure-ambivalent diagnosis, is also highlighted in Crittenden's system, which differentiates between four subclassifications of behavior that are marked by attempts to manipulate the caregiver through (i) *threatening* (confrontational), (ii) *aggressive* (e.g., demanding, punitive, rejecting, humiliating), (iii) *disarming* (i.e., coy, sweet, charming, seductive), and/or (iv) *feigned helpless* (exaggerated) actions, the aim of which is to solicit the mother's attention, comfort, or nurturance. There is furthermore a blended *defended/coercive* classification (group A/C), which highlights elements of each that are displayed either simultaneously or sequentially in response to shifts in the parent's behavior; as well as an *anxious depressed* category (group AD), which signifies extreme mood symptoms, affect dysregulation, disorientation, and/or behavioral panic during separation from the parent. While there are both convergences and divergences between the Cassidy-Marvin system and the PAA, and increasing empirical research supports each assessment protocol (see Teti 1999), neither has undergone the same rigorous testing that the strange situation has

Attachment Assessments

endured (Fonagy 2001). Despite this, they prove to be useful diagnostic indices of disorganized attachment behaviors.

Other recent endeavors have been made to measure and classify insecure and disorganized attachment in children and adolescents with the Child Attachment Interview (CAI), a self-report interview technique based on the Adult Attachment Interview (see Ammaniti et al. 1990), and the Attachment Q-Sort (AQS), which largely relies on naturalistic observations of the child–parent dyad in their home over the course of a few hours (preferably on different occasions) rather than on laboratory-based experiments (Posada et al. 1995; Waters 1995; Waters and Deane 1985). Each of these assessment techniques is useful when conducting formal attachment assessments as well as providing diagnostic information on parent–child interactional patterns. But what is garnering increasing empirical support and proving its diagnostic clinical utility in adult populations is the Adult Attachment Interview (AAI), a semistructured protocol developed by Carol George, Nancy Kaplan, and Mary Main (1996), which examines self-reported attitudes, memories, and characterizations of subjects' relationships with their parents from childhood onward. The interview is conducted in a similar fashion to a clinical interview yet analyzed through verbatim transcriptions from tape recordings, and questions focus on phenomenological descriptions and subjects' qualitative experiences as recounted through self-generated narratives. The analysis of responses includes examining adjectives subjects choose to convey about their relationship with their parents when they were a child, who they were closest to and why, parental responsiveness during times of injury, illness, and death of a relative, and whether their parents were threatening or abusive—as well as various perceptions of disappointments, trauma, and so forth. Rather than classifying subjects with respect to the security of their attachments to particular dependency figures in the past, the AAI codes individual differences with regard to a subject's *current* state of mind toward his overall attachment history and the degree of coherency, organization, or reasonable integration with respect to his personal experiences.

Four primary categories of the AAI determine whether a subject is (1) *secure/autonomous*, (2) *dismissing*, (3) *preoccupied*, or (4) *unresolved/disorganized* with regard to his or her parents and attachment-related experiences; these categories further correspond to (1) *secure*, (2) *avoidant*, (3) *resistant/ambivalent*, or (4) *disorganized/disoriented* behavioral classifications characteristic of the infant strange situation (Hesse 1999; Siegel 1999). Based on naturalistic observations of early maternal responsiveness and infant reaction to the strange situation, secure and insecure infant classifications have produced astonishingly accurate predictions of how these individuals will score on the AAI later in life (Main 2000). For example, unresponsive interactional styles by mothers toward their infants produced dismissing AAI statuses when the children reached adolescence (Beck-with, Cohen, and Hamilton 1999); while secure attachment responses in infancy successfully predicted secure/autonomous protocols in individuals by the time they reached early adulthood (Waters, Hamilton, and Weinfield 2000). While Main, Hesse, and their colleagues stress that AAI coding statuses only reflect current states of mind with regard to attachment, which are subject to transformation, the burgeoning empirical literature in this area points toward the ubiquitous influence of early attachment experiences on later attachment organizations and maternal-infant relatedness practices. Put simply, infants who experience attachment insecurities are more likely to grow up and carry those disturbances into their adolescent and adult years, which will in all likelihood deleteriously affect the way they parent their own children. It is my contention that attachment disturbance in infancy and early childhood will likely lead to some form of disorder of the self.

Eagle (1996) argues that avoidantly attached adults tend to be dismissive toward attachment needs, are rigidly self-reliant, and deny their own dependency yearnings as an effort to defensively distance themselves from their own attachment-related conflict. He cites empirical evidence showing that when these adults are confronted with attachment themes, they show heightened physiological arousal despite the denial of experiencing any negative affect. This conclusion mirrors research in children who have been classified as being avoidantly attached in the strange situation, appear detached when their mothers are present, do not protest when their mothers leave the room, and openly rebuke or ignore them upon reunion. Yet, when equipped with heart monitors, these children show significant elevations in heart rate both when their mothers leave the room and when they return (Sroufe et al. 1977). This research has been replicated by monitoring cortisol levels (Spangler and Grossmann 1993) and EEG asymmetry in brain electrical activity (Fox and Card 1999). This leads Erreich (2003) to perspicaciously conclude that disorganizational attachment patterns are defensive attempts at compromise formation represented on the level of unconscious fantasy due to thwarted wishes to feel safe via proximity to the mother.

Fonagy (2000) notes how many attachment disordered adults with character pathology have limited self-reflectivity and cannot adequately monitor or anticipate the internal mental states of others. This is particularly germane when mothers are not capable of sensing or responding to the immediate emotional needs and intentional states of their infants' minds. When an attachment figure characteristically and chronically fails to respond to her child's cue solicitations, make reparation for deficient responsiveness or absence, or provide auxiliary soothing functions, the child will not be able to sufficiently assimilate or resolve the conflict cognitively. This failure will result in the attenuation of the child's attention, behavioral orientation, and goal-directed activities, thereby impeding the child from forming coherent attachment strategies in the first place. Bowlby tells us that segregated systems or attachment pathology can occur under real or perceived conditions of separation or loss, evoked threats of rejection or abandonment, and direct punishment from the mother for the infant's attachment-seeking activity (e.g., physical discipline, scolding, or shaming the child for seeking attention, etc.). As a result, the attachment figure can exacerbate the infant's attachment-related anxieties during the very moment when he needs consolation, thus simultaneously activating the child's attachment system by threatening or angry displays of behavior followed by maternal rejection or withdrawal (Solomon and George 1999).

Children who feel helpless to regulate their own attachment motivations due to imposed maternal conflict are likely to construct self and object representations of vulnerability, fragility, unworthiness, and negativity concurrent with dysregulated affective tensions and behavioral manifestations in response to feeling a lack of protection and reassurance from the mother, thus creating more fear and distress. As a result, the infant will fail to adequately develop organized and cohesive attachment strategies; therefore, the child will be predisposed to a developmental trajectory marked by structural deficits of the self. In more extreme, maltreating families or environmental circumstances marked by absence, abandonment, loss, or abuse, the development of a cohesive, unifying self will largely be impaired and replete with lacunae in regulatory functions and negative self/object representations, which will inevitably exacerbate relationship-based anxieties and preclude the formation of healthy attachments. The potential clinical maladjustment in later development shows no restrictions: depending upon the unique contingencies that govern infant-maternal attachment, child, adolescent, and adult adaptation may be colored by polysymptomatic profiles including depression and mood disorders, chronic anxiety and panic, pervasive insecurity, phobic and obsessive conditions, paranoia, social avoidance and withdrawal, dependency, underachievement, delinquency and antisocial behavior, aggressivity and rage, complicated grief or unresolved mourning, addictions, eating disorders, somatization, conversion manifestations, borderline organization, narcissism, dissociation, psychotic processes, multiplicity, and severe character pathology.

What is fundamentally and repeatedly neglected in the attachment literature is how attachment deficiencies and developmental traumas universally activate and sustain acute *unconscious* anxiety states, fantasy systems, and depressive reactions with overwhelming affective intensity that inevitably permeate subjective conscious experience. And it is precisely these residual and unresolved, unconscious structural conflicts, which continue to saturate conscious experience and impinge upon interpersonal

adjustment strategies, that accompany so many clinical forms of attachment pathology. Until such unconscious disruptions are addressed and ameliorated, capacities for healthy relatedness, connection, and intimacy with others will be progressively impaired.

The notion of disorganized attachment provides an auspicious point of reference for conceptualizing the attachment disordered self. Here I am not necessarily so concerned with new taxonomies in descriptive research as I am with extending a general theory of attachment disorganization to clinical populations. Based upon my experience as an applied clinician, relying mainly on phenomenological and qualitative analyses of data culled from extensive case studies grounded in psychodynamic observation and treatment, attachment vulnerabilities of some kind may be said to be present in all clinical populations as well as the general masses. Although legitimate and noteworthy in its own right, the current research focus on the D classification is, with qualifications, preoccupied with recording and labeling attachment disordered phenomena rather than explicating the conditions that make their appearance—let alone their treatment—possible. While these developments pave important and exciting new directions in the attachment field, for our purposes, attachment disorganization refers to the structural deficits and anomalies of the self that infiltrate and attenuate ego resources, capacities for holistic self and object representation, and cognitive-behavioral strategies directed toward self-regulation, perceptual integration, affective stability, self-reflectivity, and rational adaptation to the vicissitudes of personal existence.

Due to the multiple, overdetermined factors that affect enacted capacities for relational connectedness, which in turn influence the integrity and fortification of psychic structure, attachment-related pathology emerges on a continuum of functional adjustment and abnormality. While Solomon and George (1999) warn us that not all attachment disorganization leads to attachment disorders, a position not unlike Ainsworth's (1963) belief that insecure attachments can be reversed, there are certain developmental vulnerabilities that must be compensated for at the very least—thus giving rise to myriad defensive maneuvers designed to regulate the self and preserve the attachment system—or they will invariably lead to more pathological forms of self-deficiency and relational disruption. When the structure of the self is understood in terms of its overdetermined dialectical organizations,[9] then attachment pathology can be viewed in part as a compromise formation (see Brenner 1982, 2002) or symptom substitution in response to primordial anxieties that alert the ego that it is in imminent harm. Put another way, disorganized attachment and its related manifestations are a compromise, alternative, or reactionary symptom construction in response to danger. As Freud (1926) reminds us, anxiety is a signal to the ego that it is in a dangerous situation; thus, paramount defenses of self-preservation must be

mobilized in order to ward off death anxiety and accompanying annihilation panic that imperils the self. Disruptions in attachment—from frightening to avoidant, resistant, and chaotic experiences, and so on—can signal these basic organismic anxieties, which must be mitigated through defensive strategies that ultimately form the yoke of sustained modes of self-structure that constitute personality. Character attachment pathology is therefore one such outcome, a circuitous adaptation to real or perceived experiences of disconnectedness, psychic injury, organismic panic, or annihilation anxieties that besiege psychic survival.

MOTIVATION AND ATTACHMENT

As classical attachment theory became more biologically focused, the range and complexities of intrapsychic and relational experience dominated by unconscious conflict became displaced. In other words, attachment theory does not adequately capture the domain and intensity of unconscious life. Yet, despite the biologicalization of attachment motivational sources, there are many parallel, overdetermined processes operative within the psyche that perform multiple functions (Waelder 1936); therefore, our appreciation for unconscious motivational forces cannot be emphasized enough. Even evolutionary psychology is premised on *unconsciously derived* determinants directing human behavior—including attachment patterns (Belsky 1999; Simpson 1999), such as those genetically imprinted within the nucleotide sequence of DNA (Bradie 1986; Kriegman 1998; Ruse 1986; Wuketits 1990; Wilson 2002).

From an evolutionary perspective, desire for close proximity to an attachment figure and its behavioral enactment establishes self-preservation and safety, mollifies fear, and insulates the infant from predation. Partially based on naturalistic observations of nonhuman primates in addition to children, Bowlby's attachment theory is ethologically justified. Motivation to maintain close proximity to a caregiver is in response to the fear of death: infants would surely die without parental feeding, protection, and shelter from the natural elements. In extending Freud's (1920, 1923) dual drive model to include a primary impetus or striving for relational attachment based on human survival, Bowlby made a clearing for new discourse on the nature of interpersonal motivations.

It is generally confirmed that small infants originally form attachments to primary caregivers within the first seven months of life, but attachment-related motivations can be readily observed throughout the life cycle in a variety of modified forms and contexts. In this regard, attachment has a contiguous developmental trajectory and is not merely age or stage specific. We learn as young children to adhere to our parents or identified surrogates and tend to form very few and select attachments based on the

unabated need (1) to establish and maintain close proximity to these selected others; (2) to use them as a secure base (Bowlby 1988), among other
things, during times of exploration, especially in unfamiliar environments;
and (3) to retreat into them as a haven from danger when real or perceived
threat is introduced. Main (1999) argues that it is the infant who selects his
primary attachment figure based on contingent social interactions, although strong biological processes (Emde 1988), emotional variants, and
caring solicitation, engagement, responsiveness, and physical contact with
caregivers are inevitably coextensive contributions influencing attachment
selection. It is interesting to note that children are fundamentally motivated to form attachments even if attachment figures are maltreating, neglectful, or abusive due to instinctively motivated pressures impelling attachment-related activities; and it is only under anomalous circumstances
that children remain unattached (Main 2000). This shows the power and
universality of the *need* for relational contact with original love objects
even when relationality is bound to trauma.

Historically, psychoanalytic theory may be readily viewed as a science
of motivation addressing the multiple sources, variants, and gradations of
mental phenomena that impel people to act. Freud's metapsychology emphasizes the various forces, energies, and resistances that govern psychic
activity, especially the unconscious mind. While Freud's drive theory has
generally been subsumed or displaced within contemporary paradigms,
we must not dismiss Freud's contributions to understanding the role and
significance of drives in human motivation. For Freud (1915b), a drive,
impulse, or urge (*Trieb*) is the basal foundation of psychic motivation
based on the ostensive fact that we are embodied; hence, the source of a
drive is biologically determined as part of our corporeal existence. But
Freud is far from being a material reductionist (see Mills 2002b). In fact,
he tells us that the essence (*Wesen*) of a drive is its impetus, pressure, or
activity, which *must find an object* in order to fulfill its aim of satisfaction.
Here we may see how Freud paved the way for the object relations
movement within psychoanalysis. An object is the most variable aspect of
a drive, and thus we may see why motivations for attachment, object relationships, and the procurement of selfobject needs entail parallel,
overdetermined motivational processes. For Freud (1923, 1933a), the ego
is the locus of organized mental life—itself the modification of unconscious structure (Freud 1926; Mills 2002c)—harnessing the energies of the
drives in the service of ameliorating various tensions that materialize
from competing motivational valences within the psyche. When we jux-
tapose Freud's thinking with Bowlby's theory of attachment, we see that
attachment to objects advances self-preservation and fulfills many ego
strivings. While motivations for attachment are innately prewired (evolutionary) urges inherent to the organism, objects of attachment, strictly
speaking, are not: these are determined and selected by the ego. There-

fore, drive is mediated by intentional choice that is unconsciously derived. This makes attachment motivation a teleological (hence purpose-
ful) expression initiated by unconscious agency.

Joseph Lichtenberg (1989) has attempted to provide a coherent theory
of human motivation based on preprogrammed, interconnected biological systems oriented toward (1) the maintenance of physiological equilib-
ria, (2) attachment affiliation, (3) aversion reactivity, (4) active exploration
and assertion, and (5) sensual stimulation; he further takes into account
self-preservative, sexual, and aggressive aims. Of course, motivation patterns extend far beyond preprogrammed neurobiological persuasions and
become developmentally and experientially differentiated, reorganized,
and instantiated within psychic structure, intentionality, behavioral action, and subjective self-conscious social life. More recently, John Gedo
(1996) has proposed several modalities of motivational patterns that gain
increased presence, interdependence, and complexity, thus corresponding
to various maturational contingencies enacted in early development and
extended throughout the lifespan. These purported modalities emanate
from and build on our most basic physiological contingencies and
progress toward more cultivated forms of psychological sophistication,
starting from (1) our inborn, constitutional motivations (such as those
proposed by Lichtenberg) and moving to (2) differentiation of pleasure
from nonpleasure gradients, (3) consolidation of stable self-organizations,
(4) internalization of ideals and imperatives, and (5) habituation or learning requirements that are necessary for adequate adaptation. We can readily see how the process of motivation suffuses all these developmental domains that may be operative at once and thus corresponds to our various
subjective experiences.

IDENTIFICATION, RELATIONALITY, AND INTERSUBJECTIVITY

While attachment motivation based on biological processes informed by
evolutionary currents is a *necessary* condition directing attachment-related
behaviors, it is far from a *sufficient* condition for capturing the unconscious complexifications and conscious motivations governing interpersonal relations and intrapsychic dynamics. In addition to ignoring the primordial role of the unconscious, the attachment literature further
underemphasizes the *emotional process* of attachment based on our primary identifications with our parents. It would be a reductive, naturalistic fallacy to boil everything down to biology (Mills 2002b): to borrow
Freud's (1900, 1933a) dictum, we must resist the temptation to view psychical processes solely from materialistic strategies. Beyond the biological
motivations associated with attachment behavior lie the psychological
contours of affectivity and the emotional significance bound to the

process of object relatedness. The role of emotions and affective attunement is garnering greater attention in psychotherapy and becoming the
subject of burgeoning new advances in contemporary psychological theory and research that extend far beyond psychodynamic practice. We may
currently observe cross-disciplinary preoccupation with the role and
meaning of emotions in neuroscience, cognitive psychology, philosophy
of mind, process-experiential therapy, developmental research, the humanities, and contemporary psychoanalytic thought. It was Freud (1921),
however, who advanced the notion that identification constitutes an *emotional bond* based on a feeling of attachment or connection to a significant
love object.

It may be argued that after his introduction of the signal theory of anxiety, Freud (1926) was the first to emphasize the importance of attachment (Sandler 1989; Tyson 2000) and threats against separation and loss
(Freud 1933a). During his mature period, Freud (1931) identified the
"primary relation" between children and their mothers (225), claiming
that the maternal object is the "prototype of all later love-relations—for
both sexes" (Freud 1940, 188). The nature and significance of attachment
is further encompassed by Freud's (1923, 1933a, 1940) view of *eros* as a relational principle (also see Reisner 1992), what he specifically delineates
on a continuum of realized possibilities and expressions including sexuality, identification, love, sublimation, reason, ethics, aesthetics, and culture, among other things (see Freud 1930). Identification becomes an architectonic function in the development and fortification of psychic
structure—being at once a basic operation of connectedness to another
through emotional mediacy, and the assimilation of universal values belonging to familial and cultural life. Identification furthermore entails the
fantasized construction of certain subjective ideals as wishful expressions that can be both a source of pleasure and conflict for each individual; and it is precisely the nature of fantasized ideal attachments that becomes a crucial aspect of the clinical encounter.

As Freud (1933a) describes, identification is "the assimilation of one ego
to another," whereby the other's ego is taken into the self: "It is a very important form of *attachment* to someone else" (63; italics added). Here
Freud recognizes the initial process of intersubjective self-consciousness:
one ego recognizes the ego of the other and wants to *be like* that other. In
fact, when we identify so strongly with another, we wish to *be* that other,
to *have* and possess her as our own (see Freud 1921, 1933a). And when objects of identification are lost or obliged to be given up, the ego compen-
sates by identifying with the lost object, which is incorporated into the
self. This often explains why objects of identification (and their ideals) are
repetitiously evoked and enacted in clinical populations through various
pathological manifestations, for example, as repetition compulsions fueled by the unconscious desire to procure a certain degree of qualitative

responsiveness, recognition, mastery, acceptance, love, and/or validation, and so forth, from an attachment figure or its symbolic surrogate.

Identification is the precursor for superego development and the internalization of valuation practices, having its original impetus in emotive attachments to parents. Because objects of choice are based on the *quality* of a subjective emotional bond with a significant dependency figure, identification is furthermore a precursor to love. In fact, Ainsworth (1967) refers to attachment as love, a claim that extends the process of attachment far beyond its biological underpinnings. She states, "We [are] concerned here with nothing less than the nature of love and its origins in the attachment of a baby to his mother" (429). Yet for Freud (1933a), love is a developmental achievement predicated on identification, for identification is "probably the very first" form of attachment (63). Identification therefore becomes an indispensable process of relationality. Extending this notion to the clinical milieu, it is often the case that identification with the therapist (parent) leads to positive internalized representations, which in turn produce positive therapeutic effects by rehabilitating or filling lacunae in self-structure.

This brings us to engage current perspectives on relational and intersubjective approaches to developmental theory and psychoanalytic psychology, a discussion that directly bears on our clinical work in treating attachment pathology. In fact, the amelioration of attachment deficiencies is a central objective of the therapeutic process, a process contingent upon the quality of relationality fostered in the patient–therapist dyad. Tantamount to the introduction or recapitulation of an optimal parent–child relation, or what we may refer to as the *relational principle*, effective therapy with attachment disordered populations requires forming and modeling a healthy relationship. Within contemporary psychoanalysis, relational and intersubjective systems approaches are gaining increased attention and demonstrating efficacy in working with diverse clinical groups. But this leads to a series of questions, both theoretical and clinical, which are important for us to clarify: How can one form a relationship with a patient who has deficits in capacities to form relationships in the first place? Can relational approaches rectify relational deficits or merely point toward a more healthy way of relatedness? Is relatedness premised on the interface between two subjectivities? Necessarily so? Is mutual recognition by each subject (the patient and the therapist) essential for healing and growth? And what precisely do we mean by relational versus intersubjective? Are the two distinct or the same?

Relational and intersubjective perspectives in psychoanalysis, each with varying degrees of specificity, have been advanced by many object relations theorists, interpersonal analysts, and self psychologists, but relational concepts and their therapeutic advance in psychoanalysis are often attributed to the work of Stephen Mitchell, Lewis Aron, and Jay

Greenberg, while intersubjectivity is often associated with Robert Stolorow, George Atwood, Jessica Benjamin, Donna Orange, and Thomas Ogden; although there are numerous proponents of this movement who together may not be inappropriately referred to as the American middle school (Spezzano 1997), or what Eagle, Wolitzky, and Wakefield (2001) refer to as the "new view" postmodern turn in psychoanalysis. With regard to theory, both schools largely converge with each other, emphasizing the nature of contextuality, emotional transmutation, meaning construction, mutual yet asymmetrical connectedness, and recognition; thus, for our purposes their respective conceptual distinctions are minimal. Relationality (Mitchell 1988, 2000), intersubjectivity (Stolorow and Atwood 1992; Orange, Stolorow, and Atwood 1997), specificity theory (Bacal 1998), and dyadic systems (Beebe, Jafee, and Lachmann 1992) approaches all appreciate the nuances of emotional subjective life, empathic attunement, optimal responsiveness, and the interdependency of relational attachment between the patient and the therapist. It is primarily for this reason (along with pragmatic considerations governing the scope of this book) that I will treat relationality and intersubjectivity as interchangeable constructs.[10] Relationality generally involves the convergence and interdependence of two or more human subjects—each with their own competing subjective processes—who form a matrix or field of reciprocal interactions that permeate the unconscious, affective, and cognitive appraisals of each person, thus giving rise to both intrapsychic and interpersonal transfigurations. But relationality also transpires within the interior of each subject, within the silent dialogue the soul has with itself (Mills 2002a); thereby, the self has a relation to its Self.

For Mitchell, Stolorow, Stern, Aron, Sullivan, Lichtenberg, and others, personality development and clinical praxis is conditioned on the relational-phenomenological field of interactional experience that constitutes subjective and communal life from birth onward. The intersubjective matrix presupposes the process of attachment and relatedness, beginning with the introjection, identification, and internalization of early parental imagoes and their value imperatives, which in turn are incorporated in and transposed onto psychic structure: this indubitably leaves permutations on self-organization and one's internalized representational world that further interact with competing, preexisting unconscious processes. Intersubjectivity may be viewed on multiple axes within the ontogenesis of each individual, from the internalization of one subject (as internalized representations of his functional properties and qualities) into the subjectivity of the other—a process initiated in infancy—to the mutual recognition that each subject is a self-conscious experiential being (Hegel 1807) who has needs, thoughts, and feelings similar to one's own. Because the intersubjective field is often asymmetrical (Aron 1996), that is, disproportionate and uneven, as in the child's unequal relation to his parents, or the patient's respect for the therapist's expertise, the degree of relational reciprocity will be contingent upon the form and parameters of the therapeutic encounter negotiated by the intersubjective unit. Not only is the analytic encounter colored by the patient's disposition, attitudes, and symptomatic profile, but it is also radically conditioned by the therapist's personality style and theoretical mode of clinical practice. Forming the intersubjective constellation is never the same process: each subject—both patient and therapist—has his own unique personality, experiences, and developmental history he brings to bear on the therapeutic context, which ensures that each intersubjective system will be created afresh, marbled by novel interaction, and mediated by situational contingencies that materialize in the moment (such as the spontaneous activation of affect; the perception, meaning, and interpretation of content; role-responsive adoptions by each subject; emotional resonance states; and the mobilization of unconscious conflict, wish and defense, resistance, transference, and countertransference, just to name a few).

As intimated above, we may readily observe a paradox in treating attachment pathology from relational perspectives. Because attachment disordered patients have endured curtailed relational experiences at best—and absent, bereaved, abusive, and/or traumatic situations at worst—which have left structural deficits of the self, how can treatment orientations bridge such lacunae in being and provide the sustenance that is so fundamental to human existence? In other words, how do we promote attachment patterns with people so relationally deprived and structurally disfigured? This becomes an ever more sustained challenge with adolescents, who are generally in their own process of identity formation, psychosocial and intellectual maturation, individuation from family, rebellion against adult authority, and cult experimentation, among other things. Those who suffer from attachment pathology are saturated with intense psychic pain, confusion, doubt, labile emotions, interpersonal alienation, cognitive disruption, and unconscious conflict, which magnifies the severity of negotiating normative development under the most favorable circumstances. As we will examine through extensive case material, what is most clinically salient is that patients who have attachment deficiencies exhibit a diverse range of symptoms, ego impairment, primitive defenses, affect dysregulation, personality deficits, and interpersonal maladjustment that continue to taunt psychic integrity and cohesive self-structure. It becomes an integral aspect of therapy to find avenues toward connectedness and emotional bonding with such patients, who are at once deeply damaged by others yet unable to disconnect from their desire for human affiliation.

NOTES

1. There is substantial debate among analytic philosophy and the hermeneutic tradition regarding whether psychoanalysis rests on a theory of causality versus a theory of meaning (see Grünbaum 1999; Jaspers 1974; Ricoeur 1970). In psychoanalytic theory, the principle of psychic determinism often presupposes causal inferences between conscious mental states and behavioral symptomatology guided by unconscious processes. While I do not wish to entertain this debate here, I do believe that both causal explanation and meaning connections pose viable complementary approaches to understanding how unconscious motivation produces affective, conceptual, behavioral, symptomatic, and interpersonal manifestations. See Rudnytsky (2002) for his attempt at consilience between the hermeneutic and scientific conceptions of psychoanalysis.

2. This causal claim imports certain qualifications: psychic structure is fundamentally forged through a primordial relational-intersubjective matrix based on the mutual self-regulation of reciprocal interactions and the internalization of primary love objects and the functions they serve; thus, various conflicts, adaptational patterns, and unconscious organizations arise. Yet, despite various unconscious pressures and developmental experiences affecting self-structure, freedom and agency are actualized in the qualitative choices made within the context of self-development, linguistic acquisition, and the culturally elaborated situations within one's social ontology. A full theory of the self and its pathological manifestations is outlined in chapter 2.

3. In the psychoanalytic literature, there are often distinctions made between the use of the terms *object*, *self/object* or *self-object*, and *selfobject*, depending upon who you consult. Here I define the term *object* as any tangible, cognized, or fantasized aspect of another person (or a part of that person) that is imbued with psychic significance (including imagistic, conceptual, symbolic, embodied, and affective properties), represented in the mind, and interpersonally related to in some fashion. The terms *self/object* and *self-object* are here employed to distinguish the self from others, yet may be conceived of as forming a unit; while *selfobject* refers to Kohut's definition of an object that is conceived of as being a functional dimension and part of the self. Kohut's selfobject theory is more thoroughly addressed in chapter 2.

4. Because we are thrown and embedded in a social ontology at birth by virtue of our historicity, there is no such thing as a solipsistic, solitary, or radically independent nominal agent. Subjectivity is conditioned on a priori events that are already constitutive of our being, and the nascent self has no say in the matter whatsoever. While we are thrown into social, cultural, and linguistic structures, however, this does not mean that the self is predetermined, only that freedom and actualization of choice transpire in the ontological context of its facticity. But just because human attachment is a necessary condition of selfhood, it is not a sufficient condition for determining the subject's modes of being. Regardless, the self would not exist without the other since selfhood and otherness are dialectically related and hence *equiprimordial* ontological conditions of human existence.

5. Recall Freud's (1916–1917) dictum: "We are *all* ill"—that is, "neurotic" (358, 457).

6. The role of the maternal object in psychic formation has been a pervasive theme in post-classical psychoanalytic theory: Klein, Anna Freud, Ian Suttie, Fairbairn, Winnicott, Sandler, Mahler, Kohut, and Kernberg, among others, have advanced this common tenet.

7. Comparative, cross-cultural attachment research unequivocally supports the observation of universal and contextual determinants of secure and disturbed attachment patterns in a representative population group of more than one billion people gathered from at least fifty-six nationalities (van Ijzendoorn and Sagi 1999). This impressive comparative-integrative analysis underscores the notion that attachment processes are universal to all human beings, with contextual components allowing for qualitative variation in adaptation and contingent modes of expression. To envision attachment strategies without contextual variance is as difficult as con-

ceiving of attachment as a ubiquitous collective phenomenon devoid of necessary universal laws governed by causal processes.

8. Alternatively, this may also suggest that some of the detached children observed had not sufficiently developed appropriate capacities for evocative memory, or at least it becomes colored under emotionally charged situations. This points to the possibility that some children may have been more insecurely attached prior to the separation experiments rather than as a result of maternal abandonment. Because evocative memory relies on the ability to internally locate and bring to conscious awareness the internalized imagoes and positive representations of the mother that aid in establishing a cohesive self over time, these processes are vulnerable to attachment disruptions.

9. The dialectical organization of the self may be viewed from multiple dynamic perspectives, including the internal pressures of unconscious drive and defense; intersubjective attunement, availability, and responsiveness from dependency figures; and environmental encroachments that mobilize anxiety, thereby affecting regulatory internalized self and object representations. These multiply determined processes in turn affect self-cohesion and the unique subjective experiences that constitute the phenomenal meaning, value, and significance of the lived encounter. Given that self-structure and personal experience are influenced and governed by these multiply contoured and contextualized processes, attachment motivations and their derived conflict will be enacted within myriad simultaneous, interconnected planes of psychic reality.

10. There are many distinctions and nuances between relational and intersubjective perspectives that deserve a thorough critique yet do not concern us within this context. However, where agreements exist, these schools of thought implicitly propound to reify interpersonal life at the expense of displacing the lived subjective *intrapsychic* experience of each individual. In my estimation, these propositions present false dichotomies that extricate intrapsychic life from the relational matrix—such as Stolorow's mythology of the isolated mind—or they banish intrapsychic experience all together, thus boiling everything down to an interpersonal ontology. In fact, Mitchell (1992) claims that *all* subjective experience is relationally mediated, while Stolorow, Orange, and Atwood (2001) have gone so far as to disregard individuality altogether, claiming that all intrapsychic experience is intersubjectively constructed. These propositions fail to account for the unconscious a priori forces that exist prior to interpersonal experience, the epistemology of internal thoughts, feelings, and experiential processes that are separate from other beings, and the lived phenomenology of somatic, affective, preverbal, and extralinguistic forces that permeate the interior of the life within. For a critical review of relational and intersubjective perspectives in psychoanalysis, see Mills (2005).

2

ଚ

The Attachment
Disordered Self

As I have said repeatedly, attachment pathology is a disorder of the self. This is a central claim we may extend to all clinical forms of attachment-related impairments, from insecure, avoidant, resistant, ambivalent, controlling, and disorganized instantiations, to those more characterologically disordered, including populations with affective, dissociative, and psychotic vulnerabilities. The crux of my argument is based upon understanding how psychic structure is defensively forged, maladaptively organized, and conflictually sustained through the disturbed and curtailed forms of object relations the self first encounters within its intersubjective milieu.

Before we specifically examine the scope, depth, and range of the attachment disordered self, a topic that will preoccupy us throughout this book, it becomes important for pragmatic reasons to provide a conceptual model of the self that purports to develop normatively. I realize that universal assertions regarding the nature of the self must take into account contextual, cultural, gendered, ethnic, linguistic, and individual differences; however, investigation into the essence of attachment pathology obliges us to consider common structural dynamics that make particularistic expressions possible. Consideration of a generic model of the self will further provide us with a touchstone to gauge when development potentially goes awry as the self is influenced by its multiple contingencies and attachment-related disruptions. Moreover, clarification surrounding our theoretical discourse will hopefully help us avoid misunderstandings with reference to terminology regarding the question and meaning of the self. Because there are so many competing theories of the self from diverse, cross-disciplinary perspectives within the social and behavioral sciences as well as the humanities (see Levin 1992), there is no unified consensus on the nature of what the self is really all about: each respective discipline brings highly selective aspects of its work to bear on theoretical, empirical, definitional, hermeneutical, and practical considerations governing an intelligible discourse on method. Because I am here interested in the psychodynamics of mind, and in particular psychopathology, I will draw on three interrelated approaches to conceptualizing the self governed by clinical, developmental, and inferential-deductive considerations.

CONCEPTUALIZING THE SELF

Throughout the clinical literature, almost all references to the self refer to a theory of consciousness: that is, the self is descriptively confined to the experiential lived reality of the subjective ego. It was Freud (1923), however, who first posited the existence of the unconscious ego (*Ich*), plagued by the anxieties generated from three ominous forces: the pressures of the id (*Es*), namely, the domain of repressed conflict governed by the drives (*Triebe*); the reality of the external world and all its social contingencies; and the critical judgment, ethical reproach, and shame imposed by the superego (*ÜberIch*). Freud referred to the psyche in its totality as the temporal clash and organization of these competing processes that begin as primitive instantiations of unconscious structure and modify into conscious and self-conscious social life throughout early development (Freud 1926, 1933a, 1940). While Freud referred to the soul (*Seele*) rather than the self (*Selbst*), we may say that the self is a supraordinate construct that encapsulates all conscious and unconscious experience. From this standpoint, there is an equiprimordial interface between unconscious processes and the relational, cultural, and linguistic interactions that influence the ontogenesis of personality development.

It is important to emphasize that the self is never totally constituted the same way for each person, primarily due to the phenomenology of affective, perceptual, and cognitive self-referents within the intersubjective field of psychosocial interaction. Thus, radical individualistic expressions and experiential organizations arise and are recalcitrant to duplication or comparison with others. Despite this experiential novelty that the self enjoys in its lived nominalistic world, there are various universal intrapsychic processes that challenge postmodern conceptions of the self as illusory, decentered, and/or conditioned by language. Among these universals, including the fact that we all desire and are conscious beings, is the primacy of unconscious mentation.

Although no longer in vogue among relational theorists, Freud's tripartite model of the mind continues to be a bedrock of psychoanalytic thought; the human being is the temporal, experiential amalgamation of the passions, the intellect or reason, and moral judgment—each dialectically opposed to the other within an invariant yet conflictual system of interdependency. And what Freud emphasizes more than any other theorist is the ubiquitous presence of unconscious activity exerting a powerful determining force over psychic organization. It is not difficult to observe how Freud's insights hold true today as they did during his era; only now they are cloaked under a new guise of relational terminology. We negotiate within ourselves and with others—as much as our patients do—the toll these processes exert over our mental lives. Our clinical work with patients affords us the opportunity to see how time and again the human psyche is besieged by unconscious repetitions and maladaptive patterns of relational enactment transpiring outside of conscious awareness, which stand in antithesis to the confines of self-imposed rational control. And when the subject is no longer exposed to tyranny from frustrating or oppressive external forces, it is impaled by self-torture due to the pervasive penetration of humiliation, shame, guilt, inferiority, and self-laceration, just to name a few, that only the self-punitive ego can employ.

Emanating from our natural, biological immediacy, the psyche or self, according to Freud (1923), emerges from its nascent unconscious configurations to experience the world of sense perception and human relatedness, hence gaining increasing zest and complexity. Note that Freud's model of the psyche is an architectonic, epigenetic achievement: higher modes of rational, ethical, and aesthetic self-conscious life are cultivated from more primitive processes that govern the unconscious mind. Because the conscious ego is an agency that is modified and differentiated from its unconscious counterpart (see Freud 1926), the self becomes a self-flourishing dynamic process of becoming nurtured by its relation to objects within its social ontology. As a result, the subject is the organization and cultivation of its various capacities, internalized experiences, and representations of self and others related to its unconscious reverberations and innate strivings. Therefore, the self emerges on a continuum of realized possibilities and potentialities enacted through the unique contingencies that govern subjective and social existence. This ensures that no two people could ever possess identical processes or properties despite having shared similarities or mutual identifications based in content or form. Despite having structural universals, the self is always wedded to context (see Mills 2002a, 2004b).

While many psychoanalytic theorists have advanced specific models of the self that deserve special attention in their own right, Winnicott, Kohut, and Stern are most instructive as we prepare for our discussion on treating attachment pathology.

Although Winnicott's theories are largely unsystematized and at times opaque, it may be generally said that self-development vis-à-vis object relations is primarily derived from *responsiveness* from objects rather than instinctual pressures, which leads to defensive fortifications designed to insulate the self from extinction. For Winnicott (1958, 1965, 1971), the essential process behind the generation of healthy self-cohesion is facilitated by a maternal "holding environment," that is, by the overall parental availability and responsiveness that is "good enough" to foster creativity, spontaneity, and play. This process is successfully characterized by the mother's ability to empathize with her baby. The degree to which empathic attunement and responsiveness is negotiated within the dyadic attachment system will largely determine how self-structure is forged.

For Winnicott, self-organization is fundamentally oriented toward spontaneous self-expression, creativity, and authenticity nurtured by maternal love. If these generic requirements are met, the self flourishes; if not, it can lead to what Winnicott (1960) refers to as a "false self." A false self is constructed as a defensive system in response to developmental conflict encountered in the primary attachment relationship, and it remains unconsciously maintained. Winnicott's theoretical framework falls within a defense model, which is intimately tied to drive theory within the interpersonal context of the mother–child dyad. While having a ground in Freudian metapsychology, Winnicott's conceptualization of the false self, however, is essentially a relational theory centering on ego-defensive maneuvers that arise in response to environmental demands. More specifically, within the infant–mother milieu, the child struggles to manage libidinal/creative impulses that are solely intrapsychic; however, this takes place within the context of the relational matrix or intersubjective field. Ego organization is in the service of adaptation to environmental encroachments and the procurement of object attachment. Therefore, within the stage of the first object relationships, various defenses are constructed in response to external demands, particularly from the demands of the maternal object. Repeated compliance with such demands, concomitant with a withdrawal from self-generated spontaneity, leads to an increased stifling of impulses derived from the natural drive for spontaneous expression and culminates in a false-self development.

For Winnicott (1960), the idea of a "true self" originates in the capacity of the infant to recognize and enact spontaneous needs for self-expression. "Only the True Self can be creative and only the True Self can feel real" (148). The self, as the center of spontaneity that has the "experience of aliveness," constitutes the core or heart of authenticity. However, the ability to enact such spontaneous gestures is contingent upon the responsiveness of the good-enough mother within an appropriate holding environment. Thus, the principal etiology of the true and false self is contingent upon the *quality* of maternal responsiveness. The true self flourishes only in response to the repeated success of the mother's optimal responsiveness to the infant's spontaneous expressions. If the mother is "not good enough," she does not facilitate the infant's omnipotence and repeatedly fails to meet the child's spontaneous gestures with appropriate attunement and gratification.

Winnicott situates the essence of both health and pathology within the primary intersubjective attachment system, where each member plays respective roles, namely, the mother's empathic capacity and delivery of responsiveness, and the infant's capacity to enact spontaneous gestures of creative self-expression. Self-development is compromised by the infant's repeated compliance with demands imposed by the attachment figure. Winnicott (1960) explains,

> The infant gets seduced into compliance, and a compliant False Self reacts to environmental demands and the infant seems to accept them. Through this False Self the infant builds up a false set of relationships, and by means of introjections even attains a show of being real, so that the child may grow up to be just like mother, nurse, aunt, brother, or whoever at the time dominates the scene. (146)

While Winnicott focuses on the particular defensive motivations underlying the false self, a process we can extend to Bowlby's notion of defensive exclusion, he highlights the imperative of relational responsiveness. Indeed, this is a central theme across the clinical, developmental, and attachment-related literature: responsiveness from love objects can largely determine the trajectory of psychic structure.

Winnicott's developmental model anticipates Kohut's psychoanalytic self psychology. Kohut built on the notion of responsiveness and emphasized how empathic attunement, validation, affirmation, and the internalization of idealized parental introjects perform invaluable developmental functions by lending psychic cohesion, malleability, and adaptive elasticity to self-structure. Kohut's (1971, 1977) paradigm of the self hinges on the subject's necessary relation to what he terms "selfobjects." Selfobjects are primarily other people—especially significant others such as a parent or surrogate—but can also be any object in reality or fantasy, and they are conceived as a part of the self that the self depends upon for psychic regulation. A selfobject, like Winnicott's conception of a "transitional object," is best understood in terms of the *functions* it serves. For Kohut, selfobject experiences are foundational: they are based on the evoking-responding-sustaining matrix of intersubjective relations that aids in building self-organization and psychic fortification.

Kohut (1984) sees human development as flourishing in response to selfobject nurturance based on three primary needs: (1) the need to be *understood*, hence to feel empathy from others; (2) the need to be "mirrored" in self-worth, hence to feel *validated* and affirmed; and (3) the need to *idealize* significant others, which are incorporated into the subject as stable-calming-soothing introjects or "parental imagoes" that form the basis for self and object representation. These ontogenetic ingredients, along with the innate strivings and ambitions that spring from within the intrapsychic configurations of the child's mind, foster and abet self-development. These innate strivings, which we may compare to Winnicott's notion of the spontaneous and creative self-expression of the infant, always stand in contrast to environmental frustrations, demands of others, and the societal values that are imposed upon the child and with which it must identify, and hence which must be negotiated within the self and through reciprocal, relational interactions. The contingent nature of intersubjective exchange furthermore influences the form, phenomenal quality, and synthetic functioning that self-organization adaptively assumes.

By humanizing the psychodynamics of narcissism, Kohut sees the self as developing on a continuum of narcissistic expression that takes on both normative and pathological variants depending upon the way in which selfobject experiences are internalized, affectively arranged, and related to the representational process. The organization and degree of self-cohesion the nascent psyche begins to forge will be directly related to the quality, duration, and consistency of parental responsiveness: over time, the accumulation of selfobject experiences becomes more solidified within psychic structure. Again, here it is important to note that when I refer to psychic structure, I am actually referring to the ontological processes that form the rudiments of unconscious organizing principles within the experiential self. As a result, self-structure is never fixed or stagnant; rather, it is a malleable, dynamic process that is yoked together by the multiply overdetermined variants (both conscious and unconscious) that compose experiential strata or parallel processes of activity within the subjective interior of the mind.

The cohesiveness of the psyche largely depends upon how attachment figures responsively interact with and mirror the child's self-expressions; this responsiveness in turn is assimilated into self and object representations affecting ongoing structural-organizational processes. Just as Winnicott offers the general prescription of providing a good-enough holding environment, Kohut stresses the optimal responsiveness of attunement to and mirroring of the child's unique talents and displays of initiative. There is no formula for self-development, however: no matter how objectively adequate parental responsiveness is delivered and maintained, the self is ultimately free to organize its own subjective experiences; this explains the potential variations of individuality in self-organization, identity, pathology, and appraisals of others.

Generally we may say that if caregivers are conscientious in their role as a focal selfobject presence, then the child will acquire healthy and adaptive structural functions of self-assertion, autonomy, control, and vitality. The positive mirroring transferences that selfobjects perform also contribute to their availability and the child's desire to internalize them within the psyche and thus make them his own. Here we may see how Freud's notion of identification manifests itself within Kohut's system. The child imbues the parent with idealized qualities and properties that perform vital selfobject functions of providing feelings of being omnipotent, wise, infallible, and so forth and then symbiotically transposes and internalizes them within the self, thus fortifying psychic structure. Keep in mind that selfobject experiences are integral to self-development and contiguous throughout the lifespan: they are never abandoned as such, only modified, because they more or less form the foundation of personal subjectivity.

Deficiencies in selfobject responsiveness give rise to a slightly different developmental picture, one that is destined to be structurally flawed if intersubjective contingencies are misaligned. Selfobject experiences of absence, lack, deprivation, and frustration from a caregiver—to overt ridicule, rejection, invalidation, and shame—all impact on attachment patterns and representational constructions of self and others. These developmental traumas, no matter how slight or malignant, leave a lasting residue on the child's inner representational world. Pathological narcissism has the potential to develop on a continuum of *selfishness* to *selflessness*, thereby explaining the contours, limits, and range of how subjectivity becomes experientially expressed. On the developmental plane of self-organization we may observe extreme forms of disorders of the self on opposite poles of the continuum—from the typical self-centered narcissist to depressed, vapid, masochistic, and dependent personality constellations. For example, the proverbial spoiled brat whose omnipotent, exhibitionistic self was overgratified and never challenged could potentially explain, within limits, the extreme displays of grandiose behavior, entitlement, exaggerated self-inflation, and brazen disregard for others (who are seen as nothing but objects to use and exploit) that the classical narcissist manifests. Likewise, the child who is perpetually devalued, denied affection or understanding, and forsaken from familial affiliation will likely grow to feel worthless, vilified, and unlovable; in this case, the developmental traumas the child experiences leave depleted, anxiety-ridden, fragmentary, and maligned self-attributions that belong to a fragile and/or damaged self.

Both of these developmental scenarios reflect deficits in self-structure as a result of attachment disruptions. In fact, if the self becomes defined in relation to the parent's own narcissistic needs, capacities for self-soothing and self-esteem regulation will be impoverished or compromised altogether. When selfobject failure imperils psychic cohesion, various defensive maneuvers must be employed to protect the self from depletion, fragmentation, or disintegration, each with varying degrees of success. Winnicott's false self is one such possible outcome, along with proclivities toward withdrawal, depression, disabling anxiety or panic, dissociation, and/or detachment from others through schizoid mechanisms. Disruptions in the behavioral attachment system observed among small children reflect how parental responsiveness patterns ostensibly affect psychic structure and future adaptation.

Defense mobilization is the key to psychic survival; from a very early age, relationships with others are associated with pain, and these relationships become transferential templates for all other forms of object relations. Even when defensive strategies successfully insulate the self from being accosted, it is not without cost, and we may say that structural deficits are present to some extent within us all. In more extreme forms of structural emptiness or depletion, when the self cannot ameliorate internal anxiety states, dysphoria, melancholic affect, or recurrent bouts of meaninglessness, the deficit self resorts to other selfobject attachments to perform these coveted functions. This explains how addictions to food, alcohol, drugs, gambling, work, or spending; sexually acting-out behavior; incessant masturbation; frenzied impulsivity; manic flight; dangerous risk-taking ventures; and so forth serve as compensatory, regulatory strategies.

Clinical and developmental models of the self have typically favored and relied on one of two methods to derive their theoretical frameworks: (1) analysts conceive the self by retroactively applying adult clinical material (i.e., material gathered from free association, dream analysis, memories, narratives, therapeutic transactions, etc.) to reconstruct plausible hypotheses about early childhood development; or (2) developmental researchers conceive the self through direct observation of child behavioral, social, and interactional patterns. While both of these approaches have utility and value, very little has been said on self development during infancy. Here Daniel Stern becomes instructive to our discussion.

Because we have no way of directly observing the contents and subjective experiences of the infant's mind, Stern (1985) offers an inferential-deductive approach to elucidating the phenomenology of the infant's subjective experience and augments it with developmental-observational considerations. Stern recognizes the epistemological limit to behavioral science when applied to the observed infant and hence situates his inquiry within the realm of logical speculation that can be derived from inferences about the infant's inner subjective life. Although this methodological procedure is commonplace among rationalist philosophical traditions, his approach is novel within the psychoanalytic developmental literature.

Stern rightfully concludes that we must attempt to conceive of the self in its initial, most rudimentary forms based on inferences that describe a working hypothesis of the infant's subjective mind, and he shows how the mind becomes a progressive developmental organization fueled by the relational contexts the child encounters within his original interpersonal environment. Stern takes his point of reference from the interior of the infant's burgeoning sense of self, which constantly confronts transformations of form and content based upon interactional contingencies. For Stern, senses of self, originally materializing in infancy and early childhood, emerge on a continuum and are retained and contiguously operative throughout the lifespan. Stern (1985) chronicles "the sense of a self that is a single, distinct, integrated body; there is the agent of actions, the experiencer of feelings, the maker of intentions, the architect of plans, the transposer of experience into language, [and] the communicator and sharer of personal knowledge" (5).

Stern is especially insightful in elucidating the senses of self that exist in preverbal forms as inner experience prior to the acquisition of self-consciousness and language. Here the term "sense" means simple or immediate non-self-reflective awareness that forms "invariant" patterns of organization that the infant experiences in his subjective immediacy, which later become verbally and conceptually mediated through speech and language. Stern envisions the self as a burgeoning agency encompassing several progressive forms on a developmental acclivity toward increased complexity and unification. These forms are as follows:

1. The *emergent self* (from birth to two months) is the elementary, predesigned awareness of self-organizing processes. At this crude level of organization, the infant experiences states of undifferentiation with the mother, albeit not totally, and is also selectively responsive to environmental stimuli and external social events.
2. The *core self* (from two to six months) is sensed as a separate, more or less cohesive, physical embodiment that is enduring in time and is the experiential center of agency, affectivity, and self-history.
3. A *subjective self* (from seven to fifteen months) is sensed as the negotiation of various developmental tasks that are partially based on the dialectic of fulfilling needs for autonomy and individuation, but always within the larger context of fostering and seeking an intersubjective union with others. This primarily involves the self-experience of subjective organizations such as the content of one's own mind—thoughts, representations, intentionality, will—and the quality of feeling states that can be shared with others.
4. A *verbal self* (which forms after fifteen months and onward) allows the self to experience itself and others through verbal and conceptual mediums, namely, as narrative, linguistic expressions.

At this point a brief digression is in order. Although Stern does not address this directly, the infant is ontologically thrown into an intersubjective milieu: it does not recognize itself or others as participating in an interpersonal system composed of dyadic or tertiary (or more) reciprocal relations. The self at first does not apprehend itself as a subject, nor does it view others as subjects, only as objects. The recognition of subjectivity as self-conscious agency is a developmental conquest, as is the recognition that others are autonomous self-conscious beings. Hence intersubjectivity is originally an object relation, that is, the mutual relation of two differing subjectivities that stand in proximity to one other. The recognition that another is in fact a subject rather than an object is a mediated relational dynamic that occurs well beyond the infant's experiential world.

Like many existential and phenomenologically oriented theorists, Stern sees the self as a burgeoning agentic process that transpires within a domain of emergent, core, and intersubjective relatedness to others, thus evoking many interpersonal capacities, each having sensitive periods within each respective formative phase of self-development during which they fulfill their role as primary organizers of subjective experience. Therefore, the self is not merely stage specific but rather a continuous epigenesis that incorporates previous forms within its evolutionary-transmutational-experiential holistic structure. In its totality,

> Such senses of self include the sense of agency (without which there can be paralysis, the sense of non-ownership of self-action, the experience of loss of control to external agents); the sense of physical cohesion (without which there can be fragmentation of bodily experience, depersonalization, out-of-body experiences, derealization); the sense of continuity (without which there can be temporal dissociation, fugue states, amnesias, not "going on being," in Winnicott's term); the sense of affectivity (without which there can be anhedonia, dissociated states); the sense of a subjective self that can achieve intersubjectivity with another (without which there is cosmic loneliness or, at the other extreme, psychic transparency); the sense of creating organization (without which there can be psychic chaos); the sense of transmitting meaning (without which there can be exclusion from the culture, little socialization, and no validation of personal knowledge). In short, these senses of the self make up the foundation for the subjective experience of social development, normal and abnormal. (Stern 1985, 7–8)

While the nuances of Stern's phenomenological analysis of the self challenge some object relations models (such as those of Klein and Mahler, Pine, and Bergman 1975)—which is not without controversy—this critique does not concern us here. For the most part, his account complements (if not converges with) many features of developmental psychoanalytic thought and attachment theory.

Now let us attempt to offer a working hypothesis of the self based on these contrasting psychodynamic models. The following constitutes my theory of the infantile mind:

a. The nascent ego is at first a primitively organized sentient activity influenced by its a priori constituency of unconscious regulatory processes, including the drives, biological motivations, affective pressures, and organismic dispositions that immediately confront external reality and relational interaction upon birth.

b. The incipient mind is primarily engrossed by its newly awakened sentience and sensory capacities, which are mediated by the intrapsychic processes that make consciousness possible. This awakening is never in isolation from the immediate absorption the infant encounters in its contingent relation to its mother.

c. The burgeoning self immediately confronts the sensory manifold of objects, which it attempts to incorporate and synthesize as an amalgamation of impressions, affective resonances, and qualitative valences that it experiences and introjects, albeit imperfectly and always under the tempest of unconscious impulses, anxieties, and fantasy distortions. The presentation of objects is mediated by primitive receptive capacities that the infant encounters more or less incoherently. We may infer that the temporal apprehension of object presentations in the infant's experiential immediacy is imbued with quasi-functional meaning or usages and emotional properties (see Mills 2000a), which largely become the formative basis of the process of self and object representation.

d. The introjection of objects or part-objects occurs simultaneously with concurrent defensive maneuvers, which become increasingly more efficient, complex, and organized throughout the infant's subjective experience with caregivers and the broader environmental encounters he incorporates.

e. The institution of defense is paramount to psychic survival: defenses give protection, structure, and cohesion to the fray of psychic incoherence that the primitive mind in its immediacy is bound to weather. Defenses are transposed on the multiple parallel processes of internalization that are based on primary attachment motivations and identifications with dependency figures (which include their responsiveness styles, the quality and content of those relational experiences, and introjected material that is assimilated and/or defended against—constantly under the sway of transmuting unconscious dynamics).

f. Quantitative and qualitative variations in the form, content, and duration of parental introjects provide the backdrop for the inner representational world of the infant, a process that serves as the prototype for object relations throughout the lifespan.

Here I wish to distinguish between *introjection*, which is the immediacy of incorporating a presentation or highly specific piece of subjective reality, and *internalization*, which is a complex intrapsychic process of integration and transformation of self and object representations that takes place over maturation. Introjections in many ways provide incremental, architectonic functions for building psychic structure: they are the substance of what is immediately incorporated, rejected, or disavowed from psychic absorption. Introjects of various amounts, frequency, and quality are received by the psychic register, are gathered together by the unconscious ego, and form deposits or clusters of associational representations—each standing in dialectical relation to the subject's self-representations—which may become objects of pleasure, fixation, affection, horror, and so forth. The accumulation of introjects is furthermore emotionally imbued with qualitative significance and self-reference. Taken over time, introjections are affectively charged, mnemonically imprinted, somatically organized, semiotically arranged, and related to the tableau of self and object representations that define psychic structure, constantly under the influence and flux of unconsciously enlisted variants.

Internalization is always a process of transmogrification over time: it involves a more totalistic, synthetic, holistic appraisal of the qualities, attributes, properties, behaviors, ideals, and limitations that define self and others. If the overall preponderance of introjects over early childhood development are positive, let's say, then self and object representations may be said to correspond to more cohesive, integrative, and realistic attributions regulating self-structure. If introjections are mainly negative, however, then appraisals of self and others will be mired in negation and conflict and will thus deleteriously influence regulatory capacities that function to integrate part into whole self and object representations that serve to form a cohesive unit.

Furthermore, internalization draws on evocative memory for regulating psychic structure, quells eruptions from unruly affect, modulates internal panic and anxiety states, and provides holding-soothing functions that lend containment and cohesiveness to the self. I was once treating a patient who was deprived of consistent maternal responsiveness and was emotionally abandoned by his father as a child, which resulted in profound problems in internalization. He could not remember much of his childhood, including what his parents looked like and how they treated him during his toddler and elementary school years. He was prone to panic whenever he was reminded that he was alone, and this panic opened into a gulf of unremitting frenzy and internal emptiness. It was as though he had very few internalized objects or soothing resources to draw upon for comfort during times of distress. After many months of treatment he told me that when he grew upset, he would think of me and pretend to have conversations as though we were in session, which helped him process and ameliorate his discomfort. He also told me, in his own way, that I had become a positive introject he could draw on from his fund of memory, and that instead of carrying on a dialogue with himself in his head, he would often think of my face or imagine talking with me during nights when he could not fall asleep in order to allay his anxieties. This is an example of how internalization becomes an evoked and sustained selfobject function that lends cohesion to the ego and fortifies self-structure; we may literally see this function as a substitute for a child's transitional object, such as a security blanket or pacifier.

Although the internalization process gradually becomes more refined, it is far from ever being complete or resolute; the self is continually imperiled by both positive and negative polarities of experience that it must try to reconcile and synthesize despite the fact that various introjects will become compartmentalized and maintain a secret life of their own. Take, for example, a former eighteen-year-old male patient who was hospitalized for the first time because he was suffering from clinical depression after undergoing a deep humiliation. Upon his first sexual encounter with a female cohort, she commented on the small size of his penis, which produced immediate impotency (both physically and psychically). The trauma to his narcissism was so great that he soon became hopelessly suicidal. During his stay in the hospital, the patient was obsessed with reliving the details of the injury over and over again as a repetition compulsion; he was unable to rid himself of this horrid introject, which he experienced as a fixed presentation in his mind. As his depression worsened, he wanted electroconvulsive therapy (ECT) to remove the memory of the whole event. This is an example of what we may call *toxic introjective fixation*: when shame is too humiliating for the psyche to bear, it must be excised.

Now let us turn to an overview of our conceptualization of the self. The self is to be normatively conceived as a supraordinate, progressive epigenetic construction achieved through relational attachment, defense formation, creative self-expression, and the dialectically mediated intersubjective dynamics that govern psychosocial life. From its inception in infancy and onward, the psyche is constitutionally endowed with its biological facticity, attachment motivations, unconscious pressures, and affective resonances, all of which are operative organizational processes within intrapsychic subjective experience. As the infant instinctively enacts the attachment-bonding process to the maternal object, thus attempting to satiate various constitutional needs and emotional longings, ego sensory and motor capacities flourish, concomitant with defensive fortifications brought about through relational encounters and environmental contingencies. Attachment security, mobilization of defense, transfiguration of drives and affect, and augmentation of ego resources are contiguous developmental tasks that incrementally acquire increased organization and zest. Contiguous with the introjection and representation of objects inherent to the process of internalization, personality maturation becomes increasingly more intersubjectively dependent and later becomes subject to verbal and linguistic mediation. Anaclitic affection, selfobject responsiveness, empathic attunement, validation, and recognition continue to be necessary (albeit not sufficient) conditions in the formation of a structurally cohesive self. As self-organization progresses throughout early childhood and beyond, ego functions crystallize through cognitive maturity, elasticity, and adaptability. Through the sublimation of more primitive unconscious impulses, which is fostered by relational and institutional practices, the self cultivates higher forms of moral judgment, rational thought, and ethical, social, and aesthetic self-consciousness. However, not all individuals will attain these higher modes of self-conscious life: in fact, we are all vulnerable to cultivate these faculties and sensibilities in only a partial manner. Yet, despite individual and social differences governing the constitution of the self, we may nevertheless say that the self as a supraordinate construct is a dynamic self-articulated complex totality encompassing its historical past, present, and future orientations (Mills 2002a, 2005).

THE REPRESENTATIONAL PROCESS

As noted earlier, an important feature of subjective intrapsychic life is how an object serves a functional purpose; that is, how internalized objects become the sediment of unconscious representational processes of self and others, and how they are used to both bind primordial anxieties and fortify psychic structure. In our conceptualization of the attachment disordered self, it becomes important to highlight how the representational process is constituted via object relations theory.

The process of representation is a fundamental component of the basic cognitive operations of perception, thought, and overall mental functioning; however, it has special psychodynamic significance for attachment-related processes. Theoretical developments on representation have produced much conceptual overlap across many fields within the social sciences and humanities, including classical philosophy (*intuitions*), psychoanalysis (*internalized object representations*), cognitive psychology (*schemas*), attachment theory (*internal working models*), postmodernism (*constructivism*), poststructuralism (*symbolics*), semiotics (*signification*), and, more recently, mind studies (*propositions*). From late modern philosophy through to German idealism and French phenomenology, Kant (1781), Fichte (1794), Schelling (1800), Hegel (1807), Husserl (1950), Sartre (1943), and Merleau-Ponty (1962), just to name a few, were preoccupied with explicating the process of cognition, hence delineating the epistemological foundations for thought and knowledge, rational judgment, and the phenomenology of consciousness. Presentation (*Vorstellung*)—meaning the process of how objects of perception are organized and presented to consciousness—holds a key function in the dynamic operations of mind, and in many philosophies it is mediated by imagination and fantasy. The presentation of objects from the external world arises within the ego of consciousness (see Freud 1933a) and is thus mediated by our perceptual faculties. In effect, objects of perception are intuited or sensuously mediated by a priori intrastructural processes, manipulated by the dynamics of imagination, and cognized as conceptual thought, which is sequentially internalized and ordered within the self, thus mnemonically inscribed within the deep reservoir of the unconscious. What object relations theorists refer to as internal objects are the *re-presentations* of other people retrieved from memory in the subjective mind. These internalized objects are usually significant dependency or libidinal figures and part-object experiences (e.g., a mother's face or touch, a bottle, a blanket, etc.), and the generated functions they serve within psychic economy. Because the process of representation comes under the direction of imagination (see Kant 1781; Fichte 1794; Hegel 1817, 1978), it becomes easy to see how object representations can readily be distorted by unconscious fantasy, anxiety, and dread; this distortion leads to repetitious cycles of negativity, projection, and introjection (hence, projective identifications) that saturate attributions of self and others.

Concerned with the neurobiology of interpersonal experience, Daniel Siegel (1999) argues that the process of representation is contingent upon the interaction of activity patterns of neuronal groupings within the brain that arise within the relational context of both verbal and nonverbal communication with others, thus affecting our modes of information processing and our subjective construction of reality. Siegel claims that the brain consists of asymmetrical, differential modes of processing information, rooted in the genetic and evolutionary maturation of the nervous system, that thus produce distinctly different patterns of mental representations. These functional asymmetries influence our intrapsychic and interpersonal organizations of how we construct our lived phenomenal reality of self and others, which vary from person to person. He states, "Repeated patterns of neuronal activations help to establish a continuity in the individual's representations of reality across time. How two individuals come to share their individual representational worlds is a fundamental part of 'feeling felt' and establishing a sense of interpersonal connection" (161).

Information processing and mental representation take many forms, including sensation, perception, symbolic coding, conceptual or categorical classification, and linguistic signification. These cognitive activities are inextricably connected to memory acquisition, storage, and retrieval; imagination; emotional arousal; and the idiosyncratic, developmental organization of brain laterality vis-à-vis object relations that affect the phenomenology of consciousness and the activation of unconscious processes within each hemispheric division and specialization. Because of the unique contingencies that govern the maturation of individual brain asymmetry, the process of representation will developmentally unfold according to variegated influences governing individual differences. This means that lateral hemispheric differentiation regulating information processing will involve the recruitment of unique patterns of neuronal group activations in each individual. What is of particular relevance to understanding attachment processes is that different attachment patterns will correspond to different levels of asymmetrically organized neuronal activity. Siegel argues, for example, that emotionally detached and avoidant children, as well as their dismissing parents, may disproportionately enlist linear, linguistic, and analytically based modes of communication processing within left hemispheric functioning, thus accounting for the marked deficiencies in emotional filtering we may observe among attachment disordered populations.

While Siegel's work can be criticized for being causally reductionistic, he nevertheless underscores the point that human connectedness shapes the neuronal connections from which the mind emerges. More specifically, the degree, localization, and activation of neural arousal directly correspond to the emotional organizations that are inherent in attachment-related processes. Because the ability to organize emotions is such an integral product of healthy attachments—the origins of which stem from our primary object relationships—emotional information processing directly shapes the construction of representations and the capacity for the mind to integrate subjective experience into meaningful units and adapt to future relational pressures.

Peter Fonagy (2000) and his colleagues (Fonagy et al. 1991) substantiate Siegel's assertions. What is of immense value in Fonagy's work is his claim that attachment disordered populations have crippled abilities to read and anticipate the hypothesized mental states of others' minds. This is particularly true with respect to compromised capacities to intuit or think about the internal emotional states of others, especially in affectively charged interpersonal situations. While Fonagy's contributions to attachment theory will be explored more fully in the next chapter, his research evokes many profound questions.

What is the process of representation like for the attachment disordered mind? Are internalized objects necessarily impregnated with negative qualities, such as cruelty and lack, or is there a simultaneous dialectical process of preserving the idealized or fantasized qualities of the object despite such negative presentations? How do protest and despair, avoidance and withdrawal, ambivalence and disorientation affect object representation? Are these defensive maneuvers designed to protect the ego against the horrors of real or perceived trauma? And how do those internalized experiences influence the structural ontogeny of the self? While there are many viable models of object relations pathology, I wish to specifically explore these questions within the context of attachment in the theories of Klein, Bion, and Fairbairn.

BRIDGES TO OBJECT RELATIONS PATHOLOGY

For Klein, the ego exists at birth and is plagued by anxieties characteristic of psychosis that it attempts to fend off and control through the primary defense mechanisms of splitting, projection, and introjection, giving rise to the "paranoid-schizoid" and "depressive" positions that mold object relations. While Klein refers to these defensive maneuvers as "mechanisms," they are not mechanistic. Ego activity is never characterized by fixed or static operations taking the form of predetermined tropisms; rather, psychic organization is the continuity of subjective temporal processes. It is more accurate to conceptualize these early mechanisms as defensive *process systems* comprising the ego's intrapsychic relation to itself and its object environment, initially the maternal object. This makes ego development and object relations an intersubjective enterprise.

Klein's theory of splitting has revolutionized the way we understand ego development. In her seminal essay "Notes on Some Schizoid Mechanisms," Klein (1946) proclaims splitting as the original primordial defense, a process she started analyzing as early as 1929. Beset by the death drive (*Todestrieb*), the immature ego deflects the destructive impulse by turning it against the object and engages in oral-sadistic attacks on the mother's body, thus triggering persecutory anxiety. Splitting is the very first in a series of defenses that are never completely separate from one another and hence form a dialectical cycle Klein labeled as "projective identification." Klein coined the term in 1946[1] and conceived of it as an aggressive discharge of certain portions of the ego *into* an external object, the aim of which is to dominate or consume certain aspects of the object's contents in order to make it part of the ego's own internal constitution. By amalgamating Freud's death drive into her developmental paradigm of paranoid-schizoid and depressive organizations that constitute the primitive psyche, she necessarily imbues the process of internalization and object representation with aggressive, persecutory, and depleting features.

Negativity is a primordial normative facticity of the infant's mind. The ego's original activity is one of negation: it defines itself in opposition to what it is not. Following Freud, Klein speculates that splitting mechanisms arise in an effort to subvert the death drive that threatens the ego with internal destruction. Splitting is a defense against felt or perceived annihilation. In fact, splitting itself is a violent cleaving operation that divides subject from object. Not only does splitting disperse the destructive impulse, but splitting itself is destructive—it destroys as it negates.

What implications does this have for attachment motivations? How does object representation unfold according to this developmental paradigm? If the infant psyche is saturated with negativity and conflict that it fights to discharge through expulsion, then it is bound to experience intense and foreboding terror of its return; projection is only a temporary measure—a fleeting moment, for it comes back to haunt the psyche as persecutory anxiety. *There is something worse than nonbeing*, namely, paranoiac torment—bootstrapped to eternity in purgatory. Schizoid mechanisms of splitting, denial, and alienation of affect through projection always return in a form that the infant must defend against, assimilate, and reincorporate back into its internal structure. By implication, part- and whole-object representations must be split and compartmentalized into "good" (affirmative) and "bad" (negative) configurations; therefore, attachment figures take on both coveted yet feared qualities and properties. The premature mind knows no continuity; time is merely *the moment*. When contentment wanes, bad introjects protrude.

For the inchoate ego, the internality of subjective experience is fragmentary and uncohesive, hence split or fractured into units of experience containing a rigid dichotomy vacillating between two antithetical poles. Splitting helps contain and preserve positive experiences, ideals, wishes, and impulses directed toward a good object or part-object—namely, loving feelings for the mother—while negating, devaluing, and destroying (via fantasy) bad attributes associated with an object that threaten the valued integrity of its idealized counterpart. Thus Klein speaks of the infant's split relation to the mother's breast—or by extension her smell, touch, face, and eyes—as being both gratifying and persecutory. The task of the ego is to keep terrifying experiences at bay, including deprivation or the absence of gratification, which immediately introduce the fear of annihilation. Therefore, the ego at first operates on a simple economy of introjecting the good and projecting the bad. In fact, because the psyche is pure activity, there is a constant flow of projective-introjective forces and content directed toward regulating psychic anxiety. Here it is easy to see how psychic structure is the instantiation and fortification of defense.

Not only is the object split into sundry dialectical parts, but the self is as well. The ego splits itself into rudimentary good and bad units that consist of various attributes, qualities, and properties the ego strives to differentiate. While the bad is expunged, the good is retained; therefore, both internal self and object representations compose the ego in its primitive constitution.

Klein explains how the sadistic and destructive aspects of the infant's fantasy life enter the material object (or whoever dominates the scene) and inevitably come back to assail the psyche with horrific force—the return of *death*. The paranoid-schizoid position is therefore one that the nascent self constructs based on its negative relation to objects and their internalized representations. From this standpoint, attachment processes are plagued by anxiety and dread even under the most favorable circumstances. This is why, for instance, a small (securely attached) child immediately panics when he notices the disappearance of his mother. Because the child is unable to evoke and sustain a calming-soothing introject or image of the loved or coveted object, the horror of invasion and assault stalks the psyche—a return of its own projection—and it identifies and reappropriates this horror as persecutory torment.

There is always something that stalks the ego. Even in the most well-adjusted individual, feelings of inadequacy or self-reproach invade the mind, as do memories of discontent or failed selfobject experiences. But what we largely want to escape from are our own negative internal representations that constantly plague us even when our external world is equally hostile. From this perspective, you can never get away from the *Thing*.

Although Klein has been largely criticized by many contemporary developmental researchers, who charge her with misattributing adult clinical reconstructions to infant experience, we nevertheless cannot deny the value of how she attempts to explain the etiology of unconscious primitive processes that prefigure and inform clinically observed forms of defense that appear in attachment and personality disordered populations. Furthermore, the primacy of negativity is ontologically justified based on the fact that pain and human suffering is a process that begins at birth and is experienced in multifarious forms and relational contexts. When attachment systems are disrupted, neglected, or subjected to developmental trauma, these most basic defensive operations are even more negatively charged. To ensure survival, the behavioral attachment system must react to preserve or restore the security and connectedness it needs for self-cohesion.

Another unabated truth about the psyche is that melancholic currents resonate within us all. This is one reason why Klein needed to account for its normativity in the ontogeny of the self. We can never escape from the fact that lack, loss, abandonment, loneliness, rejection, devaluation, and injuries to self-worth are developmentally experienced by everyone and thus are preserved within the unconscious abyss of the psyche's primordial organizing principles. As we have seen in Kohut's model of the self, depletion is a structural constituent of the mind that drains the self of adhesion and vitality. Klein attempted to explain how this is structurally prepared in what she called the depressive position.

While the paranoid-schizoid position is characterized by anxiety and aggressive attacks against the ego's own projections, the depressive position is characterized by fear and despair over loss of the material object. In other words, what is paranoiac to the ego is that it will be destroyed by bad objects, so it must attack. But in the depressive position, the ego is anxious that it *has destroyed* or *will destroy* the objects it loves and depends upon, so it enters into deep despair. Depressive anxieties spring from ambivalence the infant feels in relation to its dependence on love objects. Here the intensity of projective mechanisms is lessened while introjective processes are accentuated. The ego at this stage now acquires more awareness of its dependence on (independent) objects that are likely to go away. What is even worse than real or perceived abandonment and loss is the fear that the ego has destroyed its valued object; this fear sends the ego into guilt and self-hatred over its iniquity. In either case, the infant is enveloped by depressive anguish.

In the depressive position, the rigid, split dichotomy between self and object representations starts to recede, and the ego now becomes incrementally more aware of its competing, antipodal appraisals of self and others. During this time, internalized objects become slightly more integrated so that the infant can experience and preserve ambivalent feelings of both loving and hating an attachment figure. This creates a great deal of inner diffusion and pain for the ego, which is condemned to oscillate between these mixed emotional states; this oscillation generates more anxiety and leads to regression to paranoid projections as a means of defense. The ego at this stage may be said to experience an intense dysphoria filtered through a restless, agitated sadness over loss of the love object that it fears it annihilated. The psyche is subjected to a plethora of guilt, longing, helplessness, and hopelessness over the uncertainty of regaining the lost object and making reparation for its transgressions. While in the paranoid-schizoid position, the ego is terrified by the haunting from its own unrecognized projection; here, in the depressive position, the ego is haunted by its own recognized deed—thus the psyche falls into bits.

The depressive position can never be entirely overcome but only ameliorated through the internalization of positive introjects and sustained identifications with secure attachment figures. This is why anxiety and depression are pervasive aspects of normative human experience that may be reactivated or regressed to during times of loss, guilt, and feelings of ambivalence toward significant others throughout the life cycle. Infants who are not able to evoke and minister positive introjectory experiences of dependency figures are on even more precarious ground. They are likely to be dogged by anxieties of lack, persecution, and abandonment and will be unable to successfully draw from the mnemonic fund of good internalized introjects, thus leaving the ego impoverished. Under these developmental conditions, the structural integrity of the self may be severely compromised, thereby predisposing the child to attachment pathology, schizoid organizations, and even regression into psychosis.

What is particularly interesting about Klein's developmental model is that she anticipates much of what attachment researchers today refer to as insecure or disorganized attachments. Anxiety and dread over abandon-

ment and loss may be seen in the splitting mechanisms and defensive exclusions of withdrawal, disorientation, and detachment; the projective
mechanisms associated with the acting out of anger or destructive rage;
and the depressive reactions associated with protest and despair over
parental separation and desertion. These developmental-clinical scenarios observed in toddlers in relation to attachment, separation, and loss all
corroborate Klein's basic insights on the primitive organizational
processes of ego development and adaptation.

While Klein (1946) first defined projective identification as a defensive
process expressed through splitting and schizoid mechanisms, she later
(1957) suggested that envy was intimately embedded in projective identification. In this conception, the ego forces itself into the psychic reality of the
other in order to destroy its coveted attributes. Shortly after this theoretical
modification, Bion (1959) distinguished normal from pathological forms of
projective identification, which has further led revisionist Kleinians to
articulate many distinct yet related modes of projective-identificatory
processes (Hinshelwood 1991).

Bion, himself analyzed by Klein, was the first psychoanalyst to recognize normative functions of projective identification embedded in normal
thought processes. Bion (1959, 1962a, 1962b) distinguished between two
alternative aims of projective identification marked by difference in the
degree of violence attached to the mechanism. The first, *evacuation*, is
characterized by its forceful entry into an object, in fantasy, as a means of
controlling painful mental states. Evacuation is directed toward relief and
is often aimed toward intimidating or manipulating the object. This is a
pathological manifestation of projective identification. The second, *communication*, is a more benign attempt to communicate a certain mental
content by introducing into the object a specific state of mind, a function
often seen in the process of *containing*—a process in which one person
contains some part of another. This is a normative function. It may be argued that evacuation is itself a form of communication, and thereby the
distinction becomes blurred; but for our purposes, evacuation highlights
the thrust, intensity, and urgency of the need to expel psychic content. In
all likelihood, evacuation and communication operate in confluence and
are separated only by their motives and force of violence enacted through
projection.

In his influential essay "Attacks on Linking," Bion (1959) presents his
mature view of projective identification as a form of communication taking on both normal and abnormal valences. Drawing on Klein, Bion argues
that pathological forms fall within a range of *excess*, such as the degree of
aggressivity of splitting, hatred, intrusion, omnipotent control and fusion
with the object, the amount of loss or diffusion of the ego, and the specific
awareness of destructive intent. Normal projective-identificatory
processes, however, play an adaptive role in social reality and are ordinary

operations of communication and empathy that furthermore transpire within the process of thinking itself.

Bion's (1957) model of thinking, linking, and fantasy is preliminarily addressed in his effort to differentiate psychotic from nonpsychotic personalities with special emphasis on the awareness of psychic reality. For Bion (1954), drawing on Klein's (1930) and later Hanna Segal's (1957) work on symbol formation in the development of the early ego, the awareness of psychic reality is contingent upon the capacity for verbal thought derived from the depressive position; yet this process goes back even further. Linking— the capacity to form relations between objects or mental contents—serves a functional purpose; this process is derived from the paranoid-schizoid position. Bion (1957, 1959) envisions psychotic organization to be largely plagued by violent attacks on the ego—particularly on the links between certain mental contents—and the awareness of inner reality itself. As a result, the schizophrenic lives in a fractured world of terror where mental links are "severed" or "never forged." Fantasy formation is fragmented, persecutory, and horrific. Attempts at creating links or making connections between objects are all but destroyed, and when minute links exist, they are impregnated with perversion and cruelty.

How are Bion's reflections germane to those with attachment vulnerabilities? Are evacuation as aggressive projection and communication as benign transmission processes that are operative within the behavioral attachment system? Under situations of separation, abandonment, frustration, or empathic failure from dependency figures, for example, evacuation becomes a means to protest intrapsychically against the intolerability of the loss, absence, deprivation, and so forth that are evoked in the moment. Albeit maladaptive, the forceful entry via fantasy into the maternal object is an attempt to gain order and control and manipulate the type of responsiveness the child desires. But evacuation runs the risk of spoiling the object and rendering it sullied and flawed; thus, object representation may become too colored by negativity. If the linking of object experiences with internal resonance states becomes mired in aggressivity, then destruction will be interjected and dispersed into the coveted but hated attachment figure, and it will become an invariable bad object. Links to feelings and symbolic formations of security, contentment, regulation of anxiety, suspension of dread, and so forth may be impartially forged or cleaved altogether. This is why the positive form of projective identification as gentle or benevolent communication is what Bion emphasizes, further highlighting the ego's need to contain such destructive impulses and to be contained, mollified, and reassured by a responsive caregiver.

What is of importance in understanding the normative functions of projective identification is how Bion conceives of the phenomenology and evolution of thinking. Bion (1957) informs us that "some kind of thought, related to what we should call ideographs and sight rather than to words and hearing exists at the outset" (66), and this capacity is derived within the nonpsychotic part of the embryonic psyche. He continues to tell us that this crude level of thinking "depends on the capacity for balanced introjection and projection of objects and, *a fortiori*, on awareness of them" (66). Ultimately, for Bion, both preverbal and verbal thought necessarily require an awareness of psychic reality.

Throughout the course of his theoretical contributions, Bion explicates three phases in the process of thinking. The first relies on the presumption of a priori knowledge, whereby an innate *preconception* meets a *realization* in experience, which results in a *conception*, the product of thought (Bion 1959, 1962a). Bion's notion of preconceptions is similar to Segal's (1964) notion of unconscious fantasy used as a means of generating hypotheses for testing reality. A preconception may be understood as a predisposed intuition of and expectancy for an object, such as a breast, which "mates" with the realization of the actual object in experience, thus forming a conception.

The second phase depends on the infant's capacity to tolerate frustration. A positive conception is generated when a preconception meets with a satisfying realization. When a preconception encounters a negative realization—say, absence—frustration ensues. Klein shows that when the immature ego encounters *absence*, it experiences the *presence* of a bad object, or, perhaps more appropriately, a bad self/object experience. Bion, however, extends this idea further and posits that the experience of absence is transformed into a thought. The notion of absence, lack, or nothingness is conceptually retained. Yet this process is contingent on the infant's ability to modulate frustration. If frustration tolerance is high, the transformation of absence into a thought serves the dialectical function of suggesting that presence is possible; that is, the absent object, such as the breast or bottle, may appear or re-present itself at some later time in the future. Affirmation and negation are dialectically conjoined, separated only by their moments. With application to Bion, *nothing* stands in opposition to *being*, which, once realized, is expected to return. If the capacity to manage frustration is low, the experience of nothingness does not advance to the thought of an absent good object but rather remains at the immediate level of the concrete bad object experienced in the moment, which must be expelled through omnipotent evacuation. Bion (1962a) believes that if this process becomes arrested, advances in symbol formation and thinking are deleteriously obstructed.

The third phase of thinking involves more advanced levels of projective identification, which Bion (1962b) describes as the "container–contained" relationship. Here the infant has a sensory experience, feeling, or need that is perceived as bad, and the infant wishes to banish it. This type of projective identification evokes within the mother the same type of internal sensations experienced by the infant. If the mother is adequately well balanced and capable of optimal responsiveness, what Bion calls *reverie*, she will be able to contain such feelings and transform them into acceptable forms, which the infant can reintroject. Bion labels this process of transformation the *alpha-function*. In normal development, the container–contained relationship allows the infant to reintroject the transformed object into something tolerable, which eventually results in the infant's internalizing the function itself. If successful, this process aids in the increased capacity to modulate frustration and developmentally strengthens the infant's cognitive capabilities to conceptualize and generate symbolic functions, which generally leads to the fortification of the ego. Not only does Bion breach the sharp schism between feeling and thought that has dogged philosophical rationalism, but he also shows how emotions are made meaningful within the broader conceptual processes of thinking (Spillius 1988).

How aware is the vulnerably attached self of its own psychic reality, of its own emotional life? Following Bion's conceptualization of the process of conceptualization, can the small infant have nonverbal thought of the notion of "good" as a desired qualitative presence that can be evoked during times of frustration or the mother's absence? As I have said before, the ability to solicit and induce positive introjects—such as images and their associated feelings and meanings—is a vital function that regulates internal anxiety and depleted emotional conditions. In fact, it is a prerequisite of the structurally cohesive self. This requires some degree of evocative memory to recover the lost presence of good internalized object representations for soothing purposes. This is facilitated by maternal reverie as part of the container–contained relationship and hence is reciprocally animated within the mother–infant dyad. This becomes a two-way relation. For example, the benign communication of feelings or longings conveyed through the baby's nonverbal gestures and facial expressions can immediately pull for a specific responsiveness from the empathically attuned mother, who thus gratifies the immediate cry of desire administered through nonverbal states. Over time, when the infant better learns to modulate frustrations—as benevolent communications are adequately contained and reintrojected innocuously through maternal facilitation—the evocation of consoling images, memories, and semiotic formations in fantasy and conceptual signification quells the panic and trepidation that often accompany this stage of psychic development. If attachments are strained or jeopardized, however, bad introjects permeate psychic topography. Even worse, they can infiltrate and dominate evocative capacities. This leads to a crisis the inchoate ego must attempt to reconcile through the balance and synthesis of positive and negative self/object representations. But what if object representation is disproportionately bad? That is, what if there is mainly negativity? Here enters Fairbairn.

Fairbairn's contributions to understanding object relations pathology are particularly instructive when we examine how he conceives of internalization. For Fairbairn (1943), we are bombarded with a preponderance of negative introjects from early childhood onward that become unconsciously deposited as "bad objects," thus experienced as traumatic incidents leaving permanent effects. In other words, we acquire a fundamental acuity for introjecting bad objects that we strive to repress, dissociate, or compartmentalize and keep at arm's length. There is a propensity for the psyche to be attracted to negativity, which it absorbs and retains assiduously. Speaking scatologically, *we take in bad shit*.

Fairbairn placed a great deal of emphasis on how early childhood trauma could imprison the ego in emotional pain and anguish. His reasons for this are straightforwardly simple: bad objects become so readily internalized in childhood because our parents are too powerful to be resisted. In his clinical work with traumatized patients, from those afflicted by "war neuroses" to children who were physically abused or sexually molested, he found that children in particular were reluctant to concede that their parents were bad even when, for instance, they had been violently beaten by a drunken caregiver. Conversely, they were more likely to feel ashamed, defiled, and guilty and otherwise regard themselves poorly.[2] While this response may be in part socially and historically informed by the contingencies of his time—and indeed may be experienced differently by today's standards—Fairbairn concluded that this was a reaction formation or "moral defense" as an attempt to turn the parents into good objects so they could be internalized properly in order to provide the child with a sense of security. Because children's identities and self-representations are primarily based on the types of identifications they form with their parents, children would feel themselves to be bad if they allowed themselves to harbor contemptuous feelings toward their parents. It is intolerable for the ego to be reminded of these bad objects that it associates with evil and endangerment; therefore, they must be repressed. In effect, the ego preserves the idealized parental imago it so desperately wants to identify with and incorporate. Perhaps this is why so many attachment disordered populations show high degrees of ambivalence interspersed with flagrantly distorted idealizations of their parents.

In order to safeguard itself against the intrusion of bad objects, the ego bulwarks its defenses in order to tame the austere nature of internalization. Fairbairn reasons that the powerful exertion of bad objects cannot be rejected because, despite their imposition, the child needs them. Through internalization, children attempt to control such negativity, but, as a general rule, the bad objects' dint converts them into persecutory spirits that possess their owners. Bad objects have a hold on us we are unwilling to release. In other words, we cannot give them up. In fact, Fairbairn (1941) saw various forms of the psychoneuroses (e.g., phobias, hysteria, obsessionality, paranoia) as *techniques* of attempting to rid the psyche of bad objects without really having to lose them. Here we may be reminded of Lacan

(1977): some patients love their symptoms too much, because they provide familiarity and meaning, to the point that they are not willing to relinquish their *jouissance*—their pleasure in their destructiveness, hence their pathology. To resist internalizing one's parents is to risk psychic impoverishment, so we assume the onus of their inherent negativity, which we turn onto ourselves in order to ensure that we have a reasonably good (albeit illusory) interpersonal environment. Fairbairn's ideas anticipate in many insightful ways how the behavioral attachment system, internal working models, defensive exclusions, and attachment patterns of avoidance, ambivalence, disorganization, rejection, panic, and dread in response to separation are motivated out of relational anxieties under the press of these negatively internalized objects.

The implications of Fairbairn's thought have even farther-reaching consequences: *internalization begins with bad objects.* We are attracted to the negative, to trauma. There is a perverse appeal to pain, a primal destructiveness experienced as sadomasochistic inwardness. Developmental traumas leave lasting impressions. This is why it is often the case that we remember clearly and poignantly negative experiences—perhaps even more so than positive ones—in recollecting our earliest memories. We are drawn to our traumas, even fascinated by them, refusing to let them go; traumatic fixation is a necessity the psyche is impelled to perpetuate, an unconscious tarrying with the negative.

We take in bad shit—that which terrifies us, desecrates us, *deracinates* us—in order to rework our traumas and make them more docile. And we hope—we pine—for reprieve, for mastery and control over that which controls us. Even when we transcend our traumas, they never leave us. There is always the affective residue that creeps into consciousness from time to time, bringing forth its poisonous effect, reminding us of our inner being—our past, unabated and envenomed. Negative internalizations never completely go away; they are superimposed on all other forms of representation.

NOTES

1. When Klein republished her 1946 paper, "Notes on Some Schizoid Mechanisms," in *Developments in Psycho-Analysis* (London: Hogarth Press, 1952), she added the term *projective identification* as a way of explaining the process of splitting in connection with projection and introjection (300).

2. From the perspective of contemporary cognitive psychology, it may be argued that children form simple isomorphic relations between traumatic events and self-blame because, developmentally, children engage in naive cognition dominated by preoperational thinking; thus, they are unable to think critically or rationally synthesize causal attributions and belief systems from the accuracy of perceptual processing during traumatic events, which further fuels unconscious fantasies that justify parental abuse (see Erreich 2003 for a discussion).

3

⊘

Borderline Organization, Trauma, and Attachment

Borderline pathology has remained an enigmatic and contentious clinical syndrome since its conceptual introduction. The American Psychiatric Association (APA 2000) views borderlineopathy as a specific type of personality disorder usually not diagnosable until early adulthood; hence, its attribution to adolescent personality functioning is even more controversial. Furthermore, there is good evidence to allow us to conclude that borderline conditions have various specified developmental sequelae that are evident in childhood (Pine 1983), despite the fact that the DSM-IV-TR and the ICD-10 classification systems do not endorse childhood borderline pathology as a separate diagnostic entity. When borderline features and symptoms are clinically identified in children, they are typically labeled as conduct disordered or oppositionally defiant, often with an accompanying diagnosis of attention-deficit/ hyperactivity disorder (ADHD).

There has been some attention in the literature to the interface between attachment pathology and borderline states (Fonagy et al. 1995); however, attachment- and personality-related research have largely inhabited separate domains. Practitioners who focus on the psychodynamics and treatment of borderline conditions, however, may readily observe severe attachment deficiencies that saturate the characterological, structural integrity of this population group. It is for these reasons that, as a practicing clinician, I am more inclined to view personality disorders in general, and those falling on the borderline spectrum in particular, as encompassing a disorder of the self with attachment vulnerabilities etiologically informed by early developmental disturbances in object relations and, subsequently, structuralization.

In this chapter it becomes important for us to turn our attention to how attachment pathology is largely organized on borderline levels of functioning that stem from disorganized self-states manifested on the structural level, which in turn stand in relation to the persistently disturbed interpersonal relationships that unequivocally accompany this disorder. As we have seen in our previous chapters, attachment pathology in early childhood is causally overdetermined yet dynamically informed by real or perceived developmental traumas and repeated failures in responsiveness by caregivers, which preclude secure attachments and healthy capacities for relatedness. As a result, the vulnerably attached child will inevitably suffer from truncated ego resources and impoverished representational processes that detrimentally fuel primitive defensive organizations and structural deficiencies of the self. It is often the case that these early attachment deficits prepare a developmental trajectory of character pathology in later life that is largely organized at the borderline level; however, personality disorders of all kinds are predicated on deficient attachments. While I do not wish to exhaustively examine nor critique the etiology, course, and/or nosology of borderline conditions, it will be important for us to conceptually outline the psychodynamics of borderline attachment pathology and the polysymptomatic profile that is often coextensive with or superimposed on this primary disorder. This exploration will help prepare us to specifically examine treatment implications for working with such attachment disordered populations.

POLYSYMPTOMATIC PROFILES
AND BORDERLINE CONDITIONS

A half century ago, clinicians began to recognize a subgroup of atypical children whose disturbances in ego functioning and object relations were far less severe than those of children suffering from psychotic conditions, yet they were not organized at the neurotic level (Mahler, Ross, and De-Fries 1949; Weil 1953). Mahler and her colleagues (1949) articulated the notion of a benign or "borderline" psychosis and placed these children on the mild end of the developmental and clinical continuum that comprised autistic and symbiotic childhood psychoses. Borderline conditions were conceived to be on a schizophrenic spectrum yet represented a more incipient, attenuated, or less severe variant (Bleiberg 1994).

Soon after, Ekstein and Wallerstein (1954) used the term "borderline" to classify children who were not likely to become psychotic yet presented with a characteristic pattern of unpredictability marked by rapid shifts in ego functioning, disturbed object relations, and fluctuations in reality testing that vacillated between psychotic and neurotic perceptions. A number of early psychoanalytic investigators (Geleerd 1958; Marcus 1963; Rosenfeld and Sprince 1963) attempted to systematically delineate the development and clinical course of borderline children and identified a wide range of clinical features, including developmental asymmetry, impulsivity, low frustration tolerance, regression, withdrawal into fantasy, lack of ego structure, separation problems, sleep difficulty, somatic complaints, and pervasive anxiety accompanied by many neurotic conditions, such as phobias, obsessive-compulsiveness, and ritualistic behavior. Despite these pioneering efforts to classify child psychopathology, today the term *borderline* almost exclusively refers to severe character pathology in adulthood.

Specialists in the assessment and treatment of borderline personality have emphasized various pathognomonic features, intrapsychic processes, and interpersonal disruptions that differentiate themselves from other clinical syndromes; however, it is generally an uncontested fact that borderlines present with highly polysymptomatic profiles. This is especially evident in disturbed adolescents, where a barrage of presenting complaints and symptoms is more the norm rather than the exception. Because borderline conditions are disparate and variegated, the therapist may be confronted with a spate of clinical impressions that leave him with unabated differential diagnostic questions. For example, in the initial consultation, borderlines may present with flagrant anxiety, depression, posttraumatic stress symptoms, suicidality, obessionality, phobias, dissociation, hypochondriasis, conversion hysteria, hypomania, paranoia, grandiosity, confusion, emotional decompensation, and brief psychotic experiences, including delusional constructions of reality. In addition to this possible range of overt symptomatology, let us further observe primary diagnostic features, defenses, and behavioral manifestations that are often discerned during the initial interview:

a. Presence of intense or dysregulated affect, for example, anger, rage, negativity, lugubrious dramatic gesticulations, emotional volatility (profuse sobbing, or even screaming), detachment, and blunt, compartmentalized, or dissociated affect

b. A litany of complaints directed toward others (often family members or significant others), authority figures, social institutions, and/or life circumstances with poor self-reflectivity and little recognition of the subject's own personal involvement or responsibility

c. Marked conflict in interpersonal relationships that vacillate between transient and shallow encounters, often centering around sex and/ or alcohol or drug use, and intense, dependent, and manipulative encounters marred by neediness, connivance, demandingness, and devaluation

d. Disturbed, confused, and/or ambivalent self-representations; identity diffusion; and superficial identifications with and/or overidealizations of others

e. Life histories tinged by impulsive behaviors (whether episodic acts or more chronic patterns of behavior), usually involving aggressive actions, polymorphous sexual behavior (often as a means to procure affection or validation or quell internal anxiety states), alcohol or substance abuse, numbing behaviors, illicit activity, and self-destructiveness, including forms of self-mutilation (e.g., cutting, burning) or body modification (e.g., piercings, tattoos)

f. Confusion over interpreting inner experiential states: emptiness, loneliness, melancholia, anomie, anhedonia, void—even the reported absence of emotion, alexithymia, and/or the persistent feeling of lack

g. Developmental histories marked by parental absence, separation, abandonment, neglect, abuse, and/or trauma that point toward severe deficits in attachment

With the possible range and deluge of presenting complaints and symptoms, the neophyte clinician is often left scratching his head and contemplating what test may narrow down the diagnostic options. And even when psychological testing is conducted, the results often generate more confusion. For example, performance during psychological testing often reveals bizarre, illogical, and/or primitive responses on unstructured tests (e.g., the Rorschach), marked by regression, deviant thought processes, and affective embellishment to simple percepts characteristic of psychosis; yet on structured testing, such as standard IQ assessments, ordinary reasoning approaches are observed (Gunderson and Singer 1975). Because the range of social functioning and adaptation for borderlines may vary—from those who generally present with an appropriate appearance, adequate manners, social awareness, and a history of achievement or success to those who appear flagrantly disturbed with traumatic and shady histories—even the most experienced clinician may face diagnostic challenges. To illustrate by case example, let us consider the following patient from a diagnostic standpoint.

The patient was a forty-one-year-old, divorced female who is the mother of four daughters. She presented to the emergency room of a general hospital accompanied by her fiancé and stated that she had been experiencing severe anxiety attacks for the past two years, and that in the past five days they had been almost continual. Three weeks prior to this particular visit, she had several contacts with mental health services, including being seen on an emergency basis and then in outpatient follow-up care a few days later by her psychiatrist; she also attended an orientation session of an outpatient day-treatment program, only to present herself again soon after to the crisis intervention team of the same hospital, and then again in emergency the next day following an overdose of Clonazepam.

The patient reported that she experiences several anxiety attacks each day, characterized by a tingling sensation in her arms, shortness of breadth, vomiting, and tachycardia. She has frequent crying spells, wants to sleep but is too agitated, complains of irritability and feeling numb, has a lack of sexual interest, suffers from poor short-term memory and concentration, reduced appetite, and experiences passive suicidal ideation. The patient denied any abuse of alcohol or street drugs, and no delusions or hallucinations were noted. She was diagnosed by the attending ER psychiatrist as having major depression and panic disorder and was admitted to the inpatient psychiatry unit where I was employed.

The patient's regular psychiatrist had diagnosed her with recurring depression and anxiety as well as antisocial personality disorder, primarily because in the past she had tried to run her fiancé over with her car. The psychiatrist requested that she undergo a psychodiagnostic assessment with me in order to rule out the possibility of malingering because she was currently complaining that her panic and depressive symptoms were too overwhelming for her to work and was requesting to be placed on a disability certificate.

When I met with the patient, it soon became apparent we were dealing with more structural deficits associated to trauma and attachment pathology than had been previously identified.[1] Before we examine the diagnostic nuances of her developmental and psychosocial history, let us observe how this patient scored on the Minnesota Multiphasic Personality Inventory (MMPI-2), a standard objective clinical measure (see figure 3.1).

Notice that her validity scales are within normal limits and are the result of careful item responding rather than a random response pattern. She apparently understood the item content and endorsed symptomatology that was indicative of her current level of functioning. Now observe her clinical profile: all of the clinical scales are significantly and severely elevated, most notably the Schizophrenia (Sc) and Paranoia (Pa) scales. This type of diagnostic picture is reflective of someone experiencing a florid psychotic process that includes personality decompensation, social withdrawal, disordered affect, and erratic, possibly assaultive, behavior. A standard, computer-generated interpretative report tells us that she is confused, disoriented, withdrawn, and preoccupied with occult or abstruse ideas and feels that others are persecuting her because of her beliefs. She can appear quite apathetic and aloof, preferring to retreat into fantasy, and suffers from delusions and hallucinations, blunted or inappropriate affect, and hostile, irritable behavior, which further suggests she may behave in unpredictable, highly aggressive ways. This MMPI-2 clinical profile reflects chronic maladjustment and is often attributed to patients who suffer from paranoid schizophrenia or a paranoid disorder: personality decompensation, disorganization, and thought disorder are likely to persist.

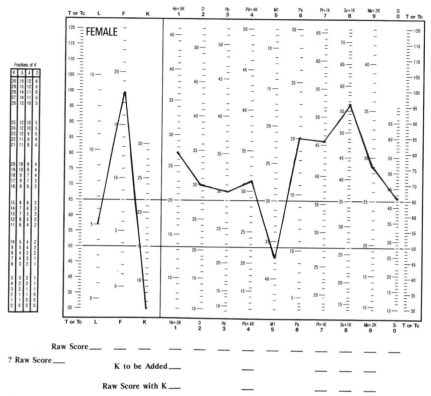

Figure 3.1. Minnesota Multiphasic Personality Inventory 2 (MMPI-2)

This patient's testing protocol resembles a classic psychotic tetrad, when she is in fact a traumatized borderline who presents as a schizophrenic. If one were to focus primarily on her overt symptomatology, as did her previous psychiatrists, her structural deficits, trauma, and attachment pathology could be easily overlooked. Let us now examine more closely her developmental history.

The patient reports having a very chaotic and bereft early childhood. Her father abandoned her and her mother when she was three years old and reportedly was the head of a biker gang, was a volatile alcoholic and addict, and engaged in much violence and subversive criminal activity. She was raised primarily in an extended family home environment: she lived with her grandparents, uncle, cousins, and mother, who was frequently in and out of the home. Her father would visit infrequently, but she felt special when he would occasionally pay her some attention. She reports that her grandmother was her primary caregiver and that her relationship with her mother was always strained, overly controlling, and inconsistent.

Between the ages of seven and twelve, the patient alleges to have been repeatedly sexually molested by a family friend in the home. When she was thirteen, her father moved to another province, which precipitated a second abandonment crisis. She began to rebel as a young teenager, got involved in the "wrong crowd," abused alcohol and drugs, and reports being raped at the age of fourteen while having a knife held to her throat. She furthermore reports having other traumatic, horrific experiences, including having a gun pointed in her face on one occasion and held to her head on another while she was forced to have sex with an eighteen-year-old boy when she was fourteen. To make matters worse, she later married the rapist when she was nineteen years of age.

She reports that her husband was a very emotionally cold, abusive individual, who on several occasions beat her physically. After having four daughters with this man, the patient finally kicked him out of the house for good and sought a divorce. Their interpersonal relationship can be described as extremely chaotic and volatile, yet pathologically dependent. She reports that they would often get into fights with one another, where yelling and cursing threats were administered as a way of controlling and hurting the other, followed by prolonged sessions of passionate sex. This was a repetitive, ongoing cycle of aggression, rejection, and withdrawal, followed by periods of loving contrition and reparation.

The patient reports approximately two years ago having a delayed-onset, posttraumatic stress reaction that was triggered by the experience of being harassed and threatened by a male coworker. She claims that the man was intimidating her at work on a regular basis and indirectly threatened her life and the lives of her children. At one point, she reports that he took a razor to his arm, whereby she immediately became terrified and paranoid. The event dredged up her earlier traumatic experiences of being raped and molested. She reportedly sought psychiatric and psychological care following this experience and saw different doctors and counselors; however, she states that her condition only worsened as she developed more depressive and generalized anxiety symptoms.

At the time of my assessment, the patient was undergoing extreme fragmentation anxiety in association with feelings that her ex-husband no longer loved her or cared about her, nor was available as an emotional object. She was extremely obsessed, needy, and very dependent on her ex-husband, despite being engaged to another man. Yet she was also consumed with feelings of rage and hate directed toward him for his rejecting, devaluing, and past abusive behavior. Through repetition, she felt compelled to maintain this self-destructive, *violent attachment* to him.

In response to feelings of being discarded and emotionally maimed, and in order to stave off extreme abandonment depression that threatened to open up into an empty inner void, the patient mobilized and directed a plethora of rage and hate toward her ex-husband, whom she would have liked to destroy—but also, ambivalently, whom she would have liked to secure as a responsive love object. As a result of these ambivalent, contradictory desires, her mood was labile and dysphoric, thus attenuating her capacity to regulate inner anxiety states and extreme emotional upheavals. Her self-identity and object representations were diffuse and lacked integration, and in her fantasy life she vacillated from feeling both tranquil and angelic to feeling overwhelmingly hostile, homicidal, and suicidal in nature.

Despite her divorce from her husband some years ago, she apparently could not let him go, even though she had retreated into a replacement object whom she used for sex and as a means of stabilizing her self-worth, as well as to punish her ex-husband by flaunting her new relationship. But this man was no better than the rest, and in many ways he represented cruel transference figures from her past. It may be obvious to the reader that the patient was entrenched in a repetition compulsion of seeking out abandoning, abusive men who were surrogates of her father and other authority figures who had violated her and ruptured any element of self-cohesion.

As observed from her extreme polysymptomatic profile, this patient shows severe psychiatric distress, is likely to regress to more tenuous states of ego-adaptation, displays signs of dissociation and underlying psychotic thought processes, and is more likely to be impulsive and act on her unmodulated affective states when anticipating threats of abandonment or rejection by dependency figures. During her stay in the hospital, she had cut herself with a razor (perhaps as a compensatory identification with the aggressor) in the attempt to gain her ex-husband's attention and sympathy; this was consistent with a pattern in their relationship where one would threaten the other with suicide or with physical pain.

While I cannot address every dynamic of her case here, I have chosen to highlight the traumatic history and structurally deficient aspects of her personality organization rather than her clinical depression, anxiety, and psychotic proclivities, which I believe are superimposed on her structural pathology. This is a very damaged person whose personality is organized at the borderline level in response to early developmental trauma and chronic, horrific childhood sexual abuse. Her profound distrust, suspiciousness, and paranoia toward others' motives and intentions are no doubt understandable due to her past history of violent sexual assault and repeated abandonment, neglect, and abuse by attachment figures whom she trusted. While I found no evidence of Schneiderian first-rank symptoms or observable delusional thinking, she is inclined to distort and misperceive her environment, to experience perceptual inaccuracies, and to insidiously project certain fears and aggressive impulses onto others that may drastically warp her experience of reality and thus haunt her as persecutory projective identifications.

Her chronic, residual, and complicated trauma due to unresolved (unprocessed) abuse predisposed her psyche to adapt through a primary borderline (dis)organization of functioning, where it oscillated between fragmentary and depleting structural dynamics that were particularly sensitive to experiences of abandonment and annihilation panic. This was prepared and compounded by the profound developmental traumas she experienced in her fragile attachments to her parents and their subsequent abandonment of her. Her major depressive and anxiety-ridden profile is characteristic of the chronicity of her instantiated posttraumatic symptomatology, which is *epigenetically superimposed* on her character pathology. My point here is not to negate the presence of what are customarily referred to as Axis I disorders, only to emphasize that they are the outgrowth and developmental elaboration of earlier etiological currents influencing the patient's personality constellation and defensive adaptation to trauma. Because her symptomatology is epigenetically superimposed over her character structure, the symptomatology itself may be viewed as a compromise formation produced through the unsuccessful transmogrification of original trauma; hence, her depression, panic, and dissociative phenomena are not the cardinal disturbance but rather they are the symptomatic expressions of trauma.

Axis I symptoms are often the target of treatment interventions and seen as problems in themselves, when, in a case like this one, they are the epigenesis (hence magnification) of developmental and structural pathology. Diagnostically, this is easy to miss; and when it is noted, the patient is typically thrown into a mixing bowl of diagnostic labels with no real understanding of the parallel processes or multiple functions that are operative, nor of the intersection and indissolubility of communicative-symptomatic confluence. Furthermore, when mainstream intervention paradigms value symptom identification, diagnostic categorization, behavioral management, and the medicalization of treatment rather than understanding the psychodynamics of personality structure and underlying pathognomonic etiology, patients often get labeled with concurrent or comorbid disorders with little comprehension on the part of the clinician of how they may be interconnected. Here I am suggesting that superimposed Axis I disorders are not the same as concurrent disorders because superimposed symptoms are more like overlays or grafts that are forged *from within* personality organization via unconscious defense and adaptation. Concurrent disorders are often conceptualized as discrete and separate clinical entities, when they are in actuality a confluence of conflictual psychic processes manifesting rich and overlapping complexifications, expressions, and polysymptomatic profiles that are characterologically, hence structurally, informed.

Because personality disorders, especially borderline conditions, reflect disordered self-states vis-à-vis object relations development, they

are informed by attachment deficits organized at different structural levels of functioning. In other words, borderline patients may be highly
functional in certain aspects of their life, such as at school or work when
ego resources are less compromised, but they have highly disturbed interpersonal relationships, mainly due to early attachment disruptions.
In adolescence, borderline functioning is generally less organized than
the more entrenched defenses and relational patterns that compose
adult character formation, and it is typically accompanied by a clinical
profile peppered with multiple, overdetermined symptoms; yet, as we
have seen, this observation may extend to more severely organized
adults.

The relationship between attachment pathology, developmental
trauma, and structural deficits cannot be emphasized enough. In my circumscribed world of clinical experience, this observed triad has become
part and parcel of my clinical phenomenology. Many patients, in fact I
would say most, who present with Axis I pathology are cursed by a dark
meridian of structural despair and anxiety inflicted by the hands of an attachment figure. For these patients who suffer from structural deficits in
personality organization, or what we may not inappropriately call *ontological insecurity* (see Mills 1997, 2002a), the kernel, yolk, or navel of such
deficiencies lies in the nature of faulty attachments.

THE SPECTRUM OF BORDERLINEOPATHY

I am in general agreement with Otto Kernberg's (1975), James Masterson's
(1981), and Gerald Adler's (1985) compelling work supporting the claim
that borderline conditions reflect disturbances on the level of personality
organization that have common developmental and structural features despite vast differences in clinical symptomatology. Kernberg (1975) argues
that many personality disorders, including schizoid, paranoid, narcissistic,
and antisocial classifications, generally function at the borderline level,
and this accounts for why there is so much overlap in personality traits,
defensive features, and dysfunctional patterns of behavior among this
cluster of disorders. For these reasons, it may prove useful to view borderlineopathy on a continuum of organizational levels of severity, from more
benign manifestations to chronic instantiations, each showing functional
degrees of variance in symptomatology and etiological influence.

Because I view borderline conditions as reflective of a curtailed and
compromised level of structural development, we may dispense with the
rigid notion that borderline functioning represents a discrete type of personality disorder as described in the *Diagnostic and Statistical Manual*
(DSM-IV-TR) established by the APA (2000). Instead, we should envision
borderlineopathy, both theoretically and clinically, as falling on a spec-

trum of disorders of the self that potentially have variegated clinical pictures despite sharing structural similarity.[2] That is, borderline functioning is conceived as being on a continuum of organizational processes governed by deficits in self-structure; this accounts for dimensional diagnoses with vast clinical features informed by parallel structural deficiencies.

Historically, the psychoanalytic literature has stressed various clinical features over others that distinguish borderline pathology from competing personality disorders. Kernberg (1975) emphasizes primitive defenses, affective coloration and instability, aggression (primarily rage), self-destructiveness, polysymptomatic neurosis, perverse sexual trends, addictions, and poor impulse control. Masterson (1981) stresses failure to adequately negotiate the separation-individuation process, split object relations, lack of ego integration of self and object representations, and abandonment depression. Donnelly (1979) emphasizes an uncohesive and fragmented sense of self, unintegrated ego nuclei, temporal discontinuity, and lack of an observing self. Adler (1985) emphasizes developmental failure in the formation of holding introjects, ambivalence toward whole objects, insufficient internal soothing functions, annihilation panic, and a fundamental, painful aloneness or inner emptiness. Giovacchini (1972) stresses identity diffusion, adaptational failure, vague and generalized life dissatisfactions involving interpersonal maladjustment, mood symptoms, anxiety, paranoid preoccupations, and transitory psychosis. Finally, Fonagy (2000) emphasizes a lack of self-reflectivity or mentalization, hence the inability or incapacity to think about mental states in oneself and in others. Fonagy's work in particular has gained increasing attention and has direct implications for understanding borderline attachment and trauma.

Fonagy and his research colleagues have focused on the question of intentionality in attachment disordered populations, and particularly on how individuals read, understand, and anticipate the internal states, desires, beliefs, and actions of others. In philosophy this is generally known as the "problem of others' minds." We all pose hypotheses or theories about others' states of mind, and this cognitive process, which begins in childhood, helps us comprehend and function in our social world. Fonagy draws on work from developmental-cognitive psychology, attachment theory, and psychoanalysis to argue that borderline patients often confuse internal mental states with objective reality due to attachment-related deficits. For example, consider the following experiment. A child is taken into a room and shown a tube with a candy wrapper fastened around it and is asked what he thinks might be in the can. The child immediately answers, "Candy." The researcher then opens the lid and shows that the tube is actually full of pencils. The child is then asked what his friend in the next room will think is in the can when it is shown to him. The child quickly answers, "Pencils." Here the child assumes an isomorphic correspondence between what he knows as reality and what he attributes to his friend. In other words, the child equates his experience with the internal state of the other's mind. Fonagy claims that a similar process happens for the attachment disordered mind and results in a poor capacity for reflectivity. In fact, Fonagy et al. (1991) have shown that mothers and fathers who have high capacities for reflectivity are three to four times more likely to have securely attached children than those parents whose reflective capacities are poor. Therefore, the capacity for reflective awareness in a child's caregiver increases the likelihood of secure attachments.

Borderline attachment disordered individuals often develop problems in mentalization, or what Donnelly (1979) refers to as an observing self or ego. I would equate this with stunted or arrested psychic structure. Most borderlines do not realize how they come across to other people or how they misinterpret others' mental communications or actions, and they thereby impute their own internal processes to others. And when self-reflexivity is present, it is usually highly specific or sensitive to shifting levels in affect or self-states in others that evoke or correspond to one's own. As we have seen with Klein and Bion, this process parallels other simultaneous, unconscious operations and cognitions such as primitive defenses including projective identification and atrophied capacities for forming holistic self and object representations.

Fonagy emphasizes a transgenerational model of personality disorders and cogently argues how attachment pathology is inherently intertwined with deficit levels in reflective functions as well as the appreciation of mental states in self and others. I see this process as coextensive with sustained and unresolved developmental trauma, thus key pathogenic factors. Concurrently in the literature, some forms of borderline functioning have begun to be viewed as developing in response to repeated chronic trauma, abuse, and/or victimization (Bleiberg 1994; Gabbard 1994), especially physical and sexual abuse (Goodwin, Cheeves, and Connell 1990; Herman 1992; Herman, Perry, and van der Kolk 1989); but a variety of other adverse events may be phenomenologically experienced as traumatic as well, including loss, death of a family member, parental unavailability or unresponsiveness, financial hardship, the inconsistent setting of limits or boundary violations, and demands for maturity, and so forth (Breier et al. 1988; Harris, Brown, and Bifulco 1986).

Fonagy (2000) notes that borderlines have predominantly *preoccupied* attachments that revolve around unresolved traumas and are concomitant with strikingly poor reflective capacities. Fonagy et al. (1996) speculate that personality disordered patients were traumatized as children and coped with their abuse by failing to conceive of their attachment figure's thoughts toward them, thus avoiding having to think about their parent's wish to harm them. This is not unlike Bowlby's notion of defensive exclusion or Fairbairn's notion of denial as moral defense in order to preserve the fantasized good qualities of parents in the service of constructing a sense of security and safety. Attachment vulnerability and trauma defensively inhibit capacities to mentalize and to develop reflective internal working models, and thus to form healthy and holistic (integrative) self and object representations, and to internalize positive, holding-soothing introjects that may be mnemonically evoked during times of stress in order to regulate affective disruptions.

Bleiberg (1994) nicely illustrates how traumatic states may become transitional factors leading to borderline organizations. The extreme dyscontrol, helplessness, inertia, and disorganization that attachment disordered children experience is often turned into self-victimization. Rather than waiting for abuse to happen to them, these children induce or evoke it as an unconscious attempt at reversing their trauma and helpless passivity. Self-victimization brings a secret sense of power and control over the abuse: if the child victimizes himself, there is some illusory sense of mastery. The hyperarousal that often accompanies disorganized attachment is actively turned or converted into thrill-seeking behavior; thus, subjects induce excitement as a means of numbing themselves or acting out the trauma. This is why food, substance use, and self-mutilating behaviors such as cutting are seen as a means to numb inner pain through dissociative, self-induced hypnotic states. Or, conversely, self-victimization is also a way to jar the psyche and intensify emotive states that are normally inaccessible to conscious awareness. A patient of mine who was a cutter once put it this way: "At least I can feel something." Consider, for example, the following case.

Billy is a ten-year-old boy who has a bleak and impoverished developmental history of parental separation, abandonment and loss, emotional trauma, repeated physical abuse by his stepfather, a series of tenuous foster home placements, behavioral acting-out problems at school, home, and foster care placement, oppositional defiance, poor school performance, aggressive and violent actions directed toward authority figures and other children, and a history of ADHD. His biological mother is mildly mentally retarded, was sexually and physically abused as a child, has been on welfare most of her life, has picked a series of abusive men, and has had a litter of children since her midteens whom she has neglected and not cared for appropriately, which has led to several apprehensions by the regional Children's Aid Society. Billy has been removed and replaced in his mother's home since he was one year of age, and he was subjected to physical abuse by two of his mother's partners for at least a two-year period. His mother's current husband was convicted for physically abusing Billy, and, although the abuse has stopped, Billy still sees him on regular visits to their home. He has been placed in at least five different foster settings in his lifetime, has witnessed the physical abuse of his mother and siblings, has been separated from his sisters due to various foster placements, and was completely abandoned by his biological father.

Billy has a history of poor psychosocial and school adjustment, has run away from foster placements, disobeys and swears at authority figures, assaulted his previous foster mother, has hit, bit, pinched, and spit at other children, and more recently was caught tying a kid to a tree and attempting to strangle him with a jump rope. On another occasion, he was swinging a bat at other children during baseball practice. And, even more disturbingly, he tried to suffocate a little girl with a pillow. When I assessed him, he spent a great deal of time internally preoccupied and was picking at scabs on his body, causing them to bleed. When I asked him why he was doing such a thing, he told me that it felt good. Take a look at one of Billy's drawings (figure 3.2).

This represents an extremely disorganized, impoverished, primitive, and regressed projection of Billy's internal self-representational world. The large head with shading and messy hair suggests aggressive and expansive tendencies, anxiety, confusion, unmodulated anger, and fantasy as a primary source of escape and satisfaction (see Ogdon 1988; Urban 1963). The omission of ears may or may not be of relevance, since it is common for well-adjusted people to omit such details; however, it suggests that there are certain things he does not want to hear or know. But what is most conspicuous is the strongly reinforced and deformed nature of the eyes: this is palpably paranoiac. The fragmentation of body parts, including the crude and bare torso with stick legs and arms, points to a seriously disorganized and traumatized personality. Billy's impulsiveness, aggression, and hyperarousal (notwithstanding his ADHD diagnosis) point toward severe attachment pathology and unresolved trauma. His tendencies toward self-victimization, thrill seeking, aggressive acting out, and self-harm may be interpreted as residual and complicated overexpressions of trauma.

Brenda was an eleven-year-old gregarious little girl who was polite, friendly, cheerful, and very verbal. She seemed to take an instant liking to me and was extremely forthright if not verbose about her many years of sexual and physical abuse by her biological father. She was energetic and hyper and displayed a constant need to talk and laugh. She was very fidgety and expressive throughout my assessment, and she presented as quite regressed and immature in appearance and behavior. For example, she brought a doll and a stuffed animal to hold during her visits. She appeared comfortable with me and was cooperative and well behaved, although she was overly distracted and internally preoccupied when attentional and concentration skills were required. She was emotionally demonstrative and overly dramatic and at times preferred to physically perform what had happened to her rather than merely verbalize her self-disclosures. For example, she physically demonstrated how her father

Figure 3.2. Draw-a-Person Test

and mother used to beat her by jumping around my office and rolling on the furniture and floor.

Brenda reportedly had a horrific, violent, and traumatic developmental history of prolonged sexual and physical abuse by her father starting when she was five years old. She claimed to have lived in constant terror and was violently beaten for the slightest infraction, particularly when her father was drinking heavily or when she refused to submit to his sexual molestation. She lived in constant fear, anxiety, and dread, and through these developmental experiences she began to acquire more dissociative patterns of coping at a borderline level of functioning organized around her chronic repeated trauma. The most palpable and egregious of these experiences, which had the most etiologic influence on her personality structure, was reportedly her father's insidious ongoing sexual molestation, followed by physical beatings, verbal devaluations, and death threats. She was subjected to such severe abuse that she feared for her life because her father warned her that if she told anyone he would kill her.

According to Brenda, her father had made her perform fellatio on a regular basis for the last six years of her life, and he would demand this from her on almost a daily basis. She claimed that he would make her close the blinds so that he could lie on the couch and have her "lick" and "suck" his "nasty thing," only to have him ejaculate in her mouth. I asked Brenda to draw me a picture of what her father forced her to do (see figure 3.3).

Brenda further confessed that he would shave his pubic hair for hygienic purposes, would instruct her on how to perform orally, including licking his "balls," would finger her in her vagina and on her buttocks during fellatio, and on several occasions attempted to rape and did indeed penetrate her. From Brenda's account, it appeared that he was attempting to groom her as his lover, and he made her do all the cooking and cleaning of the house as if she were his spouse.

Brenda showed classic signs of posttraumatic stress symptoms that had been organized on the structural level of her personality: she was chronically agitated, restless, paranoid, distrustful, hyper, and distractible; had a short attention span; was afraid of new situations and of being alone; had somatic complaints of aches and pains; clung to trusted adults; re-

Figure 3.3.

gressed to baby talk; was hypervigilant and easily hurt; daydreamed and fantasized; was easily frustrated; got overexcited; and was poorly aware of her surroundings or time of day. Many of these symptoms can be mistaken as ADHD indicators, when in fact they are residual and complicated forms of unprocessed complex trauma. She was also having more active posttraumatic symptoms, such as frequent nightmares and night terrors that her father was trying to kill her, accompanied by perceptual flashbacks of the abuse that made it difficult for her to discern her present experience from her past memories.

Brenda had temporal epilepsy and frequent seizures and had been on medication for her disorder since it was diagnosed in early childhood. While medical documentation supports a neurological explanation for her seizures, this does not preclude the psychological etiologic influence of the sexual abuse on her behavioral symptoms. I am of the opinion that her seizures, which the patient specifically stated began when she was age five, are reflective of conversion symptoms directly associated with the act of performing forced fellatio. Brenda reported that a seizure typically involved a tingling in her throat as her lips would start to quiver. She would begin to breathe in air rapidly, thus at times hyperventilating, which was accompanied by a gag reaction. She further felt as if her stomach were coming up in her throat, and she reportedly needed to spit up. The revulsion associated with the act of forced fellatio and the spitting up of her father's semen may be readily seen as symptom conversions manifesting as neurologically informed seizures, when these were further fueled by posttraumatic conflicts redirected through somatic expressions.

Brenda had a compulsion to reenact what had happened to her by dramatically performing certain aspects of the abuse. This repetition was a defensive function that allowed her to attempt to assimilate what had happened to her into a more safe, congruent, integrated picture for purposes of gaining more mastery and control over the abuse, albeit illusory. However, she had a very disoriented/disorganized attachment profile and had compartmentalized painful affect through denial and segregation strategies. At the time of my involvement, she had surely not begun to work through the emotional impact of her trauma and had attempted to flee from such intrusion by way of her hyperactivity and incessant need to talk in order to ward off the anxiety, paranoia, and fear of fragmentation. In fact, she showed inappropriate and antithetical affect when discussing her abuse, for example, laughing, which appeared highly dissociated and split off from her suffering. She was also uncomfortable hearing empathic and validating comments from me, quickly dismissing them or minimizing their import, which further suggests that she had defensively detached herself from the actual events.

This girl's tendency toward regression, such as reverting to baby talk or age-inappropriate immaturity, was in the service of dissociative denial as a way of compartmentalizing her pain. As long as she remained a child, in her mind she would not view herself as a sexual object with sexual feelings. But the effects of the abuse had led her to be highly sexualized at a young age. This was evident by the fact that Brenda had been observed talking about masturbation. When I asked her about her auto-erotic activities, she confessed that she had masturbated almost daily since she was five, and she typically would rub her clitoris with her hand before going to sleep. This may have served as a self-soothing function to ameliorate anxiety. It further suggests that she developed premature sexual impulses due to the abuse and may have had conflict over finding certain aspects of her sexual contact with her father pleasurable despite having ambivalent feelings of helplessness, revulsion, and guilt. She claimed that her masturbation was a "bad habit" due to her father. It is very common for children who are victims of sexual molestation to have contradictory feelings of both love and hate for the perpetrator and for oneself. Brenda is likely to be inclined to blame herself for the abuse in the future. This is further complicated by what I observed and interpreted to be seductiveness on her part in relation to me. For example, she acted quite flirtatious at times toward me, smiling and laughing, looking directly into my eyes for recognition, sprawling all over my couch with her legs spread apart, and prancing around my office as a much younger child would be inclined to exhibit. She further initiated touching my body on three occasions. For example, I have a visible scar on my hand from a burn. During a particular test I was administering, she reached out and started to rub it uninhibitedly. While this may be viewed as an identification with my physical pain, she also touched my arm on another occasion and gave me a warm hug when we were finished with the assessment. On one level, these may be interpreted as endearing and innocuous signs of affection, yet this is highly unusual for a molested child who is paranoid, traumatized, and fearful of men. But the affectionate gesture of the hug may also be interpreted as the need to express appreciation and emotional warmth for my concern for her well-being, and it shows how she is starving for more secure attachments to loving dependency figures.

Brenda was confused, uncertain, and ambivalent about her parents, fantasized about having a loving family with parents who were nurturing and giving, yet was confronted with the brute fact of abuse and fear that she attempted to stave off, mitigate, and deny. Easily prone to rejection, she was coy yet restless and rambunctious, had problems making and keeping friends, was easily hurt by others' actions and words, and would readily cry. The mere fact that she still clung to a transitional object (e.g., a stuffed animal) for soothing purposes shows how she had not internalized calming-soothing representations of positive parental imagoes and experiences that allowed her to regulate inner anxiety states.

When she did not directly reenact her emotional chaos through physical expression, a retreat into Pollyannaish fantasy was her primary mode of refuge. She displayed a histrionic wish for her current life to be happy and positive and desperately wanted to see the world through rose-colored glasses, but she ultimately felt maimed and persecuted. Her sense of self and personal identity was inferior, damaged, and dysphoric and pointed toward a deprived, disorganized, and traumatized personality. Her tendencies toward hyperarousal, dissociation, sexualized activities, and generalized fear and anxiety in unfamiliar interpersonal environments underscored her attachment deficits and residual overexpressions of trauma.

An important notion of borderlineopathy rests on understanding the split or fissure in the traumatized psyche as a fundamental division of polarities between internal objects and the uncohesive organization of self-representations that are rigidly compartmentalized yet temporally exist in juxtaposition to each other through systemic reciprocal dialogue on the level of unconscious fantasy. Dissociative and numbing tendencies that typically accompany borderline conditions may be viewed as a way of bringing internalized trauma states and their reciprocal fantasies under the illusion of control. Furthermore, the aloneness, inner emptiness, unconscious guilt, and sense of isolation that often accompany traumatic events may be turned into manipulative, exploitive, and assaultive engagements with others for desired attention, involvement, and interpersonal control; this leads to conflictual and hostile relationships dominated by anger, manipulation, and abuse. Splitting becomes a necessary means to keep intrusive, persecutory, and "bad" alien self-representations at bay, to preserve idealized "good" objects, and to channel the primitive emptiness, hate, and rage that rumbles within into the hostile world. Borderline organizations spring from developmental trauma and attachment pathology that eventually lead to a pattern of negative, volatile, and unfulfilling relationships, whereby others inevitably become the emotional whipping post and primary source of pain and mental agony. But hate and rage also turn into entitlement: "The world owes them something because they have suffered so much" (Bleiberg 1994, 191).

STRUCTURALIZATION AND ATTACHMENT PATHOLOGY

As noted in the previous chapter, it becomes important to reemphasize that when we refer to psychic structure we do not mean to imply that personality comprises fixed or static attributes, properties, or foundations that adhere to a substance ontology; rather, structure should be conceived as *unconscious organizational processes* that provide functional semblances of continuity and self-cohesion. Structure is constituted via an agentic system of processes that provide organizational and adaptational functions to psychic experience; these functions are relatively enduring and invariant. But this does not mean that structure does not change: on the contrary, the self is always in a state of unrest and activity (even if such activity is inhibited, lulled, or pacified). Such structural invariance is always evolving and transforming through a variety of adaptational pressures and contingencies; therefore, psychic structure, like the ontogeny of the self, is a dialectical process of becoming continually plagued by conflict and negativity.

Patients with attachment pathology organized on borderline levels generally present with disorganized, aggressive, detached, and/or traumatized profiles, often with fragmented or depleted self-structures marked by extremities in clinical presentation. In my clinical observations, I have identified five subgroups of patients that I frequently encounter presenting with varying clinical profiles and self-states organized at different developmental-structural levels: namely, those with (1) structural trauma; (2) structural fragmentation; (3) structural depletion; (4) structural vacuity; and (5) structural aggressivity. While these categories are by no means exhaustive nor conclusive, I am more concerned here with conceptualizing key organizational valences of psychic structure gathered from clinical phenomenology.

Structural Trauma

Patients with structural trauma often see themselves as hopelessly damaged, maimed, flawed, and defective. There is a fixation on being abused and spoiled, like a sullied object permanently mangled; therefore, self-representation and personal identity are rendered helplessly molested and repetitiously victimized by an ongoing internalized sense of violation and deformity. This fixation is experientially realized by patients as a gaping wound in their being, a slash in their very existence. Psychic pain remains organized around the trauma, a relentless assault on the integrity of the self. The phenomenology of inner experience centers around being desecrated, torn, and left for dead. Patients with this structural disconfiguration have a *damaged core*, dislocated and polluted. The acute feelings of helplessness, shame, and humiliation heighten the intensity of devaluation and psychic pain. Often patients with structural trauma have severe attachment deficits and dissociative profiles: they are profoundly mistrustful, distant, and aloof. Feelings of detachment and derealization are common defensive organizations that allow the self to survive. While the traumatized self survives, it is broken, if not destroyed—sodomized and then tormented by the sadistic brutality of memory.

Consider the case of Patrick, an eighteen-year-old white male, who was the victim of years of multiple forms of sexual, physical, and emotional abuse by several perpetrators, a case I will give extended elaboration in a later chapter. Patrick has a dissociative orientation to his very presence: inwardly preoccupied, almost oblivious to his environment, he never looks anyone directly in the eye. He will frequently bump into objects in his physical surround, such as the door frame at the entrance to my office. He is plagued by various details of his traumas and the affective aftermath of being violated, defiled, and used as an object for others' dirty pleasures. He recalls his perpetrators' mesmeric eyes, the control and possession they had over him, his incessant screaming and helpless passivity during moments of domination and abuse. He was always afraid to go to sleep and would be petrified for days after an abusive episode. With a night-light on next to his bed, he would tie a string around his wrist and to some object on the nightstand, hoping it would fall and make a noise to wake him if he turned over in his sleep, or if someone entered the room. Now an insomniac, as a child he would sleep under thick covers in the summer and with no covers on in the winter, knowing he would eventually wake from the disparate temperature.

One of the most painful inner experiences is the feeling of being thoroughly damaged and sullied. Spontaneously in one session, he associated to a fantasy he used to experience while lying awake at night in bed: he imagined himself tied up with rope on the ground while others were defecating on him. Then he realized the connection. His abusers would often remind him, "You're a worthless piece of shit! The only thing you're good for is a toilet." He will often dissociate when describing to me certain details or fragments from his memories, and I have caught my own dissociative countertransference reactions, which mirror his, on numerous occasions as I have tried to escape the horror of his pain. What was perhaps as terrifying as the abuse itself was having no one to hold him or mollify his agitation and fright. Attempting to provide himself with a soothing function in the wake of such unbearable isolation, he would talk to his teddy bear at night, holding and snuggling it, saying reassuringly, "It's all right, Teddy, it'll be all right." It is indeed difficult at times to suppress a tear.

Structural Fragmentation

Patients like Patrick suffer the horrible exposure, humiliation, and affective resonance of bearing a damaged psyche, mauled and discarded. With trauma as severe as this, psychic structure is always fighting the experience and tendency toward fragmentation. Patients with structural fragmentation often present in a constant state of agitation, hovering on panic and doom. When the self begins to fracture, it leads into an abyss of annihilatory, disintegrative, and decompensating inner experiences. Structural fragmentation corresponds with looming annihilation anxieties: anticipation of fragmentation induces annihilation panic, and the self begins to undergo a breaking apart, a splintering of consciousness. Here patients descend into a spiral regression of persecutory and disembodied torment. Patients with this level of insidious regression plummet into a *psychotic core*. As self-structure attempts to organize itself around pockets or semblances of containment, psychotic anxieties often become too overwhelming. Paranoia—even delusions and hallucinations—are internally constructed and projectively superimposed onto external reality as a crude means of preserving the self and protecting it from total annihilation (also see Lacan 1955–1956c; Pao 1979). Psychosis thus becomes a means of imposing some control and order on the imminent disintegration of the self. Fragmentation panic occurs when psychic structure is imperiled by experiential dysregulation—a fracturing, cutting up, and dismembering of self-continuity and cohesion. Here the self becomes divided and diffuse. What is most horrific is the anticipatory fear of complete deracination, namely, the *expectation of nonbeing*.

Cliff is a forty-two-year-old gay man who is epileptic, with a long history of rapid-cycling bipolar disorder, and has been hospitalized more than a dozen times for his illness; his is another case I will return to at length in a future chapter. He was raised in a strict Anglican, religious home environment, was never shown physical warmth or affection by his parents, and was never told he was loved. He was beaten as a child by his father for the slightest infraction and was battered for years by his first homosexual partner, who reportedly threw him from a two-story balcony, thereby fracturing his hip and pelvis and further triggering the onset of his epilepsy. Cliff remains extremely conflicted by his homosexual identity, which he believes is a sin. After the breakup of a four-year relationship, he became hopelessly depressed and suicidal. This was the longest and most significant relationship he had ever known, and his partner's abandonment of him was for another lover, which Cliff construed as a reflection of his inherent worthlessness and lack of lovability and as punishment from God. He has been characteristically dysphoric, panicky, and intermittently manic, suicidal, and psychotic since he began treatment with me more than four years ago.

In one moment during the early phases of therapy, I greeted the patient with a perfunctory handshake at my office door. I noticed that he reluctantly accepted my greeting with an ambivalent expression, and an uncomfortable limp extension of what felt like a wet fish followed. His palms were sweaty, which communicated to me that he must have been anxious, but I sensed that something else was wrong with the very nature of my gesture. Upon our sitting down in our seats, I commented on my observation that it seemed as though he did not want to shake my hand, and I was wondering why that was so uncomfortable for him. He told me that he does not like the feel of human skin except during sex; and that even when lovers in the past would try to show him nonsexual physical affection or warmth, he would "cringe." He further associated to how once his former partner had accidentally brushed his hand against his while they were taking a walk, and this had made his "skin crawl." I acknowledged how my unsolicited social gesture understandably had intrusive significance for him, yet he became apologetic. I suggested there may be more meaning behind his aversion and asked him why he found human touch so repulsive. Upon this question, he began to cry uncontrollably. When he composed himself, he described the emotional pain of not feeling connected to anyone, nor being truly cared for or loved. When others reach out, he withdraws because he fears being hurt and would prefer not to feel any closeness at all, knowing that it will never last. All he has known is deprivation and abuse; when others show genuine concern, it *cuts*.

Yet the patient paradoxically and repetitiously creates the very thing he does not want: he unconsciously picks bad objects that exploit and abandon him, thus reinforcing that he is not deserving of love nor interpersonal happiness. Cliff wants emotional warmth and acceptance so badly that he defiles himself, grovels to others' expectations, and allows people to use and take advantage of his money and goodwill. During manic episodes, he is easily manipulated and buys his so-called friends lavish gifts he cannot afford. When he was arrested for writing fraudulent checks, he experienced even more acute structural fragmentation and became psychotic. Over the years, he has slowly been able to internalize a positive introject of me as a calming-soothing presence. He often tells me that during moments when he feels upset, paranoid, or on the verge of suicide, thinking of me or imagining being in my office helps him calm down. He tells me he often calls my office after hours to listen to my voice on the answering machine, which evokes and sustains, even if temporarily, a holding-soothing imago.

Cliff feels he deserves to die for his forbidden desire and sinful lifestyle, and he thus unconsciously orchestrates his own self-destruction. Patients like Cliff seem to be always living on the precipice of annihilatory anxiety, what I would refer to as *psychic purgatory*. Fragmentation threats summon paranoiac and psychotic anxieties, further triggering annihilation panic, primitive splitting, and a fracturing of the psyche. As a result, the self becomes dislocated and persecuted by the fear of deracination. When schizoid mechanisms fail, the self is imperiled by the return of projected persecutory fantasies, oppressive guilt, self-flagellation, and death wishes.

When crippling anxiety, panic, and psychosis is not present, the traumatized self tends to find another avenue in order to survive. Here enters the realm of detachment, impoverishment, and depression.

Structural Depletion

So far, I have been presenting extreme cases emphasizing the effects of trauma on character structure; but there are more benign, less insidious forms of developmental trauma informing attachment vulnerabilities and dysfunctional adaptation patterns that organize around more depleted aspects and qualities in self-structure. Patients with structural depletion fall on a continuum ranging from those who display more agitated, restless, and dysphoric tendencies—those harnessed from more fragmentary propensities—to patients who are more structurally depressed and internally empty. Let us first look at structural depletion proper.

Depleted psychic structure is vapid and deflated and lacks vitality. Patients have a very blunted inner life and restricted range of emotional expression. They often complain of not feeling connected to their inner affective states, which seem to be segregated, detached, and compartmentalized. There is a very weak and torpid sensation of absence and melancholia. Clinical depression is a very common dimension of their life histories and can organize around loss, complicated mourning, abandonment, rejection from dependency figures, emotional estrangement, and alienation, to numbing and anaclitic depressive manifestations. Patients with structural depletion have a *depressive core*, a characterological dysthymia. Those with dysphoric or hypomanic proclivities may slip into restlessness, agitation, and/or fragmentation accompanied by regression and depressed mood. They often absorb a pervasive oppression and meaninglessness to their existence; lack interest or enthusiasm in life activities; are physically lethargic, languid, and apathetic; are somatically focused; and can retreat into substances, addictions, or food for numbing purposes.

Consider the case of Winny, a thirty-nine-year-old divorced white female, who sought out long-term psychoanalytic treatment because psychopharmacological intervention proved to be of little help. She had been on four different types of antidepressants, including SSRIs, for the past eight years with no substantial change in her depressed orientation. She had deliberately sought out many thrill-seeking behaviors and activities, such as bungee jumping and obtaining her pilot's license, hoping to engender vitality and liveliness in her sense of self, but to no avail.

Winny complained of feeling like a whipped dog with a broken spirit; she was unable to shake herself loose from the melancholic grip of indifference and lethargy that drained her very sense of feeling alive. During our initial consultation I asked her what she believed to be the ultimate cause of her malaise, and she replied that she didn't have a clue. It soon became apparent that Winny had suffered in silence from many developmental traumas that had left a wake of characterological depression. She had endured an early childhood marked by constant parental negativity, emotional invalidation, and a plethora of devaluing remarks about her selfhood and capabilities that she internalized and adopted as her inner self-representational world. She left home at fifteen, had a child out of wedlock when she was seventeen, abused drugs and alcohol, and was on her third marriage at the time of our treatment. Her son's father had died n a fire before he was born; he literally "burned to a crisp." She began a life of promiscuity and substance abuse, and she severely neglected her son's needs, which later left her with oppressive guilt and self-reproach. Her first husband was an unavailable alcoholic, while her second husband was emotionally devaluing and verbally aggressive. She described her current husband as "nice but aloof." She had an entrenched repetition of picking cold, volatile, and humiliating men like her father, who was verbally abusive, dismissive, and shameful and showed no warmth or love, as well as her mother, who was emotionally unavailable and delivered beatings with a belt strap when Winny challenged her authority. The patient reported scant memories of her early childhood, and those she had were tainted with negativity and parental neglect.

Winny described a chronic pattern of self-blame and fixation on being inferior, as though she were lacking something, and she said she always felt wrong in comparison to other's beliefs or actions. In fact, she believed that everyone else was "normal" but her. She was so confused about her own inner intentions, beliefs, and autonomy that she would habitually question her judgment and reality testing during interpersonal situations. Furthermore, she was disheartened by the fact that she could not "correctly" identify her inner emotional states at all, which made her feel even more inadequate. She would typically blame herself for creating conflict in interpersonal encounters even when there was reasonable evidence to the contrary, or she would fantasize that people would inevitably see her deficits and reject her attempts at friendship. In the end, she would still feel "bad" about whatever course of action she took and believed she was ultimately to blame for all disappointments she incurred.

Throughout our treatment, the patient began to realize that she had incorporated many negative introjects and endured many developmental traumas that had formed the sediment of her depleted psychic structure. Her parents' deprivation and critical judgment of her became the foundation of her impoverished representational world, and their lack of physical affection and warmth left an anaclitic neediness that she compensatorily acted out through her promiscuity and substance use. During the course of some deeply painful emotional work, the patient reported a screen memory of being abandoned in her crib and left utterly alone, helpless and terrified. This association was followed by a memory of being told by her mother, "I wish I never had you." Upon making this disclosure, she remembered asking her parents during early adolescence, "Why don't you love me?" Winny felt that she was not worthy of love, and this explained why she was never given hugs nor told she was valued.

In piecing together her past, a past she had buried yet converted into structural despair and anguish, Winny realized how her very being had been methodically beaten down into a state of passivity and defilement that she identified with and made her own. "I didn't live, I just existed," she confessed. The patient could not have genuine feelings, for they were stifled, invalidated, and disallowed—especially her anger, which, in a more classical, dynamic sense, was turned inward and redirected onto her self. She had turned herself into a Winnicottian false self in order to survive her oppressive and belittling environment.

The screen memory of being abandoned in her crib bothered her enough that she asked her mother about the incident. Her mother reportedly told her that she was always an angry child, although the patient could not recapture nor identify these feelings at the time, and that often she was so angry that her mother would have to place her in her crib and shut the door because she was screaming uncontrollably. This discussion evoked a certain psychic shift in the patient's repressed hostilities, which she later more appropriately directed outward toward others rather than harboring contempt for herself. Getting in touch with disavowed and segregated aggression allowed her to mobilize certain defenses and creative energies she had not enjoyed before. Until then, her original traumas were inverted, sequestered, and not permitted channelization through external expression. Yet they were granted a secret life of lulled, self-contained attacks on her structural integrity. When the potentiality of her lulled aggression was realized, awakened, and allowed a voice, I encouraged its expression.

Over the course of therapy, Winny gradually became more assertive, self-assured, and capable of discerning her own authentic emotional states. When she realized that she had repetitiously allowed others to devalue and use her unjustly as an unconscious attempt to win her parents' recognition and love, she was able to disengage from her maladaptive pattern of manufacturing unavailable and exploitive relationships, and she began to more accurately perceive her interpersonal environment and set appropriate boundaries and limitations when conflict arose. This shift allowed a vitalization of her psyche that combated her depressive core: the genuine engagement of her inner experiences further served as a catalyst that allowed her to enact more spontaneous and creative self-expressions of her individuality and autonomy.

Structural Vacuity

When depletion advances further, it enters into a no-man's-land of emotional detachment, isolation, and dissociative void. I wish to distinguish between the phenomenology of structural depletion and structural emptiness, the latter being a more severe manifestation of characterological depression. Here the psyche is shut off and enveloped in a vacuum of solipsistic withdrawal and isolation, disengagement from the intersubjective world, and unfathomable aloneness. Patients with structural vacuity have an *empty core*, a lacuna in their very being. Patients with this profile may appear to be in a state of derealization, as if they were going through the motions of living and routine banality. Schizoid and schizoidtypal patients, as well as those with the dissociative and more classic borderline conditions, compose this subgroup, where depression is taken to the extreme mode of numbing and anesthetized detachment. People merely become things, robots—zombies, dulled to the inner fluctuations of affective life and social participation. These patients seem to be too far gone, unable to feel or reach into the yolk of their existence: they appear to be simply devoid of emotions, which are in actuality sealed off in an airtight container, suffocated—strangulated by death. Such patients have the appearance of the walking dead: they are often so horrifically traumatized by their past that they kill themselves off—their inner experience—and don't grant it a life (let alone a voice), so that they do not have to live with the pain and anxiety that threatens to torment their souls.

Patients with such empty structures are plummeted into a black abyss of *nothingness*: they are consumed by *lack*, absence, and void—a hole in being. Subjective reports of emotional experience are described as though there were something missing, as if feelings and desire had been surgically removed. Psychosocial development appears almost arrested: they are literally loners and interpersonal hermits. This is not merely existential alienation or isolation, but disembodied automatization—living death. While there are multifarious and qualitative degrees of emptiness and aloneness that plague structural integrity in a variety of clinical syndromes, those with vacuous character structures have entered the realm of horrific excess and have been swallowed by a dark pit. All need for human connection has been renounced; they literally lack the capacity for attachment.

Warren, a twenty-four-year-old, single white male, was hospitalized for suicidal ideation and chronic depression. He was admitted three times to psychiatric facilities in his late teens and was followed by three different psychiatrists, who prescribed a cornucopia of mood stabilizers, antidepressants, and antipsychotic medication, none of which were effective. He further entered a residential treatment facility for six months and received both individual and group therapy, but he claimed that these interventions had no impact either. When I assessed the patient, he had been diagnosed with an anxiety disorder, social phobia, and avoidant personality disorder; it became salient that he had a primary schizoid presentation concomitant with chronic characterological dysthymia.

Warren reported that he had never felt happy as a child and in fact confessed that he did not even know the experiential meaning of the word. He could not recall one memory of his parents when he was a child, let alone describe to me what they had looked like. As he told me, "I can remember their bodies, like being in the house or something, but not their faces." The transgenerational transmission of attachment pathology in this family was more than obvious. He reported that his mother was a depressed, aloof, bitter alcoholic who was sexually, physically, and emotionally abused as a child; and his father was a cold, distant, insensitive, and hostile individual with a bad temper who was never home. Warren said that he never felt as though they were truly his parents, and he wondered if he had been adopted. Apparently his parents had had a very rocky marriage, slept in separate bedrooms for years, and divorced when the patient was thirteen after his father discovered that his mother was having an affair.

The patient reported that he had always felt odd and excluded, and ridiculed and picked on by other children, and that he never formed any friendships or attachments to his peers. He described his childhood as replete with anxiety, instability, rejection, social ostracism, and being physically bullied and beaten up. To make matters worse, he had moved approximately every year and a half until his parents divorced due to the nature of his father's work, which created more difficulties in adjusting to his novel social and school environments.

Warren's early attachment deficits predisposed him to develop a very empty core structure; the very fabric of his personality was dearth, dread, and internal aloneness enveloped by a bleak ocean of nothingness. This had left a massive void of agitated depletion, and as a result he struggled with a chronic dysphoria peppered with social rejection and aversion that was exacerbated in various interpersonal contexts. His social phobias and anxieties were particularly related to being judged, disparaged, and shamed by other people, including his parents, who had given up hope that he would "just snap out of it." He developed an avoidant pattern of behavior very early in life in order to remove himself from situations in which he would potentially become subjected to humiliation, abuse, or social denunciation. As a result, he withdrew, shut down, sealed off his emotional life, and retreated into his own stoical universe; the detachment and renunciation of his need and desire to connect with others was a way to protect his inner self from annihilation. He learned that he could trust no one, and he developed a paranoid wall of impenetrability to prevent others from hurting him, yet at the same time he could not escape their painful intrusions, abnegation, and devaluing insults, which he absorbed like a sponge. Alcohol dependency was a substitute for the anaclitic and relational craving he had to deny within himself in order to survive such a depriving and hostile reality. But his structural emptiness and depression had left him with the preoccupation of ending his life. He reportedly had no vision of a future, for all hope of a better existence was expunged from his realm of possibility. According to the patient, he had burned all bridges toward getting an appropriate education, was financially impoverished and dependent on welfare, and feared "flipping burgers" or being a laborer living in a "cheap house." The absence of attachment, coupled with structural trauma that devolves into unremitting depletion and emptiness, is truly a tragic and unbearable subjective reality: "I have no joy in anything, and I feel like I'm just waiting to die."

Structural Aggressivity

As we have seen, trauma can lead to many different orientations and degrees of psychic organization and functional adaptation, from more agitated, fragmentary, and hyperaroused structural processes to more depressive and vacuous instantiations. The degree to which the psyche is oriented toward a primary structuralization over another is largely based on the unique subjectivity of each individual and the contingencies she faces. Recall that structure is the succession of organizational processes influenced by unconscious teleology and is largely the constitution of defense. Defense becomes organized into functional patterns of behavior and adaptability and is never ontologically separated from one's social and interpersonal world, hence one's object relations. But what happens when the psychic register identifies with the violence that is imposed upon it by trauma—so much so that it becomes violence? Here enters another subgroup of attachment disordered patients, namely, those with structural aggressivity.

Patients with aggressive organizations are saturated with negativity, hate, rage, and destruction. Their psychic structure is suffused with chaos, invasion, animosity, and militancy that are internally absorbed (via introjection, identification, and internalization) and externally split off, projected, and violently channeled. Developmental trauma is perceived and felt as a pernicious assault on the structural integrity of the self, and it is combated with the same fierceness and level of barbarity. Defensive manifestations are mobilized around survival, and the most primitive impulses are summoned and sustained in order to fend off the perceived onslaught on the self. While the destructive principle is turned onto the self in fragmentary and depleted structures, we may conjecture that in aggressive structures, psychic energy is activated and cathected from the death drive, deflected from inversion, and primarily redirected toward the object world. Perhaps informed as well by evolutionary currents to fight and aggress, there is a primal identification with those who inflict trauma as a primitive reaction and bid for intrapsychic survival. Unfortunately, this soils character structure with an unremitting, sadistic, and violent negativity. The Other becomes the generalized enemy, not to be trusted or loved, but distanced if not destroyed. But the aggressed and aggressive self wages an inner war that cannot be won, for brutality is ultimately enacted through tormenting internalized representations and self-destruction. Attachments to others are violent, unpredictable, cruel, and manipulative, as often seen in the paradigmatic antisocial and borderline syndromes. Psychic reality is embroiled in havoc and ruin, always tarrying with the negative.

Patients with this psychic structure have an *aggressive core* marked by conflict, conflagration, and inner implosion. The world becomes a nemesis that is ruthless, persecutory, and dangerous, and this becomes the prototype for human relatedness. Human tenderness and vulnerability are disavowed if not aborted altogether out of fear of exploitation, sabotage, and death of the self. The self hostilely defines itself in relation to opposition, which the self must negate. As a result, the Other becomes an antagonistic and malignant imposition that must be opposed, contained, controlled, and dominated. Patients with this personality structure are tormented with negativity; they can find no refuge or peace from the condemning, malicious, and haunting introjects, memories, and developmental traumas that have formed the sediment of their inner representational worlds and self-identity.

As in many clinical populations that shield the pain of developmental trauma, overwhelming feelings of helplessness, exposure, humiliation, vulnerability, weakness, and cowardliness rupture psychic equilibrium and militate ego capabilities to cope with intersubjective strain. Shame, or any condition that evokes feelings of inferiority, inadequacy, and so forth, triggers hate and narcissistic rage because of the intolerability of injury to the self. When this occurs or is solicited, objects uniformly become sullied, bad, and combative, to the point that splitting is employed in the service of a rigid, simple economy of negation and difference. The blaze within is fueled and increasingly stoked. At the extreme, those who are cast as the enemy literally become things that oppose and transgress on the structural integrity of the self. Primitive survival mechanisms convert them into predators that must be predated on before the self is surprised, ambushed, and devoured. Confrontation is psychically realized as a battle to the death where only the patient's subjectivity shall be affirmed. In more sadistic instances, the other shall be made to crawl and show humiliating deference to the illusory superiority of the patient, who is now the one to shame, dominate, and vanquish. The Other is turned into an object that has no feelings, needs, desires, or rights of its own for the simple reason that, whether in reality or fantasy, it *can kill* the self. The psyche follows a primitive economy of rigid identification with itself and its own subjectivity, whereby opposition is radically split off, violently cleaved, and condemned. Here we are reminded of Bion; there is an omnipotent evacuation of self-negativity (as bad self-representation) and a violent attack on linking the Other to qualities of mutually shared human experience. The aggressive self cannot recognize the authentic subjectivity of the other because attachments to others are drenched with pain. Because the self feels that it has been harmed, it does not see nor recognize the harm it does to others; and when it does, its actions become quickly justified as deserved punishment.

Less severe forms of aggressivity come out in competition, intellectual argumentation, interpersonal command, and exhibitionistic power—and range to taking pleasure in inflicting pain on others through oral means, such as verbal remarks, sardonic deprecation, and manipulative threats. For example, Steve, a thirty-six-year-old successful entrepreneur, saw me for "anger management." He worked fourteen-hour days in a highly stressful and competitive job, never saw his wife or children, and when he was home on the weekends, he would displace his frustration on his family by initiating arguments, which escalated into yelling rampages where he would physically kick and bang objects. He reported feeling tense and angry throughout most of the day for years, and he was constantly gritting his teeth and clenching his fists in his office, swearing at the slightest irritant, and becoming so exasperated at the littlest things that he would become enraged and explosive. For example, he got his coat stuck on the door handle, and instead of removing his coat gently, he ripped it off. He would arbitrarily smash items in the garage , and the family dog would become the object of routine beatings when it disobeyed. People were always a source of opposition or simply in his way. Road rage was a daily occurrence. Even his dentist told him that if he did not stop grinding his teeth, he would require serious surgery. After many verbally hostile and profane exchanges with his wife, she threatened to leave him if he did not get help.

Upon my initial consultation, I asked him how long he had felt angry. "My whole life," he replied. Steve revealed that he was systematically picked on, bullied, chased home from school, and beaten up on almost a daily basis from the time he entered kindergarten until eighth grade. His parents were concerned but passive; they were not very helpful in protecting him, nor were school authorities. He would suffer horrible humiliations in front of his peers and classmates, and his beatings were pervaded with shame and depredation. For instance, gangs of kids would swarm over him on the playground or on his way home, corner him at school, and incessantly tease, ridicule, and badger him. He lived in constant fear and panic. In many ways Steve stood out as the class "geek." He was always a tall and lanky kid with glasses who was nicely dressed, and he was from a rich family; yet he was quiet, shy, and withdrawn. He had a heart murmur from infancy onward that interfered with his respiration, and as a result he could not participate in sports or gym. The other children, mainly boys, but girls as well, would verbally degrade him through name-calling and would often surprise him in the hall, knock books out of his hand, steal his belongings out of his locker, throw gum in his hair during class, and, when he was older, hit him on the top of his head with their class rings. He would often be made to fight younger kids, and he was warned that if he won, the older bullies would beat him more severely. He was made to beg for mercy—only to be hit and laughed at after doing so; he thus sacrificed his self-respect and dignity.

When the patient was eight, two older boys pummeled him in an alley and made him get on his knees to perform fellatio. When he refused, he trembled in tears as they urinated all over his face, hair, and body. Then they beat and kicked him and smashed his bike. The unimaginable shame and defloration coarsened his psyche with hate and murderous rage, which he had to indignantly swallow his whole life. During our initial meeting, he told me that he had not thought of nor told anyone of his childhood pain and rage for more than twenty years; the shame and vulnerability from his confession was so unbearable that he had an abreaction. It was reportedly the first time he had cried about it since the incident. Throughout therapy, Steve began to trace back elements of his own misogynist feelings to his mother, who used to call him a "sissy" for not fighting back, as well as to girls at school who would instigate other boys to pick on him. He came to realize that his hostile feelings toward his wife were partly due to this early affective coloration, and his generalized rage toward the world was the result of unprocessed trauma, which was besieging his psychic cohesion.

The channelization of negativity outward is an abortive attempt to protect the self from annihilation, and in this regard it is generally a more adaptive defense than succumbing to the downward plunge of fragmentation anxiety or depletion; but this style is ultimately just as pathological. There is a continual immersion in the trauma that is continuously retraumatizing—to the point that psychic structure becomes trauma, both violently inflicted and assimilated. The self cannot rid itself of such atrocious violence because its essence is violence as such—Being qua Negation! The psyche cannot rest and is flooded with the desire for revenge, which ultimately comes back to taunt and haunt structural integrity.

Gregg, a twenty-seven-year-old father of an infant daughter, was separated from his common-law wife when he sought treatment for his uncontrollable bursts of anger. He had hit his wife in the face on one occasion while allegedly experiencing an enraged blackout and thus had no conscious recollection of the event. He was not under the influence of alcohol or drugs at the time. On another occasion he grabbed her arm and dragged her to the refrigerator door when she complained that there was not enough food in the house. He almost dislocated her shoulder. Their relationship was replete with volatility, verbal abuse, and screaming matches, followed by mutual distancing and passive-aggressiveness. The patient later learned that his wife was having an affair, and he sought to avenge his wounded ego by falsely reporting her to the authorities for child abuse in order to seek custody of his daughter.

The patient was rarely physically disciplined as a child, but when he was, he experienced it as harsh and unjust. He was routinely subjected to cruel verbal debasement by a cold, detached, and embittered father; nor would his mother ever stand up for him or protect him from his father's vicious acts of shameful humiliation. When Gregg was four years old, he threw a ball into the lake. His incensed father made him strip down to his underwear and fetch it in front of his sisters and some neighbors who were visiting their cottage. He was always a chubby boy, and he remembered how they had all laughed at him after someone said he looked like a "beached whale." When he was eight, he had difficulty learning to read, so his father would make him read out loud in the car during trips. For every word he failed to pronounce correctly, he received a smack on the hand with a stick. One such trip was reportedly two hours of sheer hell. While they were playing football in the yard, his father threw the ball in his face as a lesson to him to keep his hands up. In addition, his father would frequently disparage the patient at the dinner table until he was brought to tears.

The patient's psyche was consumed with hate, rage, and negativity. As an adolescent, he would deliberately seek out conflict and initiate fights as a means of discharging his tension. Alcohol and substance use was a frequent means to self-medicate, and his relationships with others were based upon personal gain, exploitation, possession, and pleasure. He had suffered from migraine headaches since latency age, and he developed blackouts during times of intense emotional upheaval beginning in early adulthood. He would realize later that he had often trashed his room during such episodes. From his descriptions of his relationship with his wife, I suspected that she too had a personality disorder. She would devalue his occupation as a skilled laborer, shame him about his sexual performance, goad him into arguments, and humiliate him publicly in front of his friends. When she finally confessed to seeing another man on the side, he told me, "I almost put her fuckin' head through drywall."

We have seen how developmental trauma—both horrendous and moderate—erodes healthy attachment capacities and predisposes psychic structure toward borderline and schizoid levels of organization. It should be noted that anyone with these clinical profiles can potentially exhibit structural shifts in self-states; these self-states can be contiguous with one another, such as with dysphoria and paranoia, and show overlap in inner organizational processes, content, and form. In other words, each of these clinical subcategories may possess shared qualities and experiential functions with the others, thus producing hybrid manifestations in clinical phenomenology. While neither conclusive nor exhaustive, these five subclassifications of structuralization are merely appearances or forms of attachment-related developmental trauma. It is mainly for conceptual and descriptive purposes that I propose these distinctions, for ultimately psychic structure is ontologically undifferentiated. Psychic structure shares the same essence, namely, conflict or negativity (see Mills 2000a, 2000b, 2002a). Because psychic structure may mutate and transmogrify, it can exhibit combinations of these complex and overdetermined states, it can modify and adapt to various contingencies, or it may regress to earlier developmental constellations and more primitive aspects of being and experiencing.

To some degree, we all have to endure anxiety as children and field the blows that threaten our structural integrity. As we weather this negativity—from the little jabs of criticism, rejection, and shame that chip away at our self-esteem to the anxiety of competition, success, and failure—we profoundly seek out acceptance, validation, recognition, and affection from others. When attachment disruptions lead to characterological disorders, the greater faculties of autonomy, empathy, intimacy, love, and mutual recognition are eclipsed by structural deficits and stunted capacities for relatedness. Working clinically with attachment pathology becomes immensely difficult when engendering healthier ways of relatedness and emotional involvement remains a primary goal.

NOTES

1. An explanatory note is in order here. In Canada, psychiatric health care is part of the provincial health service benefits for every citizen, and therefore there is no direct fee to the patient. However, government statistics show there is a shortage of psychiatrists and other mental health workers to provide timely and thorough services. As a result, patients may have to wait for months to get an appointment to see a psychiatrist, and they often consult their family doctor for medication while they wait to be seen by a specialist. When they do get in to see a psychiatrist, by and large patients are often subjected to brief, if not cursory, intakes that focus on symptom identification and medication management. Thorough psychosocial histories are often not conducted since initial consultations are not uncommonly restricted to only thirty-minute interviews. Furthermore, psychiatry is largely psychopharmacological in nature, hence not psychotherapeutically oriented; therefore, many physicians prioritize seeing people quickly and prescribe medication as the primary form of treatment.

2. The same argument can be made for how personality disorders in general are rigidly classified and diagnosed by the DSM-IV-TR through a behavioral-symptom checklist rather than an understanding of their structural, functional, and adaptive manifestations reflective of disorders of the self. I am of the opinion that many of the personality disorders grouped into clusters, which are designed to highlight overlapping traits among disorders, really describe enduring patterns of defense, for example, avoidant or passive-aggressive, rather than underlying character structure that motivates defense. This classification may simply be for pragmatic reasons governing the need for an intelligible criterion and reliable method for purposes of diagnostic taxonomy. Nevertheless, it does not deter us from viewing personality formation as the epigenesis of universal psychic processes that emanate from a developmental monistic ontology. Instead, I envision personality disorders as reflecting core deficiencies in self-structure largely due to attachment pathology that conditions both similar and disparate forms of dysfunction to arise, including cognitive, affective, behavioral, and interpersonal sequelae. As a result, there are many forms of borderline functioning that are differentiated by their defensive and symptomatic profiles yet nevertheless share core structural deficits informed by disorganized attachment processes, including schizoid, antisocial, paranoid, narcissistic, dysthymic, dependent, and obsessive-controlling profiles, just to name a few.

II

TREATMENT PERSPECTIVES

4

⊚

Beginning the Treatment

It is my intention in this chapter to provide some guiding principles in the treatment of attachment disordered populations; but this section can also be viewed as a primer on initiating analytic therapy. While I consider this an introduction to the psychotherapeutic process, more advanced clinicians may appreciate the frank discussions of the difficulties in establishing optimal parameters for treatment in juxtaposition to the inevitable exigencies that militate against such a possibility. Among these challenges are convincing patients of the value of treatment, financial concerns, cultivating a secure therapeutic alliance, negotiating professional and personal space, and navigating through the awkwardness and intersubjective assertion of autonomy and self-expression that occur in the development of an authentic relationship. For better or worse, I will provide the reader with an intimate look into the way in which I clinically work, which is open to critique and criticism, and attempt to provide justification for approaching the therapeutic encounter the way I do. As did Freud contend, this way of practice is peculiar to my own personality and suits my style of therapeutic relatedness; other clinicians may prefer to operate differently because it is more conducive to better outcomes. Regardless of our differences in personality, style, and tack, I find it of value to bring into critical dialogue what we actually say to patients and how we actually practice in the consulting room. In this way I hope to address things they don't teach you in graduate school, including confronting the real as opposed to the ideal dimensions of treatment, the pragmatics of how to run a successful practice, how to truly get started in initiating therapy, what bodes well for success in keeping patients involved in treatment, and dispensing with myths that are typically taught as sacrosanct in the psychoanalytic literature. Let us first begin with the question of theoretical orientation and developing a relational philosophy of treatment.

DEVELOPING A RELATIONAL TREATMENT PHILOSOPHY

I was trained in the psychoanalytic tradition in Chicago, where the presence of Heinz Kohut, Bruno Bettleheim, and Merton Gill, among others, heavily influenced the scope of my clinical education and the analysts who supervised me. Although I initially favored a classical approach to theory, and indeed heavily immersed myself in the classical literature, my personality and communication style were better suited for an interpersonal approach to treatment. Despite being indoctrinated in the value of the communicative approach to psychoanalysis developed by Robert Langs (1988), in my clinical work, I gravitated toward more object relations and self psychological orientations that allowed me more freedom of play in the consulting room. After receiving supervision from Merton Gill, I still felt in need of a method that would allow me more liberation from the shackles of trying to follow a rigid formula or emulate a contrived procedure culled from a technique book. Ironically, although Freud (1933a) denounced psychoanalysis as a *Weltanschauung*, I found partial solution through a personal philosophy of living derived from psychoanalytic principles.[1]

By contemporary standards, I would be said to favor relational and existential orientations to practice, informed by my training in self psychology, the interpersonal schools, and phenomenology; but unlike any identification with a particular theoretical movement, this acknowledgment carries certain qualifications. Given my background, I never liked being classified or pigeonholed into a certain theoretical camp because this tends to limit the scope of self-identity and professional perception as well as dilute the rich and multitextured conceptual body the psychoanalytic domain serves to offer as a whole. Although I largely work as a relational analyst,[2] I may be more accurately considered a contemporary Freudian heavily indebted to many great intellectuals, practitioners, and contemporaneous trains of thought.

Among these, first and foremost is Freud, who has been greatly misunderstood and maligned by relational schools today. Many of his theories have been fundamentally misinterpreted and distorted from their original context and have not been critically evaluated within the evolution of his mature theoretical corpus.[3] This is partly because many have not bothered to consult his original texts written in German and have been conditioned by incompetent expositors and introductory textbooks that have little appreciation for accurate scholarship. Therefore, I am not in agreement with the uncritically accepted and erroneous characterizations of Freudian theory as adhering to a one-person psychology (Greenberg and Mitchell 1983; Mitchell and Aron 1999) or espousing the belief in a solipsistic, isolated mind (Stolorow and Atwood 1992), just to name two popularized propagandas circulating today. In my opinion, these claims are invalid, fueled in part by ignorance about what Freud actually said, including the corruption of classical thought by Anglo commentators that is carelessly perpetuated in contemporary training institutes, as well as political idolatry advocated by the American middle group of relational psychoanalysis, which is radically opposed to classical paradigms.[4] By the subjective accounts of his patients (Lohser and Newton 1996; Roazen 1995), Freud was quite relational, personable, and flexible in his approach to treatment; but unlike many relational clinicians today, he turned a critical eye toward continually uncovering and understanding the myriad unconscious processes that suffuse the analytic encounter, including the interpersonal dynamics of resistance, transference, repetition, and working through. While I do not wish to belabor points of contention between relational and classical thought, suffice it to say that I do not see the radical divide that is professed to exist. Where important and valid discrepancies do exist, they tend to lie in the nature of specific theoretical disputes and renunciations (e.g., feminist psychology), extensions, and revisionist expansions of technique, which are something radically different from the broad philosophical and technical innovations embedded in the classical tradition that relational perspectives seem to discredit. As I have said elsewhere, psychoanalysis is merely a footnote to Freud (Mills 2004a).

I cannot emphasize enough the need for beginning therapists to develop a firm theoretical orientation to their work and to be able to justify its merits and limitations. While there is often a schism that exists between theory and practice, your theoretical orientation guides you on how to think conceptually about case material and informs your approach to treatment. Theory and method are not necessarily synonymous, and they are often confounded to mean one and the same thing. In practice, however, the clinician is informed by multiple perspectives at any given moment and therefore must be open and flexible to seeing points of connection between the patient's reported lived subjective reality and the diverse theoretical models that may be applied in attempting to lend order and meaning to that process. Beginning therapists need to develop a firm grasp of their theoretical orientation and preferred mode of working clinically for the simple reason that it provides structure and direction for informed therapeutic practice. Whatever preferred mode of conceptualization one adopts in the end, the clinician can never escape from the fact that theory only serves as an orienting guide to the treatment process that is constantly being challenged and confronted by new emergent data and the intersubjective contingencies that arise in the lived encounter. Just as theory takes on its own dynamic, thus introducing contradiction, evolution, and change, so is the therapeutic dyad itself informed by the psychodynamics and phenomenological novelties of forming a new relationship among strangers. When it comes down to it, you and the patient, each with your own competing subjectivities and individual personalities, are thrown into an unfamiliar encounter. This is the existential dimension of treatment that cannot be eluded nor disavowed, for it is here that a new intersubjective reality is forged and negotiated.

Existential, phenomenological, and continental perspectives in philosophy complement psychoanalytic discourse, thus providing a fecundity of overlap in conceptual thought and practice that the relational schools have been increasing acknowledging over the past two decades. It can be said that psychoanalysis is fundamentally a theory and method geared toward insight, truth, and the amelioration of human suffering, while philosophy is the pursuit of wisdom, truth, human excellence, and rational meaning, what Freud (1927) himself identifies as *Logos*. I see these two disciplines as embracing similar convictions that human existence is ultimately about developing our potential, fulfilling our possibilities, and living an authentic life through liberation from ignorance and the malicious forces that threaten our happiness. This takes courage and fortitude, but it first and foremost takes awareness; for we can only be free through knowledge. In this way, therapy is a *liberation struggle*—Know thyself! This Delphic decree is the psychoanalytic motto. Insight or self-knowledge takes a commitment to educating oneself to what truly lies within—the complexity and competing flux of the inner world—and this is never an easy endeavor. It takes another to nurture and draw this out, to validate and reinforce, to encourage and to guide, to hold and reassure. This begins with the most primary of all relations, the relation of the embryonic self to its mother, then to its family and community at large, and finally to the social institutions that foster and beget the cultivation of self-consciousness. This is why a relational approach to treatment mirrors the natural process of self-development, for the self is given over to the other equiprimordially, and the other to the self: the subject–object split is foreclosed. Each is dynamically informed by a dialectical system of mutual implication, interaction, exchange, negotiation, and force.

It becomes difficult to define the overall purpose or meaning of therapy because the clinical encounter is always mediated by context and contingency. For rhetorical purposes, if I had to pinpoint the essence of treatment, I would say that therapy is a *process of becoming*, a process of creative self-discovery, a process that requires the presence and influence of the other. Therefore, therapy is about forming and being in a relationship, one that is healthier and more genuine than what patients know only too well in their private lives. Patients' having the opportunity to say what they truly think, and feel how they truly feel, is one of the most beautiful experiences and more curative dimensions of analysis; and having this recognized, understood, and validated by another serves to encourage and instill a new set of values and ideals for what it truly means to have a fulfilling relationship. When this occurs, over time the patient comes to identify with and pursue a new way of being that is modeled on authentic relationality.

What patients remember the most about you is not necessarily what you say but how you relate to them, how you model a way of being; and this is what gets internalized and transmuted within psychic structure. When I was a predoctoral intern at Michael Reese Hospital and Medical Center, I was assigned a training and supervising analyst at the Chicago Institute for Psychoanalysis to supervise two of my cases. When I first met the man, he opened his office door onto a vestibule where I was sitting, which was used as a common waiting area for several other offices. When he called me by name, I stood up and entered his office, greeting him with a handshake and a hello. He pointed with his hand to where I should sit and then walked over to his chair and promptly sat down. He stared at me and said nothing. I was waiting for some sort of an appropriate social greeting, introduction, or question, but instead I received the cool impression that I was to be observed and analyzed; he was acting toward me as I imagined he behaved toward his patients. Close to a minute had passed before I broke the ice and began to speak. It was clear to me that I was not going to be treated as a colleague, nor even as an advanced graduate student about to receive his doctorate, but as an object under a microscope. Whether this was the man's personality or his style of clinical supervision, the immediate impression he created was indelible: he was an asshole. Whether he was a brilliant supervisor or not is inconsequential; his very mode of relatedness was enough to create unease, intimidation, and resistance. This was not the way I wished to be treated, and I immediately thought about how this must feel for patients, who are in an even more vulnerable situation. Simply put, his behavior was uncalled for and certainly not the treatment approach I wanted to emulate.

There were many instances like this one during my training where I learned more about how *not* to act than about the so-called appropriate technique or demeanor I should adopt as a therapist. Ask yourself this question: How would you feel if you were in the patient's shoes? In the real world of private practice outside the academy, this type of behavior is a good way to lose business; if people are made to feel interpersonally uncomfortable, then they are more likely than not to discontinue treatment because they feel as though you have already judged or demeaned them. It is common throughout the psychoanalytic literature to encounter authors who are quick to blame or condemn patients as acting out or being resistant, deficient, limited, disturbed, narcissistic, or pathological in some way when they fail to return or commit to treatment, when in actuality they may be simply reacting to the normative feeling of being belittled in some fashion—even dehumanized—by a cool, staid, or threatening first impression that the analytic encounter can sometimes generate. And dependent and deprived patients will sometimes masochistically submit themselves to this form of treatment with the unconscious hope of winning over their analyst's approval, when in all likelihood this acquiescent submission is motivated by abnormal forces dictated not only by transference repetition but by the recalcitrant need to win recognition from a cold, depriving object in the here and now. While the analyst is always a transference figure, he can also generate extratransferential phenomena that may be more the result of unspoken or expressed power differentials that truly belong to the analyst's pathological inclinations. If you act aloof, removed, and clinically detached, then the message is clear: you don't want to get too close. So how could you expect patients to open up or trust you? If you create the slightest impression of being contemptuous, then the patient's "shit detector" immediately turns on and the relational milieu becomes soiled. Putting aside for the moment the notion of projection and transference, you are accountable for how you come across; your subjectivity, demeanor, interpersonal style and accord, and so forth influence the patient's perceptions, defense activations, relatedness patterns, and the negotiation of individuality within the intersubjective frame of treatment. If you don't concede that you bring something into the picture, then you can erroneously collude with the false impression that the patient is solely responsible for the reaction she orchestrates in others, when in actuality this is a two-way relational street.

Therapy is a *way of being*, not some contrived state, nor just another job, role, or hat one puts on only to remove it at the end of the day. I once had a patient whom I worked with for a few years. Approximately a year and a half into the treatment, during a particularly poignant disclosure, I commented that I felt for her in that moment. In a dismissing tone she told me, "That's your job, you're supposed to." Since we had already reached a degree of intimacy in the therapy, I was surprised at her dismissal and replied, "As if I couldn't possibly truly care about you." This led to her confession that it hurts when others show her sympathy or genuine concern because she feels that deep down she does not deserve it, so she brushes it away by finding an ulterior motive in the other's behavior. When you develop a genuine relationship with a patient, you cannot help but open up your own soul to the experience of the other and feel *with* him and *for* him, even though you may not disclose this directly. When this happens, and when it develops naturally—thus is not acted or manufactured—I find this to be an aesthetic supplement and intensification of empathy, what Heidegger (1927) calls care or concernful solicitude, or what Binswanger (1962) calls an extension of love.

I am always suspicious of those who say that they leave their occupation at the office. How can you just turn off your mind? I simply cannot shut off my fundamental orientation toward existence, namely, to think dynamically and critically about most aspects of life, and to open up my emotional world in the process—my total being. Deep understanding gives me a greater sense of purpose and meaning, even if certain discoveries are unsavory or distressing. Regardless of what we encounter or come to know through the analytic process, psychoanalysis makes our suffering more tolerable. Establishing a sound theoretical orientation for treatment efficacy takes thoughtfulness, justification, critical review, and revision. The lazy therapist who is only worried about what to say and not how to think dynamically will be eaten alive by certain patient populations, such as those with character disorders, and personally embarrassed when confronted with more intellectually sophisticated clients. One needs a personal commitment to ongoing professional development, and that means personal development. It means reading the literature (both disciplinary and interdisciplinary) and critically thinking about your own thoughts and experiences rather than consulting the identified expert on what is acceptable and what is not. Along with introspection and ongoing self-analysis, this critical function is a necessary (albeit not sufficient) condition for lasting professional growth that transcends the ossified dogma that can potentially serve to create stasis and prevent the actualization of genuine potential.

In many distinct ways, one's theoretical orientation often complements one's personality or individuality, and, consequently, what is more often the case than not, the personality of the therapist largely determines the course of the therapy. It is the analyst's personality that allows for genuine engagement, thus making a clearing for authentic relatedness. One cannot help but interject one's own personality in every aspect of the treatment, for every disclosure is value laden and communicates a great deal about the clinician, even during silence.

In order to establish and maintain ongoing professional identity, the therapist needs to think critically about his own worldview and adopt approaches that are congruent with that worldview in order to appear trustworthy and credible to patients. Beginning therapists often ask themselves, What do I do or say when the patient says x or y?—as if there were a bag of tricks or general skill set to apply to each and every situation when a similar dynamic unfolds. In my experience of teaching and supervising graduate and postgraduate students, it appears to be a common phenomenon that what they initially want is a tool bag to reach into in order to fix something in the patient. They have done some reading, have some pat phrases down, and are testing out or playing a role, hence trying it on for fit and size, rather than consulting their own personality and tempering it with thoughtful self-awareness and the process that guides it. Those who take the "bag of tricks" approach will be mediocre at best and will usually stifle the treatment because patients will inevitably feel that they come across as gimmicky, stilted, pedantic, and unnatural. This does not foster genuine relatedness, which is what patients with attachment disturbances need in order to live more fulfilling and functional lives.

A personal treatment philosophy should authentically reflect the way in which clinicians actually live their lives in order to be genuine to the patient. Do you really believe what you tell patients? Do you hold yourself to the same standards? If not, you should reevaluate your premises and the reasons that dictate your approach to treatment. Clinical and theoretical refinement demands work, reading, experimentation, thoughtfulness, contemplation, supervised experience, and ongoing training. You are only going to take a person as far as you have been yourself (Erikson 1964). If you can't recognize the dynamic forces that influence your own psychic reality, then how will you recognize what is going on in others? As a conscientious clinician, you should know thyself, get personal therapy or undergo analysis, and live an introspective and contemplative life. This is both a preparatory and ongoing attitude or sensibility that grounds your theoretical beliefs and convictions, guides your clinical work, and offers stability in professional identity and therapeutic efficacy. This takes time and erudition, experience and technical refinement, openness and flexibility, creativity and humor, and, as Kohut (1971) would say, a "modicum" of wisdom.

CREATING THE CLINICAL ATMOSPHERE

I have the luxury of a home office. While most of my colleagues shy away from such an arrangement, I find it the best of all possible professional worlds. Many therapists and analysts prefer to keep their private lives separate from their professional ones, and they have many valid therapeutic and personal reasons for why having a home office may be a dubious and even potentially detrimental practice; these reasons include the risk of contaminating the transference, potential violation of personal space and privacy, and concerns about individual safety or the possible endangerment of family members, just to name a few. Let me address each of these concerns in turn.

Because all interpersonal experience mobilizes transference elements (Freud 1912a), one can hardly escape their occurrence. Transference cues or triggers occur in a variety of different contexts and environments, and my office is no exception. Although my office may elicit certain unconscious material that may not have been evoked if I indeed had an office in a different location, it is all therapeutic grist. I use such material as an opportunity to bridge the transferential past with the immediacy of the interpersonal present and, when appropriate, to consider what it tells us about our relationship. I find that instead of hindering or contaminating the mobilization and analysis of the transference, it stimulates and accelerates this natural process. It is not uncommon for clinicians who want to radically separate their professional and personal lives to actually fear (perhaps more unconsciously) the demands for interpersonal intimacy that a therapeutic relationship arouses. I welcome this intimacy as a fundamental aspect of any therapy and encourage its mutual exploration.

My professional space and personal space often overlap, and I find it convenient on many practical levels to have easy accessibility to my office and the resources and amenities it affords. I had my office custom designed to my specifications to meet my needs and those of my patients. When I am not seeing patients, I spend a great deal of time reading and writing there, where I have my computer and extensive library. It is as much my private space for solitude, reflection, creativity, and enjoyment as it is for clinical work. I had wall-to-wall oak bookshelves built to generate the ambiance of scholarship and academic excellence to which I aspire, not to mention the fact that my research resources are merely footsteps away from my writing desk. I have several pieces of antique nineteenth-century European and domestic furniture in my office and waiting room, as well as Persian rugs that cover my maple hardwood floor. I prefer antique floor lamps to conventional lighting, except for a halogen system that highlights the bookshelves. Like Freud, but not so assiduously or elaborately, I have collected antiquities for many years and have a cornucopia of effigies and cultural artifacts from many ancient societies that surround my office in display cases. Original paintings and artwork adorn the walls, along with various prints, diplomas, busts, and so forth. I have created the ambiance of a small, private antiques shop. This is both professional and private space. In sum, comfort matters.

I realize that other professionals do not have the need, resources, nor the inclination to go to such aesthetic extremes, but I find it a necessity for my work. In the words of Mara Reissberger, commenting on Freud's consulting room at Berggasse 19: "In the scholar's environment, there will always be a number of objects which may be counted among the most expensive luxuries. However, they are necessary for the scholar's comfort, and therefore it is appropriate that they should be there" (cited in Engelman 1998, 55). Aesthetics deliver multiple meanings on multiple psychic levels of both organized and primitive experience; they activate many overdetermined processes that are both germane to the therapeutic encounter and significant in their own right. Even when clinicians are faced with working conditions that do not favor indulgence in such amenities, such as in hospitals or clinics, keep in mind that clinical space engages psychic space and sets the stage for work. The right ambiance stimulates introspection, cogitation, and emotionality, whereas plain, antiseptic, or bleak environments often do not. I once had a patient tell me that the last therapist he saw had her office in the back room of a hair salon, and this was the reason why he contacted me instead. Needless to say, he was pleased with the change in ambiance. If you take your clinical space seriously, so will your patients.

The question of safety often arises when one is contemplating a home office. First of all, I have a separate entrance to my office that is segregated from the rest of the house, which protects patient confidentiality and my family's privacy. Although I treat many patients with character disorders, I do not accept forensic populations into my practice; and if I were made to feel uncomfortable or unsafe by a patient, my professional involvement would likely end after the initial consultation. With regard to the question of physical endangerment, I am a man of large stature, command a presence, and am not easily intimidated—not to mention the fact that I have a black belt in Taekwondo and was an active competitor for many years; therefore, this is not an issue for me as it may be for others, especially women, who have to be more streetwise to potential danger.

There are many pragmatic advantages to having a home office: it is cost effective, it saves one from having to pay rent, and one enjoys a hefty tax exception, including the ability to legally deduct for the cost of antique furniture and office art. In sum, my professional space provides an ambiance that is aesthetically pleasing and essential for my work and well-being, facilitates a mood for clinical reflection and productivity, and is part of the joys of private practice. I realize that many practitioners may have little control over office space that is typically assigned and often communally shared in certain employment environments, but this does not mean that one cannot bring a personal, aesthetic touch to one's clinical space in an effort to provide an atmosphere conducive to optimal work.

ANTICIPATING THE INITIAL
CONSULTATION: THE PHONE CALL

Therapy begins the minute you answer the phone or return a call. I never get into heavy details or the minutiae of a patient's problem on the phone; this is properly left for the initial meeting. On the phone I generally book an appointment time, briefly discuss my business practices, such as my fee and method of payment, and provide directions to my office. Sometimes patients are distressed, are in need of explanation or reassurance, and/or are merely shopping around for prices. I usually explain that I prefer to wait to get into the specifics of things until our initial consultation, at which time I can determine whether I can be of help. When callers grill me with twenty questions on my credentials, experience, and so forth, I refer them to my website for details rather than engage in a sales pitch. This way I maintain a professional comportment, avoid unnecessary justification or competition with other practitioners, and don't waste my time. A professional website is a very practical way of disseminating information about your practice that is both visually impressive and business savvy. I list my credentials, training background, and experience; clinical services offered, including areas of specialization and expertise; and other professional and academic activities that are germane to my practice and reputation as a practitioner and a scholar. The main reasons behind this phone practice are that it (a) provides a frame or structure for containment, (b) clarifies appropriate expectations and boundaries, (c) establishes professional authority and direction, and (d) sets the initial parameters for treatment.

INITIAL GREETINGS

Unlike my supervisor during graduate school, I greet my patients in the waiting room with a welcome and open reception usually accompanied by polite, brief recognition. I introduce myself by first name rather than by title, which indirectly extends an invitation to relatedness, makes a clearing for interpersonal comfort, and gives the patient permission to address me more informally if so desired. It also serves as a quasi-diagnostic aid; I allow the patient the option of addressing me either informally or formally, and his choice of address communicates to me the type of structure and relationship he prefers or expects. Those clinicians who introduce themselves formally and request being called "doctor" may give the impression of clinical aloofness and/or the need for distance and control. I particularly find that those who insist on being addressed by their title, which is a common phenomenon among fresh Ph.D.'s, often come across as arrogant, insecure, entitled, and/or condescending in their need to demand respect.

With men, the initial greeting typically results in a handshake as part of customary social exchange. As a general rule, I usually allow women to initiate handshakes at their discretion out of respect for personal comfort and because I do not want to intrude upon bodily space for obvious reasons. But this is not a hard and fast rule: context determines everything. I then invite patients into my office and ask them to have a seat on the Chippendale sofa against the wall in front of them rather than on the analytic couch (a large Edwardian chaise lounge), which is placed beside my chair opposite the sofa. I have patients sit on a sofa rather than in a chair because I also see couples in therapy and perform regular psychological assessments involving testing, so I therefore use the sofa for multiple purposes. Patients also find the sofa more comfortable, roomy, and relaxing, and it can accommodate larger or heavier patients more readily.

Throw pillows are also ready at hand for personal comfort and back support when needed.

SEATING ARRANGEMENTS

Rather than lying on the couch, many attachment disordered populations need face-to-face therapy because of their lack of internalized positive introjects, emotional engagement, recognition, and genuine human connection, of which they were deprived. Having ready access to seeing my face and my immediate responsiveness serves multiple attachment functions that have been missing from their lives; and over time, these are gradually internalized, incorporated, and transmuted within psychic structure. While I use the couch with higher-functioning patients, with patients with attachment-based disorders I adopt a seating arrangement similar to Fairbairn's (1958), which consists of sitting comfortably about four feet apart from one another with our furniture tilted at slightly different angles. This allows for direct eye-to-eye contact when required or if solicited, but it also allows for eye aversion and prevents from distraction or interference during free association. It also affords the patient some refuge from the impingement and gaze of the other, while at times cushioning the shame and vulnerability, for example, crying, associated with disclosing painful material or emotions (D. Downing, pers. comm., 2002). This posture allows patients a secure base or to remain held by the therapist, and it avoids the awkwardness and drawbacks associated with direct face-to-face confrontation as well as the total removal of cue-related human facial expression that occurs when the patient is lying on the couch.

This arrangement is of benefit to the therapist as well as the patient. I prefer this setup because it also affords me pensive diversion when thinking about multiple processes at once (e.g., content, affect, transference, communicative processes, etc.) that could be easily missed or lost if I were staring at the patient directly in the eye, which requires other attentional processes that could potentially take me away from the analytic task. This is the way in which I optimally work as well as provide (in theory) an optimal clinical milieu. Recall that Freud developed the couch technique as a way to insulate patients from his actual facial expressions, which could serve to interfere with the free-associative process (e.g., to distort pure transference projections), as well as to provide himself with the opportunity to think without having to be cognizant or self-conscious of how his facial expressions were being perceived. Angled chairs, or, in my case, chair and sofa, allow me to perform holding functions and be fully present as a responsive, calming-soothing introject and container, and they also provide "potential space" for optimal relatedness and attachment.

GETTING STARTED

Each new clinical encounter is different, and there are no pat methods that one must strictly adhere to or rigidly follow without running the risk of appearing awkward, stilted, or simply weird to the patient. You must be yourself rather than present a front or facade; patients see right through this, and this merely leads to their apprehension, ambivalence, and/or mistrust. Following my personality style, I act naturally, perhaps responding socially to the patient's comments or questions, yet I get down to business right away by asking the patient why she has come to see me. This sets the stage for work and does not collude with the patient's natural defensive tendencies to want to minimize or flee from the problem through idle chitchat, as is often the case. Through direct engagement, you also communicate that you are not shy about wanting to confront issues directly in order to understand the patient's experience of what is often personally distressing.

Patients have multiple reasons and needs for seeking out treatment, and their agendas and concerns must be addressed and respected even if yours are different. When appropriate, I explain that during this initial consultation period I am interested in understanding the patient's view of herself, her problems, and her experiential world, and by the end of the hour I will offer an initial impression of what I think would be most beneficial in the form of treatment. Here the process of information gathering for assessment purposes and/or diagnostic considerations must be delicately weighed along with the need to make the patient feel safe and secure in telling her narrative to you, who are experienced as a stranger, hence an immediate transference object. Above all else, I am conscientious to comport myself as someone who is genuinely interested in understanding the patient's life and current experience with the intention of communicating an attentive, responsive, empathic, and validating presence. This sets the tone for future relatedness and facilitates an increasing comfort level in the patient for disclosing often difficult and painful material. It also proves to the patient that I am not like others, and that this mode of relatedness has the potential for an entirely different type of relationship.

For qualitative purposes, I wish to distinguish between a formal assessment and the initial consultation. During a formal assessment, large amounts of information need to be amassed for diagnostic purposes and for reasons of treatment, including professional recommendations. This usually requires the administration of a battery of psychological tests. When I am asked to serve in this capacity, my professional role is quite different from my role when I am screening a patient for treatment purposes. During a formal assessment I take copious notes, but during initial consultations and during the regular course of treatment I do not. In fact, it is imperative not to take notes during the consult because the consult is already the initiation of therapy. Clinicians who are more worried about jotting down everything the patient says communicate to that patient that she is a clinical object rather than a person, and this potentially creates distance, alienation, and disconnectedness—the exact opposite of what you want to engender. Taking notes during the initial consult or during therapy proper is bad technique and should be avoided. It also shows that the clinician is uncomfortable with the emotional immediacy of the lived encounter and that he needs to introduce a barrier (for whatever reason) to buffer the genuine exchange of sensory information. The unconscious perception of the patient is typically this: "He doesn't really care. I'm just another number." Introducing an inanimate medium is also very inconsiderate if not insulting to the patient's feelings and state of vulnerability and only serves to weaken optimal responsiveness and attunement.

Here the analytic attitude or sensibility is one of attunement, responsiveness, and empathic validation with an emphasis on the understanding of personal lived experience. I often emphasize the value of understanding as a quest for insight into unconscious processes that are always operative and inform conscious behavior. Therefore, not only does the initial consult present a model of relationality, but it also introduces the educative imperative of self-knowledge. Because the consult is the patient's foray into understanding her malaise or pathology, I attempt to offer suggestive direction and structure through educative collaboration, which almost always includes some form of interpretation when I am offering diagnostic impressions. More on this later.

PRELIMINARY CONSIDERATIONS FOR ASSESSING ATTACHMENT PATHOLOGY

Among the stock and trade of any good clinician is the capacity to form sound theoretical conceptualizations and dynamic formulations regarding the patient's present symptomatology, life history, defenses and adjustment, and his patterns and quality of interpersonal relationships. This requires astute behavioral observation and listening on multiple levels for subtle communications regarding how content and affect are organized around key relational and psychogenic themes. You get an initial sense or impression of attachment capacity by observing how patients initially relate to you, carry their body comportment, and show whether they are tuned into the present experience. The way in which a patient shows or discusses affect often suggests his range of comfort level with emotional expression. When the patient is prompted to consider emotional expression, a paucity of feelings or confusion surrounding emotional states, especially toward others, may be indicative of structural deficits, compartmentalization, alexithymia, and/or numbing or dissociative tendencies. The level of eye contact is a powerful source of information; frequent eye aversion or the intolerability of making eye contact or looking at the therapist's face often points toward bereft attachment experiences, or those populated by conflict or trauma. The gaze of the other also implicitly invokes a power dynamic of domination, submission, accommodation, and control. Levels of distractibility, such as looking around the room, inattentiveness, and drifting into fantasy or daydreaming, not only communicate potential defensive maneuvers or core symptomatology but also display discomfort in relatedness; the patient would rather be elsewhere than in-relation to you.

Avoidant, ambivalent, dismissive, resistant, preoccupied, controlling, angry-resentful, denigrating, disorganized, and/or incoherent patterns of associations, behavioral descriptions, reports of internal representations, and verbal narratives of interpersonal relationships often correspond to the adult attachment categories discussed in our theoretical section and underscore structural deficits of the self. What is of particular import is how patients describe the qualitative aspects of their relationships—whether their descriptions are vague, Pollyannaish, impressionistic, uninsightful, dismissive, uncertain, or ambivalent, or whether they are preoccupied with how they were treated—including their understanding and felt experience of developmental traumas and how they are currently organized. I always ask about significant relationships in the initial interview and particularly about experiences and attitudes toward parents. This sometimes includes earliest memories, incidents, and dreams, but I typically ask for qualitative descriptions of parents, siblings, lovers, or partners and the perceived impact they have had on the patient's personality. I particularly fish for adjectives and emotions directed toward significant figures, patients' impression of the quality of their relationships with these figures in childhood and currently if applicable, their levels of disappointment, regret, resentment, loss, and so forth, and their subjective experience of what went wrong in past. When I deem it appropriate, I will ask patients about their most traumatic childhood experiences and the impact they have had on their lives.

More secure or autonomous patients typically present with more coherent and collaborative discourse while describing their attachment-related experiences and their subsequent impact, whether favorable or negative. These patients tend to value attachment, intimacy, interpersonal warmth, and emotional connection, and they are capable of maintaining some degree of critical reflection or objectivity when discussing particular experiences or relationships. In contrast, dismissive-avoidant patients attempt to normalize their experiences or provide overly positive, Pollyannaish descriptions of parents that are unsupported or contradicted by specific incidents reported. For example, patients might say that it is "normal" to get hit with a belt as a kid, or that the past has no relevance on how they feel about themselves now. Denial is also manifest in overly positive, histrionic descriptors, such as how their mothers were "totally wonderful" people. Negative experiences are said to have little or no effect if they are not negated altogether. Narratives about patients' relationships are brief and lack qualitative detail, and there is often a repeated insistence on lack of memory. Patients with a preoccupied profile ruminate or perseverate over certain experiences and can be seemingly angry, confused, passive, fearful, and/or overwhelmed. Narratives of early parental relationships have many diagnostic indicators that correspond to Ainsworth's strange situation response, such as resistant-ambivalent behavior, and can be long, tangential, digressive, detailed, irrelevant, and even vague. There are also tendencies to display emotionality that are typically associated with borderline character pathology.

Because I like to work from natural conversation as a participant-observer and explore the immediacy of the moment, I do not dominate the session with any more questions than I need to ask in order to provide a preliminary assessment. As noted earlier, because I do not consider the initial consult a structured, formal interview, nor an interrogation where I need to gather large amounts of information quickly for other professional reasons, I am continually mindful of the relational ambiance I wish to nurture.

OFFERING DIAGNOSTIC IMPRESSIONS

In the initial consult, I always form working hypotheses about patients' personality structures and their possible pathologies; these are open to modification and revision, especially when more dynamic complexity and evidence present themselves. More toward the middle to the end of the session, after I have gathered enough information to form a preliminary understanding of the patient's presenting complaints, symptomatology, and psychognomonic past, I offer initial diagnostic impressions. This may be more straightforward when standard diagnostic criteria are fully met, but I tend to shy away from placing patients in a category or reifying them as a clinical entity. This can inadvertently create the impression that you don't see them as a human being but as an object or thing. However, I do not minimize the severity of symptoms or pathology, when present, by dismissing clinical nomenclature, such as by saying that mental illness is merely a myth (Szasz 1960) or a social construction (Foucault 1965), since this tends to invalidate the patient's lived subjective reality of his pain. As the Latin term *patiens* signifies, patients are those who suffer.

In communicating my clinical impressions, I tend to focus on the *process* of how patients' present symptoms are mediated by many developmental contingencies and conflicts that are unconsciously informed and rooted in their relational and genetic past. Patients inevitably engage in the reiteration of certain relational patterns that serve as unconscious templates partially informing conscious object choice. The repetition of relationships in all their myriad forms usually translates to recognizable behavioral manifestations that are both defensive maneuvers organized on the structural level as well as paradigmatic expressions of conflicted object relations and attachment vulnerabilities.

Thinking processentially requires thinking on multiple levels about ongoing organizing principles in the patient's object relations, self-representations, defenses, and symptomatic profile. It requires thinking about the patient's immediate conscious state of mind by tracking the content, affect, process of association, and the intersubjective milieu of therapist–patient exchange, as well as thinking about the unconscious level of communicative defenses, transference projections, resistance, and the process of symptom emergence. What guides me in pointing out this process is to first focus on the precipitating, disturbing events that triggered or informed the current disturbance and explore how current symptomatology stands in relation to myriad conscious and unconscious disturbed meanings and/or internally conflicted resonance states that are activated or invoked in response to the disturbing events. It is often the case that one can trace a certain dynamic pattern of symptom formation that emerges from the breakdown of various defenses that are alerted when the ego is besieged by anxiety. This conceptual scheme has its rudiments in classical theory derived from Freud's (Breuer and Freud 1893–1895; Brenner 1982, 2002; Freud 1900, 1914a, 1916–1917) notions of compromise formation, conversion, and repetition. Rather than seeing symptomatology as the problem in itself, for example, depression or panic disorder, from this framework, we can conceive of symptoms as the conscious behavioral expression of unconscious conflictual manifestations that appear in many altered, disguised, and distorted forms that serve multiple unconscious functions. Conceptually, the clinician may use this approach as a template for forming initial diagnostic impressions that are wed to an understanding of the process and emergence of symptomatology etiologically informed by dynamic currents. Rubin (N. Rubin, pers. comm., 1988) depicts this process through a pathological sequence outline, or what I refer to as the process of symptom emergence (see figure 4.1).

1. There are always precipitating or disturbing events that trigger, fuel, and exacerbate current symptomatology; so it becomes a matter of ferreting out the details or specific contingencies and content that are related to more archaic conflict and primal anxieties.
2. Patients have multiple disturbed meanings with varying degrees of intrapsychic significance that are activated on both conscious and

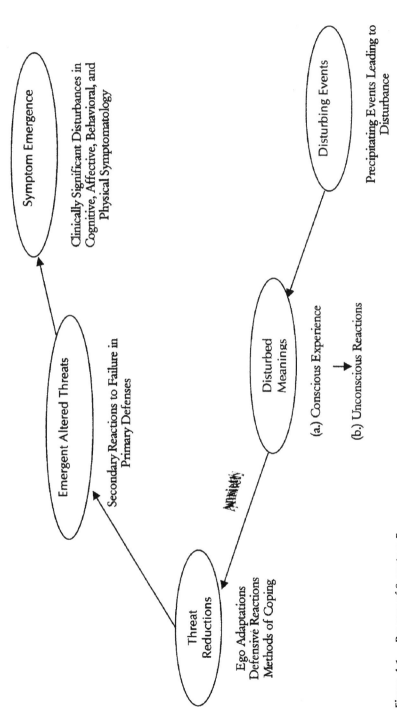

Figure 4.1.   Process of Symptom Emergence

unconscious levels in relation to the disturbing events. Consciously, patients will report their subjective experiences, cognitions, emotional reactions, fears, and so forth, while on the unconscious level a plethora of conflict, affective eruption, and primitive dangers are activated. The latter are organized on many planes or realms of unconscious experience informed by multiple and overdetermined psychogenetic, developmental, dynamic, relational, and self-referential structures, along with their parallel processes. The potential wealth of unconscious experience is certainly beyond lucid comprehension or conceptualization during this stage in the interview; however, many general themes and content areas may be noticed and related to the corresponding precipitating events.

3. What is often evident is that the patient has come to treatment because of some identified stressor, disturbance, or event that motivates the patient to get help. Anxiety is a common reaction to the disturbing events and disturbed meanings that are experientially processed by the ego on multiple levels. Following Freud's (1926) theory of signal anxiety, the ego realizes it is in a dangerous situation that it must protectively combat through the mobilization of various defenses that allow functional adaptation. By the time patients present themselves in the consulting room, however, clinical symptoms are typically already present, which suggests that more primary defenses that typically allow for functional methods of coping and adaptation have already eroded or become tenuous.

4. When primary defenses fail, secondary defensive reactions emerge in response to altered threats that continue to plague psychic integrity informed by internal pressures and external stressors. These emergent altered-threat reductions are often desperate attempts to regulate disabling affective states and disturbed meanings associated with the precipitating events and/or excavated internal disruptions. For example, when efforts to deny, repress, or avoid painful or threatening material are ineffective, more regressive forces and behavioral acting-out impulses may be enacted, such as heavy drinking, binge eating, sexual promiscuity, compulsive or ritualistic behavior, excessive exercise, sleeping, and other forms of withdrawal, escape, or numbing activities. Often, more acute symptoms or problems emerge and by this time are severe enough to compel the patient to seek treatment if certain threat reductions or attempts at resolution fail.

Let us see how this conceptual model applies to a clinical case. Mrs. Z was a forty-eight-year-old white female with a presenting clinical picture of paranoid agitation, domestic violence, and suicidal gestures in response to her suspicion that her husband was having an extramarital affair. She was voluntarily admitted to an inpatient psychiatry unit of a general hospital after she was found intoxicated and standing in the rain nude, which she had been doing for approximately two hours. Upon confronting her husband about the alleged affair, the patient had reportedly slapped and hit him and then set a blanket on fire in the upstairs bedroom of their house before running outside in the cold with no clothes on, refusing to come back inside and saying she would rather die. She deliberately tried to hide from a small neighborhood search party but was eventually located and brought to the emergency room by the police. This was the patient's first hospitalization, and she had no previous psychiatric history. I began treating her on an outpatient basis after her release from the hospital three days later.

Mrs. Z had been married to her husband for twenty-three years and had a twenty-year-old daughter who had recently got married and moved out of the home. Following her daughter's marriage, the patient was removing something from her husband's car when she noticed that there was a crack in the upholstery of the driver's seat. Apparently the seat was splitting at the seam in the upper right-hand corner, yet she paid it little attention. A week had passed when she noticed that the rip in the seam had widened, and with panic she immediately fantasized that her husband was having vigorous sexual relations with another woman in the car, thus causing damage to the seat. The patient reported that upon having this fantasy, she recalled an event that had taken place approximately four months prior to her daughter's wedding when she had thought she smelled perfume on her husband's shirt while doing the laundry, something she dismissed at the time. This recollection further revived a painful twenty-year-old memory of when her husband blurted out another woman's name during intercourse, leaving an unabated narcissistic injury; yet he assured her at the time that his slip was only a fantasy and that he had never been unfaithful, an explanation which she had believed.

After she discovered the torn seat for the second time, Mrs. Z's suspicions started to assume more paranoid qualities, thus producing obsessional preoccupations that her husband was cheating on her each day as he went to work. She started checking and cleaning the car every night as he returned home, hoping *not* to find evidence to corroborate her intuitions. One evening, however, she found a small piece of wire fencing underneath the passenger's front seat and concluded that someone had been in the car. When she asked her husband to explain how it got there, he could not and only suggested that she must have overlooked the object when she previously vacuumed the car.

The patient now started to record the gas mileage each day as her husband drove to and from work. She had already driven the same route he normally took and recorded the mileage so she could have a baseline for comparison. When the mileage on the odometer proved to be significantly higher than expected on his next return from work, she confronted her husband about the discrepancy and accused him of having an affair. He vociferously denied any such thing and told the patient that she was paranoid, thus engendering confusion, doubt, and panic. It turned out that he was indeed cheating on the patient, but he lied, manipulated the patient, and distorted the events sufficiently to cause her to question her own perceived reality. Mrs. Z's symptomatology eventually mushroomed to the acute state that brought her to crisis and psychiatric admission.

While I cannot go into every nuance of her case here, a topic I treat at more length elsewhere (see Mills 2003b), the patient's original disturbing event was her daughter's marriage and subsequent move away from home. This mobilized various disturbed meanings triggering abandonment anxieties the patient was susceptible to experiencing, based upon her past. These anxieties erupted more fully upon the recent salient disturbing event—noticing the rip in her husband's car seat—which precipitated an unfolding series of fears surrounding rejection, betrayal, injury, and guilt with regard to relational attachment and her own sexual inadequacy. Developmentally, the patient was raised in a tumultuous home environment dominated by an alcoholic father who was unloving and perceived as threatening during drinking binges, while he was cold, detached, or absent when sober. She reportedly had a clingy-dependent relationship with her mother that was mutually encouraged and reinforced, and she later transferred this relationship onto the role expectancies of her daughter, who was also a surrogate and buffer for the tension that existed between the patient and her husband due to their own strained marriage. Furthermore, there were reasonable suspicions that the patient may have been subjected to sexual abuse, and to this day she is frigid and finds no pleasure in sexual activity. This was a great source of frustration for the husband, who, in the end, found gratification elsewhere. When the patient's denial, self-deception, and avoidance of confronting the truth of her husband's infidelity broke down, alcohol abuse, verbal arguments, passive-aggressive withdrawal, and eventually domestic violence were more desperate secondary defensive attempts at threat reduction.

Coming to grips with her own paranoiac knowledge of her husband's transgressions brought on an overwhelming abandonment depression as she realized that her marriage could not be repaired nor salvaged. The mobilization of disturbed meanings had even farther-reaching unconscious significance due to the fact that her first husband had committed suicide. Notwithstanding the traumatic impact and his immediate physical desertion, she had always fantasized that his suicide was indirectly because of her, and this belief left an aftermath of oppressive guilt and self-blame. Her current husband's infidelity ruptured profound narcissistic wounds surrounding her sexual disgust and inadequacy, which further evoked the felt recognition that her lack of sexual interest drove him to the affair; this conviction confirmed her self-deficiencies as a wife and a woman. In her mind, this was the third man who had found her unworthy of love. Abandonment depression led to fragmentation anxiety, which in turn led to suicidality.

The consequences of symptom formation can easily intensify and lead to vicious circles of reexperiencing disturbing and traumatic events that continue to feed and sustain disturbed meanings and disorganization in regulatory functions. Thus, the basic notion of repetition and the concentric, vicious cycles nourishing and perpetuating symptom manifestation are unequivocally intertwined in the developmental-relational experiences and historical past that compose personality organization and self-structure. Let us examine another example of how repetition serves organizational functions through the recurrence of unconscious pattern.

Consider the case of Martin, a thirty-eight-year-old married black male who was a successful business manager. He came to treatment in crisis after his wife discovered that he had been visiting massage parlors for sexual gratification. Martin was abandoned by his mother and father shortly after birth and was primarily raised by his great-grandmother. He moved to Canada from the West Indies when he was three years old and lived with extended family members including aunts, uncles, and cousins, moving from apartment to apartment throughout his childhood because they were repeatedly evicted for violating boarding codes. The patient never felt accepted or wanted and was told that he was living with his relatives only out of family obligation. While his cousins received what he perceived were nice gifts for Christmas, he was given inexpensive trinkets. Growing up and seeing other children warmly engaged with their parents only made him feel more displaced since he reportedly was never hugged, kissed, or told he was loved.

When Martin was eight, his biological father called him and said that he and his new wife were moving to Canada, and he asked Martin to be a part of his family. Martin was ecstatic. But when his father and stepmother arrived with their newborn infant daughter, Martin was immediately forsaken. What little attention he did receive occurred when his father would visit "lady friends" and prostitutes, but he was only to be told that he had numerous other siblings whom he had never met. He remembered one incident of sitting in the "parlor" of a woman's house having cookies and milk as she and his father were audibly fornicating in the adjacent room.

Martin's father deserted his family again when the patient was twelve years old, and he remained with his stepmother, who he felt "hated" him for his father's actions. Martin's father had a record of five marriages and divorces and innumerable illegitimate children by the time the patient came to see me; and, like his father, Martin had transgressed in his own

marriage for several years. In fact, the patient's concentric pattern of repetition was to unconsciously orchestrate the same situation he had experienced throughout his entire lifetime. Through the recapitulation of his
original abandonments, he set up the very thing he feared the most. Faced
with the anxiety of his wife's imminent desire to end their marriage, all he
could do was helplessly look back and see in retrospect how the process
came about, this time through his own hands.

Let us examine one more example. Mr. van B was the youngest of three
boys. His mother was hospitalized shortly after his birth, and he was reportedly raised by different aunts and uncles during the first year of his
life. The patient was physically bullied and beaten by his brothers throughout his childhood; felt invalidated, unloved, and unprotected by both parents; and confessed that he harbored intense and unremitting emotional
pain and generalized fear throughout most of his life. He had two previous psychiatric hospitalizations and had been on antidepressant and anti-
anxiety agents for more than twenty-five years. Mr. van B had a history of
interpersonal difficulties with others, including his wife—his marriage
ended in divorce—and other women he had encountered subsequently in
work environments. He had displayed a lifelong pattern of being fired or
let go from a series of jobs, including being a successful church pastor, and
was terminated from his most recent employer for insubordination.

Mr. van B was a man who had suffered in silence for many years due to
unresolved developmental traumas, which had disposed him toward a
lifetime struggle with clinical depression and agitated internal anxiety
states that were characterologically informed. The patient was insecurely
attached to his parents, subjected to chronic bullying and physical abuse
by his older brothers, and felt he had no one to confide in or turn to for
mollification or protection. He reportedly was never shown physical affection or proper love by his parents, was shamed and ridiculed by his
mother when he was hurt and in emotional pain, was invalidated and
dismissed by his unavailable depressed father, and was never accepted by
his family during his childhood. Mr. van B claimed that although he was
a good student he was repeatedly rejected by his family and devalued for
not possessing skills of "practical value." He experimented with homosexuality with a peer as an early adolescent and found it pleasurable, but
he was also subjected to two later incidents of sexual abuse: one where an
older boy intimidated him into performing fellatio, and another occasion
where an older man persuaded him to engage in group masturbation
with his cousins.

The patient presented with a plethora of rage and pain about his past
and was plagued by feelings of being unjustly mistreated and maligned
by others, especially women, including his previous female manager, his
ex-wife, and his mother. The precipitating events that had been most disturbing to the patient were increased fantasies of cutting the heads off of

people who had wronged him in the past. While he had started having these fantasies about a year after being terminated from his job of five years, they had increased within the month before he came to therapy, at about the time he was anticipating having to find work because his unemployment benefits were running out. While the patient reassured me by adamantly denying that he would ever act on such fantasies, he did admit that they were both a source of pleasure and were disruptively intrusive, enough so that he was prompted to tell his family doctor, who then referred him for a psychiatric consultation.

Mr. van B's decapitation fantasies were derived from his unresolved feelings of being chronically invalidated, neglected, physically abused, and verbally cut down by others, which unconsciously symbolized his own feelings of being emasculated—hence castrated—at the hands of women. For example, when the patient was a child he went to his mother in tears seeking her comfort because his older brothers had beaten him up. Instead of consoling him, she said that he sounded like a "bull calf." The shameful feelings caused by her humiliation, rejection, lack of concern, and inability to show him love were still a source of considerable inner anguish. He also harbored intense animosity toward his ex-wife, whom he felt had assassinated his character to his parishioners and besmirched his good name, which he perceived was the main reason why he lost his position as the pastor of his church. Furthermore, he believed that his previous manager and other female coworkers had conspired to get him fired. Because he felt he was never properly recognized, validated, nurtured, or understood, he was deeply embittered and harbored many retribution fantasies. This had further developed into an entrenched predisposition toward misogyny due to repeated rejection from significant female dependency figures in positions of authority. His animosity toward women inevitably led him to unconsciously orchestrate conflict and bring about the very thing he wished to avoid the most, namely, being devalued and rejected by females, who were transferential attachment figures from whom he ultimately wished to procure their validation and acceptance.

Mr. van B was a very narcissistically vulnerable man who bore oppressive psychic injuries to his sense of self. Although he largely felt that he was inadequate as a man and a failure in his career, he had developed a grandiose posture of male superiority as a compensatory defense against his feelings of inferiority. His narcissistic element of superiority over women was also partly informed by his identification with the omniscience of religious authority and his abhorrence for the "feminization" of the church and contemporary society as he envisioned it. The patient was exceptionally sensitive to being slighted or dismissed for his egotistical views, and he had suffered many blows to his self-esteem by going from a position of spiritual authority as savior to being rejected by the very people who had once revered him for his need to dominate the flock. He had a pension for creating conflict wherever he went, thus bringing about the repetition of being vilified and denounced, which only fortified his preexisting vulnerabilities that he was not worthy of being accepted or loved, a theme that had dogged him since childhood.

The therapist should never have to feel the pressure to fully understand or grasp all essential aspects of a patient's life or the dynamic complexity that informs her character structure, let alone do something about it. In fact, to attempt do so would be a presumptuous and narrow undertaking. What I try to do is put my clinical impressions in the context of my professional observations and concerns based on the patient's self-disclosures. My formulations are often brief and succinct during the first session (given the limited nature of information gathering that takes place), usually focusing on observable patterns. I typically tell the patient that these impressions need to be more fully understood through our mutual exploration and thus that they should be open to many possible interpretations from the standpoint of multiple perspectives evoking different levels of personal meaning. In this sense, I am honest about my impressions, therefore not secretive nor deceptive, which does nothing but undermine trust, and openly invite reflection through the introduction of a new way of thinking processentially about the patient's life and symptomatic expressions. In short, I attempt to model an openness through mutual inquiry into the patient's life emphasizing cooperative dialogue and concern. After offering initial diagnostic impressions, I then ask patients for their thoughts or reactions to my preliminary observations if they have not already offered them.

ENGENDERING MUTUAL COLLABORATION

In graduate school, one is often taught a generic (albeit broad) model of therapeutic intervention that in principle can be applied to most clinical encounters. This model or orientation largely forms the theoretical bedrock that in turn guides methodological considerations that justify a given practice. While our treatment philosophy and guiding principles of therapeutic efficacy may be largely defensible and merit validation within a certain pedagogical context, the clinician inevitably encounters the problem of the *universal* and the *particular*, namely, the problem of extending a universal theory and/or method to a particular experience or context that often challenges the very assumption of that universal. In philosophy, this is referred to as "the problem of the one and the many."

I make no bones about the fact that I operate from a theory-based method of treatment that guides my procedural considerations, but this is always informed by data presented in the immediacy of the clinical encounter. Theory must always be open to modification, contingency, and context, and this is a lesson we can appropriate from Freud. If clinicians cling steadfastly to a particular line of thinking with rigid identification based on an economy of conditioned learning or ideology, then they will find it very difficult to navigate through the spontaneous lived encounter of the patient's experiential world in the context of intersubjective exchange. You simply cannot superimpose an empty formalism on the dyadic therapeutic process without running the risk of ruining the treatment. Universal theories may easily break down when confronted with novel encounters that do not readily fit into what is "supposed to happen." This is why therapy is a relational qua human experiment based on emotional interaction, interpersonal negotiation, and conceptual accommodation.

In the clinical reality of the consulting room, under the pressure to procure and sustain a fee-paying patient, you are faced with the challenge of convincing patients of the value of treatment. In other words: Does it bake bread? You have to provide some kernel of hope and reassurance that the process of therapy will lead to symptom relief, transformation, insight, potential happiness, and perhaps even enlightenment—or the patient will be inclined to leave. This is simply a practical matter that comes up time after time in the consulting room and especially during the initial interview. Today's consumer is educated, and many potential patients have done some preliminary research into the type of therapy they think they need, or they have been informed by another source, for example, a family physician, on what to seek out. I routinely have patients ask me about my credentials, what my training and theoretical orientation is, how therapy works, and why I have adopted my approach over other more mainstream models such as cognitive-behavioral therapy (CBT), and, for better or worse, I often feel as though I have to sell them on the value of treatment. This is where the clinician needs to explain the therapeutic process by introducing the educational aspect of therapy. This is a most crucial time in setting the stage for treatment and engendering certain expectations in the patient. The clinician needs to be prepared to answer these questions when they arise with persuasive justification, clarification, and reassurance.

In clinical reality, the goals of therapy are dictated by contingencies. In this sense, context is everything. Some patients know what they want and others are horribly confused. Some want structure, guidance, and to be told what to do and what not to do and ask for "homework assignments," and others resist anything they feel or perceive is imposed upon them without a welcome invitation. Most want symptom relief and skills at symptom management, and they often ask for ways or techniques to alleviate their suffering. The clinician always has to work with the immediacy of the moment and weave these experiences into the larger dynamics of the emerging process. After determining the problem and identified goals of the patient, we as clinicians may form the professional judgment that what the patient wants is not what she really needs. When this is the case, I always inform patients directly of what I think is the best way to proceed, while acknowledging and validating their desires and intentions. This involves negotiating the patient's needs with the analytic task, and the clinician must be flexible and eclectic in the services he can provide and what he is willing to provide. Short-term, solution-focused work is more typically solicited than long-term dynamic therapy or formal analysis; but with attachment disordered patients, long-term treatment is necessary, and I tell them so. For example, I often have patients during the initial consult who are in crisis or have acute anxiety or depression in relation to difficulties in their significant interpersonal relationships. These types of patients under immediate duress present with an urgency to "fix" the problem. This is understandable, but they also may harbor certain illusions or erroneous expectations about what therapists actually can do and do. This is where clarification and some instruction is needed. Let us examine a clinical vignette that transpired during the initial consult with a depressed and agitated patient who had a series of failed relationships and who had been on medication for two years with little results.

Patient: All I want is for this to go away.

Therapist: I can appreciate your sense of urgency. It's obviously not been easy for you, but therapy is a process and it takes hard work in examining and resolving conflict, and that can often be a lengthy process.

Patient: How long will it take?

Therapist: Everyone is different, and it varies from person to person depending upon the issue. According to what you just told me, you've been depressed for several years and have had one failed relationship after the other—and you don't understand why; so I anticipate you will need to see me at the very minimum for six months to a year, and maybe much longer depending on how far we get.

Patient: I didn't think it would be like this. I thought it would be simpler. I thought you'd just tell me what to do and I'd get better.

Therapist: Well, I'm not a mechanic, and it's not like having an oil change. As you know, psychiatrists only give you a pill, which may take the edge off, but it won't address the underlying conflicts or reasons that are causing your problems.

Patient: You're right. It hasn't helped. But I need to know what to do now. I just want to be able to be happy, to enjoy the moment, to be like others who I see who are laughing, like they're happy. I want to be able to live my life and not worry about every little thing.

Therapist: I know you do, and I know it's painful. We can focus on what can help now and discuss things you can do to head toward those goals, but it will be equally important for us to understand the underlying causes that are fueling your symptoms. If we don't get to the bottom of things, then it would be like putting a Band-Aid on an open wound without stitching it up. My concern would be that your difficulties would only come back in the future, or in another form.

Patient: It makes sense. Then what am I supposed to do?

Therapist: I think you need to see me at least once to twice a week, and we can take it from there.

THE FUNDAMENTAL RULE

In the reality of the consulting room, patients come to you for a profusion of reasons with competing symptoms, agendas, wishes, needs, and conflicts. Not everyone will be amenable to dynamic therapy, and specific decisions surrounding treatment are left to clinical judgment and the context that informs competent interventions. Once I am prepared to take on a patient, I explain to him what I think is best for him and what I can offer. With regard to patient goals, I take the patient's lead yet introduce the analytic process. Although I am flexible in addressing various concerns, I never steer away from an analytic sensibility.

After the therapist offers initial diagnostic impressions and solicits the patient's reaction and feedback, it becomes important to discuss the purpose of therapy if this subject did not already arise in the normal course of conversation. I find it important in the initial consult to clarify and instruct patients on what to expect and the method that will be most viable. But here, context must dictate the course of action. As a general rule, I say just enough to satisfy the patient's curiosity or need for clarification or structure. I almost always tell patients that therapy is hard work and that a certain degree of discomfort is necessary in order to bring about change. I usually introduce the notion of the primacy of the unconscious in influencing and motivating mental functioning, including conscious choice and action, and often find supporting material from the interview to offer to the patient to consider for reflection. Here I may emphasize the value of insight into conflictual forces and repetitions that are typically unknown to direct reflection, and I stress that awareness of them will lead to changes in internal organization. Shifts in affect and emotion are to be expected and often constitute the very heart of therapeutic efficacy, which involves working through disappointments, psychic pain, and developmental trauma.

During the first session, I stay faithful, with qualifications, to Freud's (1912b, 1913) dictums on technique and introduce the fundamental rule.

It is a widely held misconception that the fundamental rule is an instruction to free associate, when in fact it further entails a pledge of honesty. Thompson (2004) argues that the ethic of honesty is the fundamental rule, rather than a directive to free associate; but from my reading of Freud, the method of association and the oath to be truthful are equally emphasized. After a long-winded instruction to the patient on how free association differs from a normal conversation, Freud (1913) sums it up: "Say whatever goes through your mind. . . . Finally, never forget that you have promised to be absolutely honest, and never leave anything out because, for some reason or other, it is unpleasant to tell it" (135). I typically introduce these technical principles in reverse order and tell patients something along this line: "In order for therapy to work, you must be completely honest with me and not hold anything back. It is important that you simply say whatever comes to your mind without omitting or censoring anything, even if it appears irrelevant or trivial. You need to tell me everything, no matter how difficult or shameful it may be." I also tend to emphasize that "this is the place to leave social etiquette behind," and that "it is important to suspend your own fears about my judgment in order to allow your inner process to unfold naturally." I clarify and reemphasize these principles from time to time if needed, particularly when patients become confused or when resistances such as thought blocking set in; and I sometimes find it useful to say, "It's OK if you don't know what to say. Simply tell me whatever comes into your mind at the time." Some patients may have many questions, which I attempt to answer explicitly, while others appear to accept the procedure with little difficulty. At times it proves useful to adapt Freud's analogy and say, "Imagine that you are in the passenger's seat while taking a drive in the country and you are observing the landscape that appears in your mind. Simply tell me what you see." Initially, there may be a need to encourage or reassure the patient, but usually the patient settles right into the spontaneity of associating freely.

When I receive a patient for the first time who was not referred to me for psychoanalytic treatment, I may need to explain the nature of my work in relation to other approaches to psychotherapy. Because some people are quasi-educated about psychoanalysis, from time to time I may get skeptical reactions or even derisive comments directed toward Freud that the patient has gleaned from popular culture or previous educational exposure. When this happens, resistance—even hostility or fear—is apparent. I find that it is important not to become overly zealous or authoritative in defending your clinical orientation; instead you should attempt to allay the patient's concerns. Confrontations regarding defense or the pointing out of resistance should wait until sufficient rapport is developed, which is part of facilitating a positive transference. Freud observed this through trial and error and eventually realized that until patients take you into their confidence, resistances will impede the working alliance. I find it imperative to be respectful of patients' defenses—that which protects them—and to proceed gently, lest you run the risk of scaring them away. Immediate challenge or rupture of the patient's primary defenses is experienced as an assault on the self, and the patient could likely leave. This is especially important with attachment disordered populations, who have weathered a history of developmental trauma.

Trust is never automatic—it is earned. You cannot expect the patient to automatically share confidences with a stranger, be completely candid, and unburden himself of secrets without developing some comfort level with you and the analytic process. This is the task of facilitating a positive working alliance. Not only are patients besieged by their own internal resistances to knowing, but they instinctively do not wish to subject themselves to unnecessary interpersonal discomfort. While transference projections are inherent from the start, the patient is also responding to real or perceived nuances of interpersonal relatedness facilitated by the therapist.

PROCESSING THE INITIAL SESSION

Toward the end of the session, after I have communicated my initial thoughts and impressions, I ask the patient, "Is there anything else about you that is important for me to know?" This query often surprises the unconscious, and additional information is normally disclosed. A variation of this question is as follows: "Is there anything else you would like to tell me that is important for me to know about you?" Upon following up on this open-ended solicitation, I ask patients about their experience of opening up to me. This is an invitation to relatedness. This query makes a space for engaging the nature of our relationship and allows me to anticipate the impact of my presence on the therapeutic process. This invitation activates multiple levels of meaning for the patient in relation to his hope and dread of what is to come. Patients typically talk about their feelings and comfort with me, and this allows me to say something personal in relation to them. I am inclined to ask patients whether they feel comfortable working with me, and it is here that we mutually determine whether we wish to proceed with the therapy and if so, discuss the proposed scope, duration, and frequency.

Developing a relationship is a process that cannot be ready-made or imitated, nor superimposed. While the therapist must be attuned to the role responsiveness that the patient wants the therapist to initiate and deliver, developing a therapeutic relationship is not about adopting some contrived role the other wants from you. As in real life, forming the therapeutic relationship is about being supple, is at times difficult, and takes work, intersubjective negotiation, and time.

DISCUSSING BUSINESS PRACTICES

The direct discussion of business practices is something I always save for the end. To bring these matters up beforehand would, in my opinion, potentially contaminate the treatment and stir up projected fantasies that would merely be destructive to facilitating the alliance. I often hear of colleagues who discuss all aspects of their business practices immediately, including limits to confidentiality and policies regarding the patient's being charged for late cancellations or missed appointments, which I believe sabotages the alliance and feeds negative transference from the start. This is incompetent technique. Those who operate this way give the immediate impression that all they care about are themselves. If limits to confidentiality are immediately disclosed as a caveat, then the message conveyed is that the therapist really does not want to know the truth nor anything that would threaten or jeopardize his little world. The perception is that the clinician needs to impose some type of control and limit to what can be said, and that he cannot be totally trusted—let alone told everything. This immediately contradicts and violates the fundamental rule. What is the use of this technical principle if you say to patients, "Tell me everything without holding back even one detail, except for A, B, C, and D!"? What good could this possibly serve but to protect the therapist's ass, only to discredit the therapy? It certainly is not considerate of the patient's possible subjective reality that may have brought her into therapy to begin with, and as a harbinger of treatment, it communicates that the clinician really doesn't want to know the intimate "dirty" details, because he is either afraid or doesn't really give a damn.

At the end of the session, I tell patients that I need to attend to some "housekeeping business" before we end. I start with confidentiality, or revisit the issue if it has already come up earlier. I take the patient–doctor relationship to be *entirely privileged* communication, and I tell patients so. I explain that I am like a confidant or a priest and that whatever is communicated or confessed to me will remain between us unless the patient gives me permission to disclose such information elsewhere. I find that this direct pledge of confidence also reinforces the ethic of honesty I ask of my patients, and that our relationship is based on a sacred bond of trust.

After introducing the rule of confidentiality, I give the patient a contract titled "Agreement of Informed Consent" and ask him to read and sign it if he is in agreement. In our litigious society, this is a pragmatic option, but it also has other purposes. Here I say verbally, "This tells you more about me and my background, and my business practices. If you would like to read it over, I can answer any questions you may have." If the session is rushed for time, I ask the patient to take it home and bring it back next time. The contract is organized into five sections:

1. Professional Credentials
2. Clinical Services Offered
3. Assurance of Confidentiality
4. Fees
5. Consent

Because of certain legal requirements governing my profession, as well as established ethical codes of conduct, there are some exceptions to the rule of strict confidentiality, which I stipulate in the contract under "unusual circumstances." This way I honor obligations to my field without directly endangering the climate of honesty that I have taken care to establish. However, this stipulated clause is potentially unsatisfactory and not without some compromise; but I am bound by certain exigencies beyond my autonomy. If I had it my way, therapy would be as sacrosanct as the Catholic confessional or a lawyer's office. Yet if I am ever questioned by the regulatory college governing my professional practice, I will have a tangible record.

A word here is in order about the fee. Those clinicians who address the issue of finances immediately after greeting the patient run the risk of appearing as a money-grubber who is only concerned with collecting his fee. Money is a very powerful symbol and a real practical concern for most patients. Recall, this issue is addressed initially over the phone and is almost always initiated by the patient's inquiry into the cost of treatment. I prefer to establish very clear expectations for payment on the phone during our initial discussion so there is no misunderstanding. I generally ask to be paid at the end of each session, upon which I will issue a receipt that can be turned into one's insurance provider for reimbursement. Unless I have received an ongoing, long-term therapy commitment from a patient in which I issue monthly billing invoices, I prefer to be paid after each session for the simple reason that this practice helps patients budget their finances. It is much easier to pay a smaller bill than to get a huge bill for hundreds of dollars at the end of the month. When financial constraint is an issue, I propose to see patients every other week to help them manage their money. This practice also has utility for the clinician who relies on a steady flow of earnings to support his own livelihood. In my contract I discuss in detail my policies regarding billing and fee collection, and I verbally introduce the notion in this fashion: "Because this is the way in which I make my living, I require a twenty-four-hour notice for canceling any appointment times. It is customary to charge for late cancellations or missed appointments, so I want you to be aware of this from the outset." I make sure this is verbally communicated so there are no "lapses" of memory on the patient's part when a cancellation or missed appointment occurs. After learning from experience, I further have a clause in the contract stating that patients will be charged a "nuisance fee" for returned or canceled (not-sufficient-funds) checks; and that in the event that patients refuse to pay their bill, their account will be turned over to an agency for collection, and an additional interest rate and cost for the collector's fee will apply. I have found that these practices save a great deal of unwanted headaches when delinquent accounts occasionally occur.[5]

Before ending the initial consult, I make sure to clarify that the patient understands everything in the contract, and then we schedule a mutually determined appointment time that will preferably serve as an ongoing commitment. Because I adhere to a fifty-minute hour, I place two battery-operated digital clocks at strategic, visible locations near our seats so the patient and I have immediate access to the time. This helps patients keep track of their hour and becomes a cue that helps them initiate ending at the appropriate moment. After our financial transaction, I let patients see themselves out. I conclude the session by recording the transaction for accounting purposes and then take a detailed process note reflecting on the hour.

NOTES

1. I started out my early career in academic psychology, but I rapidly grew discontent with empirical research, not to mention the fact that I was not very good at it. I was convinced that number crunching and the banal statistical procedures of research could hardly answer the proper questions that arise in the course of clinical treatment, let alone satisfy my quest for a personal philosophy of living. But it took an existential crisis of my own to help me realize that antiseptic science could not address what the clinician faces on a personal level every day, namely, Do you buy into the method you profess, or is this merely a role? Do you live your life according to the principles you claim to espouse? The fundamental questions that each clinician must face ultimately engage the larger philosophical quandaries of how to live one's life authentically. Despite all my years of formal education and technical training, I barely understood the philosophical merit of my own professional convictions, the very ones that were guiding me in my work with patients. Following the personal despair of a divorce, I began to gravitate more and more toward the philosophical literature in an attempt to find solace and meaning in my situation. After reading Rollo May, R. D. Laing, Sartre, and Nietzsche, whom Freud (1914b) allegedly "denied" himself the pleasure of reading (15), I realized that phenomenology—the study of the lived experience—is the proper domain for psychoanalytic investigation; and it was then that I realized that philosophy would be a welcome friend. I later took my Ph.D. in philosophy, specializing in psychoanalysis, German idealism, and existential phenomenology, and there I found a synthesis between the personal and the professional. While psychoanalysis has remained my first love, philosophy will always be her gracious mother (*alma mater*).

2. I wish to distinguish myself from some forms of clinical practice that are common among relational analysts today, including the overexpression of personal communications, countertransference disclosures, and the insistence on reciprocal revelations that may reveal more about the needs of the analyst than those of the patient.

3. These issues are explored in depth in my most recent contributions, *Rereading Freud: Psychoanalysis through Philosophy* (2004a) and *Psychoanalysis at the Limit: Epistemology, Mind, and the Question of Science* (2004b).

4. While I do not intend to create enemies among my respected colleagues over theoretical turf wars, I do feel it is vitally important to be open to self-critique within any preferred camp throughout the history of the psychoanalytic movement in order to be able to prosper and advance psychoanalysis as a whole. Even though I readily concede that I practice as a relational Freudian, I am not so impressed with the need to deify relationality by vilifying classical approaches. For a thorough critique on this matter, refer to my recent paper "A Critique of Relational Psychoanalysis" (Mills, in press).

5. A word about the Canadian health-care system is in order here. Health care is part of every resident's entitled right based on democratic principles that govern this country's political-humanistic commitments to its citizenry. As a result, patients do not have to pay directly out of pocket since a large percentage of their taxes go to sustain egalitarian health-care delivery for all residents. This is socially conditioned and an expected legislative right. However virtuous this system is, it also tends to produce a sense of entitlement; people are frugal, and in some cases chintzy, when it comes to paying for what they believe should be "free" by virtue of their right to health care. This equally applies to mental health care. However, psychologists, psychological associates, master's-level therapists, and social workers in private practice are not covered by the health-care system; only physicians are directly paid by the government. This becomes problematic when patients need therapy but have no free service to turn to. Because Canada is dominated by a psychopharmacological model of mental health treatment, people will often be given medication for their difficulties, which is inculcated by medical authority. By and large, individual psychotherapy is rarely delivered by the medical community, including the psychiatric community. Moreover, there is a dearth of government-funded psychotherapeutic resources in the community because they have been largely displaced by biochemical interventions. Because individual therapy is not promoted as widely as psychopharmacology, people often end up suffering rather than seeking out talk therapy through direct expense, in part because they perceive health care as a free service that is owed to them. When they do see a clinician for therapy, the significance of paying directly out of pocket is already prepared by this context. This socially conditioned attitude can surface when the patient is sick or misses regularly scheduled appointments or must cancel for some reason but expects not to pay. Entitlement plays itself out in other mental health contexts as well. Having worked in government-funded clinics, I have observed that those who don't have to pay directly for therapy value it less, don't work as hard, are inclined not to honor appointment times, and in many cases don't even bother to call to cancel. This cheapens the treatment for obvious reasons. In private practice, however, I have observed two common scenarios: either the patient gives therapeutic work higher value despite harboring certain resentments for having to pay, or having to pay may fuel certain resistances that devalue the treatment when desires for symptom relief are not adequately granted. Those who simply want the quick fix proselytized by medical propaganda (asserting mind-brain dependence as material reduction) will find reasons to leave and opt for a pill. It is often the case that many of my patients are monitored on psychotropic medication by their family physician in addition to therapeutic treatment undertaken with me.

5

❧

The Fragile Nature of Therapeutic Alliance

One of the most salient problems attachment disordered populations have is trusting and opening up to other people. As a consequence, they don't let others into their lives very readily, and when they do, it is usually under the condition of guardedness and emotional reservation. This is understandable, given that many of these patients have suffered from various developmental traumas at the hands of attachment figures and have developed a defensive constellation of distance, caution, and self-protective detachment from the perceived possibility of further disappointment, hurt, and affliction. But they have paid a great price: they have sacrificed the ability to develop and experience deep and fulfilling intimacy with others. While some patients have primarily disavowed or withdrawn from the need for attachment and have adopted various emotionally compartmentalized, schizoid, depressive, and avoidant character traits, others are more paranoid and aggressive, thus anticipating and expecting to be further assaulted, exploited, ridiculed, and/or rejected by others. Not only are mistrust, suspicion, and skepticism about the motives and intentions of others apparent from their interpersonal interactions, but these unconscious dynamics are projected onto the therapy from the start; hence, the therapist must operate with the assumption that he will be inevitably cast into a negative transference role. With regular predictability, patients are unconsciously looking for ways to be rejected or hurt in order to conclude that a secure and safe relationship is not possible, for this experience would lend credibility and justification to their way of being; so they repetitiously enact earlier experiences of misunderstanding, invalidation, abandonment, and abuse with the therapist, only to justify to themselves why they shouldn't trust others. The patient will test the therapist to see whether he is just like all the others in the patient's past. This is why, in the beginning stages of treatment, the clinician must make an extra effort to facilitate a positive alliance so that any apprehension can be breached, and the general hope of being able to connect with other people in more secure and healthy ways is rendered a further possibility.

Throughout this chapter, I will address some of the common therapeutic obstacles to forming a working alliance with attachment disordered patients, thus highlighting various defensive and transferential impasses that preclude mutual collaboration. Because patients' sundry sources of conflict and fortified structural deficits are interpersonally informed in nature, you as the therapist have to connect with patients from the start and show them (over time) that they can increasingly trust you before they may gradually let you into their experiential worlds—not to judge, devalue, or exploit them as others have done, but to understand, validate, and nurture their genuine potential and process of creative self-discovery in-relation to you. This means, in part, showing respect for their boundaries and defenses while opening a space for *approachment* and proximity.

FORMING AN ALLIANCE THROUGH ATTACHMENT

As the analyst and patient attempt to form the "working alliance" (Zetzel 1958), the "personal relationship" (Lipton 1977), or the "real relationship" (Gill 1982), as the therapeutic alliance is often referred to, resistance and transference mobilizations are there from the get-go. That is to say, contrary to claims in the psychoanalytic literature that often characterize the nature of transference as developmentally succeeding the enactment of resistance, transference may initially impede the alliance because it manifests itself *as* resistance to developing a relationship or attachment to the clinician. Negative transference is a given, and patients are unconsciously perceptive in picking up and reading into every little nuance of communication that confirms their expectations that others cannot be trusted and are not safe, so the clinician will inevitably be turned into a bad object. This makes the initial stages of forming a positive therapeutic alliance sufficiently precarious and fragile.

Not only do patients resist reliving or knowing painful aspects of their past and unconscious fantasy life, but they equally resist the vulnerability, anguish, and shame of having them exposed in the intersubjective context of therapy. When the clinician is perceived as the one who can potentially see things that the patient cannot, he may immediately become a feared or persecutory object. To form the alliance, it becomes important to give patients space for safety and to work gingerly with resistance until a cooperative bond is established. In the words of Sheldon Ross (1987), "The initial emphasis is on *attachment*, developing a loving and dependable bond. Next, there comes an understanding of the pleasures and pains that are part of this bond" (143, italics added). Giving patients initial space and respect for their defenses, from my standpoint, is part of creating optimal conditions for facilitating rapport and interpersonal comfort on the part of the patient with you as the therapist. The analyst who bulldozes over the patient's resistance with standard interpretive confrontations will only serve to unnecessarily expedite the negative transference prematurely. In the initial sessions, I make it a point to get to know the patient's experience and understanding of herself before offering interpretations of her experience, and in this way I avoid premature communications that can fuel resistance and a negative therapeutic alliance. At first, all one has to do is listen, which communicates availability and responsiveness through an empathic presence.

EMPATHIC ATTUNEMENT, AUTHENTICITY, AND THE NEED FOR RECOGNITION

Psychoanalysis has many humanistic commitments that are overlooked and displaced in the psychological literature and are usually attributed to other theoretical orientations that attempt to differentiate themselves from analytic sensibility by claiming to offer something that psychoanalysis does not. This is an unfortunate and misguided myth perpetuated by a radical misunderstanding of the nature of psychoanalytic inquiry and technique. Empathy has always been an important dimension to analytic practice, and it is crucial for making advances in the working alliance. While given emphasis by phenomenological psychologists as a "very special way of being with another person" (Rogers 1980, 137), empathy is described by Freud (1921) as "the process . . . which plays the largest part in our understanding of what is inherently foreign to our ego in other people" (108). Earlier, Freud (1913) had referred to this as "sympathetic understanding,"[1] which is the ability to form an effective transference through "proper *rapport*." He says, "It remains the first aim of the treatment to *attach* him to it [the transference] and to the person of the doctor. To ensure this, nothing need be done but to give him time" (139, italics added). Freud continues to tell us that this process leads to an attachment to the therapist through linkages to certain imagoes in the patient's past that are associated with affection and understanding, and this technical approach "carefully clears away the resistances that crop up at the beginning and avoids making certain mistakes" (139).

Freud argues that it is only through empathic attunement and understanding that more positive transferences and feelings of affection will develop and help mitigate the resistances that threaten the therapeutic

alliance. He emphatically warns against taking a judgmental or moraliz-
ing stance or acting as an advocate for another party the patient experiences conflict with, such as a parent or spouse, for it will only serve to
provoke a violent resistance to forming a bond with the clinician.

Within many clinical accounts of empathy, the emphasis falls on being
attuned with the affective processes of the patient. Helene Deutsch (1926)
provides us with an initial understanding of empathy: "The affective psychic content of the patient . . . becomes transmuted into an inner experience of the analyst, and is recognized as belonging to the patient (i.e., to
the external world) only in the course of intellectual work" (136). She further concludes that empathy involves the dialectical oscillation between
close emotional harmony with the patient's inner life and a distant objectivity afforded by intellectual evaluation. Following Freud's (1921) claim
that a "path leads from identification by way of imitation to empathy"
(110), Deutsch believes that empathy is initiated by a temporary identification with the other. Whether or not this involves a moment of merger
with the other accompanied by a simultaneous sense of separateness, she
does not say (also see Berger 1987). Yet on some level, identification
(whether transient or partial) is a key ingredient in the capacity to relate
to and understand the inner processes and experiences of the patient (see
Fliess 1942; Furer 1967).

Within psychoanalytic self psychology, Kohut (1971) describes empathy
as "vicarious introspection" and designates it as the primary method for
comprehending the inner reality of another. "Empathy is a mode of cognition which is specifically attuned to the perception of complex psychological configurations" (300). Through the recognition of complex psychological processes, empathic observation involves an attunement to
others' inner experiences: "When they say what they think or feel, [one]
imagines their inner experience even though it is not open to direct observation" (Kohut 1966, 115). For Kohut, empathy is a method of observation for collecting psychological data as well as a technique that becomes employed within the clinical encounter to seek out hidden and
unavailable archaic, painful, and conflicted aspects of development. Com-
bined with a caring comportment,[2] this operational mode of empathic observation serves as a foundation for a responsive, validating, and understanding posture that is essential for fostering the therapist–patient bond.

There are many levels of empathy that may involve attending to a complex mélange of experiences ranging from mere conceptual understanding and affirmation of the other's inner reality to affective and emotionally charged thoughts and inner conflicts that are unconsciously derived.
Schafer (1959) notes that empathic appreciation of another's mental world
goes beyond the simple emphasis on shared feelings to include an understanding of the individual's "organization of desires, feelings, thoughts,
defenses, controls, superego pressures, capacities, self-representations,

and representations of real and fantasied personal relationships" (345) on all intrapsychic levels.

Controversy over the meaning of empathy has even divided psychoanalysis, rendering it a meaningless concept to some (see Reik 1948, 357). Given the disparate terrain of possible meanings and purposes of empathy, we are still ambivalent about, as Basch (1983) points out, whether empathy should be considered "an end result, a tool, a skill, a kind of communication, a listening stance, a type of introspection, a capacity, a power, a form of perception or observation, a disposition, an activity, or a feeling" (102). Furthermore, "the impossibility of specifying the accuracy of an empathic experience and the failure to acknowledge a hierarchy of experiences or to recognize that empathy becomes more complex and accurate as [therapeutic relations] continue often make it difficult to compare and contrast empathic experiences" (Berger 1987, 22). But, regardless of these definitional disputes and experiential differences, attunement to the patient's lived subjective reality *in the moment* becomes paramount.

Balint (1968) informs us that "we have to recognize the fact that the first wish of the patient is to be understood" (93). The attempt to understand the subjective experience of the patient is a necessary condition for empathy; and when such attempts fail, the desire to understand on the part of the analyst will still be communicated within the intersubjective matrix. This communication offers a validating and affirming function that serves to promote close proximity and connectedness within the relational dyad, which can further bridge the schism of mistrust. When patients see that the therapist genuinely shows a desire to understand their lives, this serves a very affirmative soothing function that promotes attachment. In Kohut's language, because the patient has endured so many selfobject failures at the hands of attachment figures, the mirroring functions of empathic understanding and validation nurture a more cohesive self while promoting a collaborative bond that strengthens the working alliance. But what is often more powerful and personally meaningful to patients than the conveyance of mere understanding is when the therapist simply recognizes their experience in authentic ways.

To what degree does the analyst's authenticity contribute to the formation of healthier attachments by fortifying self-structure in the patient? To what extent does the analyst's subjective self-expression hinder this process? Unlike certain contemporary theorists who advocate that authenticity is merely the subjective spontaneity of the analyst's autonomy in the therapeutic moment (see Teicholz 2003), I envision authenticity as a phenomenology of becoming based upon the pursuit of an ideal (Mills 2003a). While the therapist's authenticity can be as transparent as the epistemic self-certainty of one's own internal self-states, such as the affective reverberations, desires, intentions, and propositional attitudes that populate internally mediated experience and prompt us to act, it also summons us toward a more cultivated and holistic pursuit of becoming one's possibilities. Within the consulting room, however, this process tends to coalesce around weighing priorities and the calculated risk that authentic self-expression will either facilitate or encumber the patient's process, which means that the clinician has to remain ever conscientious in discerning what is optimal for the patient in the immediacy of dialogic exchange. This can only be determined by the contingencies of the analytic moment under the influence of professional judgment, which requires staunch attunement to the intersubjective process.

The analyst's authenticity is a way of being that at once entails a genuine or congruent enactment of the subjective felt quality of one's own uniqueness within the context of being cognizant of the therapeutic needs of the patient. This is predicated on a fundamental identification of living up to an ideal therapeutic posture based upon mediative self-reflexivity, which requires an ongoing degree of self-consciousness. Of course, authentic self-expression can be misaligned with the needs of the patient, and the clinician can potentially be remiss due to our inherent human limitations, which can lead us to fall short of what we believe is optimally helpful. Because authenticity is a process of becoming, we are always dialectically meandering in and out of more genuine modalities along with our patients. In fact, we are always slipping into or tarrying with inauthentic modes of therapeutic comportment in our crusade toward being genuine with ourselves.

If we are to accept the notion that the analyst's authenticity is in part a fundamental openness to the pursuit of an ideal—itself an indeterminate and elusive question—then authenticity is always a process that is interminably courted yet never fully actualized. While empathy (for self and other) is a necessary condition of authenticity, it is far from sufficient to take into account the complexifications of intrapsychic and intersubjective life with all their competing needs and divided agendas. Being faithful to the patient's process may mean that we could be potentially led to sacrifice an element of our own at any point in the therapy. With the analyst's and patient's pursuit of an authentic way of being comes the inevitable recognition of separateness, self-differentiation, and the autonomous and creative urge for unique self-expression that solely belongs to each person's individuality within the analytic dyad. While a relational approach to promoting attachment attempts to emphasize and place value on shared experience in the analytic encounter, it must also be tolerant of the asymmetry of the patient's proportional recognition of the analyst's subjective agency. Indeed, part of the therapeutic task is to foster acceptance of individual differences and the need to express those differences differently because we have distinctive agendas as separate psychic entities. Not only is it necessary to balance and preserve acceptance of self-differentiation within meaningfully shared experience, but it is vital for the patient to develop an individuated and autonomous sense of self while maintaining appreciation for the unique specialness nourished between two subjects who mutually value the shared meaning of authentically coconstructing their relationship together.

Whether we refer to establishing the therapeutic alliance through a process of empathic attunement (Kohut 1971; Rowe and Mac Isaac 1991), optimal responsiveness (Bacal 1985; Sandler 1976), or a nurturing holding environment (Winnicott 1965), empathy and authenticity as a clinical way of being require validation of the patient's inner experience through recognition. The value of recognition in the consulting room was brought to the attention of contemporary psychoanalysis by Daniel Stern (1985), Jessica Benjamin (1988, 1992, 1995, 1999), and Thomas Ogden (1986, 1989, 1994a), but this is a lesson we learn from Hegel (1807). The longing for human recognition is a fundamental relational need. We all want to be acknowledged as an individual subject with our own unique needs, desires, wishes, aspirations, and autonomy; yet we stand in relation to other subjects who may have similar needs—but also competing and dissimilar ones that negate our own. This is where conflict ensues, and we are forever faced with the confrontation of the other's desire that stands in opposition to our desire. For Hegel, this amounts to a battle to the death— to interpersonal conflict over whose needs and desires will be recognized over the other's—to the point that each could potentially be annihilated if he doesn't conform to the other's wishes. In pathological development, the child is forced to conform to the needs of the caregiver, or the attachment system would be imperiled, and the self could conceivably (psychically) die. Defensive exclusions and dysfunctional modes of accommodation help preserve the tenuous attachment system. But the aftermath of this servitude to the perceived or actual oppression from the Other leads to disruptions in capacities for secure attachments resulting in structural deficits of the self. Here I am reminded of Brandchaft's (1994) notion of "structures of pathological accommodation": in order for children to survive in their relation to the demands of their primary attachment figures, they must subjugate themselves to colonization by the Other. But when the self is threatened with annihilation—namely, psychic death—and cannot accommodate through adopting a false self, fear, anxiety, and aggressivity become paranoically organized: the Other becomes a haunting, persecutory threat. This is why Lacan (1977) says that when others oppose us, we simply want them to vanish! In other words, we unconsciously wish them dead. Others negate us, they disconfirm our wishes—hence our very Self—and this dread can ominously lead to the fear of psychic extinction.

In the Self's struggle for recognition, the Other becomes a real or fantasized object that can hurt us and hence invalidate our own lived subjective reality. Patients bring these unconscious fears to the table every time they open their mouths, because deep down they tremble over being mis-understood, abrogated, and vilified yet again—an eternal recurrence. This is no different in therapy: patients expect to be misunderstood and inval-idated, and in many cases they unconsciously bring about the very thing they lament the most. Therefore, one therapeutic task is to communicate recognition of the patient's individuality and experiential world regard-less of whether the patient is capable of or willing to provide such recog-nition in return. For Hegel (1807), mutual recognition is a developmental achievement, where two subjects recognize the individuality and needs of the other through intersubjective validation; and often the patient is in no position to provide this reciprocal function to the clinician during the ini-tial negotiation of the working alliance. It is only after the patient comes to identify with the analyst through a positive (transferential and gen-uine) attachment, feel his empathy and availability, incorporate his holding-soothing selfobject functions, and respond to his responsiveness that we see that the therapist is internalized. Here the "real relationship" takes on a life of its own through spontaneity, creativity, and reciprocal ne-gotiation, whereby the analyst serves as a catalyst for structural shifts in the patient's self-organization and the transmuting internalizations that flower into more cohesive, integrative representations of self and others, which the patient comes to value and thrive upon. It is here where recog-nition becomes the kernel of a healthy relationship: the patient is more able to initiate new ways of relating to the analyst and to the subjectivities of others and to acknowledge the analyst's independent presence and au-tonomous self in-relation to her own; and through an ongoing exchange of mutual recognition, the patient and therapist grow together.

ALLOWING FOR BENIGN RESISTANCE

Patients present with a variety of benign resistances in the initial stages of therapy that can reflect more their apprehension toward *you* than the presence of conflictual material that resistance typically is thought to be in the service of staving off. With regard to treating the initial resistance, I usually observe this general rule: say something empathic and don't probe. When I see early manifest resistance, I find it useful to bring it into the context of the relationship rather than keeping the focus on the defen-sive function itself. For example, a patient was referred to me for long-term therapy because her psychiatrist felt that her problems were based on unresolved conflicts in her past. She had been diagnosed with chronic dysthymia with bouts of major depression that had flared up and remit-ted over the years. During the initial consultation, I told her that I thought she had been characterologically depressed for several years and that medication would be of little help in alleviating her suffering. She agreed and was initially very relieved, telling me that I was the first professional in years who had provided some sense of hope that she could overcome her malaise. She eagerly embraced my proposal to initiate long-term therapy on a weekly basis. The following week, the patient was ten minutes late to her second session and described that her husband had forgotten to gas up the car. She was also late by ten minutes for the third session and apologized for running behind. I asked her if she was nervous about the therapy, but she denied this, instead insisting that extrinsic circumstances had prevented her from arriving on time. After this justification, the patient began to associate to how her mother was always violating established boundaries in the patient's communications between her and her son. While the opportunity to examine her resistance presented itself on several occasions, I felt it best to concentrate instead on establishing relational comfort and a nonintrusive comportment unlike that of her mother, who had impinged upon her. At this time, I chose not to point out her own boundary violations and the connection between us, such as how she had cast me into a transferential role. By the ninth session, the patient had come to the appointment on time but commenced to chastise me for questioning her for being late to her previous sessions.

Patient: I've been very mad at you for questioning me about the times I was late. I told you the reasons why and you seemed to question me like I wasn't telling the truth or something, like you didn't believe me. Why did you question me?

Therapist: It's hard for me to know exactly what I said since it was so long ago, but as I recall, I was wondering if you were apprehensive about starting therapy.

Patient: But I told you I wasn't. It makes me think you don't believe what I say.

Therapist: I can see how you'd feel that way, and it makes sense you'd be mad at me, especially if I gave you the impression that you're not honest. That was not my intention. But perhaps instead of trying to figure out what was going on between us back then, we should look at how this has affected our relationship now.

Patient: It's not a big deal, it's just I don't want you to think I'm not telling the truth, since you told me to be completely honest; and after I was, you questioned that. You made me question whether others see me that way too.

Therapist: I can see how this stirs up other things for you. Why would you question whether or not others think you are telling the truth?

Patient: Because many people have questioned my believability, which I also feel about myself. I don't know if it's me or them, or is this how I really am? I used to lie and make things up because I didn't want to have to explain what really happened, because I didn't think they would believe me or wouldn't care, or they would just want to know things I didn't want to have to explain. It was just simpler. But then people would know I was lying because I didn't make sense or they would catch me or trip me up. But this time I was telling the truth, and that's why I was mad you didn't believe me.

Therapist: I'm glad you were able to tell me this directly rather than keeping it in and harboring resentment for what I said.

Patient: Yeah, me too. It felt good to say that. I want to be able to do this with others instead of just being pissed off or hurt, and think it's my fault.

This exchange allowed us to explore why in the past she had felt she could not be open with others out of fear of judgment and exploitation; and furthermore how her own deception and dishonesty created conflict with others who ended up not liking or trusting her, which led to many experiences of being rejected and alienated from others, a repetition she enacted over and over again in many interpersonal situations. My gentle query into her initial resistance also evoked anxieties that I saw her as "crazy," which were, despite being her own projection, also experienced as feelings of nonacceptance and rejection from me. My recognition of her fears and validation of her needs during this session allowed us to form a closer attachment, which advanced a more secure base for more difficult work that was yet to come.

NEUTRALITY AND ANONYMITY

One of the most distorted views of classical analysis is that the analyst is allegedly conceived to be a "blank screen," whereby the patient is "supposed" to project his own mental contents and attributions onto the therapist, who is turned into a transparent transference object based on the patient's conflicted past. While the notion of the blank screen model of psychoanalysis is a point of scholarly dispute (see Hoffman 1983), it should be noted that for the record Freud never actually used these words in his original texts; hence, this misattribution to Freud was probably due to early Freud expositors and Americanized versions of conceptualizing analytic technique. What Freud (1913) does say when he describes his technical process is that the analyst should be "opaque" (*undurchsichtig*) to patients and act as a "mirror [*Spiegelplatte*], . . . show[ing] them nothing but what is shown to him" (118). This is a radically different statement from saying that the analyst is merely a "blank" surface, a tabula rasa, as if therapists bring nothing to the interpersonal context of therapy. This is certainly not what Freud said, nor did his own therapeutic actions ever legitimately warrant such a conclusion. There is nothing blank about opacity, and a reflective surface is hardly a screen.

It is important to be neutral with regard to the patient's presentations and associations, for each presentation has value and merit within its own right, and henceforth they become equally important to understand in juxtaposition to one another. The term "neutrality" is actually misleading, for Freud actually used the word *Indifferenz* in German, which is more appropriately translated as "indifference." What he meant by this term is simply that the analyst should be equally interested in *all* aspects of the patient's disclosures rather than just some. As Schafer (1983) reminds us, "One should not take sides in the analysand's conflicts" (74). Rather, equal attention should be given to all of the patient's productions (Gill 1982, 63). This is not altogether different from what Freud (1913) refers to as "evenly suspended attention," the purpose of which is to give equal weight to each production until it is critically unpacked and analyzed more carefully. Thompson (1996) persuasively argues that Freud's notion of neutrality is mainly in service of establishing rapport and a positive transference alliance, and that the equanimity with which the analyst approaches the productions offered during free association reinforces the patient's pledge to honesty.

There is a great deal of latitude in the interpretation of what exactly constitutes neutrality in the clinical encounter. Schafer (1983) advocates for the analyst to be nonjudgmental and maintain a nonassuming attitude toward everything the patient says. He furthermore advises the clinician to subordinate his personality and conceal ordinary aspects of his character traits, which he is not accustomed to do outside of the consulting room. Some of Schafer's instruction is based on conventional wisdom following classical thought, but it is not without problems. For example, everything the analyst says or does (even during nonverbal moments) conveys value-laden communications, namely, potential judgment. Here, presumably, the point is not to judge the patient, although we are constantly passing value judgments on the patient's productions, as any good critical thinker would normally do. Therefore, our indifferent attitude is immediately put to the test when information that steers the clinician away from taking associations at face value presents itself. Moreover, Schafer's dictum to subordinate one's personality and normal behavioral traits is also a deposit of a strict analytic attitude that Freud never himself practiced. Recall that Freud smoked like a stove incessantly—throughout the entire day and night—including during the analytic hour, and he frequently had his dog lie comfortably in the consulting room while he received patients. Along with the thousands of antiquities lining his office walls, these aspects of his personality spoke volumes. But we can appreciate the spirit to which Schafer is speaking: we do not wish to project our own personal preferences or biases onto the therapeutic work, and this requires disciplined patience and poise in maintaining a neutral posture and abstaining from treating the patient as we would an acquaintance or a friend. In this sense, one's personality is curbed, more inhibited, and under the direction of professional composure focused on the task at hand.

This is certainly how I operate, yet within the parameters of relationality dictated by my own personal inclinations and idiosyncrasies.

The main objection to Schafer is that he argues that neutrality, as he defines it, needs to be employed in a relentless and uncompromising manner throughout all aspects of each session throughout the entire treatment (also see Thompson 1996). This appears overly rigid and seems to violate clinical reality and the relational focus that informs one's treatment philosophy. We cannot possibly stay neutral (nonjudgmental) with regard to everything the patient tells us; and, following Freud, if anything, we must strive to maintain the empathic attitude ("sympathetic understanding") toward the patient (thus implicitly siding with the patient) in the service of maintaining rapport and the positive alliance. This is anything but neutral. From this standpoint, "neutrality does not preclude an empathic, authentic, warm attitude on the part of the therapist, but, to the contrary, may best reflect such warmth and empathy" (Kernberg 1982, 33). Analysts cannot suppress their personality without running the risk of being unduly cold and appearing apathetic or without feelings. We cannot be affectless nor conceal all aspects of our thoughts or feelings for the patient. As Kohut (1977) says, a "lack of emotional responsiveness, silence, [or] the pretense of being an inhuman computer-like machine which gathers data and emits interpretations do no more supply [a] psychological milieu . . . than [does] an oxygen-free atmosphere" (253).

With respect to neutrality, one may still maintain an openness with regard to the associations the patient produces under the rubric of a mutual, cooperative exploration into the meanings behind such disclosures. In this way, the clinician aligns with the patient while potentially making everything the patient discloses open to examination with the aim of deriving truth.[3] This is why, at one point, Freud refers to himself as "an elucidator (where ignorance has given rise to fear), as a teacher, as a father confessor who gives absolution, as it were, by a continuance of his sympathy and respect after the confession has been made" (Freud with Breuer 1893–1895, 282). Thompson (1996) properly shows that neutrality is "the analyst's *state of mind* and the manner in which they bring their minds to bear on what their patients confide" (72).

Yet it becomes easy to see how Freud's many remarks on neutrality seem to clash with his rule of abstinence, that is, with not complying with the patient's demands for love. Freud (1915a) introduced abstinence as a technical means of keeping the countertransference in check and as an insurance against disclosing too many sentiments for the patient that may interfere with internal forces impelling her to work. This technical device was designed to serve a basic principle, namely, *noninterference*. In practice, however, we employ neutrality and abstinence selectively—not universally—across all therapeutic contexts. I prefer to view Freud's caveat on abstinence as advising us not to overly gratify a patient's need for wish fulfillment at the expense of analytic work, nor to overly frustrate or deprive the patient under the guise of analytic work. Therefore, abstinence should be employed in moderation through a neutral (open) posture that is flexible in response to the contingencies of the treatment within the defined intersubjective-relational space mutually created between the patient and the therapist.

I prefer to view abstinence within a posture of anonymity. The clinician should be anonymous with respect to certain aspects of one's personal life and one's personal views for the simple fact that they can disrupt the treatment. "What anonymity should mean is that the therapist will make every effort to maintain the focus on the patient's life and problems" (Levy 1984, 126). This is not to say that the therapist should not and will not respond to certain questions or requests by the patient, such as appropriate solicitations for responsiveness, but anonymity is also designed as a measure of containment of the analyst's own subjectivity in the service of allowing the patient's subjectivity to take center stage in the analytic process. The key here is flexibility in the analyst's responsiveness. As a general rule, unnecessary self-disclosure on the part of the clinician will introduce unnecessary anxiety in the treatment milieu and burden the patient with unsolicited knowledge that may serve to dampen the alliance on a number of levels. But at the same time, patients wish to see their therapists as human—but not too human, not with all the insecurities, ambivalence, and ambiguities patients carry themselves. Here the question of degree of disclosure, balance, and tact becomes important.

A word on the asymmetry of the relationship is in order. Under no circumstances should the therapist delude himself into thinking that the therapeutic relationship is equal or egalitarian, as some feminist and postmodern therapies promulgate. Nor should a relational stance be mistaken to assume that uninhibited self-disclosure is a necessary condition for fostering a good therapeutic relationship.[4] On the contrary, the type of relationship one aims to foster is much different from the ones patients are typically accustomed to. The therapeutic dyad is never based on equality; rather, it is asymmetrical and disproportional: there is no illusion of equivalence between the patient and the analyst, for then the patient would have no need to seek you out in the first place. The clinician is an identified expert possessing a trained skill set who may offer the patient something unlike his previous relationships, so there is nothing equal about it.

The conundrum of working within a relational framework of attachment is that certain therapist disclosures will be permitted, expected, and unavoidable, while others will not; a balance must be maintained between authentic personableness and anonymity, where the former is open to spontaneity and malleability, while the latter necessitates a secure frame. At times, and with respect to certain topics, a firm limit will need to be instituted by the therapist and observed by the patient even if this produces frustration, annoyance, or anger. For example, I may be inclined to comment on benign topics and even discuss my feelings for the patient in the clinical moment, but I never discuss my personal views on religion or politics, let's say, even if directly prompted. I recall being pressured to do so by a particular patient, to which I replied, "I could tell you my thoughts on that, but my concern is that this would make the therapy more about me and not enough about you." When asked by patients to give a personal disclosure, I tend to validate their desire or need to know my thoughts on the matter and then ask them to reflect upon what this information may mean for them. During the initial course of therapy, the issue of therapist disclosure usually arises. When it does for the first time, I address the issue directly and explain my reasons for why my personal views and opinions should remain removed from our discussions. There are the occasional times, when they transpire naturally, that I will say to the patient, "I will not offer information about certain aspects of my personal life for the simple reason that it may interfere with the treatment." Let us examine this exchange with a patient who insisted that I tell him how to behave in a certain situation:

Patient: What would you do if you were in my shoes?

Therapist: I really can't answer that; I'm not you.

Patient: But surely you have an opinion on what I should do. I know you do. I want to know what you would do if you were me.

Therapist: As frustrating as this may sound, that's up to you to decide, not for me to say.

Patient: But why can't you just tell me?

Therapist: My concern would be that it wouldn't have the same meaning for you, or it wouldn't be as significant if it came from me; besides, it is up to you to decide on how you wish to live your life, and there is no easy way around this struggle.

Patient: I would just like to know what you think—that's all! [*exasperated*]

Therapist: I know you're irritated, but I'm wondering if this has more to do with how you perceive my availability to you rather than what I would do if I were you?

Patient: It would be so much easier if you just told me what to do.

Therapist: Then tell me more about that. What makes it so hard for you to decide?

Patient: 'Cause I'm sure I'll make the wrong decision.

Therapist: And you think that somehow I won't.

Patient: You better not; that's why I'm here.

Therapist: It sounds like you're looking for someone to blame if it doesn't turn out the way you want rather than taking on the responsibility of making your own decisions.

Patient: Yeah, I'm good at that.

Therapist: Then let's see more closely how this gets in your way.

Here I was attempting to maintain my anonymity under the direction of keeping the focus on the patient's process, which led to a discussion of how his indecision and ambivalence is turned over to others at the expense of developing more autonomy and self-confidence. This clandestine pattern also served defensive functions that maintained his self-esteem during times when he failed. Through his own self-deception, by turning over major decision making to others, he insulated his more fragile and insecure ego from responsibility and shame when others' advice or suggestions proved ineffectual, and instead he mobilized self-indignant rage and reproach directed toward others for "causing" him to fail. Conversely, at times when others' advice proved helpful, he would end up feeling dependent and weak for not being able to handle such decisions himself. My refusal to gratify his wish to be rescued, and thus cast into a role he would inevitably find unacceptable one way or another, forced him to face up to his insecurities and fears more directly, thus breaching his own resistance while maintaining our working alliance.

When patients ask me direct questions about how I perceive or feel about them, they are typically asking for reassurance or are seeking my acceptance on some level. Rather than squelch the opportunity to explore the underlying dynamics motivating their appeal, I try to redirect the locus to what they are really wanting from me and how it relates to them. Consider this exchange:

Patient: You must think I'm nuts. Do you?

Therapist: What do you imagine I think?

Patient: That I'm screwed up.

Therapist: Why would you say that?

Patient: Because that's what everyone else thinks about me, so you must be thinking it too. I don't know if anything about me is normal. I'm always questioning everything I think and do—I'm constantly comparing myself to others, thinking they're normal and I'm not.

Therapist: So because you think you're screwed up must mean that I think so too.

Patient: Right.

Therapist: I'm feeling as though even if I would say, "You're not nuts!" you would still think that I was not being truthful.

Patient: Yeah, that's probably true, because I feel I am.

Therapist: So it sounds like you take your own feelings about yourself and misattribute them to what others may think about you.

Patient: I guess so.

Therapist: I got the sense that when you were asking me whether I thought you were nuts, you were really wanting me to reassure you that you're OK.

Patient: Yes, I did.

Therapist: And I can appreciate why that's important for you to hear that from me.

INTIMACY, EMOTIONAL IMPOVERISHMENT, AND COMPARTMENTALIZED AFFECT

Patients with variegated forms of attachment pathology have compromised capacities to form a bond with the therapist. This makes the task of forming an alliance that much more challenging. What adds to this challenge is when patients present with very curtailed access to their emotional life, which in many instances is impoverished, sealed off, compartmentalized from direct examination, or dissociated from their self-conscious reflective abilities altogether. Because these patients themselves are emotionally impoverished, and rely on dissociative defenses to regulate disruptive affect states, they are often not tuned into the emotional needs of others, are uncomfortable with communicating vulnerable or tender feelings, may have some discomfort or diversion from close physical contact of a nonsexual nature, for example, affection, hugs, and so forth, and are not adept at appropriate empathic responsiveness when solicited by another. These deficiencies may be informed in part by problems in mentalization, as Fonagy, Target, and their colleagues point out, but they also contribute to limiting the range and quality of close intimate attachments. As a result, attachment disordered patients often report problems in interpersonal relationships and have a limited number of friends, and when they do maintain relationships, they are more superficial or exploitive in nature. When they are involved in intimate relationships, they can be clingy, insecure, excessively jealous, and overly ambivalent about demands for interpersonal love (Holmes 1996). In addition, and more problematically, they often don't know how to be truly intimate with others, do not share difficult affective material easily, are rather clumsy when it comes to relating to significant others on deep meaningful levels of engagement, and complain of not knowing how to connect or communicate effectively about relational needs.

Intimacy with significant loved ones is a perennial problem that brings many individuals and couples into therapy. But with attachment disordered populations, there is an insidious ineptitude apparent in repeated failed attempts at intimacy, which often lead to chronic tension, stagnation, and alienation from others. Here we may observe more benign forms of attachment pathology that encompass individuals who simply feel lost when it comes to knowing how to be emotionally available, responsive, or empathically attuned to the needs or requests of significant others, such as a spouse, partner, friend, or family member.

Consider the case of Don, a forty-two-year-old Scottish immigrant, father of two sons, who was recently separated from his wife because she complained that he was not able to communicate nor express his personal feelings. She was fed up with his chronic lack of intimacy and unavailability in the marriage and threatened to dissolve the relationship if he did not seek professional help. Reluctant to admit to having any problems, Don initially presented with a version of Freud's enigmatic question: "What do women want?" After twenty-two years of marriage and two children, he was genuinely puzzled as to why his wife would initiate a separation. The patient was very anxious and talkative during the initial stages of therapy, yet he seemed to talk about everything except his problems with intimacy. After establishing some interpersonal comfort that helped soften the resistance, we were able to examine his identified core deficits associated with the inability to identify certain emotional states and motives for his feelings when he became aware of them. As he put it, "I just bottle things up, but I don't know what they are."

Don's early attachment with his parents was virtually nonexistent. He had no memories of his early childhood and could only give vague impressions of recollections from high school. He described his family as stoic, cold, and distant and felt as though he grew up in a household where no one talked; they merely went on with their daily routines and activities with very little interaction. The patient's interpersonal style was so ambiguous and awkward that one could pejoratively conclude that he was socially retarded. His capacities for self-reflective insight were virtually nil, and his structural deficits and alexithymia were so pronounced that he could not identify feeling states in the session, let alone articulate them with any verbal fluency. Gradually he began to acknowledge that he often would experience long, distressing absences of thought (as dissociation), did not know what to say to his wife even when prompted, would not know how to anticipate what was on her mind, could not read her nonverbal cues or gestures, and was quite anxious that something about him was horribly flawed.

Over the course of a few months, Don was able to slowly chip away at his happy-go-lucky facade and realize his repressed anger and emotional pain associated with his parents' relational neglect and lack of interpersonal warmth. Resentment, indignation, and rage were directed toward his mother, whom he saw as domineering and selfish, and who manipulated him through guilt-inducing statements and verbal debasement. With disturbing effects, the patient came to lament that, through repetitious enactment, he had married his mother, a demanding, withholding, and devaluing woman who blamed him for all aspects of her own disappointments. As with his mother, his primordial defense was to simply shut up and not speak, and thus he sequestered his emotional life to the self-protective chambers of communicative void.

This patient dropped out of treatment prematurely, which is not an uncommon occurrence in the treatment of attachment disordered populations. When satisfactory symptom relief is achieved, increased interpersonal discomfort and vulnerability associated with emotional disclosure and intersubjective recognition become too costly for patients' psychic economies. This is most unfortunate when primordial fears associated with emotional vulnerability, abandonment, and loss are mobilized after patients have already formed a positive therapeutic alliance but anticipate unacceptable risks associated with forming a dependency or close attachment to the therapist. When patients experience this threat as a perceived demand for intimacy placed on them by the clinician, the alliance may become tenuous and they may be more inclined to flee from therapy.

PREVENTING PREMATURE TERMINATION

Carly was a thirty-three-year-old married mother of two adopted children who had suffered a clinical depression related to unresolved trauma surrounding ongoing physical and emotional abuse by her father when she was a child. The patient reported being physically abused on a weekly basis from six to nine years of age by her alcoholic father who had a volatile and erratic temper, and she was offered no protection by her mother, who turned a blind eye and denied the severity of the beatings. Carly's parents divorced when she was twelve years old. After that, she reportedly became very secluded and withdrawn during her adolescence and left home at the age of seventeen to move in with her boyfriend, whom she married two years later. This marriage ended after two years when she discovered that her husband was having an affair. She entered into a three-year common-law relationship with a man almost immediately following the breakup, which was terminated allegedly due to "sexual incompatibilities" along with his alcoholism and controlling behavior. Following the end of her second relationship, she met her current husband, whom she has been married to for the past eight years.

The patient reported harboring a chronic sense of anxiety and depletion since childhood, was sensitive to rejection from others, and could not tolerate being alone, but she had no friends because she could trust no one, despite her professed desire to be in close proximity to others. Carly confessed that her decision to marry her current husband was based on a desire for financial and emotional security at the expense of love. The patient had a hysterectomy following a long struggle with severe endometriosis, resulting in bladder incontinence, vaginal burning, and excruciating pain associated with intercourse. As a result, their relationship was largely nonsexual, lacked physical warmth and affection, and was almost exclusively focused on their young children, who were three and four years of age. To make matters worse, he was a man twelve years her senior, was reportedly very homely and physically unappealing, and was chronically sexually frustrated and unsympathetic toward her reluctance to perform her wifely duties. She found him physically repulsive, and as a consequence, their relationship had been strained for some time and was thus devoid of intimacy and proper communication.

The early part of our work focused on her ambivalence toward her husband, who she saw as both a kind and generous man of means and security but also someone who evoked sexual abhorrence. She came to realize that her deprived needs for paternal relatedness partly motivated her wish to be with this man, who in many ways initially became an idealized Oedipal surrogate, and who, as a reportedly loving and available father to their adopted children, gave her vicarious (unconscious) satisfaction of being with a love object she had previously never known nor had. But her ambivalence was exacerbated by taboo incestuous currents associated with intercourse with her husband (father), which corresponded to her past abuse: sex was literally traumatic and torturous.

Carly retreated into her children and, unlike her parents, set unreasonable demands for herself to be the "perfect mom" as a compensatory strategy to give to herself through her children and attempt to heal her own developmental and physical traumas. She was particularly overly attached and clingy with her oldest and first adopted son, Jeremy, who she felt was like her: sensitive, dependent, prone to feeling rejected or having his feelings easily hurt, and very vulnerable about separation and loss—qualities and anxieties the child would have assiduously absorbed from the patient. During Jeremy's fourth birthday party, Carly's father made a devaluing comment about her son, which brought back a spate of painful memories surrounding her own abuse. She recalled how her father would systematically pick on her derisively through cruel teasing and taunting, and she was made to feel ashamed and humiliated when she did not show appropriate deference to her father's sadism and need to dominate. She was further reminded of how he would beat her harder with a belt for not crying enough during her punishments, which would often lead to more violence, such as once having her head slammed into a steel pole, and, on another occasion, being punched in the face with his fist.

These associations mobilized such fear, hate, and paranoia that she decided to cut her father out of her life and her children's altogether; he was not allowed any contact with his grandchildren, and she broke ties completely.

Shortly after this work was introduced in the therapy, I took my annual vacation. The patient had a distressing time during my absence, which elicited abandonment anxiety and dredged up emptiness, sadness, and unhappiness in relation to her marriage and her children. Her youngest daughter was a discipline problem, and routine interactions with both kids were triggering recollections of the abuse on a daily basis. The emotional pain associated with reliving the memories of the trauma brought on a regression followed by an intensification of her depression and anxiety symptoms. During this time, the patient was complaining that she was getting worse rather than better and that focusing directly on the abuse in therapy was too destabilizing. While we attended to strategies for symptom management, Carly ultimately wanted to flee from the demands of such emotional work. Once she began recovering from her crisis, she needed to cancel two of her appointments because of a scheduling conflict. I gradually began to feel that she was investing less in her subsequent sessions, which were now being used to discuss more banal and less affectively charged topics. I pointed out my observations and concern that she was running away from the very thing that she needed to face, namely, her trauma. This led to her confession that she was considering terminating the treatment because of the disruptive affective states that were evoked, resulting in crippling effects on her ego. Whenever she thought of or discussed her abuse directly with me, she ended up feeling exposed, ashamed, and defiled, which reinforced her desire to leave therapy.

We processed the residual effects of her feelings of abandonment by me during my holidays and the associated transference feelings of vulnerability and humiliation created by her father that surfaced in my presence. Her perception of my abandonment of her further elicited disturbed meanings associated with her first husband, who had left her for another woman, thus drawing into question her desirability and lovability. As in her past, she immediately fled into another relationship, only to leave that union when problems in sexuality arose again, this time in relation to her feeling she was with a controlling, manipulative alcoholic like her father. In many ways, my encouragement to consciously process her experiences of abuse was unconsciously perceived by her as abusive and as a manipulative attempt to control her as did others. Her impulses to terminate the therapy were motivated in part by her need to reject her father and his abuse. This was a crucial point in the therapy, because she recognized that she really wanted to avoid and escape from her own intolerable feelings of vulnerability and self-deprecation for being emotionally damaged and sexually deficit. This led to ongoing reparative discussions of what it meant to trust and be vulnerable with me, and how I could be seen as a holding-calming presence during times of working through her pain.

Over the months I developed a fondness for Carly; she came to trust me and we felt a mutual closeness. Because Carly, like so many other vulnerably attached patients, had been so chronically invalidated by her parents, she was starving for acceptance, recognition, and affirmation of her sense of self. My responsiveness and encouragement of her individuality and autonomous self-assertion allowed her to give herself permission to create a new space for relatedness with her family members. She began setting limits and boundaries about what she would accept or tolerate from others' expectant behavior toward her, and she began negotiating better communication patterns with her husband and children. While her dynamic conflicts were rooted in trauma and deficient attachments, thus informing her depleted structuralization, she was able more and more to use our relationship to vitalize her own sense of self. In this way, I believe my presence and responsiveness was introjected and organized into more cohesive units regulating her psychic structure.

What partially informed these shifts in structuralization and adaptive functioning was the ability to experience and incorporate my subjective recognition of her, grounded in the *emotional immediacy* of the therapeutic encounter in the moment. For example, during one session she began to associate to a dream she had about her father. She described how in her dream she called her father by accidentally pressing the speed dial on her phone but quickly hung up when she realized her mistake. She then described that the dream scene changed and she was at a hockey game. There she saw her father with his back to her watching the game, sitting several seats up from her, but she did *not* attempt to catch his attention. She saw him again after the game finished; he was playing with children on the ground outside the stadium. In describing the dream, she was puzzled by its possible meanings. I interpreted that despite her father's abuse, she still had a desire for an attachment with him, and that she couldn't cleave the wish for some connection even though she had cut him out of her life. The patient began to describe feelings of lack and loss of not having her father's love or recognition, and she said that even to this day she had no close friends. She sensed that people talked about her behind her back and that no one truly liked her nor would they want to be her friend. Her associations naturally led to an exchange regarding our relationship:

Patient: I know that people talk about me, say I'm too serious or I'm not enough fun—not "light" enough. I feel that they just don't like me.

Therapist: What do you think I may feel about you?

Patient: That's not the same—you wouldn't pick me as a friend if you saw me on the street.

Therapist: Do you really want to know what I think about you?

Patient: If you want to tell me.

Therapist: [*looking her directly in the eye*] I think you're a wonderful woman, I care about you deeply, and I know you've suffered.

Patient: [*begins to sob profusely for a minute without speaking*]

Therapist: What are the tears all about?

Patient: [*emotionally*] No one ever speaks to me that way. I don't get feelings from others like that.

Therapist: How did it feel to hear that from me?

Patient: It hurts. It hurts to be treated nicely.

Therapist: I know, but you deserve to be.

MALIGNANT TRANSFERENCE

All therapists at some point confront the inevitable, namely, when you are cast in the role of the bad guy without warning or consultation, and for no apparent justification other than the brute fact that you are viewed in a toxic light based upon your perceived negative presence. I refer here to the *malignant transference*, a destructive dynamic that is often unconsciously designed by the patient to sabotage the treatment from the start. As stated earlier—contrary to classical texts in the literature that claim that psychoanalysis or dynamic therapy naturally progresses from certain stages of resistance, to transference analysis, to termination—resistance and transference are there from the beginning. With malignant transference, aggressive transferential projections are conjoined with resistance and align in the service of refuting change through therapeutic protest. Unconsciously, the patient is looking for any reason to sully the therapeutic process and leave; thus, the therapist becomes the target and excuse for why therapy is predictably doomed to failure. The therapist is already cast as the oppressive Other whom patients believe they could never trust nor attach to; therefore, opposition, confrontation, negativity, and rejection are constructed and acted out through malignant behavioral manifestations. This is where things go wrong almost immediately after the therapy has begun, but this dynamic may be enacted at any time in the treatment process. Here the therapeutic working alliance is imperiled by a repugnant negativity and affective colorization based on distorted transference projections and, as a result, has little chance to survive or prosper unless the alliance is appropriately and promptly nurtured. Often this bad dynamic is beyond repair, and when addressing and alleviating it, the therapist runs the risk of contaminating all future interactions.

Consider the case of Carol, a thirty-eight-year-old artist who contacted me after having a miscarriage. The miscarriage triggered disturbed meanings of fear, insecurity, and depression associated with an abortion she had had at the age of twenty-five when she was in a physically abusive four-year relationship. Prior to being in this abusive relationship, she was abandoned by her husband of four years for another woman. The patient's developmental history was characterized by tenuous attachment, prolonged negativity, and emotional abuse in the home by her unavailable mother and devaluing, critical father who showed her no recognition. She reported a history of attention deficit disorder (ADD), trouble in school performance, and marginalization by her peer group. She currently complained of feeling insecure in her present relationship, questioned her self-worth and capacities, and constantly sought recognition from others, especially toward her art, which may be characterized as morose representational expressionism. Her need for recognition from others was not unlike her need for recognition from her father, who never validated her vocation and devalued her talents. Carol had a very dissociative presence, preferred to avoid eye contact, was easily distracted by competing associations in the initial consultation, yet was articulate and focused on her experiential affect. She commented that she felt apprehensive toward me because she did not know me personally, but that she wanted to address her many unresolved conflicts in relation to her past that had been dredged up due to her recent loss. I personally felt that the initial meeting was successful and viewed her as a potentially viable analytic case, and we mutually agreed to initiate long-term treatment. Two days later I received the following e-mail:

> I didn't feel comfortable with the therapy.
> I am going to discontinue it.
> Thanks, Carol

I was initially quite surprised by her communication since I had felt that we had had a good initial meeting; I felt that I had understood her pain and many essential features of her past and childhood that had impacted on her development, and no reservations from the patient had materialized during our session that could not be explained as normal apprehension or reticence to initiating therapy. Because I never like to leave loose ends, I responded with the following e-mail:

> Dear Carol:
> I'm sorry you did not feel comfortable, but therapy is often uncomfortable and a necessary part of change. I would appreciate knowing why you felt uncomfortable with me, certainly if you feel I did not understand you or address your needs. And I would certainly welcome you to discuss it with me.
> Best, Jon

This is the response I received. I have not edited it or altered it in any way:

> Jon, doctors are very scary, and I have a history of looking for help and then not wanting to go through with the process.
>
> There are lots of issues at play with regards to this for me.
>
> For instance, pretty well all abuse I have experienced in my life has come in the form of help from concerned individuals.
>
> I am dealing with a lot of anger and I got very angry at you. When I really examined it, it was not clear if you deserved it or if all these unresolved issues from my pass [notice the slip] made it hard to see and objectively understand.
>
> I am struggling with issues of trust. If I am going to go to those sad vulnerable times in memory—I don't want an authority sticking my pain in a box. My experience is unique and while the question/answer part of our meeting went OK—I found that the conclusions you came to were pat—they didn't hold the experience. They stuck a label on it that as far as I'm concerned is as inadequate as using language to describe emotional experience.
>
> I am looking for someone to be a guide with me on precipice of grief, regret, sorrow, anger, hate, self loathing and pain. I cannot stand to be stuck in some intellectual paradigm with all my shit clinically dissected with appropriate detachment. I'm not even sure if the intellectual paradigm you must be using to do this work is something that I believe in.
>
> I don't want to transcend these emotions—I don't want them to be taken away. I am on the precipice and I want to jump. Not because I am seeking annihilation, but because I am looking for wholeness. I want to reclaim this part of myself—not cut it off or out.
>
> I do not know much about clinical psycho-therapy—I am not sure if I would even agree with its analytical definition of health and wholeness. I just know that it is way bigger than the human intellect.
>
> For me this process requires a lot of humility.
>
> When it really comes down to it, I have to trust my feelings, your office was very stuffy—I wanted to run away.
>
> —C

This was my response:

> Carol, thank you for your honest feedback. Your experience must be very distressing: I understand your need to flee, and that we may not be well suited to work together. From my standpoint, however, I feel you have a need to find a reason to reject me and turn me into an abuser, and this probably would be beneficial for you to understand. The invitation still stands to discuss this with me rather than just table your pain. In any event, I wish you well.
>
> Jon

I recognize the inherent riskiness of my correspondence, but my rationale for providing an interpretation at this time was in the service of provocation as an invitation to process her repetition compulsion and the malignant transference dynamic that was self-evident. Suspecting that this patient had a primary borderline organization, I also wanted to attempt therapeutic reparation through reaching out to her relationally rather than merely participating in the abandonment reenactment the patient only knew too well. This was her response:

> For someone who whines about being abused, I sure don't hold my punches.—I am sorry. I know you are trying to help—and I tend to lash out at help. I spared you the brunt of it—I was much more angry in my journal. If you would like to meet and talk about it, that may be a good thing. I have not been sleeping well and I've been binging on popcorn and chocolate. But then again I'm totally premenstrual and that makes this stuff more strident. I bet you feel sorry for my Mom now don't you. C

Carol and I met to reprocess our initial session. She told me that she wanted to leave after the first five minutes of initially meeting me because she feared that I was just like her father, who was critical and judgmental. She was furious with me for asking her in the initial consultation why she had stayed in her abusive relationship for so long; she felt I was blaming her for the abuse, which further raised grave doubts for her about my capacity for empathy and understanding. She also told me that I was like her abusive boyfriend, who liked to play the role of psychologist and who would twist, distort, and intellectualize what was said only to make her more confused about her own inner states and motives. I replied with validation of her feelings and told her that we each have our own subjective realities and that we will inevitably be misattuned with each other at times. I further redirected our focus to the palpable transference parallels and acknowledged how I could indeed be perceived by her in that way, but she was mistaken about my attitudes, which I reassured her were benign. My redirected empathic alignment liberated her somewhat from the immediate affective coloration that had transpired, which allowed us to approach her own projected fears and transference anxieties more directly.

We agreed to proceed with a trial period to see if we could mend the rift and work with one another therapeutically, but in the end this proved ineffectual. The malignant transference had produced an insidious, irreparable dynamic, so I referred the patient to a female therapist. It is worth noting that the patient had introjected an invalidating dismissal that she harbored as a narcissistic injury from a comment I made during our first session. Despite the fact that she could recognize the potential value of understanding how she projected certain anxieties and expectations from her past relationships onto me in the present, thus distorting the immediate interpersonal climate, she was not about to let me off the hook for a casual remark I made (and quite unconsciously on my part) referring to her lost baby as a "fetus." When she confessed that this had been bothering her from the start, I acknowledged my gross insensitivity and how invalidating that must have felt to her. While partially motivated by my own countertransference, I felt I needed to offer her an explanation and told her frankly that my wife had had four miscarriages and I needed to view our (her) loss as merely fetuses rather than babies to protect myself from emotional pain, or else I would feel just like her. She acknowledged my self-disclosure with gratitude for my honesty, and we had a brief moment of mutual recognition. While this event is unlikely the central issue that fueled the malignant transference, it certainly did not help matters. This is furthermore a good example of how intersubjectivities can be easily misaligned because of the overwhelming presence of emotional and defensive operations that inform each subject's intrapsychic processes, her transference and my countertransference respectively.

WHEN ATTACHMENT DISSOLVES

It is a common practice in technical publications to emphasize what works well clinically and to reinforce therapeutic interventions that lead to successful results. Practitioners shy away from revealing mistakes they feel they have made, let alone intervention blunders, as well as negative outcomes of therapy. Sometimes treatment does not go the way we wish, nor can we predict with any certainty how patients will view us or come to perceive the therapeutic relationship, how we may be internalized or repudiated unconsciously, and whether we are at all a positive influence in producing structural shifts in their psychic equilibrium, cohesion, and/or organizations that aim toward integration and adaptation. What is most unfortunate is when a good treatment turns awry and the analyst is left not knowing why.

I had been working with a woman in her midthirties in weekly therapy for approximately one year. During this time we had reprocessed much of her painful childhood in relation to multiple developmental traumas, abandonments, and parental abuse, and their subsequent impact on her adult personality and melancholic disposition. Without going into the details of the case, suffice it to say that I had sufficient reason to believe that she had become reliant on me to discuss her emotional life and that she did not feel that way toward others, including her closest family members and friends, and on numerous occasions she told me that being able to disclose her true innermost thoughts and feelings to me without having to manipulatively conform to others' expectations was a genuinely liberating and cathartic experience.

When I had made the decision to leave my position at an adult outpatient clinic where I was employed and enter into full-time private practice, we had mutually discussed and arranged plans for her to continue with me; therefore, we spent no time on termination. On our last visit at the clinic, we decided that she would call me to schedule an appointment, but I never heard from her again. There was no "good-bye," no "thank you," and I can honestly say that I felt hurt and rejected by her deception and sudden disappearance from treatment. When I had not heard from her for several weeks, I decided to leave a phone message inviting her to contact me, but she did not return my call. I do not think that money was the issue, since she was financially secure and I had indeed offered her my lowest fee, which she had accepted at the time. But this may have been an underlying dynamic since she was receiving therapy for free at the clinic, and issues surrounding entitlement are not so uncommon among Canadian citizens, who see health care as part of their privileged rights. She furthermore had a depriving and traumatic childhood, and the value of our relationship may not have held much currency. For all I know, she may have been hurt and angry with me for abandoning her by disrupting the continuity of our relationship, which she had grown accustomed to expect, and this was her way of expressing her contempt. Or perhaps she grew to resent her dependency on me as well as my departure. Or was she merely taking me, and hence the treatment, for granted? Regardless of the possible reasons, this is an example of those times when what appears to be a qualitatively secure bond with the patient proves to be merely a transient experience. As to whether this is based on the functional utility of responsiveness or the transitional holding phenomena created by the clinician's presence, your guess is as good as mine.

I offer these speculations primarily for selfish reasons, namely, to search for some meaning in unanticipated loss. But I think sharing this experience is worthwhile because I often have wondered how other clinicians come to an understanding and resolution of dissolution when the therapeutic relationship terminates without epistemic certainty, justification, or cause. Therapists equally become attached to their patients and thus experience sudden termination as a derisive reflection on them. Perhaps this is the only way some patients can tolerate endings or say good-bye: disruptions in continuity, responsiveness, and availability are tantamount to loss. Sudden termination furthermore underscores the fragile nature of therapeutic alliance even when a seemingly secure attachment to the therapist had been established and embraced. Of course, it is always possible that my assessment of our relationship was merely an illusion, and that she, like so many attachment disordered patients, adopted a defensive false self role in relation to how she perceived she needed to act toward me. When I changed the rules, she no longer felt the need to play the game. Or are we merely deluding ourselves into thinking that we as clinicians really matter very much to our patients? If attachment theory has any validity, viability, or predictive merit, then I am drawn to the conclusion that what I had to offer her wasn't the kind of relationship she wanted or could tolerate. I do feel, however, that no matter how imperfect it was, or how imperfectly I executed my role, it is nonetheless still what she needed.

NOTES

1. In everyday usage, the term *empathy* has acquired a number of different meanings that imply attunement with the emotional or feeling states of another, often associated with acts of sympathy or kindness. Sympathy is distinguished from empathy insofar as sympathy involves the capacity to enter into and participate in the shared feelings of the other (which are often feelings of sorrow or suffering), while empathy involves an act of insightful imagination or projection into another's experience without necessarily having to feel that same experience. Clearly, empathy, sympathy, and insight can overlap, yet empathy implies a degree of subjective space within the intersubjective engagement of another that is distinct from the other's affective reality while still remaining positioned alongside it. In the words of Carl Rogers (1980), "being empathic, is to perceive the internal frame of reference of another with accuracy and with the emotional components and meanings which pertain thereto as if one were the person" (140). This involves "entering the private perceptual world of the other . . . [and] being sensitive, moment by moment, to the changing felt meanings which flow in this other person" (142). From this account, empathy almost requires a subjective merger through imagination and identificatory perception of what it would be like to experience the world from the other's perspective.

2. Like *Dasein*, which Heidegger (1927) conceived of as the concretely existing human being whose essential structure is care, empathy may be viewed as the disclosure of care. Although empathy may take an array of forms focusing on ideational content, affect, conscious and unconscious organizations, and the processes that characterize intersubjectivity within human interaction, care becomes its essential ontology—for the *desire to understand* the inner experience of the other would be absent without the intentional comportment of care.

3. Here when I refer to "truth" I am specifically referring to the Greek notion of *aletheia*, a topic that has been entirely ignored within psychoanalytic epistemology. For the ancients, truth (ἀλήθεια) is disclosedness or unconcealment. Rather than emphasize the relation between correspondence, coherence, pragmatic, and perspectival theories of truth in psychoanalysis, elsewhere I argue for the value of a dialectical account that embraces the notion of truth as creative self-discovery (see Mills 2005).

4. Ehrenberg (1993) goes so far as to claim that detailed self-disclosure about one's own experiences, including countertransference, is the central vehicle for analytic investigation.

6

ⓐ

Managing Primitive Defenses

Patients with attachment pathology can potentially present with every conceivable psychological profile by the simple fact that attachment-related processes are rudimentary and essential features of psychic structuralization and regulation. In other words, they form the ground of unconscious organizing principles and play a significant role in conscious motivation and expressed needs for relatedness. Because attachment pathology is a disorder of the self as the result of disruptions in attachment, it may potentially involve, as we have seen, many overdetermined conflicts and clinical symptomatology. Attachment vulnerabilities lead to the enactment of multiple defenses, from more benign maneuvers to more primitive instantiations. For those more characterologically disordered, lapses into primordial and archaic defenses are not merely regressive: they are primary forms of psychic regulation.

Throughout this chapter, I wish to highlight the therapeutic challenges of dealing with more difficult defensive constellations typically encountered in attachment character disorders. I will discuss the more rigid forms of dichotomization and splitting, confronting paranoiac proclivities, the erotic transference, ameliorating suicidality, containing psychotic anxieties, and de-escalating rage and potential violence. But first let us begin with addressing the dialectics of therapeutic exchange.

WORKING DIALECTICALLY

I am convinced that the nuts and bolts of successful therapeutic interventions do not involve following a methodological recipe, script, protocol, or set of established guidelines but instead rely on basic orienting principles dictated by the emergent process of dialogical exchange. In the consulting room, I work as a dialectician, constantly confronting and juxtaposing opposition with the patient's immediate subjective reality with the aim of directing the patient toward a meaningful understanding and integration of competing, antithetical processes. I do not know what the end process will assimilate nor entail, nor do I pretend to know what it should be for each individual. Only the process borne of the lived intersubjective encounter will dictate the teleological progression of therapy; and my responsiveness and presence is as much contingent upon the contexts of that process as it is upon the patient's unique subjectivity, personality traits, unconscious dynamics, and life history.

In contemporary psychoanalytic circles, the term *dialectic*, like many philosophical technical principles, seems to be currently in vogue; yet definitions of the dialectic are as vague as hell. Ogden, Hoffman, Ghent, Benjamin, and Mitchell, among others, use the term frequently in their writings, but, with the exception of Odgen, they don't even bother defining what they mean. Presumably, like Hoffman's (1998) "dialectical constructivism," *dialectic* implies opposition and tension. I have devoted a substantial amount of scholarship to explicating this technical principle in theoretical psychoanalysis under the rubric of what I have coined "process psychology," or "dialectical psychoanalysis"; so it is therefore beyond the scope of this clinically oriented project to go into the details here with customary philosophical rigor (see Mills 1996, 2000b, 2002a, 2002c, 2004a, 2004b). But a few remarks are in order.

Nowhere do we find a more comprehensive logic of the dialectic than in Hegel's (1812) philosophical system outlined in his *Science of Logic*. Hegel's dialectical logic has been grossly misunderstood by the humanities and social sciences, largely due to historical misinterpretations dating back to Heinrich Moritz Chalybäus, an earlier Hegel expositor, and unfortunately perpetuated by current mythology surrounding Hegel's system. As a result, Hegel's dialectic is inaccurately conceived of as a three-step movement involving the generation of a proposition or "thesis," followed by an "antithesis," then resulting in a "synthesis" of the prior movements; thus, we have the popularized and bastardized phrase "thesis-antithesis-synthesis." This is not Hegel's dialectic; rather, it is Fichte's (1794) depiction of the transcendental acts of consciousness that he describes as the fundamental principles (*Grundsatz*) of thought and judgment.[1] Yet this phrase itself is a crude and mechanical rendition of Fichte's logic and does not even properly convey his project. Unlike Fichte's (1794) meaning of the verb *aufheben*, defined as "to eliminate, annihilate, abolish, or destroy," Hegel's designation signifies a threefold activity by which mental operations at once cancel or annul opposition, preserve or retain it, and surpass or elevate its previous shape to a higher structure.

Fichte's dialectic is a response to Kant's (1781) *Critique of Pure Reason*, where Kant outlines the nature of consciousness and addresses irreconcilable contradictions that are generated in the mind due to inconsistencies in reasoning.[2] For both Kant and Fichte, their respective dialectics have firm limits or boundaries that may not be bridged. Hegel (1807, 1812, 1817, 1978), on the other hand, shows how contradiction and opposition are annulled but preserved, unified, and elevated within a progressive, evolutionary process. This process of the dialectic underlies all operations of mind and is seen as the thrust behind world history and culture. It may be said that the dialectic is the *essence* of psychic life, for if it were to be removed, consciousness and unconscious structure would evaporate.

In order to dispense with this erroneous yet well-conditioned assumption about Hegel's dialectic that is uncritically accepted as fact, I wish to reiterate myself. When psychoanalysis refers to dialectics, it often uses Fichte's threefold movement of thought in the form of thetic, analytic or antithetic, and synthetic judgments—a process normally and inaccurately attributed to Hegel;[3] or it describes unresolvable contradictions or mutual oppositions that are analogous to Kant's antinomies or paralogisms of the self. It is important to reemphasize that Hegel's dialectic is *not* the same as Kant's, who takes contradiction and conflict as signs of the breakdown of reason, nor is it Fichte's, who does not explicate the preservative function of the lower relation's remaining embedded in the higher. Furthermore, when psychoanalysts and social scientists apply something like the Fichtean dialectic to their respective disciplines, the details of this process are omitted.

Take, for example, the most sophisticated definition of the dialectic I could find in the psychoanalytic literature: "The dialectic is a process in which each of two opposing concepts creates, informs, preserves, and negates the other, each standing in dynamic (ever changing) relationship with the other" (Ogden 1986, 64). Here Ogden emphasizes difference, opposition, and preservation, but he also makes the two opposing concepts mutually creative forces. Note that he does not emphasize synthetic unification as do Fichte and Hegel, but rather his dialectic is like Kant's—opposition is firmly established in antithetical deadlock. This conceptual definition does not articulate the process of opposition, let alone how it arises, nor does it address the process of preservation, and Ogden completely omits whether his dialectic is oriented toward higher levels of development, unification, and organization. When a process of synthesis and integration is introduced in the psychoanalytic literature, the presumptive conclusion is that a synthesis cancels the previous moments and initiates a new moment that is once again opposed and reorganized. But the synthesis does not mean that all previous elements are preserved, or that psychic structure is elevated. In fact, this form of dialectic may lead to an infinite repetition of contradictions and conflict that meets with no resolve. Hegel's dialectic, on the other hand, carefully expatiates on a process by which mental activity cancels the rigid opposition, surpasses the opposition by transcending or moving beyond it in a higher unity, and simultaneously preserves the opposition in the higher unity rather than simply dissolving it. The preservation is a validating function under which opposition is subsumed within a new shape of consciousness. Thought does not merely set up over and against these antitheses, and it does not only set up a higher unity—but it also reasons a unity precisely through these opposites. Thus, the dialectic has a negative and a positive side.

What is important for process psychology, however, is understanding the essential structure of the dialectic as sublation (*Aufhebung*) denoted by these three simultaneous movements: at once they cancel or annul, transcend or surpass, retain or preserve—aspects of every transmogrification. The dialectic as process is pure activity and unrest that acquires more robust organization through its capacities to negate, oppose, and destroy otherness; yet in its negation of opposition, it surpasses difference through a transmutational process of enveloping otherness within its own internal structure, and hence it elevates itself to a higher plane. Not only does the psyche destroy opposition, but it subsumes and preserves it within its interior. Death is incorporated, remembered, and felt as it breathes new life in the mind's ascendance toward higher shapes of psychic development: the psyche retains the old as it transmogrifies the present, aimed toward a future existence it actively (not predeterminately) forges along the way. This ensures that dialectical reality is always ensnared in the contingencies that inform its experiential immediacy. Despite the universality of the logic of the dialectic, mind is always contextually realized. Yet each movement, each shape of the dialectic, is merely one moment within its holistic teleology, differentiated only by form. The process as a whole constitutes the dialectic, whereby each movement highlights a particular piece of psychic activity that is subject to its own particular contingencies. As each valence is highlighted in its immediacy or lived, experiential quality, it is merely one appearance among many appearances in the overall process of its own becoming.

Hegel's dialectic essentially describes the process by which a mediated dynamic begets a new immediate. This process not only informs the basic structure of his *Logic*, which may further be attributed to the general principle of *Aufhebung*, but this process also provides the logical basis to account for the role of negativity within a progressive unitary drive. The process by which mediation collapses into a new immediate provides us with the logical model for understanding the dynamics of the mind. As an architectonic process, the psyche invigorates itself and breathes its own life as a self-determining generative activity that builds upon its successive phases and layers that form its appearances. Mind educates itself as it passes through its various dialectical configurations and ascends toward higher shapes of self-conscious awareness. What *Geist* takes to be truth in its earlier forms is realized to be merely a moment. It is not until the subjective agent achieves a state of elaborate self-awareness or actualization as pure conceiving or conceptual understanding[4] that mentation finally integrates its previous movements into a synthetic unity as a dynamic self-articulated complex whole.

The clinical utility of the dialectic becomes apparent in the consulting room when patients present with countless antithetical, opposing, and competing wishes, desires, and/or intentions that stand in sharp contrast to their respective opposites, namely the counterwishes, desires, and intentions that oppose certain tendencies in the mind that come under attack by the rigid antipode that is established in the patient's psyche. Such impasse and opposition sets up conflict and tension in the patient's mind and lived experiential reality. Each process, self-state, or mode of subjectivity is radically misaligned when juxtaposed to others based on the simple quality of difference (each side of difference valuing competing loyalties), and this can apply to specific mental content, affect, impulses, defenses, interpersonal experience, or self-states that form certain allegiances that combat other self-states, internal objects, or competing parts of psychic organization. This agglomeration of competing processes inevitably trickles into the intersubjective medium of therapy, thus acquiring new forms of opposition and conflict that extend and magnify specific dialectical tensions that are intrapsychically realized by each subject (both the patient and the analyst). In Freud and Jung's early pivotal work, we can readily observe the dialectical tensions that populate the mind and fuel symptom substitution as failed compromise formations. Symptom formation is failed compromise by virtue of the fact that symptoms do not offer a sublated (*aufgehoben*) form of dialectical progression or unification, yet they are dialectical manifestations of opposing wishes and conflicts that have transmogrified in maladaptive forms. What becomes important in working dialectically with patients is to work to ultimately uncover opposition *within* immediate experience and attempt to bring those opposing forces to bear on one another in an effort to find some resolution through negotiation, compromise, and integration into a more comprehensive unity within the patient's dynamic organizing principles. Thus, the integration of the complex, split-off, compartmentalized, and segregated systems of mental operations and defenses into a meaningful whole becomes a central element of therapy, and this ultimately requires the enlistment of insight and reason for a full comprehension of the competing and conflictual processes under question. This is why therapy is a liberation struggle to transcend that which is unknown and operative within us via actualizing higher levels of self-conscious awareness in thought and action.

In a more concrete and simplistic fashion, working dialectically involves highlighting a specific piece of subjective reality in the patient within the immediacy of the therapeutic moment and exploring it (conceptually, affectively, defensively, transferentially, etc.) in relation to that which is not consciously spoken of or acknowledged as such. Each psychic event contains its opposite; thereby, being and nothing, identity and difference, are mutually implicative. Following the logic of the dialectic, there is presumed to be the opposite of what the patient articulates or discloses within the very nature of such disclosure (albeit in cryptic or disguised forms), and it becomes the task of the analyst to ferret out such opposition and bring it into dialogue with the particular piece of subjectivity that is currently dominating the patient's attention. There is opposition contained in every psychic experience, and often this undisclosed, unspoken opposition is a dynamic that informs the patient's immediate experience. Here we may observe the universal dictum: "Every fear is also a wish." Every fear contains its counterpart within its dialectical structure because each fear may only be experienced and defined in relation to what it is not. Therefore, it is not uncommon that when a patient fears the occurrence of a particular event, let's say the fear that her father will be in a car accident, we may also suspect a particular death wish directed toward her father that is fueling the anxiety that signals the ego to be fearful to begin with, anxiety associated with her reintrojected hatred for her father, unconsciously harbored yet consciously denied and not acknowledged. That which troubles the patient is largely because it stands in opposition and difference to another competing aspect of the patient's psyche that needs to be clarified and given a particular voice. The juxtaposition of these dualistic, ambitendent wishes creates distress when these wishes are confronted and forced to face one another directly, hence bringing about a dialectical confrontation that must be mediated by the subjective mind. This is so by the simple fact that every conscious thought and intention has its opposition contained (albeit hidden) within the very premise or proposition of the patient's stated or felt experience, which stands in competition with other dynamic aspects of the psyche that clamor for release and expression. When rigid dichotomies are brought in juxtaposition and dialogue with one another, there is an emergent process of unconcealment in the very act of such confrontation, which may now enter into the initial stages of more integration and holistic comprehension. One task of therapy is to draw out such polarities and show how this fundamental clash creates a stalemate in the mind that further sustains emotional pain and symptomatic dominance. When this task is executed successfully, elements of opposition are brought into confrontation with each other so that each side may execute a dialogue with the other in order to bring about shifts in psychic organization and structure, what Pizer (1998) calls negotiations of paradox. While the abridgment of the rigid bi-

furcation that informs various experiential self-states is a viable therapeutic task, shifts in maladaptive structure leading to fortification and
reparation are ultimately desired aims.

Patients of mine often tell me that what seems to be of most help in their
process of self-analysis (which goes on both in and outside of the office) is
my systematic use of questions. My asking pointed and probing, open-
ended questions allows patients themselves to think about their own competing thoughts, beliefs, desires, and so forth without having premature
interpretations foisted onto them, which they readily resist. What is more
experientially meaningful for patients is when they themselves arrive at
insight via self-awareness through the critical reassessments and questioning of their own premises and competing desires that clash with others.
Dialectical questioning facilitates a process of unconcealment or disclosedness that the patient undergoes by directing him to uncover and critically
examine his experiences in the moment by joining or aligning with the
value of insight in identifying and articulating competing, antithetical
processes. Working dialectically does not necessarily mean that one should
emulate the Socratic method, because the systematic dialectical questioning Socrates practiced was ultimately designed to produce a state of crisis
in the interlocutor by exposing fallacious propositions or illogical beliefs
through a form of cross-examination (*elenchus*), which serves to debilitate
the other's argument or mode of justification.[5] These strategies may appear aggressive and may be experienced by the patient as though she is being subjected to a ruthless interrogation. In the end, patients often feel
ashamed, debased, and demoralized, which further evokes earlier feelings
of discomfort associated with faulty or unsavory attachment experiences.
The Socratic dialectic resists finalization, whereas, with process psychology, integration, unification, and resolve are desired goals. Instead, dialectical questioning is designed to highlight contradiction, opposition, and
competing processes that are often rigidly segregated and held at bay from
one another in order for clarity, dialogue, negotiation, and cohesion to occur. This inevitably leads to a process of mourning, for we must mourn the
loss of the fulfillment of wishes that never reach their actualization. Some
elements of inner experience must be sacrificed to the abyss while others
are realized through synthetic integration.

Brigit was a successful director of a large corporate financial institution
when she began to develop acute panic attacks and somatic symptoms after she was reproached by a newly appointed female vice president who became her boss. Her panic disorder intensified over the months, and she was
forced to go on disability due to the unmanageable nature of her symptoms.
The interpersonal conflict with her new boss further opened up various
transference gates that transported her back to experiences in her past of
feeling unloved, stupid, deprived, and neglected by her mother, who was a
constant source of disparagement, rejection, and critical judgment. Rather

than succumbing to her mother's dismal assessment of her capabilities, Brigit developed many obsessional neurotic trends designed to help her excel in her endeavors and gain praise from authority figures despite her mother's lack of recognition. As a result, she became a workaholic and was rigidly obsessed about performing her job as optimally and successfully as possible, without having any understanding of her unconscious motives driving her professional ambition.

During the second session, the patient instantly developed a panic attack in my office after I had interpreted that her obsessional need to succeed and be perfect was in the service of gaining recognition from her mother, who had never acknowledged her, and that the stress of her corporate environment and the negative relations with her female boss were dredging up inner experiences of her mother's negative judgment and invalidation. These revelations precipitated a crisis in her psychic economy that shattered her defenses and threatened her perceived sense of stability and personal identity. All the years that she had worked so hard in her company in order to get the next raise, job title, and position of authority, and the respect that accompanied these, were suddenly rendered valueless; she hated her job and everything it stood for because she realized that she was ultimately motivated out of the need to prove to her mother that she was worth something.

Brigit lost her father at a very young age, and her mother raised two daughters virtually alone. Her father was a salesman who traveled frequently and was never home, and, consequently, Brigit's relationship with him was virtually nonexistent. Brigit described her mother as cold, bitter, affectionless, strict, punitive, and judgmental, and Brigit had always felt unloved and inferior in comparison to her sister, who had excelled scholastically and was perceived to be more attractive. The patient had been morbidly obese since childhood and reported that she would frequently binge on food as a means to cope with her mother's extreme rejection, cruel remarks about her weight and poor school performance, and overall debasement. She was literally starving for positive attention.

By the third session the patient reported feeling energetic, had had no panic symptoms since the previous session, had started to exercise and diet, was less self-deprecatory, and had new insight into her self-worth, freedom, and past conflicts. She claimed that she no longer wanted to be so driven by her job in order to gain validation and recognition, which she could receive through her husband and children, and that she valued love and attachment to her family more than money or a job title. In a reaction against her childhood, she wanted to fill her "house with beauty" and began devoting much attention to her own personal enjoyment and self-fulfillment.

During the course of our work together, Brigit decided to leave her company and began her own business as a private contractor. She began to realize and fulfill many possibilities she had denied in herself due to the internalized oppression and devaluation she experienced from her mother. Much of our work centered on coming to terms with her competing desires and conflicts that tended to cancel each other out, thus leading to impasse, rather than to cohesive integration in her conceptual understanding. The parts of her that felt damaged, inadequate, weak, stupid, ugly, and not worthy of love or success were brought into dialogue with the more confident, autonomous, and secure elements of her self-esteem that were fighting the dominance of toxic introjects she had identified with and incorporated into her psychic structure. Certain self-states would often oppose ominous antithetical self-states in reaction to certain intrapsychic threats (and bad internal objects) that were evoked in relation to her ambivalent feelings about her mother. During this process of dialectical revamping and striving for meaning and unification, she tarried with the emotional significance and rage of never being shown love or validation. At a particular point in session, immediately after focusing on her mother's lack of attunement, she associated to how she hated her husband's ex-wife for the devaluing way in which she treated the patient's stepchildren, and how she could identify with their suffering in relation to her own. This led to the following dialogue:

Patient: I see red when I think of her, I hate her so much. I was so upset, I had this dream of being in my mother's house confronting her in the kitchen. I don't know why she would be there though. Weird, eh? I wanted to make her feel the same way she made Candice [stepdaughter] feel.

Therapist: Perhaps it is really your mother you want to confront.

Patient: No, I couldn't do that. It would kill her. [*A period of silence ensues.*] When I was a teenager, I was suicidal. I just felt so unwanted by her.

Therapist: Perhaps a part of you wanted her to die.

Patient: [*Face becomes frozen.*]

Therapist: What's the look all about?

Patient: I don't want to discuss how she screwed me up anymore—it's not fair to her. I don't want to blame her. She's a good person deep down. She does all sorts of volunteer work—she's even won awards for how she's helped others.

Therapist: It sounds like you're protecting her.

Patient: I don't want to say, "You fucked me up."

Therapist: But you feel she did.

Patient: I couldn't let her know that, it would crush her—she's eighty-three.

Therapist: You're being very thoughtful toward her feelings, when the other part of you can't stand her.

Patient: She didn't accept me for who I was. I didn't want to wear those damn dresses. It was like she was saying—

Therapist: "Be this way or I won't love you."

Patient: No! Never! We never discussed love. Maybe that's why it hurts to hear nice things from you—why it hurts when Sue [husband's ex-wife] tells them that she won't love 'em if they don't mind.

What stood out for me in the course of working with this patient was how she struggled with explicating and then integrating her various dichotomous self-states into a meaningful whole. The rigid bifurcation, compartmentalization, and splitting of competing, oppositional forces is never an easy process to overcome, nor is the process of overcoming it ever fully completed. Pure synthesis or unification is only possible conceptually. Experientially, absolute synthesis or pure self-consciousness is never attained by the simple fact that opposition is always preserved, even when canceled or surpassed, and thus will inevitably resurface at times when various antithetical self-states, unconscious intentions, and interpersonal tensions create new polarities the mind will be forced to reevaluate and resolve. The upward evolutionary thrust of the dialectic in the service of individuation and liberation from oppressive internalized pressures is oriented toward achieving greater degrees of freedom and wholeness, albeit imperfectly realized. It is equally subject to regression and retrograde withdrawal under the influence of pathology (see Mills 2002a, 2005). The progressive drive or teleological direction is a process of its own becoming, and this process is never a predetermined end state but rather a process forged by the unique contingencies and capacities within the patient's own internal psychical world in relation to the intersubjective context of therapy.

During the termination of our work together, Brigit told me, "I like who I've become." She no longer felt ossified in black-and-white dichotomies and was more capable of seeing how her competing self-states were interconnected, and how her maladaptive unconscious repetitions were no longer making decisions for her. She was now "working to live rather than living to work," had become more spontaneous in her personal affairs and relationships rather than following a rigid plan or protocol, had continued to lose weight and maintain healthy lifestyle changes, and had decided to pursue activities that had been previously forbidden during her youth by her mother. To celebrate her newly acquired state of transformation and independence, she had gotten a tattoo of a sun and told me that it was to represent her new life based on "personal illumination" as well as to signify the "brightness" and "warmth" she now felt she had, unlike the coldness she experienced as a child. In the end, she averred, "I feel alive."

THE DESIRE NOT TO KNOW

Human knowledge is paranoiac—it torments, persecutes, *cuts*. This is essentially what Lacan (1953–1954) means when he says, "My knowledge started off from paranoiac knowledge" (163), because there are "paranoid affinities between all knowledge of objects as such" (1955–1956b, 39). For Lacan, aggressivity suffuses the very fabric of human knowledge, a paranoiac residue of the dialectic of desire.

Because language is a necessary condition (albeit not a sufficient one) for conceptual thought, comprehension, and meaning to manifest (see Frie 1997; Mills 1999), human knowledge is linguistically mediated. But the epistemological question—that is, the origin of knowledge—requires us to consider prelinguistic development, intrapsychic and interpersonal experience, and the extra- or nonlinguistic processes that permeate psychic reality, such as the constitutional pressures of the drives (*Triebe*) and affective states (from the monstrous to the sublime) that remain linguistically foreclosed as unformulated unconscious experience.[6] When these aspects of human life are broadly considered, it becomes easier to see how our linguistic-epistemological dependency has paranoiac a priori conditions. From Freud to Klein and Lacan, knowledge is a dialectical enterprise that stands in relation to fear—to the horror of possibility, the possibility of the *not*: negation, conflict, and suffering saturate our very beings, beings whose self-identities are linguistically constructed.

The relation between knowledge and paranoia is a fundamental one, and perhaps nowhere do we see this dynamic so poignantly realized than in childhood. From the "psychotic-like" universe of the newborn infant (e.g., see Klein 1946), to the relational deficiencies and selfobject failures that impede the process of human attachment, to the primal scene and/or subsequent anxieties that characterize the Oedipal period, leading to the inherent rivalry, competition, and overt aggression of even our most sublimated object relations—fear, trepidation, and dread hover over the very process of knowing itself. What is paranoid is that which stands in relation to opposition, hence, that which is alien to the self. Paranoia is not simply that which is beyond the rational mind, but it is a generic process of *noesis*—"I take thought, I perceive, I intellectually grasp, I apprehend," hence have *apprehension* for what I encounter in consciousness. With qualitative degrees of difference, we are all paranoid simply because others hurt us, a lesson we learn in early childhood. Others hurt us with their knowledge, with what they say, as do we. And we hurt knowing. "What will the Other do next?" We are both pacified yet cower in extreme trembling over what we may and may not know—what we may and may not find out; and this is why our relation to knowledge is fundamentally paranoiac.

For Aristotle (1958), "all men by nature desire to know" (108). This philosophical attitude is kindled by our educational systems, perhaps informing the popular adage "Knowledge is power." But whose? There is no doubt that the acquisition of knowledge involves a power differential, but what if knowledge itself is seen as too powerful because it threatens our psychic integrity? In the gathering of knowledge, there is simultaneously a covering over, a blinding to what one is exposed to; moreover, an erasure. I ~~know~~ (No)! Unequivocally, there are things we desire to know nothing about at all; hence, the psychoanalytic attitude places unconscious defense—negation/denial and repression—in the foreground of human knowledge, the desire not to know.

When we engage epistemology—the question and meaning of knowledge—we are intimately confronted with paranoia. For example, there is nothing more disturbing than the idea that a lifetime of successful inquiry into a particular field of study may be entirely debunked by the simple, arrogant question, "How do you know?" Uncertainty, doubt, ambiguity, hesitation, insecurity—anxiety! The process of knowing exposes us all to immense discomfort. And any epistemological claim is equally a metaphysical one. Metaphysics deals with first principles, the fundamental, ultimate questions that preoccupy our collective humanity: "What is real? Why do I exist? Will I *really* die?" Metaphysics is paranoia—and we are all terrified by its questions: "Is there God, freedom, agency, immortality?" *Is? Why? Why not? Yes, but why?!* When the potential meaning and quality of one's personal existence hinge on the response to these questions, it is no wonder why most theists say that only God is omniscient. And although Freud (1927) tells us that the very concept of God is an illusory derivative of the Oedipal situation—a wish to be rescued and comforted from the anxieties of childhood helplessness—He, our exalted Father in the sky, is *always* watching, judging. Knowing this, the true believer has every reason to be petrified. For those in prayer or in the madhouse, I can think of no greater paranoia.

For Lacan (1977), the paranoiac process of acquiring knowledge has its genesis in the imaginary,[7] first as the subject's misidentification with its alienated image in the reflection of the other, and second as the fundamental distortion and miscognition of external objects (also see Muller and Richardson 1982). Human knowledge is paranoiac because the subject projects its imaginary ego properties into objects that become distorted and are perceived as fixed entities that terrorize the subject with persecutory anxiety in the form of the other's desire. While the terrifying part-object experiences of the dislocated body arise in the imaginary, the symbolic register introduces another form of fragmentation. Desire and speech by their very nature impose a command. Knowledge is saturated with paranoia because it threatens to invade the subject, and it is precisely this knowledge that must be defended against as the desire not to know.

Interpreting Lacan, Bruce Fink (1997) tells us that just as patients do not possess a genuine desire for change, they further lack a genuine desire for self-knowledge. While people may show interest in knowing why their lives and interpersonal relationships are unsatisfactory, and specifically what keeps interfering with their adjustment and happiness, Lacan (1955–1956a) suggests that there is a more fundamental unconscious wish not to know any of those things. "The subject's entire subsequent development shows that he wants to know nothing about it" (12). In *Encore*, Lacan (1972–1973) further adds that "the unconscious is the fact that being, by speaking, enjoys, and . . . wants to know nothing more about it"—that is, "know nothing about it at all" (104–5). This is why patients often resist therapy and avoid the process of self-examination and change. They have no desire to know the root of their symptoms or neurotic mechanisms, what functions their defenses serve, and why they are instituted in the first place. This is why Lacan says that patients do not want to give up their symptoms because they provide familiarity and meaning: we enjoy our symptoms too much! (Žižek 1992). This is the insidious structure of *jouissance*, namely, the realm of excess, pleasure in pain, or the satisfaction individuals find in dissatisfaction, to the point that they wish not to give it up. As Ragland (1995) asserts, "The inertia of *jouissance* . . . makes a person's love of his or her symptoms greater than any desire to change them" (85). From this standpoint, the unconscious is first and foremost sadomasochistic: it inflicts a perverse pleasure through suffering at its own hands.

There is a self-destructive element to the enjoyment of symptoms, a revelry in the realm of excess to the point that truth or knowledge must be suspended, disavowed, or denied. This is why Lacan thinks that all knowledge of objects as such becomes tainted with paranoia: it threatens the subject's *jouissance* and thus must be defended against through the desire not to know.

I was once treating a patient with a severe characterological depression, a history of bulimia, and two previous suicide attempts. He reportedly had a happy marriage of sixteen years and was a successful building contractor, but he detested himself for unknown reasons and had struggled with a pervasive sense of suicidality since his early twenties, shortly after he moved away from his parents' home. He had been on several psychotropic medications and had seen two different therapists over the years, but he claimed that they never really got to the root of the problem. Initially he was very enthusiastic and motivated about engaging in psychodynamic work, until certain evoked events from his past started to create intense dysphoria. The patient confided that he was a fire setter when he was four years old and burned down an entire crop of his neighbor's cornfields. In order to teach him a lesson, his mother burned his hand on the top of the stove to deter him from ever playing with matches again. His first suicide attempt was after she died, but he was a cutter as a kid and even attempted to step in front of a moving car when he was seven years old.

The patient had suffered from many developmental traumas at the hands of his mother, including being tied on a leash like a dog to the clothesline so she could keep an eye on him. The more he began to realize the depths of the abuse and the immense lack of love that characterized his childhood, the more worthless he felt about himself and the more paranoid he became of what he might uncover next. Unlike patients presenting with typical resistances of denial, avoidance, aversion, thought blocking, missing appointments, and the like, he was compelled to delve into the unknown, hoping to recover the unconscious remnants that held the key to a new understanding. But his desire not to know was too powerful. When he said to me, "I will come here forever," this was the first signal that he was planning to flee from knowing too much.

When you as the therapist are confronted with clinical signs or personal intuitions that the patient is fantasizing (either consciously or unconsciously) about bolting from therapy, it is best to address your suspicions right away and explore the source of the patient's and your anxieties. If you wait too long to confront defenses it may be too late. Ken was a physician in his midfifties who suffered from severe social phobia with intense fears of interpersonal rejection and would sweat profusely around large groups of people, thereby creating self-humiliation and ingrained patterns of avoidance and withdrawal. As a child, he was tormented by his alcoholic father, who would emotionally devalue him through his verbal criticisms and tirades, compare him unfavorably to other children, and constantly point out every perceived personality flaw. Ken had a stuttering problem as a kid and was subjected to relentless teasing and ridicule both at home and at school. In his father's eyes, he was a family embarrassment and a failure. Throughout his life and academic training, Ken was terrified of authority figures, negative judgment from teachers and peers, and any demand for social interaction or performance in front of others, and these fears reinforced his repetitive patterns of social anxiety, avoidance, and withdrawal.

Throughout therapy, the patient began to realize the depth of hate and rage he harbored for his father, feelings he had denied in himself and repressed for years, feelings he inverted and turned on himself through his own self-deprecation and shameful condemnation. To his dismay, he had constructed a false self in order to win approval from authority, even to the degree of becoming a doctor in the hopes that his father would finally show some pride and recognition for his accomplishments. Upon his graduation from medical school, his father showed up drunk and embarrassed him in front of his graduating class, yelling uninhibitedly during the ceremony.

The patient's need for recognition and his sensitivity to judgment and rejection were dynamics that were made clear early in the therapeutic relationship when I noticed that he would frequently disparage himself for not sounding very articulate, including apologizing to me for not being clear enough in his descriptions and narrative. Like his father, I became a transference phantom who he feared was judging and devaluing him, and this exacerbated his anxieties and pressure to perform in the session in order to garner my approval and acceptance. After becoming emotional during a painful disclosure, he became self-conscious of his vulnerability and wanted to distance from the emotional immediacy of his exposure. When he reconstituted his defenses, he said:

Patient: You probably think I'm not normal—that I'm this dysfunctional person.

Therapist: I think that's your own judgment and shame talking.

Patient: I just want you to think I'm normal.

Therapist: I can see that's how you want to feel about yourself.

The following week the patient initiated the session in the following manner:

Patient: I have decided that I want to discharge myself as a patient—I need to take some time to think about life. I'm dealing with my anger better now, and I think I understand the connections to my past—I feel I'm ready to go it alone.

Therapist: Usually people come to therapy because they want to think about things in here. I'm wondering if you're unhappy with the way things have been progressing.

Patient: No—but I don't have any insurance, but that's a separate issue. I suppose you're going to tell me that I'm avoiding things again, but I don't want to be dependent on this.

Therapist: I didn't realize that finances were an issue.

Patient: They're not—not really, but there is some concern.

Therapist: My experience is that patients will look for any excuse to leave. I think you should stay.

Patient: Yes, maybe I'm avoiding it. I didn't realize it was going to be like this. I guess I was hoping for a quick fix.

Therapist: It's human nature to want to avoid pain—what are you avoiding?

Patient: I guess I don't want to keep digging in the dirt.

Disillusionment, upheaval, and emotional pain are part of any process of therapeutic change, and there are no shortcuts. Each person must traverse the domain of his own arduous process, and no process is the same, despite the fact that certain thematic dynamics universally resonate within us all. Because his disclosure about wanting to leave therapy was unanticipated, I wondered whether it was partially motivated in response to what had transpired in the previous session. I asked whether he perceived my comments regarding the question of his normalcy as an empathic failure that may have opened up more feelings of vulnerability and shame, but he quickly denied their impact. He went on to describe that he had been to three doctors and was diagnosed by the first one as having social phobia and a panic disorder. The second doctor had prescribed medication to control his profuse sweating, while the third, who was a homeopath, prescribed some herbal remedies and called him a "delicate flower." When he relayed this information to his wife, she reportedly made fun of him. It became apparent that he was concerned his wife would find out he was in therapy, and he feared she would not understand.

Patient: I know I haven't discussed Lisa. She doesn't know I'm coming here. I feel I can't tell her things.

Therapist: Why not?

Patient: Oh, I guess I don't want to burden her.

Therapist: I got the impression that you can't fully trust her to open up to her.

Patient: I guess I could tell her; she's caring.

Therapist: Does she love you?

Patient: Yes, I assume she does.

Therapist: Assume?

Patient: It would be horrible if this wasn't the case—I wouldn't want to know that.

Therapist: Do you ever talk about your relationship with one another?

Patient: Sometimes, but not really. We avoid those discussions, but I'd like to be closer.

Therapist: What would it be like for you to tell her that you want to be closer, more intimate, so you can be vulnerable with her?

Patient: I'm afraid she wouldn't really listen, or want to be.

Therapy is the one forum where people come to witness the exposure of what they don't want to know about themselves, yet it is nevertheless revealed. The desire not to know is so potent and influential that patients are looking for any conceivable excuse to run away from themselves, from their own self-knowledge, because they find it too unbearable. When this is realized, suddenly therapy becomes a nemesis that mobilizes paranoia: "Will I know too much? Will I have to change? Will I have to make a decision to act?" Ken's marriage was a farce and he knew it, but he didn't want to know. Denial, disavowal, avoidance, suppression—these defenses are primitive by virtue of the fact that they are basic, primordial operations of psychic economy. When they are dissolved under the spotlight of self-knowledge, something has to be offered to replace them—to help contain the disruption of psychic equilibrium. Insight may be enlightening, but it provides little comfort when the roof comes down. But patients eventually have to face the brute facticity of truth while dispensing with illusions; and no ploy or mental maneuver can reverse the throes of this process. We can only delude ourselves for so long before it comes back to haunt us with imperative force, a necessary preparation for change.

IMPASSE AND THE EROTIC TRANSFERENCE

It may be argued that, similar to basic animal instinct, primitive defenses (including dissociation) are evolutionarily informed in the service of adaptation. One automatic prereflective tendency is to flee from conflict, as we have illustrated in the desire not to know. Other defenses are enlisted to aggress against and combat the threat of imminent harm to the psyche; and when the self is too imperiled to weather the onslaught of anxiety incumbent upon it in times of confrontation, psychic integrity becomes compromised by regression, depletion, fragmentation, and/or inertia that strips away the person's capacity to cope and function adaptively. Sex and aggression are basic archaic pressures of the drives that find their objects and outlets of expression through relational exchange. I am frequently surprised to see how many of the leading proponents of relational psychoanalysis are quick to dismiss Freud's most basal insights into unconscious motivation, what Mitchell (1992) calls the "outmoded concept of drives" (3). Let us ask ourselves this basic question: What are the two things that make people most uncomfortable? What is so unpleasant that many people avoid conversations, let alone detailed enactments, that broach a sensitivity too close to home? Sex and aggression in all their derivative forms—from base carnality, to vulgarity, hate, and murder, to love, intimacy, and cultural sublimation—are the very aspects of human desire that bring on the most uncomfortable trepidations. But we can never escape the fact that we are sensuous embodied beings with antithetical desires fueled by passion, appetition, hostility, and might.

Transference work is often said to be the heart of psychotherapy, where the goal is to identify and resolve past patterns of unconscious repetition, and/or to focus on the reparative aspects of such enactments. Here I use the term *transference* to refer to many parallel unconscious activities, from the innately disposed, experientially derived representational templates, behavioral patterns, and/or affective schemas that are originally acquired from our interactions with attachment figures, then superimposed on all later interpersonal relationships (see Freud 1912a, 100–102), to the repetition of "latent object relations" (Racker 1968, 76), what Stern (1985) may refer to as RIGs (Representations of Interactions that have been Generalized), to the displaced past within the organizational present (in contrast, see Fosshage 1994). Just as others are filtered through the lens of our perceptual apparatus informed by our own personal histories—at once a projected repetition activated by the nuances of the immediate interpersonal environment—transference is simultaneously the coming to presence of the lost past within the process of the ceasing-to-be of the experiential present. In other words, what are unconsciously activated and transferred are elements of the past within the immediacy of the moment, which is none other than the recovery of lost presence. So, not only is transference the attitudes we take up toward the doctor in the present context based on our internal objects, self-representations, and previous interpersonal relationships, but it is also the reconstitution of the present within the past.

Whether we speak of transference in the generic sense, such as the positive and negative valences identified by Freud (1912a, 1916–1917), to the idealized and narcissistic transferences such as mirroring, twinship, and merger manifestations as described by Kohut (1971), we can never lose sight of the fact that transference is omnipresent. The inability to reconcile transference or bring it into its appropriate light can readily lead to impasse in the analytic dyad, which may further jeopardize the treatment. This is especially the case when hostile or erotic transferences become magnified with no resolve.

Because many attachment disordered patients have curtailed capacities for showing and soliciting intimacy and healthy affection, it is very common to see how their various relational needs and emotional dependence on others become sexualized. Erotic transference is bound to occur between a patient and therapist under the normative course of analytic work, even if such transferences are subdued or relegated to affectionate feelings for the therapist. It should be said that eroticism does not have to take the form of overt sexuality, and even the most homely of clinicians are not exempt from its presence by virtue of the fact that the analyst becomes a repository for the patient's wishful fantasies on multiple unconscious levels. But what happens when the patient's sexual feelings for the therapist are in the service of resistance? As Freud (1916–1917) reminds us, "The work of overcoming resistances is the essential function of analytic treatment" (451). Yet what if the patient does not see that the transference is resistance? Moreover, what happens when the erotic transference is unrelenting, intractable, and daunting? What becomes of the patient's analysis when the eroticism becomes so fortified that the analytic dyad becomes mired in a stalemate—so much so that treatment comes to a standstill?

I once had a patient who developed a very intense and unremitting erotic transference toward me about three months into therapy. She had a very bereft childhood, was shown little to no affection by her parents growing up, and had always yearned for the recognition that they were neither able nor willing to show. The patient had displayed heightened needs to procure my acceptance and approval almost immediately from the start of treatment, and over the months, fostered by my attunement and responsiveness, these desires steadily grew into feelings of sexual attraction.

The erotic transference began to become conspicuous after the patient had a particularly emotional session for the first time in the therapy while discussing her sadness over her parents' continual lack of love. After she became teary, there was a moment of sustained recognition, and we mutually acknowledged its importance, not only for the patient's process, but also for the advance in our relationship that allowed us to explore emotional pain. At the end of this session, I had commented that I felt closer to her since she disclosed her feelings uninhibitedly, and she reciprocated my gesture with a similar acknowledgment. Admittedly, the patient received a great deal of validation from me, which in part fueled the transference, but it was shortly after this event that she began to behave more superficially, seductively, and reservedly about showing further emotion.

Two sessions later, the patient disclosed that she was attracted to me and was nervous about her feelings as well as what my reaction would be to her disclosure. I invited her to tell me more about her feelings toward me and why she thought they had developed. Upon this invitation, she grew exceedingly self-conscious and confessed that she had indeed crossed over a boundary, which made her feel foolish and exposed. I remarked that I thought her feelings communicated something important about us and that we should continue to explore what they might mean. She voiced concern that her feelings might intensify and asked me to forgive her for her transgression.

Two days later, the patient called and said she had been feeling dysphoric and was crying sporadically. She confessed that she felt humiliated and stupid and thought it would be best for her to quit therapy. She was further fearful that I had recorded her comments in my case notes and that they could potentially be viewed by a third party. Upon my asking why she feared I would betray her confidence, she reluctantly disclosed that she had been raped ten years earlier by a family physician, and his records were subpoenaed as part of the court documents in his trial. I reassured her about the rule of confidentiality and requested that we process her concerns in the next session.

The day of her next appointment, she called me to tell me that her husband had inadvertently taken her keys to her car as he went to work and she had no way of getting to her scheduled appointment on time. I suggested we have a phone session instead and she agreed. She continued to talk about her feelings of humiliation, exposure, shame, and self-punishment for disclosing her desire for me, and she said she imagined that I "got a good chuckle" from the whole incident. Her fear of my ridicule was quite a salient feature in her feelings of humiliation, which further evoked the feelings of mistrust and betrayal that accompanied the assault from her previous doctor who had raped her. While she felt reassured at the end of the phone session that her feelings for me were part of the process of our work together, the erotic transference degenerated into an insidious defense against divulging her innermost thoughts, which she admitted she consciously held back because she felt too uncomfortable. Because she was no longer observing the fundamental rule of associating honestly and without censorship, the therapy soon devolved into an impenetrable impasse.

Over the next three months, we became mired by her self-consciousness and her inability to get beyond the vulnerability of her disclosures. Four interpenetrating themes emerged from our mutual analysis of the issue: (1) her denial that her feelings were transferential; (2) her inflexible belief that she had committed a taboo boundary violation; (3) her fear that I thought she was very mentally ill; and (4) her feelings that she was to blame for ruining the treatment.

Initially, we focused on the here and now of our "real relationship" and how her erotic feelings for me were natural outgrowths and extensions of the feelings of validation, responsiveness, and interpersonal warmth she experienced from me over the months. I was the first person to understand her pain and provided a holding context for her to uninhibitedly reveal her most cherished fears and secrets. The patient refuted all suggestions that her affection for me could have other unconscious motivations as well and steadfastly maintained that her feelings were "normal" and purely based in the contingencies of the analytic encounter I had fostered. As she put it, "These [feelings] are not based on my past"; she believed they were based instead in the immediacy of her experiences toward me. She averred that she was attracted to my "warm eyes" and "nice smile" and that her relationships in the past had nothing to do with the immediacy of the moment. She confessed to having fantasies of me while masturbating, accompanied by guilt and feelings of betrayal toward her husband, whom she almost told during a vulnerable moment of internal crisis. Over the weeks, her feelings did not subside, and she feared that the intensity of her affections were leading her to fall in love with me.

As an educated woman who had read Freud, she jokingly began referring to me as "Herr Professor," while she called herself "Dora." I had made the interpretation that she was attempting to seduce me as she had done with other men in her past; she would win them over and then grow tired of them and end the relationship, or else they would get fed up with her games and abandon her. In the end, she would feel unworthy of love, which was a repetition of her feelings she had experienced from her parents. While the boundaries or frame of the therapy surrounding the question of our sexual involvement was never directly stated (i.e., that we would never be intimate), she knew that I did not desire her in the same way, nor would I reciprocate with any mutual disclosures. The bane of her self-consciousness materialized when I surmised that she did not receive the responsiveness from me that she was hoping for, which she perceived as a rejection.

When I didn't respond to her seductive invitations, she would frequently threaten to leave therapy, claiming that she could no longer open up to me because she spoiled the opportunity by "opening [her] mouth" about her true feelings. She deliberately held back what she really wanted to say and then would become exasperated with her feelings of exposure, shame, and vulnerability, which would lapse into self-reproach with the desire to end the treatment, itself a manipulative threat to hurt me back. She insisted that she had violated the established boundaries of therapy, despite my instruction about the ethic of honesty during our first session with subsequent reminders. Her need for self-blame and punishment began to take on delusional elements in her thinking and rationalization for why she did not feel the need to continue.

Her erotic transference steadily became more tinged with frustration and animosity, and she would attempt to orchestrate tension and indeed became mad at me in order to make the break easier. She began questioning my technique, claiming that I was following a protocol and that, unlike her, I was not being real. She pushed the issue to the point of exclaiming that I would not tell her my true assessment of her mental stability even if I thought she was "nuts." When I said that most people don't ask me that question directly because they obviously come to see me for problems they are well aware of, she was genuinely hurt and angry with me and threatened to end therapy that moment. I responded by saying that she set herself up for disappointment by projecting onto me what she already knew about herself but was unwilling to accept now that she fantasized about having a sexual relationship with me. The patient acted out her rejection and aggravation by canceling our next appointment.

In the weeks that followed, our interchanges became more contentious and confrontational. She would challenge my observations and reject most of what I would suggest, yet at the same time she would insist that she could not honesty disclose to me anymore because she feared I would judge and "hate" her if I found out how she really was deep down. Because she could not achieve the deep level of emotional intimacy she desired with her husband, as she told me, I was more a threat to her self-esteem as a man who was judging her as a woman. She was growing tired of exerting so much effort in holding back her associations, to the point that she felt the therapy was pointless and futile.

Despite the fact that she was repeatedly testing me to see whether I would convince her to stay as a means to show that I really cared, I simply told her that the decision to leave was solely hers but I thought it was ultimately self-destructive. I interpreted that she was torturing herself with her own self-hate and was invested in hurting herself more than healing herself; therefore, I could not do anything to change that fact if she was not willing to look at it more closely with me. After I was no longer trying to convince her to stay, she relinquished the need to resist. The more I put responsibility onto her to choose, the more she began seeing the value of therapy. My previous interpretations were useless by virtue of the fact that they were not coming from her; insight had to be on her terms, derived from her process of confronting her own disillusionments. She came to realize that the minute she introduced sexuality into the therapeutic context, it destroyed her ability to be open and real about the type of interpersonal involvement she truly craved. As in her past with previous lovers, sex was a poor substitute for the emotional intimacy she longed for, and since I was not responsive to her seductions, she assumed I was not interested in developing anything beyond what she felt she could offer.

Her frustration and desire to leave was partially motivated by her resistance to accept the limits of her own wish fulfillment. What she wanted she could not have, and this simply hurt too much for her to continue, and thus to continue to subject herself to her own desire. Her primordial defense was to reject me as I had rejected her. But this relapsed back into the circularity of her own self-condemnation and conviction that she did not deserve to be loved. And hence she was able to acknowledge the seed of her transference associations rooted in her original failed attachments. It was here that she came to her own revelations that she was going to have to mourn the loss of the fulfillment of a wish—the wish to be loved by her parents.

When patients want to flee from treatment, it is often because they cannot face up to their own inner reality. I often ask patients to take a risk and muster up the courage to face their own process even though we may have no clue where it may possibly lead us. Having faith in the process is no easy task because we can never predict with any accuracy how it will turn out; it is only when we look back to see where we came from that we begin to see the teleological progression of change. The therapeutic process is a dialectical, self-articulating complex totality that can only be realized in each of its contextual moments. When bogged down by impasse, at times all we can do is let the process unfold.

AMELIORATING SUICIDALITY

We often hear of the jilted lover who takes his own life. While I was growing up in a small farm community in the Midwest, a high school boy killed himself on Halloween night in front of his girlfriend after she told him she wanted to break off their relationship. Threatening to kill himself if she did not reconsider, he drove to a nearby cemetery, parked himself in front of a tree, removed some jumper cables from the back, jumped onto the hood of his truck, fastened the cables around his neck and a branch of the tree, and then hung himself while she sat screaming in the passenger seat. While suicidal motivation is highly complex and overdetermined, self-destructive rage may be the overarching factor. Perhaps this boy's suicide was partly intended as a means to hurt and avenge his wounded ego, to punish her for her cruelty and rejection, or perhaps it was simply in response to the emotional devastation of loss; in any case, the will toward death proved to be too powerful. I always wondered if this boy was mentally ill, or if the loss of attachment was just too painful to bear.

I once assessed a man admitted to the hospital for drug-induced psychosis; a month later he hung himself. In an outpatient clinic, I was the supervisor of a second-year psychology graduate student who was as green as grass. During the first week of her first practicum placement, her very first patient committed suicide the week after their initial consultation. She was devastated. In both of these cases, there was no reasonable, conceivable way of knowing this would happen.

A clinician's worst nightmare is when a patient commits suicide. In fact, some therapists are so fearful of taking on the responsibility of a suicidal patient that they prefer to send such patients elsewhere. Crisis-intervention approaches prefer to focus on immediate stabilization and are thus inclined to ship off the chronically suicidal patient to long-term care. Even specialists in mood disorders are likely to screen their outpatient clientele carefully, and those working with severe character pathology such as borderline personality disorders are timid about these patients' characteristic proclivity toward self-harm. Take, for example, Marsha Linehan (1993), who refuses to work with patients unless they *promise* not to attempt suicide while in treatment. It is not so uncommon for seasoned professionals—let alone the neophyte—to jump the gun and immediately admit a patient to the hospital when suicidal tendencies are spoken of directly in therapy. Unease, trepidation—even paranoia—seem to be universal anxieties we all harbor toward suicidality.

Suicidal vulnerability and attachment deficits go hand in hand. When attachment disordered patients do not have interpersonal support, structural integrity, ego resources, holding introjects, capacities for evocative memory or self-soothing, or a fund of positive experiences at their disposal to retrieve during times of crisis, they can become particularly vulnerable to impulsive suicidal acting out. Not only are depressives and psychotics at risk for suicide, but so are many forms of personality disorders, as well as alcoholics and addicts, due to the strong self-destructive elements that accompany their character structures.

Addressing suicidal potential in a patient is never an easy topic, but it is one that is nonetheless straightforward. There is perhaps nothing worse than a clinician who appears uncomfortable or awkward in addressing this question, for his discomfort communicates to the patient that the therapist is just as frightened as he is. Statements such as, "I know this may sound odd but . . . you haven't been thinking about . . . I mean, you haven't had any thoughts of, you know, hurting yourself or anything like that, have you?" will only kill the discussion and shut down the whole risk assessment. The patient is likely to minimize or deny it because he knows the therapist is scared as hell and can't be trusted. Similarly, do not ask, "How do you plan to do it?"—which joins with the suicide plan that the patient may not have developed thus far. But one might ask, "Have you gone so far in your desperation that you have thought about what you might do?" (Blanck and Blanck 1974, 266). This way you avoid aligning with the plan, which further enables you to assess the patient's state of mind. I simply prefer the direct approach: "Have you thought about killing yourself?" If so, then insist that the patient spell out his thoughts and impulses in as much concrete detail as possible. Bellak and Faithorn (1981) describe that "the explicit statement of all suicidal notions may have a cathartic effect and facilitate reality testing by both the patient and the therapist" (172). This also shows that you are not squeamish about discussing the reality of the patient's inner world and thus can potentially be a container for the tempestuousness and fracturing of the psyche that accompanies this fragile state of mind.

I was once given a referral for a patient who called me stating that he was not coping well at work, and that he was upset over a relationship that he had recently terminated. He was particularly vague on the phone, sounded emotionally removed, and seemed somewhat ambivalent in the first place. We set an appointment for the following day, yet he failed to show. I simply thought he had changed his mind due to his ambivalence until I received a call two days later from a psychiatric nurse at a nearby hospital stating that the patient had taken an overdose on the same day he was scheduled to see me. I spoke with the patient and we rescheduled an appointment for the day of his discharge from the hospital.

Clive was a stockbroker in his early thirties. When we first met, he was clearly mentally confused, tangential in his thoughts and associations, unable to articulate his inner experience with coherence or congruency, panicky, and deeply ashamed of his suicide attempt. He explained how he was increasingly unable to concentrate or complete his responsibilities at work because he was too distraught over his former girlfriend. At first he spoke of her and their relationship in very ambiguous terms, only stating that he was very uncomfortable and overly self-conscious being with her, which was so disconcerting that he had to end the union. During the initial meeting he was in a frenzied state because he felt so lost about his life. One overarching theme was his obsessional preoccupation and rumination that he was not happy in comparison to others, and if only he could find certain answers to his confusion, he would be "back to normal." As he put it, "Why can't I just be like others? I see people laughing at their jobs. Why can't I just be like them? It's like my whole life has just stopped. I just want to be happy. I have to be happy now." Litman (1970) alerts us to four ominous signs of suicidal potential: (1) an impatient, agitated expectation that something must be done immediately; (2) a feasible, detailed, lethal suicide plan; (3) narcissistic pride, suspicion, and hyperindependence; and (4) tendencies toward isolation and withdrawal, living alone, or living with someone emotionally removed or estranged. Clive fit these criteria to a T, but what was overwhelming present was the urgency that he had to feel better about his entire life right then and there—at that very moment.

If suicidal trends are severe, patients should optimally be seen daily until the acute crisis is stabilized. The outlook is favorable if they feel more relieved after the initial interview, with decreased agitation and a slight lift in mood, and quickly form a dependent attachment to the therapist (Litman 1970). At the end of our first session, Clive reportedly felt calmer and stated how comfortable he felt with me. We made an appointment for two days after our initial meeting, but he called the next day feeling suicidal. We did some grounding techniques over the phone and he came to see me later that afternoon.

When Clive arrived, he was visibly shaking and paranoid, stating that he was not capable of controlling his impulses, which felt alien yet compulsory to him. I was concerned that his suicidality had by now acquired an autonomous organization in his ego that was dissociated from the rest of his self and experienced as ego-syntonic. Under these circumstances, the only way to put a floor under a patient is to have him talk about what is most important to him at that time (Semrad 1980). Rather than focus directly on the suicidality or, even worse, prematurely conclude that he needed to be hospitalized, I insisted that he tell me exactly what he was experiencing in that moment without holding anything back. He began to disclose that he found himself unable to stop thinking about Ginger, his former girlfriend, and that the constant thought of her was bringing on the urge to kill himself. He was obsessed with rehashing various aspects of their relationship, her facial expressions, their conversations—her specific disclosures of past sexual exploits with other men. He recalled how over the past four months, since he had begun dating her, he had become more preoccupied and self-conscious about his desirability, which made him question his confidence, capabilities, and self-esteem. Unable to concentrate or complete his work, he found himself fantasizing about her all day, wondering what she was wearing, how she was acting when he was not around, who she was talking to, and so forth—to the point that his whole reality as he knew it became encased in impending dread. He could not eat or sleep or carry on with the daily activities he had once enjoyed, such as going to the gym or visiting his friends, because he was constantly worrying about Ginger and her perception of him.

Clive confessed that there was something wrong from the very start with this woman, but he just couldn't seem to let go; she had an animal magnetism and he was mesmerized. They were sexual with one another within hours of meeting at a bar, and their entire relationship from then on was focused around sex. Despite the pleasure of sexual passion, he reported a fundamental discomfort in the way she made him feel: there was no emotional warmth or intimacy—just sex. He started having intrusive and disturbing fantasies at work, the gym, and wherever he went—that every man must lust after her sexually—to the point that he almost instigated fights with strangers who he perceived were eyeing his girl. Ginger had such a toxic influence on his psychic cohesion that he eventually had to end the relationship because he simply wasn't functioning. As Clive put it, "It was like I was constantly walking on eggshells. I had to watch every little thing I thought or said: I couldn't be me." She did not take his rejection lightly and began to harass him at home and at work, threatening to show up and make a scene if he did not continue to see her. In the end, she had convinced him that he was "really fucked up in the head." He rapidly decompensated after the breakup, and this is when his suicidal fantasies and impulses started to take command over his psychic reality.

During this session I was more concerned with establishing a climate of understanding, stability, and safety rather than pursuing the etiology and psychodynamics of his suicidality. Bellak and Faithorn (1981) tell us that "one must demonstrate clearly to the patient a continuity between the immediate *panic*, the *precipitating factors*, and *life history*. This gives the patient at least some feeling of control over what seems frighteningly ego-alien" (90). Clive was somewhat mollified and reassured that his panic and urgency was only a temporary reaction to unformulated and unarticulated conflictual inner experiences that we would later figure out more fully together, but for the time being he needed to focus his recovery. He had agreed to take a leave of absence from work, which relieved some of the immediate pressures he was shouldering. Given that he had never reported feeling suicidal before, nor had he ever had a relationship like this one that made him feel so disjointed and out of control, he was comforted by the conviction that he would eventually reconstitute and be able to put this behind him.

Later that evening when I was sleeping, I was awakened by a dream (if not a nightmare) that I was suicidal, that my mind was fracturing, that my life and all I knew was being compromised by the sensation that I was no longer in control of my own thoughts or impulses. Relieved to wake but emotionally shaken, I immediately felt discombobulated. What did I identify with in my patient? Did I become a container for his self-destruction; was this merely my assimilation of his projective identifications? Or was there a communicative aspect—a command hallucination—that resonated within my own dark interior? What archaic piece from my past was roused from its somnolent slumber; what uncanny death wish did this excavate in me? I instantly feared for Clive and felt the need to check my phone messages. When I went downstairs to my office, I saw the red light flashing on the answering machine and knew it was him. I played back the message, only to hear his languid voice in desperation and disquieted panic. I called him, but he did not answer, so I left a phone message on his machine explaining how worried I was about him and that I wanted him to give me a call immediately. Although I was on the verge of panicking myself, I decided to wait rather than jump the gun and run the risk of making a clinical blunder.

When he called the next day, he was acutely suicidal. He told me he had been sitting in his bathtub for an hour and a half with a razor to his wrist. I insisted that he come to my office, but he preferred to talk on the phone instead. "Suicidal patients suffer from 'tunnel vision' and only see one particular solution. It is therefore important to show them that there are other options" (Bellak and Faithorn 1981, 173). Clive told me that he did not see a way out of this, nor could he envisage a future: his entire universe was colored by lack, chaos, and upheaval. In moments like this, we are reminded that if the therapist honestly reports feelings of helplessness in himself and entertains thoughts of breaking off communication with the patient, then an emergency situation has developed and it is time for some sort of active intervention (Litman and Farberow 1970). How do you attempt to convince a person in this state of panic, dissociation, and irrationality that his solution is based on impulsive, desperate actions rather than more competent ones? How do you appeal to the autonomous portion of the ego that still has the capacity for rational engagement? How do you instill hope? This was the moment of crisis: Do I insist he come to my office? Do I go to his house? Do I call the police? Do I have him hospitalized? "We are going to get through this together," I said. "Now talk to me."

I got him grounded, he calmed down, we made a contingency plan, and he reconstituted and was more hopeful. "The prognosis is most favorable if the patient, although depressed and contemplating suicide, thinks of those who would suffer from his deed" (Blanck and Blanck 1974, 266). This mobilizes attachment and empathic motivations that cling to the value of life. I asked him to think of his family and the impact his actions would have on them. He contracted for safety, promised to go to his mother's house or the hospital if he felt unable to fight his impulses, and told me he would take a sedative prescribed by the psychiatrist to help him sleep.

The next day, he was better but disheveled. He told me that the one thing that gave him hope was my comment, "The feelings are only temporary; they will pass." We reinforced our contingency plan: he was going to seek out support from his family, go to dinner with a friend, make himself do some exercise, and spend the night with his mother rather than be alone.

The intensity of Clive's suicidality began to abate, and we were able to look more closely at the insidious dynamics fueling his impulsivity and internal turmoil. Kernberg (1984) tells us that every suicide attempt or completion implies the mobilization of intense aggression not only in the patient, but within the interpersonal field, and this is why so many suicides are intersubjectively informed. Malan (1979) further urges us to consider suicidality "as a fusion of intense destructive anger expressed self-destructively on the one hand, and love, protectiveness, concern and guilt on the other—the patient would rather kill himself than harm the other person—and it is usually the anger that needs to be brought into the open" (204). Intuiting that Clive was not telling me the whole story, I urged him to tell me what he had *really* been bothered by but could not seem to tell me directly. With intense discomfort and shame, Clive confessed that what had really disturbed him were Ginger's unsolicited and provocative sexual disclosures about her past. Over the course of their brief relationship, she had managed not to spare him a single detail about her sexual appetites. She admitted to "fucking hundreds of men," including enjoying "anal sex," and frequently cruised for men "simply to fuck" and disregard after she had her fill. Clive was particularly troubled by his observation of semen-stained sheets on her bed that she had not even bothered to wash since her previous lover; but what was even more unsettling to him was her flamboyant need to explain how the stain was from a "big black buck" she picked up at a bar. Clive's ego was assailed: he was unable to shelter himself from the pain of his own feelings of inadequacy. This threatened his integrity as a man, based on the simple economy that his "dick" was the measure of his self-worth. To make matters worse, he was a premature ejaculator, which was a source of grave embarrassment and feelings of sexual ineptitude. At one point, in a state of dissatisfaction with his performance, Ginger referred to him as "Quickdraw McGraw," thus rendering him humiliated and vilified.

Clive felt that something was wrong with him because he could not shake off the deep humiliation and significance of her disclosures. He wanted truth and honesty, but he didn't want to know such brute facticity: "That's reality, Clive, you're just goin' to have to deal with it," she told him. Clive was drowning in his fundamental ambivalence between loving this woman—this "slut"—and hating her for how she made him feel so impotent and ineffectual. He was turning his aggression on himself, protecting her from his wrath and narcissistic rage that imperiled his psyche. He started to feel guilty for judging her so negatively, and feelings of betrayal were lacerating him with the need for self-punishment. At the same time, he could not admit to himself that he hated her for making him feel so inadequate and flawed. But the injury to his ego was a nefarious, festering wound that unearthed primordial deprivations and pain associated with his relationships with his primary attachment figures.

He recalled that as a boy he was very clingy and dependent on his mother and experienced prolonged separation anxiety well into his elementary school years, and he still relied on her emotionally as his primary source of support and comfort. His father, on the other hand, was a volatile and physically abusive man who used to beat him with a belt and shame him indiscriminately. As a result, Clive became a childhood bully, was always getting into trouble, and picked on and beat up other kids as a way of expressing and reenacting his own traumas with his father. When he was older, Clive attempted to channel his aggression in more sublimated ways through sports, and he excelled in hockey. But his volatile temper and bad sportsmanship led to multiple fights on the rink, to the point that his mother was too embarrassed to attend his games, which hurt him deeply. His folks eventually divorced when Clive was a teenager because of his father's multiple affairs, yet his father blamed Clive for the breakup due to his bad behavior and for being a "mommy's boy." Ginger was a trigger for excavating deep feelings of deprivation and inadequacy related to his childhood past that led him to question his lovability. Unconsciously identifying with his father's rage and aggressivity, as well as his appetite for sexual pleasure, he made Ginger into the sluts his father was "screwing," which clashed with his desire to have a loving, nurturing woman like his mother. What intensified this identification was the fact that his father had become a depressive drunk since the divorce and had been hospitalized on two occasions for suicide attempts.

Clive came to recognize many anaclitic depressive features within himself. He described how, when he was in the hospital, a nurse had touched his face when he was sobbing, attempting to comfort him. He recounted this event as a painful ecstasy: "It felt so good," yet it *cut*. He further described a similar sensation when his mother held him in her arms, stroking his hair, just shortly after he had left the hospital, while he was staying with her and her new husband. There was a regressive yearning in Clive to return to a quiescent state of maternal blissfulness, and his suicidality was partially informed by these infantile longings that were not fulfilled with Ginger. Sex with her was not the warmth and love he truly craved, but she became a toxic introject he could not purge.

Over the weeks of his recovery, Clive's ego boundaries strengthened and he went back to work without further crisis. He began to understand more fully how he had lost his sense of self in this woman's worldview of eroticism = love, and he could see her pathology for what it was. He began to focus on seeking out substance and intimacy in a woman rather than appearance and beauty, vowing not to repeat the same pattern, and gradually started dating again. He soon met a woman and, cautiously, over time, they fell in love. During the termination of our work together, he reported feeling the happiest he had ever been in his life. The blackness that had engulfed him just a few months before was now a distant world, while his future with his new partner was bright and full of promise. He thanked me for my help, while I in turn thanked him for his gift of recognition, and the therapy ended with a mutual hug.

CONTAINING PSYCHOTIC ANXIETIES

When I was twenty-two years old, I was a first-year master's practicum student at an inpatient psychiatric facility in a rural state mental hospital in the Midwest. I remember vividly the first time I set eyes on a schizophrenic patient because it was so shocking to me at the time. I was being escorted through a locked-down unit of the acute psychiatric wing by a petite female social worker who couldn't have been more than five feet tall. I recall thinking about the sharp contrast between our respective heights and sizes, and how comical we must have appeared to others as we strolled through the corridors together. When we came upon the locked unit, my colleague reached for her keys and unlocked the door. As we walked in, much to my surprise, there was a dirty-haired old man wearing tinted thick glasses strapped into a wheelchair with a bar across his wrists preventing him from moving his arms. He was stationed squarely in the middle of the hall facing the direction of the door, greeting people as they entered. When we laid eyes on each other, he immediately said in a dark voice, "Hey baby, I'm master of the universe. Are you Catholic?" Being young and naive, without a stitch of clinical experience, I immediately started laughing. Then he started laughing hysterically. Not accustomed to seeing such bizarre behavior in vivo, I was overcome with the anxiety of the moment and handled it the only way I knew how.

A few years later, during my doctoral studies, I was completing a year-long clinical placement at Elgin State Mental Health Center, at that time the largest state psychiatric facility in Illinois. With more than 750 beds, this was a massive psychiatric compound with dozens of buildings designated for the chronically mentally ill. At this point, research in psychotropic medication was still in its infancy, and many patients were simply warehoused because psychopharmacology proved to be of little use.

Patients had to be locked away, some in restraints, while others were allowed to roam the halls with minimal supervision, or else they were gathered in one large common area observed through a glass wall. Patients were largely unmedicated and agitated; they paced around talking to themselves, some urinating in the corner, while others screamed uninhibitedly at imaginary strangers. Men and women were segregated and not allowed to intermingle. This facility literally made the movie *One Flew over the Cuckoo's Nest* look like child's play in comparison to the *real* reality of institutional life.

I was walking into a locked holding area for chronic female schizophrenics, again escorted by a woman. The minute I stepped into the unit, I was instantly surrounded by a swarm of patients—there must have been thirty of them. They were all conversing, saying various things, mostly smiling and reaching out to touch me with mild intrusion. Then the noise mushroomed. Suddenly, a woman in front of me lifted up her skirt, exposing her vagina, and the herd began to roar with laughter. I felt as if I was about to be devoured by a crazed clan of starving witches. But this time, instead of laughing out of anxiety or, even worse, becoming self-protectively physical in response to being groped, I merely smiled pleasantly, looking into their eyes with recognition. As they continued to fondle me, I slowly walked through the circle, nonviolently, unfazed by their screeching, my colleague behind me the whole way, until we reached our destination and let ourselves out of the unit.

These were two early defining moments in my career as a clinical psychologist. One has to get one's feet wet in any profession one chooses to pursue, and I wanted to know what it was like to work with those who suffered from the most recalcitrant forms of mental illness. As a result, I worked in psychiatric hospitals for years. My rationale was straightforwardly yet naively simple: if I were able to work with the most difficult abnormal populations, then I could conceivably handle any form of psychopathology. I'm still working on it.

How do you contain psychotic anxieties in another? How do you defuse them, make them more benign, hold them for the patient in a less baleful way, transform them, and then give them back in a revamped form that is more manageable and less horrific? This is what Bion means when he speaks about the container–contained relationship, or Winnicott when he speaks of the holding environment. This takes a certain clinical attitude or, perhaps more precisely, a clinical sensibility for working with those who cannot successfully modulate their own disruptive fears and inner pain. In working with psychotics, one has to learn to cultivate a clinical sensibility that insulates you from contagion of the emotional immediacy and threat of disintegration that the psychotic wishes to evacuate and place into the interior constitution of the therapist. A psychotic process can have a very debilitating effect on the therapist by virtue of osmoses: there is a semipermeable fluidity between psychic realities, and at times it becomes very easy to lose one's ego boundaries within the diffusion of projective identificatory transmissions. Recall that the Greek terms *psyche* and *noesis* signify that which is beyond intelligible mind or rationality. Psychosis is the experiential fracturing of intensities: all shields are yielded to unbounded flux and disarray that require bounded containment in order for the patient to reconstitute and find some footing to stand upon. Simultaneously, the therapist must find some space for sanctuary, for retreat from the bombardment of chaos and aggressivity that saturates the psychotic mind, a space that insulates the self from the unconscious process of absorption that inevitably transpires when one is working with this clinical population. And when it creeps in, that foreign body, that uncanny presence of persecution hovering over you like a primal darkness, paranoia sets in, rendering you *paranoos*, thus besides yourself, beyond mind (*nous, νόο*ς), hence beyond intelligible thought, simply—madness.

I was once leading a biweekly inpatient therapy group at a private psychiatric hospital in Chicago. On my left was a man who had scalded his testicles in boiling water because God told him to, while on my right was a new schizophrenic patient on the unit whom I knew nothing about. He looked frighteningly scary with dark penetrating eyes, but I felt a calm between us. He sat in silence the entire session until the very end. Just as I was ending the group for the day, he leaned over to me and said in a deep sinister voice, "Hey, check this out." A cold freeze crept up the back of my neck. I noticed that some of the patients were also taken aback by the ominous tone of his voice, which sounded like something out of a horror flick. At that moment he handed me a piece of paper with writing on it. I asked him if these were his writings and he nodded. At a brief glance, I could see that they were mainly statements with some encrypted codes. I asked him if I might keep it temporarily and said that I would return it to him later. He nodded again, so I wrapped up the group and took the paper with me. I photocopied the page and have reproduced it as figure 6.1.

What are most discernable are the grandiose delusional fantasies of importance, heroism, and omnipotence. There are numbers that appear before each proposition, which appear arbitrarily arranged, but they probably have some encrypted significance. What is most interesting, however, is that the grandiose delusions follow from an aggressive premise, and that death and destruction are thematically suffused throughout his fantasized preoccupations:

- 7.2 Billion worth of war tools exploded
- stopped a music crowd from rioting
- stopped a tornado from destroying windows
- went to Canada for the mayor to find a proton

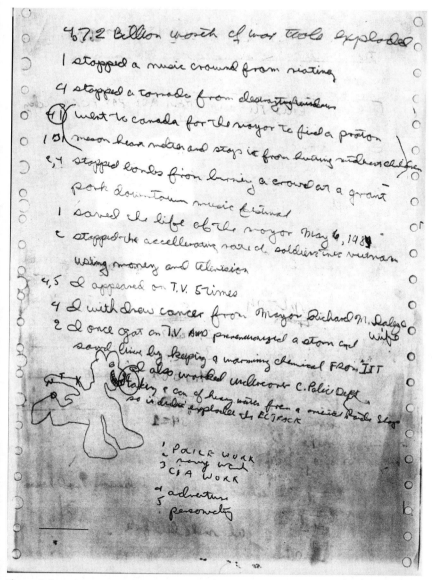

Figure 6.1.

- ... heart matter and stay in from hurting midwest children
- stopped bombs from blowing a crowd at grant park downtown music festival
- saved the life of the mayor May 6, 1984
- stopped the accelerating rate of soldiers into Vietnam using money and television

- I appeared on T.V. 5 times
- I withdrew cancer from Major Richard M. Daley's wife
- I once got on T.V. and premonized a storm and saved lives by keeping a warming chemical from IIT
- I also worked undercover C. Police Dept. taking a can of heavy water from a . . . so it didn't explode in ECJRACK

1. Police Work
2. saving work
3. CIA work
4. adventures
5. personality

I do not claim to know the internal significance of these thought fragments, but what is significant is that he wanted to share his inner experience with me—his *jouissance*—the ecstasy of pain. I felt he was reaching out to me despite his internal tempest of destruction and paranoia, showing some initiative—some advance—toward attachment. At this time in history, the Gulf War in Iraq was under way, and, as it is today, America was on edge. Images of Scud missiles and warfare were daily news occurrences on television. But these bombs were in his head, exploding, disrupting order, deracinating, spreading panic and mass havoc, spilling onto the page. He tried to confine them, to modulate and transform them, and then undo the devastation through his heroism: Did he sufficiently corral death? Was he saved? Did he save himself? Writing allows for expression, for outpouring, for giving tangible life to abstraction; but it is also a container, a distancing (if not alienation) from inner space through exteriorization, even if it is only a temporary repose. This page of cogitations, as esoteric and dismembered as they appear, is projected containment, a disordered attempt at order. The overdetermined significance of writing as both container and contained is evident.

I later met with this patient and thanked him for sharing his thoughts with me. I asked if he would like to explain what they meant, but he just sat there in silence. "I see from this picture that you like to draw," I said, pointing to the animal in the corner of the paper. The mouth and size of the front legs of the creature spoke volumes about his inner rage, the lacerating inner voice he could not speak but only show. "Would you draw something for me?" He nodded yes, so I handed him a piece of paper and a pencil. "Draw me a picture of yourself." This is what he drew (see figure 6.2).

Lacan (1955–1956c) tells us of the Evil Other who sends the psychotic on a mission. This patient was bombarded with messages, thought bombings, what we call delusions. His mind was excised, detached from his body—his own sensuous impulses—which was merely an amorphous, appendageless mass resembling an excised tooth, itself an instrument for

Figure 6.2.

devouring flesh. Were these antennae receiving messages from the Evil Other, from his own death fears/wishes—passively absorbed, eyes wide open—such divine, illuminated revelation, aborted on paper? We will never know. How can the psychotic form an attachment to the other when the other is a perceived source of danger and death? I began experimenting with projective drawings in assessing clinical populations many years ago; they tell a personal narrative without speaking. I once asked a schizophrenic man to draw me a picture of his mother's face. This was his production (see figure 6.3):

This is what introjection looks like: ghastly, menacing, enraged, domineering, encroaching—apocalyptic. This hideous reconstruction is his primary attachment figure, this orally devouring, all-engulfing, sadistic attack on linking, on psychic cohesion, seeing through you with cold steel hate and vacuity, a real monster—dear ol' Mom. Profile drawings of faces often convey paranoia, uneasiness, and evasiveness. It becomes easy to see why psychotics have malignant attachments, if they have any at all. How can you feel love from this? How can you cuddle up to such horror? "Now draw me a picture of yourself," I requested (see figure 6.4).

How exposed, how feeble this poor man was, with no eyes to see and no feet to stand. When there is no capacity for action, the only thing mobilized is dread and annihilation panic. With his large expansive head full of apprehension and deformity, his mouth wide open in oral passivity yet unable to communicate, on top of this massive square-shaped heap of unsatisfied yearnings, arms stretched out for interpersonal connection where there are only feelings of inadequacy and deprivation, these blemished and damaged limbs riddled with a crippling lack of autonomy—here is the self-portrait of a horrifically disorganized personality. I too would feel frantic, helpless, unbalanced, searching for ground, groping for something but resigned to nothing.

When one is working with psychotics, one of the best strategies to assume is simply to be nonthreatening, to sit in still peacefulness, open and receptive to whatever the moment brings forth, without superimposing an agenda on the patient or bombarding him with one question after another; but rather to convey empathy through a nonverbal presence of concern and comfort and acknowledgment that he is suffering but unable to express his suffering as such. "Is there something you wish to tell me?" In their silence, their solitude, we may ponder, "Is there a way I can reach you? You can connect to me; I am not like the others."

DE-ESCALATING POTENTIAL VIOLENCE

With psychosis and paranoia come the potential for violence. While this is more an exception rather than the rule, paranoiac processes distort reality

Figure 6.3.

testing and can lead to the fantasized construction of perceived threats to the self that do not genuinely exist. This is particularly intensified when a patient is in an acute psychotic state, under the influence of persecutory delusions, and perceives that his environment is encroaching, hostile, and/or tyrannizing. A simple economy of "attack before being attacked"

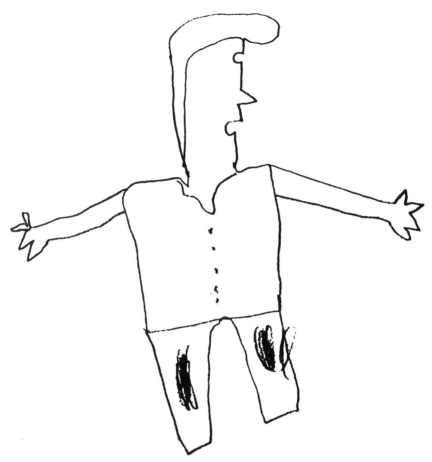

Figure 6.4.

is formulated in his head, motivated by deep destructive and self-preservative elements the patient cannot contain in himself, which are therefore evacuated into his surround, only to hover over the patient, who is filled with the pernicious dread of them being reincorporated back into his psychic structure as a potential death of the self. Violence also occurs when the ego is eclipsed with rage that mushrooms into a psychotic colorization of perceptual processes, where the bad self is disavowed, projected onto the other, and taken as a nemesis that can harm the vulnerable split-off portion of the ego that needs to be protected. "Strike before being struck": a simple yet effective economy for immediate survival.

For clinicians working in inpatient psychiatry, unexpected violence and the need for physical restraint of patients are frequent occurrences. Front-line staff, such as psychiatric nurses, typically weather the brunt of such

outbursts, and it is not uncommon for mental health technicians and workers to get hit or injured during physical take-downs that are deemed necessary in the moment to secure safety and order on the unit. Fortunately, I
have never been assaulted, although I have encountered a few occasions
where the threat of violence was imminent. I have found that my large
presence and soft voice serve as a bridle, constraint, or container for psychotic anxieties; there is a holding and soothing function to my physical
size, which signals and allows others to keep their own aggression in check
while experiencing safety in the moment, and my gentle voice (as I am
told) alerts the patient that I am affable and nonthreatening rather than
dangerous. At times of interpersonal conflict on the unit, all I had to do
was walk in the room and people would calm right down. I realize that
these personal characteristics are traits that cannot be easily emulated by
others by virtue of my personality and body type, but I think they further
reflect the clinical sensibility I was attempting to convey earlier. Deep
down, patients who are out of control, or on the verge of acting out aggression, are actually hoping that someone will help them harness their
impulsivity, gain some semblance of order over their inner rupture, and
contain what they cannot seem to confine or subdue through their efforts
alone. Before enactments of aggression, patients typically give many warning signs and opportunities for intervention, either verbally or nonver-
bally. There is also a pleading quality to these communications, especially
during precipitating moments just prior to affective escalation, before desperation gives way to acting out. These pleas and communications are attempts at reaching out for connection, for some attachment to a calming-
soothing presence that the mental health professional personifies.

But how about when the threat of violence emerges in the session? In
my circumscribed experience—and this is certainly not meant to be a
blanket generalization—women have tendencies to panic more than men
in these situations, to read into danger that is not there, only to frustrate
and exacerbate the situation, which can then make it potentially unsafe.
While this observation is merely subjective, and contingent on the clinician's level of professional training and skill acquisition, I have seen this
discrepancy more often than not, both clinically and in academic instruction and supervision. In formal graduate training, we are taught to be
afraid about unpredictability and the potential for patient violence, to
keep our backs to the door in the event that we need to make a fast escape,
and not to see patients in the office building alone, especially after hours,
to the degree that some female clinicians even have panic buttons to press
just in case there is an assault. Of course, some institutional settings require us to be on guard and take necessary precautions, but this attitude
toward safety can easily be overblown to the point of unwarranted fear-
fulness. In my experience as a clinical supervisor training graduate-level
practicum students and doctoral-level interns, women are the first to read

danger into their work with men. From the male side of things, I am cautioned by male colleagues to document everything very carefully because I will never know when a complaint to my college is coming, or when I may be accused of sexually assaulting a patient in my office. Having a home office is even more risky. There are strong deterrents to having an isolated office, let alone one in the home, and clinicians who decide to go this route often curtail their treatment population to avoid "at-risk" patients, such as antisocial individuals and forensic clientele. And those who have home offices don't typically receive new patients in the evening, or they restrict their practice to women. These are real issues and concerns, and I am not attempting to make light of them here, for even the most conscientious practitioner is not free from warranted paranoiac proclivities. Yet the reality of private practice is that one should expect to get a complaint at some time in one's career, which is an occupational hazard of our profession, and all we can do is continue to uphold an optimal standard of practice. I am especially at risk since I treat so many character disorders and conduct routine assessments in my home office. But as with any venture into unpredictability, risks should be calculated and based on solid rationales as well as personal levels of comfort.

There is always a certain degree of personal awkwardness, intimidation, and discomfort that comes with being a therapist. The therapeutic encounter is very intimate and nerve-racking, and patients and analysts alike must navigate through such discomfort together. If the clinician is uncomfortable in his own skin, then the therapy is compromised. Patients readily pick up on your own fears; trepidations; anxieties; ambivalence about personal disclosure or reticence in treating them; hesitations; the strictness or permeability of the treatment frame; and the need to exert power and control, to set limits around what is permissible, such as what are appropriate and inappropriate expressions of emotion. Anger—let alone rage—directed at the therapist is usually a big no-no. I have heard of therapists who as a general rule abruptly terminate the session if and when patients display their anger by raising their voice, even if it is not directed at them. This attitude is not only palpably rigid and paranoid, but it appears grossly incompetent. How are therapists capable of helping patients if they themselves are unable to handle raw emotions? The real relationship is borne out of negotiation, spontaneity, and flexibility, and this means allowing emotional processes viable outlets for expression. This may mean that unhealthy displays of affect have to occur before more temperate and modulated ones can transpire. This is especially the case when one is working with personality disorders who use emotionality as a vehicle for pathological expression.

I was once coleading a weekly therapy group with a female psychologist for inner-city black youths who lived in a group home. As part of the conditions of living in the home, group therapy was a mandatory requirement; however, this created much resistance and animosity for the teenagers, and they were not shy in voicing their disdain and dissent. They had all been largely abandoned by their parents or seized by child-welfare agencies because their guardians or caregivers were deemed unfit. Most of the boys had been involved in crime, drugs, and gang affiliations and were subjected to many developmental traumas and abuse. For all practical purposes, they were largely psychopathic and used threats and intimidation to get their way. My coleader was virtually terrified to be alone in the room with these boys due to their vulgar communications and unpredictability, and on one occasion we had to cancel the group because I was unable to make my appointment that week.

One boy was the identified leader of the pack, and the rest of them were discreetly afraid of him. For example, if a member of the group attempted to participate in a genuine manner, all the leader would have to do was look at the boy contemptuously, and the discussion would soon be dead, or else it would slip into crude expletives aimed at women or devaluations directly aimed toward us. The typical group dynamic went something like this: they would arrive late, sit down in protest, begin to goof off, and then follow the leader's lead in derisive attacks on me and my coleader, only to suck up to him with their affirmative jokes and laughing. Running this group was always a source of anxiety and confrontation, for the uncertainty of control and safety was a lingering question on the brink of my consciousness. During a particular group exchange, the boys were making sexually uncouth and misogynistic comments about women, to the chagrin of my female colleague. Because most of the boys were merely going along with their identified leader's provocations, I took this opportunity to point out that they didn't seem to have minds of their own because they were "too afraid to go against the top dog." At this point the leader said that I was going to have to pay for my remark, and he continued to threaten that if I didn't give him a dollar, something might happen to me. In the tense hush that ensued, I replied, "What I think you really want from me is my respect, but threats can never buy respect. You can make people afraid of you, but that's not the same. Respect is never automatic; it's always earned." This intervention defused the confrontation, and we ended the group normally without incident. It could have gone in a more insidious direction, but fortunately this confronting yet validating interpretation allowed the boy some distance from his need to demonstrate dominance while letting him maintain his pride.

On another occasion, I was seeing a patient in weekly therapy who had earned his Ph.D. in biochemistry from Harvard. During his graduate school training, he would spend large portions of his day conducting experiments in the lab. Over the course of his graduate program he became addicted to inhaling chemicals, which he stole on a regular basis. After his graduation, his addiction became uncontrollable and he was unable to work or function. The continued use of inhalants further precipitated a severe psychotic break that was surmised by many mental health professionals at the clinic to be tantamount to a reactive schizophrenia. He moved back home with his parents, who monitored his condition while he was allowed to attend a day treatment program where I was employed. One afternoon, during our scheduled appointment time, the patient came to session after apparently getting high on glue. He sat in his seat and appeared visibly rankled, and then without provocation he began to yell at me in a high, whiny voice that sounded like a small child's cry during a temper tantrum. "You are a child!" he shouted uninhibitedly. "You are a child and need to be punished! You're not my father!" I sat still for a while and then said, "Why are you mad at me?" "Be quiet. Don't talk back!" he insisted. Because he was so psychotically enraged and unpredictable, I uncrossed my legs and shifted my seat to get into a more protective position just in case he was going to charge. "I don't understand why you're yelling at me, but you're scaring me and I don't feel safe." At that moment he stood up and began to rush toward me, but I scooted my chair back out of the way. He stopped and then started to pace, shouting, "Shut up! Shut up! You're not my father!" Remaining in my seat, I said, "Perhaps it would be better if you left and call me later when you've calmed down so we can talk." In a huff, swearing the whole way out, he left my office without incident. By this time, staff were waiting in the hall, and we had him hospitalized.

When destructive rage is mobilized in a patient, the therapist becomes the immediate transferential target for displacing such rage. Rage is often a defensive manifestation in response to perceived attacks on the self that have a network of unconscious associations and meanings that imperil psychic integrity. For example, it can be in response to narcissistic injury, abandonment depression, and/or paranoid feelings of persecution, just to name a few, that become temporarily dissociated from the ego. When this happens in the session, containment and reparation need to be immediately established so the self-reflective ego can regain its grip on reality testing.

Kurt was a twenty-one-year-old white male who had been admitted to the inpatient psychiatric unit of a general hospital when I first started to see him in therapy. From a diagnostic standpoint, Kurt would be considered by most clinicians to be a psychopath, but he was organized on the borderline level of structural development. He was muscular, of average height and weight, had hoop earrings off each ear, shaved his head, and wore a goatee. He had an intense, agitated presence with piercing eyes, and he brandished facial grimaces that gave the aura of impenetrable hate and rage. What was even more malevolent about his appearance was the fact that he exhibited two large tattoos: one was a Japanese symbol on the left side of his neck, while the other was the word *PAIN* branded in Old

English script on the nape of his neck visible for all to see, even when he was wearing a coat. He looked indubitably dangerous and virtually unapproachable.

Kurt voluntarily admitted himself to the unit because he was having uncontrollable panic attacks and impulses to hurt himself and others for no apparent reason. When I first met with him, he was visibly trembling: his legs were shaking, he was moving up and down in his chair, and we had virtually no eye contact throughout the entire session. I asked him why he was in the hospital. He said that he was angry but didn't know why. He told me that he was agitated and had racing thoughts "about stupid things." "Like what?" I replied. "I feel stupid and weak for talking to nurses." He showed me several circular scars on his forearms from burning himself with a cigarette. He went on to say that he would get so angry that he had to hurt himself in order to feel better and calm down. He was preoccupied with intense feelings of aloneness and regret for making people mad at him, which only produced more sensations of loneliness and alienation.

I asked him what was troubling him most of all. He told me that his parents had abandoned him when he was small. When he was two, his parents separated and he and his mother and two older sisters moved into his aunt and uncle's home. His father had completely forsaken him. When he was seven, his mother left too.

Kurt was able to tell me that he thought his rage was in response to pain, and that is why he had the tattoo engraved on his neck. He further remarked that it was painful to have the tattoo placed there because it is the most sensitive part of the neck, a reminder of his sensitivity and vulnerability to his own pain. "It gives the impression that you want to cause others pain," I said. "It's just a tough guy defense," he replied: he would scare people, drive them away, so he could protect himself from further rejection and hurt. He lived with two lesbians much older than him and was afraid of losing their friendship. The older of the two was like a surrogate mother, which he readily admitted. "I hate my real mother—I wish she was dead. I told her that once on the phone." Surprisingly, Kurt claimed that he was not bothered by his father's desertion. Despite the fact that his father had sent back all the family pictures of his life with Kurt and his sisters, his absence seemed like an inconsequential blemish on Kurt's psyche (obviously a product of denial); a mother, on the other hand, "is supposed to be there for her children." "I like you, I feel comfortable with you," he said, if not for the simple fact that we both shaved our heads. "I felt stupid when I got here. I told the doctor that I just wanted to be taken care of, but he laughed."

During our second session, the patient told me that the night before he had to be restrained on the unit because he yelled, cursed, and tore up his room after his doctor failed to visit him as promised. He was panicky and out of control. I suggested that perhaps our previous discussion was up-setting for him, and he associated to how he remembered when he was seven years old standing in the kitchen doorway at his uncle's home begging his mother not to leave him. He recalled how frightened, dejected, and vulnerable he was then, which later gave way to anger and caustic bitterness. He then associated to an incident that happened approximately three weeks before his hospitalization. Kurt worked as a janitor on the midnight shift and cleaned office buildings after hours. He was taking a break outside, having a cigarette and a Coke, when a man in his twenties walked by and began "to size me up. I said, 'What the fuck you starin' at?' and he said, 'You'!" At that point, Kurt started a fight with his provocateur and ended up chasing him into an apartment building, where he pummeled him until he lay motionless. Afterward he said he felt good. "You want to inflict pain on people like your mother did to you," I interpreted. He replied, "It makes sense . . . a part of me wants to get hurt." Kurt recounted how physical violence and abuse of substances had a soothing, pacifying effect on him: drugs, alcohol, fights, self-inflicted abuse = calm. He was intimately aware of his self-destructiveness; his physical appearance invited confrontation, and he had even been hospitalized in the past after being hit in the face with a beer bottle. "I almost drowned in my own blood. I'd be better off dead."

Later that week, Kurt attended a regular therapy group I ran on the inpatient unit. He sat quietly throughout most of the session slumped over in his seat. A particularly nasty borderline who was previously irritated with me for not paying enough attention to her while she attempted to monopolize the group's time became irate with me for a particular comment I made to another patient. My attempt to focus on the group process rather than on her only added fuel to her rage and stoked a litany of insults and devaluations directed at me. As other group members came to my defense, she only became more incensed, until Kurt exploded from his quiet solitude, threatening, "Shut the fuck up you stupid bitch, he's my friend."

Kurt's attachment pathology was organized on the borderline level of structural aggressivity. Rage was his primary emotion, generally in response to real or perceived feelings of abandonment. His rage was in the service of staving off an abandonment depression and fragmentary anxieties and thus left him in a permanent state of structural flux and dysphoric agitation. When his anger became intensified, it would breach the threshold of psychosis, and a falling away of his ego boundaries would ensue. In a psychotic rage, he would deliberately seek out fights in bars, or with strangers on the street and in parking lots—anything to physically discharge his unarticulated tension and inner rupture. He needed to experience pain in order to bind his psyche, to provide containment, to remind himself of his past, to reassure himself that he could feel something and was alive.

In our next session, we began by processing what had happened in group. I asked him why he felt the need to protect me, and he said he didn't know. He began to associate about another conflict he encountered on the unit. A schizophrenic had taken Kurt's milk, which had been saved for him, out of the refrigerator, and he drank it. When Kurt confronted him on the theft, the other patient flipped him the finger.

Patient: I wanted to murder him.

Therapist: What's so intolerable?

Patient: I don't want to be weak, like a bitch.

Therapist: Why the impulse to hurt others?

Patient: I have to stand my ground.

Therapist: What would happen if you just walked away?—Like with the other guy, if you would've just took your Coke and went back inside?

Patient: I have to keep fighting, I can't let it happen. If I would've fought to keep my mother, she would've stayed.

Therapist: You feel it was your fault?

Patient: Yeah.

Therapist: Why?

Patient: She would've cared more if I put up more of a fight.

Therapist: Is fighting going to change that now?

Patient: Probably not.

Therapist: I can't help but get this image of you as that little boy in the doorway, pleading, begging for your mother not to go, not to abandon you like your father did.

Patient: [*agitated*] If I would've fought, she would've cared more.

Therapist: Then you're the reason why she left.

Patient: [*staring at me hatefully, fists clenched, gritting his teeth*]

Therapist: Are you angry?

Patient: Yeah.

Therapist: Feel like hitting me?

Patient: Yeah.

Therapist: I know this is painful . . . and I know that I'm assaulting you by forcing you to think about these things. I'm sorry it's upsetting you.

Patient: That's why I didn't hit you, it's not your fault.

Therapist: I'm glad you restrained yourself. It's not your fault either. You're not the reason she left.

Figure 6.5.

Kurt allowed me into his inner world, drenched with pain, hate, and rage. The desire to fight was a symbolic refusal to accept that his parents were just simply disturbed people who were not capable of giving him what he needed and deserved, namely, love. The repetition of aggression, enacted behaviorally and structurally organized, was in part in the service of an unconscious omnipotent fantasy of undoing the original abandonment, of proving to himself that he was not at fault, that he did not fail but continued to long for his mother. In his mind, if he gave up his aggression, he would no longer care, and he would be just like her. His anger and pain gave meaning to his life, and without them he would have to face his shame and bereavement. To blame his mother would mean that he was deserving of love and self-worth, but it would destroy his wish that she would someday come back into his life. Over much work, Kurt came to realize that his rage was a protection against his sadness over loss. No matter how hard he fought, no matter how much he protested or begged, he had to mourn the loss of his mother, the loss of the fulfillment of what she meant to him, the loss of a wish.

Kurt continued his treatment with me in outpatient therapy once he was discharged from the hospital. Shortly after he left the hospital, he sent a thank-you letter to the unit as a token of his appreciation. Enclosed was a self-portrait (see figure 6.5), along with a note on the back.

i drew this picture when i first was admitted. i felt as if i was falling. But things changed, because of the staff on this floor. First I'd like to thank the nurses. Especially a few concerned ones. Sandra who helped me to open up & took care of me when everything started to crash. Lee, although I only had you once you sat and talked me threw a panic attack & showed me it's O.K. to be scared. As with Bonnie who kept checkin' in on me to see how I was feeling. Yvonne & Diane pushing me forward when i felt stuck. Barb who I never had as a nurse, but it was nice to see a familiar face. Ronda who was also a familiar face & showed some compation. Filip for making me smile & Leslie for also pushing when I needed it. Lastly Dr. Mills for being sincere & telling me I'm not alone. I've noticed when patients leave they manage to say goodbye & tell other patients they will miss them. For me however I'll miss you people the most. I hope to see you again, but as a visitor only. It's been a <u>crazy</u> 39 days! I thank all of you.

P.S. Gorrette, I did not leave you out. Maybe the pin you gave me can share it's wings so i no longer will fall.

NOTES

1. In his *Wissenschaftslehre* (secs. 1–3), Fichte (1794) discerns these three fundamental principles or transcendental acts of the mind.

2. Cf. Immanuel Kant (1781), *Critique of Pure Reason*, 2nd division, *Transcendental Dialectic*, bk. 2, chaps. 1–2.

3. For example, see Donald Carveth's (1994) incorrect assessment of Hegel's *Logic*, 151.

4. For our purposes, we may view the striving for self-consciousness to be a process of self-actualization that one can never fully achieve but only approximate through laborious dialectical progression. We are always oriented toward higher modes of self-fulfillment, whether in action or fantasy. It is the striving, however, that forms a necessary aspect of any transcendental orientation or philosophy of living; and like the pursuit of wisdom and contentment, it is a process of becoming.

5. This is clearly expressed by Meno: "Socrates, before I even met you I used to hear that you are always in a state of perplexity and that you bring others to the same state, and now I think you are bewitching and beguiling me, simply putting me under a spell, so that I am quite perplexed. . . . You seem, in appearance and in every other way, to be like the broad torpedo fish, for it too makes anyone who comes close and touches it feel numb, and you now seem to have had that kind of effect on me, for both my mind and my tongue are numb,

and I have no answer to give you. Yet I have made many speeches about virtue before large audiences on a thousand occasions . . . but now I cannot even say what it is" (Plato 1981, 68–69, 80a–b).

6. While Donnel Stern (1997) has focused extensively on unformulated experience and dissociation, this notion was originally addressed as a psychoanalytic concept by Harry Stack Sullivan (1953, 185), but it stands in relation to Sartre's emphasis on prereflective consciousness that he culled from Franz Brentano. Moreover, what is largely unknown to psychoanalysis is that the notion of unformulated prereflective unconscious experience dates back even further to the whole tradition of German idealism, finding its most vivid expression in Hegel's (1817) *Philosophy of Mind*, originally prefigured by Fichte (1794) in his *Wissenschaftslehre*.

7. Because readers may be unfamiliar with Lacanian theory, it is necessary to provide a preliminary overview of his ontological treatment of the human condition, which he situates in three realms or contexts of being, namely, the imaginary, symbolic, and real. It may be useful to think of three main periods that characterize Lacan's work. While his early period (1932–1948) focused on the role of the imago, his middle period (1948–1960) concentrated on the nature of language and its subordination of the world of images to linguistic structures and practices. During his late period (1960–1980), Lacan was preoccupied with a formal systematization of psychoanalysis via logic and mathematics that sought to provide a coherent explanatory framework involving the three realms or registers of mental life. As a cursory definition, we might say that the imaginary (*imaginaire*) is the realm of illusion, of fantasy, belonging to the sensuous world of perception. In contrast, the symbolic (*symbolique*) is the formal organization of psychic life that is structured through language and linguistic internalizations and thus becomes the ground of the subject; while the real (*réel*) remains foreclosed from epistemic awareness within the abyss of unconscious desire. The real is delimited—the *Ding an sich*: it remains the mysterious beyond, the heart of desire. For Lacan, desire is persecutory by virtue of belonging to the Other; it first originates in a specular imago and then is constituted through the domain of language and speech.

The imaginary, symbolic, and the real are not mental entities; rather, they are *orders* that serve to position the individual within a field that traverses and intersects her (Bowie 1991). The word *order* suggests a number of important connotations for Lacan. In his conception, these orders are analogous to botanical or zoological taxonomy in that (1) there is a hierarchical arrangement of classes whereby (2) internal principles of similarity and congruence govern membership in each class. Furthermore, (3) higher levels of classification have superior cognitive status, suggesting that (4) a series of commands or orders is being issued from some undetected source—presumably the real, the night of the mind. No limitations are placed on the Lacanian orders; they may be used to explain any form of human condition, from the most banal mental mechanism to the most severe forms of psychopathology. Within the three Lacanian orders, each perspective is realized from its own unique vantage point and reveals an insight into psychic organization that forecloses the others, yet envelops them. However, by themselves, each fails to fully represent and articulate the greater dynamic complexity that characterizes the parallel processes and temporal unification of the three orders.

As multiple processes, the three Lacanian orders are not stable, fixed entities; rather, they are under the constant pressure of evolution, vacillating between antithetical movements of progression and regression, construction and decay. The three orders pressurize each other constantly, having short-term moratoriums. In other words, the three orders are in conflict with each other and, when operative, attempt to exert their own unique influence over the other orders. This in turn creates overdetermined and multiple, dynamic levels of psychic reality. In their dialectical transitions, each order encroaches on the other—the symbolic defining and organizing the imaginary, the imaginary hallucinating the real. Furthermore, the real always wedges its way through the gaps of conscious intentionality, giving desire a voice through the medium of perception and speech. At any given moment we live in all three realms of being, and each operative and dynamic within their own orders are parallel to each other, yet they are integrative, structured, and complex. While the real is the most obscure concept for Lacan, it reintroduces a vibrant theoretical life to psychoanalytic inquiry that underscores the primacy of an unconscious ontology that Freud was so instrumental in advancing. Despite its mysterious appeal shrouded in inconceivability, the real is the reverberation of its own truth disclosed on its own terms and understood through its own language, the idiom of desire.

7

⊘

Embracing Countertransference

A female patient of mine recounts her week. I listen with interest, waiting for her to arrive at particular conclusions. She has suffered a great deal and still does but prefers not to dwell on it. My interest turns into patience as she continues to talk but circumvents her discontent. She's adroit at avoidance but easily offended when I point such things out. "I'd better wait," I think. I grow more aware that I must encourage her digressions. I feel frustrated. Getting farther and farther away, she skirts the issue with supple grace, then strays off into tangentiality. I forget her point and lose my focus, then get down on myself. The opportunity is soon gone. I glance at the clock as her monologue drones on into banality. I grow more disinterested and distant. There is a subtle irritation to her voice; a whiny, indecisive ring begins to pervade my consciousness. I home in on her mouth with aversion, watching apprehensively as this disgusting hole flaps tirelessly but says nothing. It looks carnivorous, voracious. Now she is unattractive, something I've noticed before. I forget who my next patient is. I think about the meal I will prepare for my wife this evening, then glance at the time once more. Then I am struck: Why am I looking at the clock? So soon? The session has just begun. I catch myself. What is going on in me, between us? I am detached, but why? Is she too feeling unattuned, disconnected? I am failing my patient. What is her experience of me? With some lament, I confess that I don't feel I've been listening to her, and I wonder what has gone wrong between us. I ask her if she has noticed. We talk about our feelings, our impact on one another, why we had lost our sense of connection, what it means to us. I instantly feel more involved, rejuvenated, and she continues, this time with me present. Her mouth is no longer odious but sincere and articulate. She is attractive and tender; I suddenly feel empathy and warmth toward her. We are now very close. I am moved. Time flies, the session is soon over; we don't want it to end.

Countertransference used to be considered a very undesirable—even pathological—aspect of the therapist's internal experience of the patient. Among many forms of mainstream therapies today, it is still seen as a detriment when evoked or encountered, a dirty word. Nonanalytic clinicians prefer not to discuss such matters, and when they do arise, countertransference is either viewed as an unsavory dimension of the therapist's prejudicial attitudes, or it is shirked as an extraneous variable, thus deemed irrelevant. Moreover, many clinicians prefer not to disclose their innermost feelings and conflicts with other colleagues, let alone with their patients, out of fear that they will be negatively judged, exposed, and professionally criticized. In the professional analytic literature, however, countertransference is one of the most discussed therapeutic topics and most debated clinical phenomena.

This chapter will broadly address the nature of countertransference and its therapeutic implications for working with attachment disordered populations. While I do not intend to offer an inclusive account of countertransference, I do wish to highlight a few important theoretical considerations under contemporary scrutiny and therefore champion clinical recommendations that have to do with the therapist's experience. I believe, as do many others, that facing and understanding one's own countertransference can largely determine the efficaciousness of successful therapy. This is particularly germane when one is working with characterologically disordered patients. Rather than shy away from one's own inner conflicts and dynamic processes that are indubitably bound to spill over into the therapeutic matrix, I feel it is incumbent upon clinicians to embrace their own processes—no matter how sordid or unrefined—in order to manage, if not eclipse, the destructive elements that besiege a successful treatment. After emphasizing a few proposed therapeutic considerations for working with attachment pathology, I will turn our attention to an extended case treatment of working with an extremely aggressive borderline woman, where unabated countertransference was an ongoing occurrence of my clinical reality.

PERSPECTIVES ON COUNTERTRANSFERENCE

> We have become aware of the "counter-transference," which arises in him as a result of the patient's influence on his unconscious feelings, and we are almost inclined to insist that he shall recognize this countertransference in himself and overcome it.
>
> —Freud (1910, 144–45)

Freud said very little about countertransference, but he implied that it was based on pathological manifestations as a result of the analyst's own unresolved conflicts and hence was an obstacle to treatment. In "Observations on Transference-Love," Freud (1915a) further speaks of the need for restraint of the analyst's desire and for abstinence from gratification of the patient's need for love in order to keep the countertransference in check. It was not until the 1950s, however, that countertransference began to garner more attention among the psychoanalytic community.

Paula Heimann is generally credited with the first definitive contribution to the literature where the analyst's countertransference was viewed as constructive rather than entirely pathological (Langs 1990). Heimann (1949) tells us that, while largely troublesome and in need of self-analysis and rectification, the analyst's experience of countertransference can also be used to help understand the experience of the patient. Rather than perpetuate the avoidance and anxiety associated with countertransference discussions among professional colleagues, this made a clearing for displacing countertransference as a taboo subject. Before this, analytic clinicians were inclined to emulate the emotionally detached android who shut himself down and felt nothing but manufactured benevolence in order to avoid his own inner processes via remaining focused, albeit illusorily, on the patient's experience. It is no wonder that the psychoanalyst used to be depicted as a cold, staid, inhuman "blank slate" that emitted no personal feelings.

Ironically, it was Ferenczi (1933) who readily acknowledged that the therapist had myriad emotional responses to the patient, and that he at times should express them openly, a concept that has gained wide acceptance among contemporary relational analysts today. However, this was not readily accepted by the mainstream of his day. Heimann (1949), on the other hand, recognized the value of the analyst's emotional responses to the patient and advocated that they can become a profound tool in understanding the patient's subjectivity, especially as "an instrument of research into the patient's unconscious" (140). Not only should we turn our "own unconscious like a receptive organ towards the transmitting unconscious of the patient" (Freud 1912b, 115), but we should especially cultivate an emotional sensibility (viz., allowing free emotional responses to flourish) in order to be attuned to the emotional resonance states and unconscious fantasies of the patient.

Heimann (1949) viewed countertransference as a one-way relation: she saw it as "the patient's *creation*" and thus "part of the patient's personality" (142). This surely cannot be entirely the case, but her writings nevertheless stressed the value of the therapist's inner emotional reactions to the analytic relationship as a vehicle for understanding the dynamics of treatment.

Annie Reich (1951) was one of the first analysts to focus on the intrapsychic dimensions of transformation in overcoming the disruptive factors of countertransference. As in analysis itself, what she advocates for is the ability to face our own unconscious and use our unconscious as a tool for therapeutic transmutation. Just as transference is a projection onto the doctor, so is countertransference a projection onto the patient by the analyst himself. In effect, the patient becomes an object of the past for the clinician's attitudes in the present. Countertransference is based on an unconscious identification with something in the patient that, like a mirror, reflects back something that is intolerable. The task in overcoming the countertransference is to achieve a sublimation of the therapist's conflicts through "desexualized" psychological insight into the patient and into himself, which transforms impulses toward acting out into higher faculties of reason necessary for mutual understanding and change, which is what analysis is all about.

In her seminal paper "Counter-Transference and the Patient's Response to It," Margaret Little (1951) further advanced our understanding of countertransference as an intensely interactional phenomenon. She saw countertransference as potentially encompassing any of these four dimensions:

a. The analyst's unconscious attitude to the patient.
b. Repressed elements, hitherto unanalysed, in the analyst himself which attach to the patient in the same way as the patient "transfers" to the analyst affects, etc., belonging to his parents or to the objects of his childhood; i.e., the analyst regards the patient (temporarily and varyingly) as he regarded his own parents.
c. Some specific attitude or mechanism with which the analyst meets the patient's transference.
d. The whole of the analyst's attitudes and behaviour towards his patient. This includes all the others, and any conscious attitudes as well. (1951, 144)

Here Little emphasizes a two-way relation, namely, the inseparable relation between the patient's transference projections and the analyst's unconscious and conscious reactions to them. Little argues that countertransference has both normal and pathological variants, and these variants are proportional to what is elicited by the patient and the unique contingencies of the analytic dyad. Little unequivocally emphasizes the interpersonal, intersubjective, or relational dimension to countertransference phenomena and argues that no countertransference experiences are the same. What she means by this is that every countertransference reaction is different, for it resonates within the therapist in peculiar ways that stand in relation to his own dispositions and certain aspects of his personality. In fact, Little sees countertransference as a compromise formation whereby projection and introjection play a significant role. Here she alludes to Bion's notion of projection identification as the identification and incorporation of a piece of the patient's projective fantasies. Little rightfully shows how the patient becomes the object for the analyst's conflicted fantasies and unconscious urges, and not merely the other way around. Her work on this subject is so rich with relational nuance, complexity, and insight into the therapeutic situation that it is surprising that her ideas are so underrecognized.

While Heimann (1949) saw all responses to the patient as countertransference, Tower (1955) defined countertransference as the analyst's transferences to the patient. In fact, Tower privileged countertransference as an *"emotional understanding"* (165) of the patient's transference neurosis. Winnicott (1949), on the other hand, mainly spoke of "objective countertransference" as "the analyst's love and hate in reaction to the actual personality and behavior of the patient based on objective observation" (70), the term *objective* being in desperate need of an operational definition. Ferenczi (1950) preferred to focus on the affectionate, positive, loving, and/or sexual attitudes one takes up toward the patient, a point Balint (1950) highlighted by returning to Freud's (1912a) observation that every human relation is libidinous. Harry Stack Sullivan (1949) emphasized the analyst's "parataxic distortions" of being "in participant observation of the unfortunate patterns of his own" (12), patterns that Cohen (1952) claimed were always derived from the presence of anxiety in the analyst. This issue led Frieda Fromm-Reichmann (1950) to distinguish between the personal and professional responses of the analyst under the influence of countertransference, a position that brought Alexander (1948) and others to ultimately conclude that countertransference is simply any and all attitudes the analyst has toward the patient.

Racker (1972) perhaps provides the most comprehensive consideration of countertransference in the classical literature, showing the inextricable nature of intersubjective processes in the therapeutic dyad, including the projective elements of the analyst's transferences and the identificatory aspects of the patient's responsiveness to the analyst's projections as an interactional pathology. He is particularly perspicacious in highlighting the defensive functions of the clinician's reticence in addressing countertransference in both professional and personal space.

Racker distinguishes many forms of countertransference, namely, (1) *concordant identifications*, which are the therapist's identifications with a patient's internal object or self-state, such as in the example of the analyst whose ego or superego identifies with the ego or superego of the patient; and (2) *complementary identifications*, whereby the patient treats the analyst as an internal (albeit projected) object, which the analyst himself assumes; that is, he identifies himself with this object. Racker further distinguishes countertransference experiences within two classes: (1) *countertransference thoughts* or fantasies and (2) *countertransference positions*, or behaviorally manifested or enacted roles, which may lead to persistent role adoptions and/or acting out by the analyst.

While Gitelson (1952) describes countertransference as "partial" reactions to the patient, Heimann (1949) views countertransference as a phenomenon that "cover[s] all the feelings which the analyst experiences towards his patient" (140), a view that Kernberg (1965) refers to as "totalistic" or all embracing. Kernberg, as does Tower, emphasizes the total emotional reaction of the therapist in the treatment situation, which encompasses both conscious and unconscious reactions to real and fantasized events. Kernberg, as does others, highlights the interactional, hence intersubjective, nature of countertransference as an ongoing interpersonal negotiation between the lived intrapsychic experiences of both parties who form the relational matrix. Here, as with Menninger (1958), the therapist's conscious experience of countertransference is accentuated, although it may be said to have originated from unconscious determinants. Kernberg (1965), as does Masterson (1983), alerts us to the potential danger of countertransference fixations, which typically correspond to regression in patients during analysis. In effect, the more primitive or neurotic dimensions of the therapist's personality become overidentified as "counteridentification" with the patient's regressed psyche, and a resurfacing or repetition of the analyst's own conflicted character traits is superimposed on the therapeutic process.

There is still contemporary debate regarding appropriate definitions of the term *countertransference* and its implications for the consulting room. Eagle (2000) argues against past and current popular trends to equate anything and everything the analyst thinks or feels toward the patient to countertransference. In fact, there is so much confusion about what exactly constitutes countertransference that some advocate for abandoning the term altogether (Aron 1991; McLaughlin 1981). At one extreme, there are some intersubjective theorists who readily object to the whole phenomenon of countertransference, claiming instead that there is no such thing within an intersubjective system of mutually regulating interactions and reactions. However, despite the fact that there are arguably cotransferences that transpire in the session as well as in everyday interpersonal life, I find it important to retain experiential distinctions between the analyst's transference toward a patient and the analyst's actions based on how such a transferential phenomenon is subjectively filtered, interpreted, distorted, and acted upon during a therapeutic moment within the analytic milieu. Just because a therapist experientially processes an unconscious artifact that by definition applies to all people in every interpersonal situation does not mean that the therapist will act on such transferences in such a way that they obfuscate the coming to presence of the analyst's developmental intrapsychic history from the urge to act during the immediacy of the clinical encounter. In other words, one can become sufficiently aware of transferential forces operative within the analytic moment without the felt compulsion to behaviorally execute them. It is for these reasons that I find it both pragmatic and necessary (as a technical principle as well as for theoretical purposes) to maintain conceptual nuances between the analyst's transference to the patient and the analyst's countertransference, the former being a universal dynamic of every relational encounter, and the latter being a therapeutic enactment.

In a recent article titled "Countertransference and the Analytic Instrument," Richard Lasky (2002) judiciously distinguishes between the analyst's internal experiences that impede the therapeutic process verses those that facilitate it, although the criterion by which to determine this is not altogether clear and is open to multiple interpretations and contingencies. Lasky does, however, distinguish between various definitions of countertransference from what he calls the "analytic instrument" by classifying them into general groupings (69–70). Therefore, it may be helpful at this point to summarize three main kinds of definitions of countertransference generally observed in the psychoanalytic literature, each carrying different meanings and significance depending upon which author or school of thought one consults:

(1) Countertransference should be conceived as a specific response or set of responses by the therapist to the patient's transference relationship to that therapist. Countertransference can be constructive or destructive, healthy or abnormal, and can either help or hinder the treatment depending upon the degree to which the analyst is capable of bringing his personality to bear on the therapeutic process.

(2) Countertransference is primarily seen as a dynamic that is destructive to therapeutic efficacy and is marked by the analyst's negative and harmful reaction to the patient's transference. This approach would differentiate between the neurotic or pathological portions of the analyst's personality that are brought to bear on the therapeutic dyad independent of the patient versus those that are specifically mobilized in response to the patient's transference, thus impacting on the analytic work in differing ways. From this view, countertransference is a purely negative phenomenon. It is only in the wake of the clinician's understanding of his pathological reactions that the countertransference can be attended to and overcome, thus moving beyond the throes of the analyst's negative responsiveness that creates an impasse to therapy. Here the analyst can come to use the countertransference experience in a more productive light: such insight not only adds illumination to the unconscious dynamics of the patient but can also be harnessed as an avenue for engaging the therapeutic encounter in more beneficial and propitious ways. This model observes the presumption that the countertransference can be left behind through a process of self-analysis that then frees the clinician to adopt a more favorable role and attitude toward the patient's dynamics uncontaminated by the subjectivity of the analyst.

(3) Countertransference is tantamount to the inner life and total experiential reaction of the analyst at work in the context of therapy. This is not necessarily predicated on the patient's transferential relation to the therapist, but it certainly encompasses this primordial dynamic. Every part or dimension to the therapist's personality is potentially at play and evoked in the therapeutic encounter, whether unconsciously organized, expressed, or consciously realized. Based on ego identifications by the analyst, countertransference can have positive and negative valences, is both normative and pathological, and can equally boost or hamper the analytic process.

So after all these decades of debate, do we have a better understanding of countertransference? Or has this concept become so varied, elusive, and/or potentially watered down that it loses its original significance? Recall that Freud identified countertransference as a specific reaction (as internal protest and rebuttal) to the patient's transference. Lasky's solution is to make the analytic instrument the means, method, and expression of the analyst's subjective inner condition—thus, the analytic instrument draws on the therapist's entire personality—but not to equivocate or equate the analyst's personality with the therapeutic sensibilities he brings into the consulting room. Countertransference is neither the preexisting character structure of the therapist nor everything the analyst experiences toward the patient. This view to me seems correct. There is a big difference between what the clinician experiences internally in the context of treatment and what he does with such experiences, both intrapsychically and through behavioral enactments. This can make all the difference between using the countertransference as a therapeutic corrective versus conducting and perpetuating bad therapy.

But this still leaves a conundrum. If we are to adopt the criterion that the therapist's conduct versus his inner experience is the defining characteristic that distinguishes the countertransference from the analytic instrument, then how are we to reconcile the enactment of countertransference when by definition behavioral comportment is internally mediated by the analyst's subjectivity? While inner subjective experience is a necessary condition for therapeutic action, are we conceptually justified in bifurcating thoughts, fantasies, intentions, beliefs, and attitudes (viz., the domain of the analyst's intrapsychic activity) from the expressed behavioral manifestations that inform his interventions (e.g., body posturing, nonverbal cues and communications, physical gestures, emotional utterances, and verbal, linguistic expression)? Are the inner motives, unconscious emotional resonance states, neurotic evocations, internal precipitous reactions, and the analyst's conscious understanding and reconciliation of such processes capable of being separated from countertransference based on behavioral activity alone when these behaviors are predicated on such mediated inner experiences to begin with?

Perhaps we can only make the distinction between countertransference (as behavioral phenomena) and the analytic instrument[1] (as subjective agency) by looking back at the process retroactively to see how the therapist's internal attitudes and emotional reactions affected his therapeutic demeanor. This would make the criterion of what justifiably constitutes countertransference a process of intersubjective mediation and not necessarily a solitary one performed by the therapist alone. This process involves a twofold dialectical relation between each subject in the intersubjective system, which in turn generates a new phenomenological field in the treatment process, what Beebe, Jafee, and Lachmann (1992) call a "dyadic system" of reciprocal mutual influence, what Stolorow and Atwood (1992) call the "intersubjective field," or what Ogden (1994b) refers to as the "analytic third."

From the standpoint of the analyst's subjectivity, there are at least three levels of self-reflective mediation required: (1) the clinician needs to be introspective enough to discern and identify various internal disruptions that are potentially motivating or fueling tendencies toward certain interventions in order to contain (or at least curb) acting-out episodes from transpiring in the first place; (2) there is a need to self-monitor one's precipitous reactions, internal resonance states, and overt behaviors that directly affect the patient and the emergent, altered intersubjective system; and (3) one must be self-reflective enough to examine one's own past actions that have affected the therapeutic climate in order to make various correctives or reparation within the treatment itself (because, presumably, countertransference phenomena are largely unconsciously motivated enactments; therefore, it is often the case that not until such unconscious motives are consciously realized do we have more insight and mutative control over their instantiations). Yet this process of observing and ameliorating countertransference is contingent on the patient's receptivity and subjective response to the therapist's interventions through ongoing relational exchange and interpersonal negotiation. Even though an analyst may be internally motivated to act out his countertransference behaviorally, catching it and modifying one's behavior beforehand will limit the countertransference tendency before it detrimentally spews over into the analytic process. But even if it does, the patient may or may not experience the analyst's countertransference as detrimental per se, and perhaps even conversely, it may be facilitative of moving the treatment into auspicious directions. This makes the criterion of determining the impediment or efficacy of countertransference an intersubjective phenomenon and not necessarily one based on either the therapist's internal experience of the patient alone or his unconsciously motivated determinants and conscious intentions that govern overt interventions.

Whether we are considering the patient's view of the analyst's attitude toward the patient (Gill 1983), the patient's interpretation of the analyst's experience (Hoffman 1983), or the patient's experience of the analyst's subjectivity (Aron 1991), we must include the patient's intrapsychic *and* relational stance toward the inner life of the therapist (and vice versa) in our equation of what constitutes countertransference. This is why countertransference cannot be dissected or removed from the intersubjective environment of therapy and exclusively attributed to the analyst. This furthermore ensures that countertransference is not something that can be overcome because we are always embedded in a relational ontology. This is a reason why I prefer to view countertransference as a mutative and transforming interpersonal phenomenon rather than one that is solely attributed to the "affectively rich internal environment of the analyst" (Lasky 2002, 93). Countertransference is an ongoing trajectory of relational exchange that can be seized upon and continually altered, revamped, and reincorporated into the variegated nuances of treatment, which is always in flux as a process of becoming. This means that as certain countertransference processes are evoked, sustained, transmuted, and surpassed (yet simultaneously preserved), they are reconstituted in other intratherapeutic forms or replaced by ongoing, overlapping, and overdetermined multiplicities of mutually interjective psychic processes within intersubjective analytic space. We cannot get behind or beyond countertransference by virtue of the fact that it is part and parcel of the relational matrix.

In countertransference, there is always something that is not said, the presence of absence—of negation, of "the *not*." Countertransference is a call to embrace our inner being in the mode of its immediate appearance within the moment of felt resistance to or from the Other—in the moment of being bombarded with otherness to the point that it fractures our secure little world we have hitherto made for ourselves in our preferred pathways of defense. We often experience countertransference as an assault on our inner being—on our self-integrity—that repudiates our essence. But countertransference is the coming to presence of a coconstructed reality where no single agency manufactures it alone; it materializes out of the moment-to-moment tensions of breaching psychic union with the other's subjectivity. In this sense, countertransference, like transference, is a resurfacing, a *re-presence* (as re-presentation) or reintroduction of the interjection of our being into the being of the other.

FACING COUNTERTRANSFERENCE HONESTLY

Throughout my first analytic treatment, my analyst, who trained with Bion, behaved in various ways that were palpable enactments of countertransference. For example, he would frequently eat his breakfast muffin during our session and then attempt to share it with me if he happened to notice I was looking at him while he ate his food. On one occasion, he failed to show up for our scheduled appointment. Later he told me he had slept through our appointment time because he was jet-lagged from returning home from a trip. Another time, he lightly dozed off in the session and then denied that he had fallen asleep, even though I had to wake him. After these events, he started to invite me to his condominium for sessions rather than his office. I recall the sense of specialness I felt as a result of being privileged to be in his home, but I was only to find that his phone was a constant source of interruption because of his reluctance to turn off the ringer. When I brought these incidents to his attention, I asked him if he felt his actions were due to his countertransference. I had suspected that he had resented taking me on as a graduate student for a reduced fee. When he acknowledged that this could be happening, I asked him if he would share it with me, but he declined. He told me that he didn't work that way, but he would think about it. Although frustrated, I was respectful of his candor and saw the necessity of preserving the asymmetry of the relationship through a firm boundary. It is only in retrospect that I feel he should have handled the matter differently.

What becomes a hindrance to the patient's growth is the therapist's inability to recognize and understand his own dynamic conflicts that spill over into the treatment environment in a deleterious fashion. In this respect, Freud's (1910) attitude is as prevalent today as it was a century ago: the analyst must "overcome" the countertransference. We often hear of caveats for working through the countertransference, as if it were something we could put "behind" us. Natterson (1991) further tells us that we can get "beyond" countertransference through self-scrutiny. But is this possible? Is it possible to overcome or get beyond our human condition— our subjectivity? These propositional attitudes only view countertransference as an interference to treatment, when it can potentially become an ally to understanding and facilitating a better treatment approach to our patients. Little (1951) supports this claim: countertransference "cannot be avoided, it can only be looked out for, controlled to some extent, and perhaps used" (151). Well, it certainly can be used. I am under the persuasion that it is not possible to overcome or even transcend our countertransference because we are always immersed in it. Instead, we must *embrace* our countertransferences in order to transform them—not to transcend[2] them, which is neither possible nor practical, but rather to accept, incorporate, and evolve them through self-reflective mediations.

The phenomenology of our inner subjective experiences and prejudicial dispositions will always saturate the clinical encounter, and no amount of self-deception or professional instruction will eradicate this fact.[3] Likewise, no amount of therapy or personal analysis can erase countertransference, for these processes are as natural as breathing and continue to be fueled by the therapist's unconscious affective resonance states and/or neurotic proclivities that repetitiously resurface in conscious life. Equally, countertransference is not in and of itself an anomalous quality or emergent property of therapy that can be tabled, bracketed, or completely abandoned. Countertransference is nothing other than the phenomenal manifestation and admission of being human, and it commands us to acknowledge our own lived subjective reality by observing and nurturing our unconscious disruptions. Just as transference is a ubiquitous phenomenon of every interpersonal encounter, so is countertransference: both are equiprimordial processes. Countertransference is a communication to the self that speaks to us when we increasingly draw our attention to it. We can never come to sufficiently know all our unconscious "blind spots," just as certain surreptitious satisfactions of infantile needs will continue to press for fulfillment through the various attitudes and reactions we come to harbor toward *all* patients. Here I wish to emphasize the need for professional and personal honesty; although the psychoanalytic community long ago recognized the value of countertransferential acknowledgment, the psychological community in general—especially mainstream academe—needs to recognize and openly admit that countertransference is a natural phenomenon, not an inherently pathological one, and therapists need to put aside the veneer of denial, secrecy, or fear of exposure or admonition by professional colleagues that they perpetuate by pretending that they are "above" or "beyond" falling prey to their unconscious shortcomings.

Countertransference is never left behind through a process of self-analysis—as if you could think it away? As if you could liberate yourself from your humanism, your subjectivity—whether pathologically motivated or not—in order to achieve a state of unadulterated responsiveness and sensitivity to the patient's need for wish fulfillment? What we may optimally strive for is to embrace and immerse ourselves in our countertransference, to repudiate yet savor every emotive moment, to grapple with and attempt to understand it courageously, and, once this is sufficiently achieved, to transform our facticity through determinate freedom, what the ancients would call wisdom.

The didactic training of therapists today is riddled with the pretentious, illusory belief that a certain skill or technique, when delivered correctly, is the right, absolute standard upon which to judge the success or failure of an intervention. We all know this is bullshit, but we placate instructors, supervisors, or training analysts in order to assuage their narcissism, receive their praise, and get our degrees so we can practice autonomously without having to remain enslaved to the concessions of authority. Many students—perhaps most—are terrified to be honest to their supervisors about their true thoughts and feelings when treating patients because of the fear of negative evaluation, condemnation, and potential retaliation, such as the supervisor's failing them in their course, practicum placement, or candidacy as an analyst in training. They are also adept at adopting a false self in order to appease the supervisor because they intuit or know that the other expects a certain degree of compliance and conformity to their wishes. They also know when professors or supervisors are pretending or lying about a professed belief, attitude, or sensibility that they themselves could not possibly uphold, let alone expect others to emulate. Here I have in mind the need for the profession to repeat inauthentic platitudes such as the idea that we should all attempt to cultivate a presentation of altruism (if not unconditional regard) in order to be good therapists, and that negative dispositions about our patients only point toward a limited or pathological person who has no business being in the profession. This is endemic to some forms of clinical instruction, such as CBT (cognitive behavioral therapy) or person-centered therapy. The admission of extreme negative feelings about a patient is typically met with consternation, if not moral reproach for being so brazen (and remiss) in offering such a candid confession. As a result, students and clinicians alike are discouraged from discussing their true feelings in professional space (e.g., the classroom, supervision, conferences, journal publications) due to a culture of dishonesty and fear that is promulgated from within the academy and analytic institutes regarding standards of training and professional identity.[4] As a profession, we must cease being phobic and disingenuous with ourselves about our conflicted feelings and difficulties in working with patients, and equally we must stop being paranoid that countertransference is an unwelcome, taboo subject not capable of being professionally discussed openly among colleagues.

How often do we hear psychotherapists admit their profound hatred or uncontrollable lust for patients in the presence of other therapists? Not often. And when we do, we are careful in what we say, let alone disclose back, only then to wonder about the ramifications of such conversations. I once had a colleague confess that the way he discharges his rage for certain patients is to imagine their faces as he chops wood for his fireplace. On other occasions, the uninhibited comfort in discussing vivid and lurid sexual fantasies about various patients has proved to be powerfully transformative and containing. We all know that it is not uncommon for therapists to masturbate while thinking about certain patients or fantasize about them during sexual intercourse with their partners. Under these circumstances, forbidden wishes may be fulfilled through circuitous displacements that transfigure and convert the countertransference into manageable forces that are more safe, curbed, subdued, and restrained; hence, the countertransference is prevented from being acted out. Yet the question of using a patient as an object of functional gratification as a means to an end becomes an indissoluble moral dilemma.

It is not enough to merely become aware of one's countertransference feelings toward patients, but one must understand these feelings within an ongoing climate of self-scrutiny and self-analysis, thereby linking the present experience in the clinical encounter to dynamic vulnerabilities from one's own past and character structure, in order to transmute them within the interpersonal medium of therapy so as to effect and bring about a new mode of therapeutic relatedness. But how is this possible?

THE SPECTRUM OF COUNTERTRANSFERENCE PHENOMENA

When contemplating countertransference, we often think of extreme emotions or impulses that are aroused, such as the dialectic of love and hate, which hinder our capacity to treat our patients in the most competent and optimal manner. This is far from the case. There are benign and malignant countertransferences just as there are forms of cancer, yet each may potentially have a detrimental effect on the success of therapy if it goes unnoticed and is merely enacted through the guise of personal mannerism, preference, or intersubjective therapeutic play.

Countertransference enactments are as myriad as possibility itself. Boredom during the session, for example, is one of the most universal manifestations of countertransference; even when the patient is legitimately boring, the mere fact that the clinician remains on the level of banality points toward a failure to intervene. We may even observe the opposite scenario: Lacan would tell his patients that he was bored five minutes after the session began, blame it on them, and then ask them to leave, thus passing off his invalidation and rejection as a legitimate technique he called "scansion."

Within the clinical literature, we may readily observe a preoccupation with various forms of countertransference phenomena that continue to summon our attention, such as the analyst's denial and repression (or re-repression) as resistance to his countertransference; the inability to understand certain kinds of material because they touch on one's own vulnerabilities and personal problems; depressed or uneasy feelings before or after the session; the propensity to act out hidden, unconscious conflicts that neglect the patient's welfare; dislike as a failure to understand the patient; the inability to restrain verbalizations of one's annoyance, anger, or direct outbursts; the need to enter into competition with patients, such as getting into critical arguments or belittlements; engaging in rationalization or staying on the intellectual level as a way of avoiding emotionality; and the sadistic withholding of reassurances and validation—or, conversely, overly consoling and gratifying patients in response to anxiety. Countertransference has no bounds and may appear in a variety of extreme forms, ranging from a sense of total dedication to a patient or the exploitation of the erotic transference, to feelings of emotional discontinuation, microparanoiac attitudes, paranoia as the mobilization of strong aggressive impulses toward the patient, and feelings of regression, dissociation, fragmentation—even transitory psychosis—as an overidentification with the patient's regressed or decompensated clinical condition.

Although the phenomenal qualities and nuances of countertransference are different from therapist to therapist, for didactic purposes, it may prove useful to examine the more miscellaneous forms of countertransference we commonly encounter. While neither exhaustive nor inclusive, table 7.1 contains a list of potential countertransference phenomena (unconsciously motivated yet typically manifested as qualia of consciousness) that clinicians should be alerted to. I have categorized them in terms of subjective experiences therapists may notice during (1) *therapeutic enactments*, that is, behavioral instantiations pertaining to the session, as well as various thoughts, feelings, and fantasies that materialize and coalesce around experiential self-states, such as the presence of (2) *passivity*, (3) *anxiety*, (4) *aggressivity*, (5) *eroticism*, and (6) the *narcissistic vulnerabilities* that are evoked in the analyst during the therapeutic encounter. These countertransferences do not necessarily need to be grouped into these thematic categories, nor are they inclusive to these experiential self-states. Countertransference phenomena cross over into a wide array of therapeutic contingencies and subjective experiences that have multiple, overdetermined meanings and significance governed by the unique personality constellations of the therapist–patient dyad; it is only for descriptive purposes that I list them here in this fashion.

We must admit that the compendium of countertransferences listed in table 7.1 is highly specific to each analyst's peculiar subjectivity within the contextualization of the therapeutic milieu; therefore, a universal application to all clinicians would not be warranted. Despite this caveat, we may notice various patterns or thematic repetitions that have a tendency to universally emerge, which lends credibility to countertransference generalizations that may be observed over time regardless of their historical, cultural, and/or gendered instantiations. It is up to the clinical judgment of each practitioner to discern what applies to him or is irrelevant.

PROJECTIVE IDENTIFICATION AS
UNCONSCIOUS COMMUNICATION

In psychoanalysis, there is much complexity in what we mean by identification in its various forms. For Freud (1921, 1933a), identification is the earliest form of attachment to an object based on an emotional bond, which involves many introjective and projective maneuvers throughout the process of internalization, a subject matter we previously addressed in chapter 2. In fact, the term *identification* is used in so many theoretical contexts that it is hard to precisely determine its elemental value in psychic

Table 7.1. Six Categories of Countertransference

Therapeutic Enactments
- accepting what the patient tells you at face value
- carelessness with regard to patient arrangements
- forgetting about a patient's appointment time
- arriving late for the session
- allowing the session to go overtime
- not charging for no-shows or late canceled appointments
- letting a patient accumulate a large bill
- overcautiousness or therapeutic overeagerness
- avoidance of direct discussions
- inability to analyze, think critically, or address resistances
- mistimed or wrongly emphasized interpretations
- the patient's misunderstanding of the therapist's interpretations
- being hesitant, reticent, or not firm
- taking on a passive, obsequious, or masochistic role
- failing to address maladaptive defenses
- fear of confrontation
- need to elicit affect from the patient (e.g., via provocation or drama)
- parapraxes, significant slips, or faulty achievements
- didactic, authoritarian comportments; playing the role of the expert
- prolonging treatment when therapeutic goals have been achieved
- inappropriate self-disclosure

Passivity
- unevenly suspended attention
- inattention, distractibility
- difficulty in concentrating and/or remembering
- inability to identify with the patient
- persistent drowsiness, somnolence, dozing off
- disinterest, boredom
- indifference
- insouciance, apathy
- lassitude, lethargy
- aloofness
- preoccupation with other matters or personal affairs
- daydreaming

Anxiety
- laughing readily or out of context
- verbalizing spontaneous thoughts
- confusion
- avoidance
- helplessness
- lack of confrontation, evasion
- overt anxiety in the session
- feeling intimidated
- carry over affects from the session
- premature reassurances to defuse the experience of anxiety in the patient
- inability to gauge points of optimal frustration

Table 7.1. (*continued*)

- dreams about patients (especially involving acting-out episodes)
- disturbing feelings for the patient
- dread associated with seeing the patient on appointment days or pervasive discomfort during the session
- stereotypical or prejudicial attitudes
- phobic reactions, recognized fear
- masochism (allowing oneself to be emotionally abused by the patient)
- paranoiac attitudes
- patient's overconcern about the confidentiality of the therapist's work

Aggressivity
- negation, criticism, invalidation
- overdirectiveness, overactivity
- dissatisfaction, disapproval, dislike, contempt
- aversion, disgust, repudiation, repugnance, revulsion
- frustration, peeve, scorn, exasperation
- arguing with the patient
- becoming increasingly disturbed by the patient's accusations and reproaches
- resentment, anger, outrage, rancor, indignation
- rage, wrath
- loathing, antipathy, animosity, abhorrence
- hate/hatred for the patient, or self-hatred
- feeling trapped, controlled
- paranoiac fantasies (as projection or introjective aggression)
- violent emotions, fantasies, daydreams, or dreams
- feelings of revenge or desire for vengeance
- cruelty, sadism
- death wishes

Eroticism
- attention paid to the patient's body
- compliments paid to the patient's appearance or clothing
- visual orientation toward a female's figure, breasts, legs, or genital area
- visual orientation toward a male's physique, chest, shoulders, crotch, or buttocks
- special attention paid to one's own appearance, dress, or hygiene before the session
- seductive body posturing or positioning
- initiating self-disclosures about one's personal life
- perceptions of seduction (when dubious or ambiguous)
- unacknowledged flirtation (either sensed, received, or reciprocated)
- idealization of the patient's personal qualities
- avoidance or lack of confrontation regarding sexual matters
- sexual curiosity
- special interest in or preoccupation with sexual material in the session
- initiation of discussing sexuality
- voyeurism via encouraging detailed explication of the patient's sexual fantasies
- suggesting extratherapeutic contact
- invitation to social functions
- giving patients cards or gifts

(*continued*)

Table 7.1. (*continued*)

- titillation or sexual excitement
- feelings of lust
- direct or overt eroticization
- sexual fantasies or dreams
- homosexual thoughts, desires, or revulsion; homophobia
- self-disclosure with regard to personal relationships, including feelings for the patient
- falling in love with the patient
- sexual transgressions

Narcissistic Vulnerabilities
- excessive preoccupation with the patient outside of the session
- talking about oneself, one's accomplishments, etc., out of context
- seeking to impress the patient
- need to get assurances/praise from the patient
- increased need for gratification
- overidentification with or idealization of the patient (e.g., the analyst's "best" patient)
- jealousy/envy
- feelings of competition
- manufactured arguments or debates
- feelings of superiority
- entitlement
- guilt
- shame
- narcissistic injury, narcissistic rage
- need to see the patient as special
- becoming the object of unbridled adulation or idealization
- being overconciliatory or overly gratifying or reassuring
- need for the patient to identify with the therapist
- tendency to think that the patient should be like the therapist (at the expense of his own individuation)
- asking patients for favors
- helping a patient in extratherapeutic ways (e.g., giving practical advice, helping secure a loan)
- using the patient as a mirroring selfobject
- intolerability of the patient's autonomy or self-assertion
- dependence on the patient's narcissistic supplies
- encouraging illusions about the analyst's therapeutic prowess as a healer (e.g., as the magic cure)
- engaging in exhibitionist, professional gossip or boasting about a patient
- feeling that the patient's recovery and health reflects on the therapist's reputation and prestige

economy. Since Klein's introduction and Bion's subsequent modification of the term *projective identification*, identification has been primarily employed in the context of defense. As we have seen, Racker refers to direct, concordant, and complementary identifications in the countertransference with reference to their defensive functioning, and this may be said to extend to other forms of defensive identification, such as ego/superego identifications, disidentifications, counteridentifications, introjective identifications, projective counteridentifications (Grinberg 1962), and so on. When we refer to specific modes of defensive identification, it is important to keep in mind that these are merely temporal intrapsychic phenomena enacted in a particular moment of intersubjective exchange. Just as Lasky (2002) informs us that the convoluted nature and interface between countertransference, intuition, and empathy is highly complex and intertwined, so is the process of projective identification.

The psychic process known as projective identification has become a familiar tenet of psychoanalytic doctrine, yet depending upon which model you consult, the term can mean a variety of different things. As described earlier, projective identification was introduced by Klein (1946) in the context of splitting, where it was conceived as an aggressive discharge of certain portions of the infantile ego into another (usually the mother) via unconscious fantasy, the aim of which is to control or incorporate certain aspects of the other in order to make it part of the ego's own internal structure. Not only did the introduction of this concept revolutionize Kleinian theory, but further developments paved the way toward its progressive application in understanding a number of mental processes, pathologies, and clinical encounters. To be sure, projective identification may be viewed in multiple fashions: (1) as a general process of mental activity, from unconscious structure to conscious thought, (2) as a defensive maneuver motivated by intrapsychic conflict, and (3) as an intersubjective dynamic affecting object relations, especially the process of therapy. But with a few noteworthy exceptions (see Bion 1959), projective identification has been largely overlooked as a basic element of psychic organization.

Elsewhere, I have shown that Hegel's anticipation of Klein's and Bion's theories of projective identification as the process of the self returning to itself following its own self-estrangement adds to our understanding of both the normative and pathological processes of mind (Mills 2000a). In health and illness, the ego projects certain aspects of the self onto the object world, which the ego then identifies with and finally reintrojects back into its own subjectivity. In effect, the self rediscovers itself in the product of its own projection and then reintegrates itself within itself as reunification. This is the generic structural movement of the Hegelian dialectic (*Aufhebung*), whereby internal division, external projection, and reincorporation function as a mediating and sublating dynamic.

Although Klein discovered projective identification, which further led Bion to advance the distinction between its normal and pathological variants, Hegel was the first to articulate the formal structural processes of projective identification as having their source and origins within the unconscious mind. Since Bion, a less pejorative attitude toward patients' use of projective identification has been adopted among clinicians, which has further led to attempts to define different aspects and subtypes of this phenomenon differentiated by form and motive—such as the degree of control over the object, the attributes acquired, the need to protect certain positive qualities or to avoid separation, their relation to splitting, the force of evacuation, communication, containment, and so on—all subsumed under a general rubric (Spillius 1988).

More recently, projective identification has been given special attention in its relation to countertransference and empathy. Tansey and Burke (1989) view projective identification "as a psychological operation with defensive, adaptive, and communicative properties" (44). They affirm a Bionian interpretation of projective identification as both normative and pathological, as do Malin and Grotstein (1966). Following a Kleinian analysis, Ogden (1982), on the other hand, emphasizes the pathological aspects of projective identification as primitive defense, as does Kernberg (1975). This view has direct clinical utility for working with attachment disordered populations since the clinician is often the unconscious target of the patient's projective identifications. For Ogden, the projector is able to induce in the object certain internal states, which the object then metabolizes and gives back to the projector, who in turn reinternalizes them. Generally we may say that within the context of therapy, the patient projects onto the therapist certain disavowed and repudiated internal contents that the therapist unconsciously identifies with, such as the behavioral fantasies, attributions, or personal qualities that are the objects of splitting, which the therapist then introjects as a function of his own ego (hence introjective identification), and this leads to conflicted inner states that the therapist must manage. If the therapist's countertransference reactions are too strong and/or remain unrecognized as the internalized projected attributions of the patient, he may potentially act out such negative states within the therapeutic encounter, which could thus potentially lead to further internal disruptions in both parties that would negatively affect the intersubjective field.

Although projective identification is a psychic process that may be either intrapsychically or intersubjectively evoked and instantiated, it may be helpful to view projective identification as an unconscious communicative process of inducing interpersonal patterns of behavior in the therapist that are designed to cause the therapist to respond in certain circumscribed fashions. Here the therapist becomes the target and repository of the patient's negative experiences, thoughts, conflicts, and behavioral fantasies, which the therapist unwittingly identifies with and takes into his psyche. As a result, the therapist is unconsciously induced to behave in certain ways in response to the patient's projective identification, which inevitably gives rise to countertransference reactions that are triggered as a result of the emotional schemas that are aroused and henceforth prodded on toward action. As Ogden (1982) tells us, the patient desperately wishes to rid himself of a distasteful or threatening piece of psychic reality that endangers the self (including internal objects) by depositing the unconscious fantasy in a powerfully controlling way into the receptacle or container of the analyst's mental apparatus: "The projected part of the self is felt to be partially lost and to be inhabiting the other person. In association with the unconscious projective fantasy there is an interpersonal interaction by means of which the recipient is pursued to think, feel, and behave in a manner congruent with the ejected feelings and the self- and object-representations embodied in the projective fantasy" (2). Therefore, projective identification involves a series of subjective and intersubjective processes whereby the subject discharges or evacuates various unwanted attributes of self into the subjectivity of the analyst with the intention of manipulating the other to act in desirable circumscribed ways.

It should be clear that in this model, projective identification is a form of unconscious communication (or, more accurately, a series of meta-communications) directed toward the unconscious receptor of the analyst. At this point, it becomes important to question the degree to which an unconscious communication of this sort is possible, if at all. What is the epistemological criterion for determining whether a projective identification is indeed coming from the patient and is not merely the constructed fantasies of an overly imaginative analyst? Is the patient really capable of taking something (quite literally) from within her unconscious mind and then transmitting and placing it into the mind of the therapist? Is there really some form of isomorphism transpiring between two subjectivities? Or are we merely treading into the realm of speculative, creative fantasy as a means of tolerating a clinical phenomenon that is not so easy to comprehend nor constrain? Is conceiving of projective identification in this manner not a means of superimposing some form of order on that which we experience as beyond our control? Is countertransference a reliable touchstone for understanding the unconscious life of the patient? Is projective identification capable of inducing such countertransference enactments? Does this speak to the patient's projected internal world or does it tell us more about the therapist's? These are indeed difficult questions to answer, and all of them hinge on the defensibility of epistemological justification. Perhaps we have no other recourse than to rely on the bona fide associations from patients and the use of introspection and self-analysis from the therapist in order to establish the possible verity of these solutions. Perhaps we may only use the analytic process as our guide, thus open to interpersonal negotiation if not an amenable critique (and possible consensus) of the objective dimensions of external reality (e.g., what was actually said, invoked, enacted, etc.) concomitant with the discursive intersection of competing experiential subjectivities that inform the therapeutic dyad.

I take as a presupposition that unconscious communication transpires and is evinced in a number of normative psychic operations, behavioral observations, physiological arousal levels, and clinical situations, many of which are open to empirical investigation and critique. Despite the fact that the concept of unconscious communication has been espoused since the early days of psychoanalysis, nowhere do we see such a preoccupation with this subject matter than in the much underrecognized and underappreciated work of Robert Langs, who founded the strong-adaptive approach of communicative psychoanalysis (see Langs 1992, 1993; Smith 1991, 1998). Langs has devoted his entire professional career to studying the processes by which encoded perceptions and unconscious fantasies are communicated on manifest and disguised levels of associational interaction that are often consciously unrecognized and unacknowledged by both the patient and therapist at the time they arise. While it is beyond the scope of this immediate context to explore these ideas fully, Langs cogently argues for the empirical verification of unconscious communication. If unconscious communication were not possible, then we would not emotively react to others so strongly; they would merely be filtered through our perceptual apparatus just as any other piece of objective data would be experienced in consciousness and hence processed, assimilated, and then stored as information. The mere fact that others arouse in us intense and unremitting ruptures of internal protest, dread, anxiety, conflict, and so forth points toward an intersubjective, dialectical tension arc of mutually inflicted and reciprocal unconscious interactions.

The dynamics of projective identification as unconscious communication and their implications for acknowledging countertransference can be grasped once the therapist becomes aware of the specific experiential states that are being induced in him during clinical exchange. In countertransference, we normally act on impulses or emotional reactions (based upon the peculiar contingencies of our psychic registers) rather than realizing in the moment that they are being cajoled, exhorted, or goaded by the patient as a particular form of manipulative wish fulfillment. Moreover, the reason why we often react rather than act is because we experience the projective identification as an exploitive intrusion on our psychic constitution. Despite our being able to differentiate self from other, the knee-jerk reaction is to unwillingly absorb the patient's alien projection as an ego-dystonic identification because we feel it so forcefully—to the point that it becomes confusing to discern the place of its origin, hence the term *projective identification*. Because we are epistemologically more aware of our own immediate internal experiences than we are of the process of inducement, it is no wonder that projective identifications trigger strong countertransference reactions.

Cashdan (1988) argues that in projective identification, the patient unconsciously enlists the therapist to experience the feelings associated with the patient's disowned internal dramas and then pressures the therapist to act on such fantasies and behave accordingly—such as to become submissive (a projective identification of dependency), dominating or hostile (a projective identification of power), sexually aroused (a projective identification of sexuality), or obsequious or self-sacrificing (a projective identification of ingratiation). Cashdan shows that these four major forms of projective identification can be used to understand the relational stance and the induction the therapist is being enlisted to participate in:

a. A projective identification of *dependency* elicits a relational stance of *helplessness*, whereby the unconscious communication is "I can't survive," which induces feelings of *caretaking* in the therapist
b. A projective identification of *power* elicits a relational stance of *control*, whereby the unconscious communication is "You can't survive," which induces feelings of *incompetence* in the therapist
c. A projective identification of *sex* elicits a relational stance of *eroticism*, whereby the unconscious communication is "I'll make you sexually whole," which induces feelings of *arousal* in the therapist
d. A projective identification of *ingratiation* elicits a relational stance of *self-sacrifice*, whereby the unconscious communication is "You owe me," which induces feelings of *gratitude* or appreciation in the therapist

Projective identifications are often attempts to repair, undo, or mitigate serious levels of psychopathology in the self. Fortunately, the internalized osmotic representations and behavioral fantasies of the patient as introjective identifications can be transmuted once the clinician becomes rudimentarily aware of them as such. The realization of being drawn into a projective identification can be turned into an empathic tool in order to make or reestablish a connection to the patient. Tansey and Burke (1989) point out how the patient's use of projective identification may stir up in the analyst similar experiential self-states that mirror or complement the immediate experience of the patient. When the therapist becomes aware of a temporarily heightened internal emotive experience that is qualitatively different from more usual or neutral self-states that he experiences while in interaction with the patient, then the therapist may suspect that a projective identification is in play. When I am led to believe that I am being seduced by the patient's projective identification, I use this as an avenue for speculation and hypothesis testing about the therapeutic situation. Once I become aware of my own internal emotive (countertransferential) states, I pose the hypothesized question in my mind of whether the patient is experiencing something similar to what I am experiencing (viz., modifying Racker's notion of complementary or concordant identifications) and hence question what this may potentially tell me about the patient's inner reality as well as the relational climate between us. So, for example, if I notice an immediate surge of annoyance or repudiation of what the patient is associating about, I wonder whether the patient may be experiencing similar emotional states about me or others (that have been displaced onto me) that have not yet been directly addressed between the two of us. This process more often than not affords me a more harmonious understanding of the patient's immediate subjective experience that aids me in making desirable empathic, responsive, and validating connections in the here and now of therapeutic dialogue. Beres and Arlow (1974) nicely conclude that

> the affect which the therapist experiences may correspond precisely to the mood which the patient has sought to stimulate in him. . . . Empathy in such instances consists of recognizing that this is precisely what the patient wishes to provoke in the analyst. The affect experienced is a signal affect alerting the therapist to the patient's motivation and fantasy. If the therapist does not recognize this, then empathy has failed and countertransference takes over. (35)

Because attachment disordered populations often have noncontiguous and incongruent emotional processing capacities, projective identification becomes a primary method of regulating psychic structure and disruptive inner self-states. A key technical principle in turning a potential countertransference rift into a bridge for empathy is being sensitive to signal affect and abrupt shifts in experiential self-states in order to reverse the impulse toward malignant countertransference reactivity and direct it instead to affective attunement and facilitative identifications necessary to make empathic linkages.

COUNTERTRANSFERENCE WITH ATTACHMENT DISORDERS

Because countertransference is a relational phenomenon and not merely an intrapsychic one, it becomes reasonable to hypothesize that when the clinician notices countertransferential experiences within his own subjectivity, we may further speculate that strong emotional ruptures are equally being mobilized and unconsciously transmitted by the patient as well and are thus informing the intersubjective field. It is more often than not that a patient's experience of me unconsciously mirrors my own experience that I have either assimilated and/or defended against as a form

of projective identification from the patient's unconscious and precon-
scious communications. While commensurate with many of the countertransference phenomena already mentioned before, there are certain experiences I notice time and again while treating attachment disordered
populations. Not surprisingly, these countertransference reactions and
repetitions tend to echo various attachment styles characterized by ambivalent, avoidant, angry-resentful, dismissive, controlling, disoriented/
disorganized, dissociated, and detached behavioral patterns. While these
observations may be peculiar to my caseload and my own personality
and/or unconscious subjective processes, I offer them as suggestive
orienting events that point toward potential countertransference enactments other clinicians may notice or experience (see table 7.2). These
attachment-related countertransferences are communications about the
paucity of affective and relational involvement the therapist has with the
patient. When these experiential self-states arise in the course of therapy,
they often represent particular anxieties about the bond and level of connection or trust established between the analytic dyad, and they present
an opportunity to examine the nature of the therapeutic relationship.

TRANSMUTING COUNTERTRANSFERENCE

Since strategies for managing countertransference with attachment
pathology are really no different from those one would use with any other
clinical population, the first task is to become aware of it. But how do we
know when we are embroiled in a countertransference when by definition
countertransference is unconsciously motivated? Perhaps it is more conscious than we may want to admit. In addition to noticing the sundry possibilities of countertransference described above, we may also notice
changes in our patients, such as coming late to sessions, late cancellations,
remaining silent, or acting different in sessions in comparison with their
typical, customary manner. When we are enmeshed in countertransference, we often have myopia or tunnel vision because our self-reflective capacities have been overshadowed by forceful emotional pressures that do
not afford us the critical distance we need in order to see more vividly the
multiple, parallel processes that are simultaneously operative and transpiring before us. Because of his lassitude, the lazy therapist who does not
think about his patients outside of the consulting room is more prone than
others to ruin the treatment or perpetuate bad therapy.

Detection and recognition of certain signal experiences is the first step,
and as mentioned earlier, signal affect is often a good touchstone to alert
the therapist that something is happening. When clinicians begin to focus
their self-consciousness on the unearthing of such signal experiences, it
should be an indication to step back, reflect, and examine the process

Table 7.2. Attachment-Related Countertransferences

Security/Insecurity
- fear of rejection, abandonment, or loss
- fear of cultivating dependence
- fantasies/wishes that the patient will drop out of treatment
- providing unnecessary reassurances as a form of security seeking
- questioning the patient's autonomy
- feelings of instability/precariousness
- helplessness as a failure to intervene
- fantasies of holding, soothing, protecting, or rescuing the patient
- precipitous feelings of love/eroticism
- using the patient as a fantasized dependency surrogate
- becoming parental, overnurturing, or overvalidating
- feeling overly obligated or dutiful
- lacking assuredness or confidence in interventions
- naïveté about the quality of the therapeutic relationship or the therapist's importance
- being overzealous, too friendly, or worried about appearing nonthreatening to the patient
- fantasies that the patient will not pay his bill

Ambivalence/Preoccupation
- uncertainty, obscurity, abstruseness regarding feelings for the patient
- prolonged confusion/ambiguity about the patient's communications
- emotional misalignment
- therapeutic clash due to misperception or misunderstanding
- inability to achieve empathy when the patient's associations pull for such
- aversion/diffidence
- overpreoccupation about the patient
- resistance to accepting the patient's explanations/associations
- contradictory feelings, inconsistency of attitudes
- fluctuation in mood about the patient
- persistent hesitancy, indecision, doubt
- anger, contempt
- passivity

Avoidance/Dismissal
- boredom, somnolence
- apathy, indifference
- focus on problem solving
- tendencies toward intellectualization
- normalizing the patient's experience
- ignoring, averting, overlooking important material or responsibilities
- evading questions
- fantasies of rejecting the client or terminating treatment
- reluctance to examine attitudes and feelings about the patient further than immediate impressions or emotive reaction
- lassitude or inability to confront defenses
- avoidance of intimacy or discussing the patient–therapist relationship
- pessimism about success of treatment

Table 7.2. (*continued*)

- discouragement, disillusionment, dissatisfaction
- discontentment, despondency
- excessive abstinence
- making excuses for irresponsibility
- discounting the patient's experience

Disorganization/Disorientation
- distractibility, inattention, inability to concentrate
- facial or gaze aversion
- thought suppression
- bewilderment, feeling perplexed
- feeling head is cluttered
- unremitting confusion
- being lost, dazed, or misguided
- emotional blocking
- freezing up, emotionally barricading oneself
- feelings of incoherence, disjointedness
- feelings of disconnection, discontinuity
- dissociation during the session
- frenzied, haphazard approaches to interventions
- spontaneous, undisciplined interpretations in order to gain reorientation or interest

Detachment
- daydreaming, fantasizing
- withdrawal
- isolation and compartmentalization of affect
- paucity of affect
- lack of emotional involvement
- affective abandonment/detachment of affect (e.g., when the patient is upset, the therapist has no emotional reaction)
- removal of warmth
- pervasive sense of disconnectedness (e.g., disidentification)
- extreme feelings of alienation
- failing to take good process notes
- no interest in seeking out supervision
- feeling as though the patient is a thing, an automaton, or a clinical object of study
- not thinking about the patient at all outside of sessions

---

transpiring within one's own subjectivity *and* between the intersubjective field. When certain disruption threats are noticed, such as ruminating about the patient, or focusing on narcissistic injuries, assaults, rage, and so forth, there is a danger situation brewing, and as in Freud's notion of signal anxiety, the ego is alerted to peril. In these situations, one's self-image is torn or flooded with feelings of rejection and ineffectiveness. These feelings mobilize retaliatory impulses to dump back onto the patient or to block out from awareness the emotional significance of the onslaught inflicted on you as therapist. Under these circumstances, Lubin

(M. Lubin, pers. comm., 1990) advises us to examine the good and bad self-representations of the therapist qua therapist that are evoked in such a dynamic polarity and entertain a process of internal release and elaboration of the fantasies mobilized within. This potentially allows for a discharge of internal frustrations that are controlled and confined to a safe atmosphere characterized by self-acceptance and internal transmutation.

By allowing one's internal fantasies a contained and sublimated outlet for expression, one affords oneself a more harmonious self-experience without having to suppress or avoid discomfort, and this process furthermore becomes an impetus for the therapist to shift into a different psychic field with affective utility. Rather than renouncing or blocking disruptive countertransference experiences, one should sustain one's own internal activity in order to see it through to some therapeutic end within oneself and within the analytic dyad. Silently welcome your countertransference rather than repudiate it; if you don't get through the initial shock and intrusion, then you won't fully understand it or transform it into more productive catalysts for change.

As a general rule, it is best to curb or inhibit your initial reaction to act so you may sit back and reflect on the impulses and affectivity that are triggered within, thus allowing for linkages and parallel associations to surface and to be processed. Despite the press to react, if you delay, you may gather your sensibilities and potentially realize the myriad parallel processes that are operative. Think about the precipitating events that triggered your reactions and relate them to your own developmental contingencies, life history, and the broader frame of the established therapeutic context.

Once you have come to notice the experiential shifts in your own self-states and the associational connections to your own inner subjective world, it becomes essential to think of this as an opportunity to form an empathic link to the patient's inner experiential habitat. How do you empathize with someone who repulses you? How can you feel a connection with a patient whose behavior is so appalling, disruptive, or aversive that you wish you would never see him again? These strong affective reactions communicate to us that we are intimately conjoined to our archaic past. What kind of intensive identification is unearthed when we have such affective coloration in the moment? When this happens, we are transported back to certain life or childhood experiences in our developmental histories that still live within our deep interior. These trigger events stoke the unconscious stove of emotional resonance states that we find most incomprehensible and horrific. But they can be harnessed as an ally toward broaching an intimate and empathic connection to the patient once they have been corralled and brought into self-reflective containment.

Countertransference obliges us to open ourselves up to our own childhood fears and anxieties that are in response to, parallel, or mirror our present experience of the patient. When focusing on shifts in self-states or induced emotive countertransferential reactions, ask yourself, When would *I* have acted as the patient is acting? When would I feel that way? Put yourself in the patient's shoes in order to recall a previous time in your life when you may have felt or behaved in such a fashion as the patient, or at least begin to imagine what events would bring you to experience such a similar lived encounter, such as during conditions of extreme frustration and pain. For example, if you feel devalued by the patient, then think to a prior point when you may have been perceived to have devalued him. Regardless of what your internal shift, signal experience, or emotional reverberation is about, the patient is transmitting a certain unconscious trajectory of unarticulated or unformulated experience by making you feel the way you have made him feel, and as a result, he is communicating to you, via projective identification, such experience. Use this as a guide or orienting principle toward speculation and further investigation. If you are able to do this, then you will move past the projective identification and transform the initial countertransference reaction into a more appropriate empathic attunement with the patient's projected self-states, and you will thus afford yourself distance from your emotional reactivity in order to provide containment and understanding. This is similar to what Bion (1962b) had in mind when he spoke of *reverie*—namely, the adaptive accommodation and transmutative metabolism of projective identification given back as empathic responsiveness and interpretive insight.

The nature of when the therapist should or should not disclose or openly interpret the countertransference cannot be considered here. Much of this depends upon the unique contingencies of the therapeutic moment, the conditions and purpose such communications would serve, the affective climate, the motivations and conflicts operative within the analyst and the patient at the time, the capability of the therapist to have attained necessary critical distance versus acting out, the anticipated receptiveness of the patient, and, of course, the hypothesized subsequent impact on the therapeutic relationship that such countertransference disclosures would likely produce. There is no pat formula one can apply because each intersubjective context is different. The therapist must learn to navigate through the analytic process as it unfolds in the lived experiential moment, a skill that is always transmuting and open to refinement.

DEFUSING BORDERLINE RAGE: FROM PROJECTIVE IDENTIFICATION TO EMPATHY

The following case study is based on a two-year, biweekly treatment of an attachment disordered patient whose personality was organized around repeated developmental trauma from family members through ongoing verbal devaluation, interpersonal rejection, and emotional debasement that left a highly entrenched aggressive self-structure. This patient stands out, more so than others, as one of the most viciously hostile and verbally assaultive borderlines I have ever encountered in my practice. The aim of this section is to explicitly address technical considerations for defusing destructive rage in the immediacy of the clinical encounter by closely examining an intervention segment taken from a tape-recorded therapy session. I have specifically selected this particular session because of how I attempted to transform my own countertransference reactions in the moment through empathic linkages to the patient's emotional pain.

Cheryl, a female of Ukrainian descent, was thirty-six when I first began treating her through a university counseling center where I was employed. She was divorced from a man twelve years her senior who was a professor at a prestigious university but was recently remarried to a schoolteacher and accomplished jazz musician. She was a nontraditional, full-time student majoring in psychology at the time she entered therapy under the mandatory directive of the dean for cursing out a professor in class. Apparently the patient initiated an argument with the instructor in a course on feminine psychology that escalated into a heated debate; unable to contain her composure, she told the professor to "fuck off."

When I first met Cheryl I thought she was manic. She was talking a mile a minute with pressured speech, rapidly shifting from topic to topic, and I was barely able to follow her train of thought. She preferred to pace the room and gesticulate with her hands while she recounted her recent preoccupations and biographical narratives. I preliminarily assessed her current mood, affect, and behavioral symptomatology and thought that she may have had an undiagnosed bipolar disorder. She told me that she had been depressed several times in her life and that she used large amounts of cannabis on a daily basis as a means of calming her mind, which she reported was always racing with multiple thoughts. Expressing my concern, I asked whether she would mind seeing a psychiatrist to determine whether medication might help with her symptoms. At the end of our initial meeting, she expressed interest in seeing me on a weekly basis at my suggestion and accepted a referral to the clinic for a consultation with the psychiatrist.

During our second session, Cheryl told me that she had gone to see a physician at the clinic but claimed that he was an "asshole"; she had left during the intake consult because he was not listening to her. Her character pathology soon became more apparent as she described a history of intense and conflictual interpersonal relationships with men always ending in volatile and acrimonious ways, ambivalent relations with women, ambiguity over her identity and what she ultimately wanted to do as a career or pursue in her life, a lifelong addiction to marijuana, rage as a primary emotion, and a very angry-preoccupied fixation with multiple developmental traumas she had incurred from her family. Her borderline personality was organized around structurally aggressive self-states primarily in response to how she felt emotionally abused and invalidated by her father and older brothers, while her silent and detached mother passively observed and never bothered to come to her defense. Yet fortuitously, she felt she was married to "the best man in the world," whom she described as a loving soul mate she cherished.

Cheryl immediately took a liking to me, and an idealized transference arose within a couple of months. I was described as a "wonderful" therapist who understood her and acknowledged her pain as her family members did not, and my personality was described as "warm" and "accepting," unlike that of her previous therapist, with whom she could not feel comfortable or open. The first year of treatment largely consisted of forming a positive working alliance where I adopted the therapeutic role of an empathic and mirroring selfobject by validating her past deprivations and emotional hardships with her family of origin, as well as recognizing her unique talents and potential. The transferential symmetry with her husband, Jonathan, was quite apparent as I was raised to a pedestal just below his level of import and stature.

During this stage in the therapy, the patient had delved into much genetic material and realized that her first marriage was to a man—identified as a bipolar alcoholic—who was a surrogate of her father, himself a first-generation immigrant who became a physically disabled, emotionally combustible, degenerated alcoholic. Feeling dislocated from his own country and having to learn a new language, her father was forced to enter into manual labor and injured his back. As a result, he took out his rage over his lack of professional and financial success on his family. Because he had acted out and displaced all his frustrations on his children, especially his sons, the systemic anxiety, hate, and bitterness trickled down to Cheryl, for she was the youngest child, who was perceived as the most helpless and vulnerable member of the family whom others could disparage and control. Her mother was identified as an unavailable depressive who simply accepted her fate in life and had little energy to combat the climate of lability and misogyny that defined the family unit. The patient's addiction to "pot" was a means of self-medication to cope with the affective aftermath of growing up in an "emotional concentration camp." Her husband, Jonathan, was identified as being her salvation from a life of misery.

The patient was so motivated to examine her dynamic past and its effect on her personality that we increased the frequency of our sessions to twice a week, which continued until the end of the academic year. At this time, I had accepted a new job at a mental health clinic of a general hospital in the same city and would assume my new position in midsummer. The patient agreed to continue her treatment with me there once she returned from her summer vacation with her husband. Because he was a teacher and she was a student, they planned to take the summer off to do some traveling and visit his family in the midwestern United States. She was to call me to arrange an appointment once she returned from her holidays.

Once I settled into my new position, the summer soon passed into early fall, but I had still not heard from my patient. Since we ended things on a good note, I assumed that she felt her life was going well and found it either unnecessary to return to therapy or difficult to continue for some reason that may have been related to her improvements or perhaps the idealized transference. Then one day I received a page on the unit, only to find Cheryl on the other end of the phone in a state of suicidal desperation. I asked her to take a cab to the clinic, where I soon met her. Cheryl was visibly upset and hysterical, claiming that Jonathan was a chronic drunk who had recently battered her, and now she was seeking a divorce. Because the events had just transpired a few days beforehand, she was devastated, overwhelmed, and feeling suicidal. Astonished by the turn of events, I attempted to ground her emotionally and shore up her functional defenses so she could begin to recover her faculties. After two hours of crisis intervention, Cheryl was feeling much calmer and in control. Feeling reasonably sure she was now feeling safe and would not engage in self-harm, I informed her that I had other scheduled responsibilities I needed to attend to and that I wished to see her the following day to resume our therapy so we could process and work through the unanticipated trauma. But as I attempted to end the session for the day, Cheryl claimed she was suicidal and could not promise me that she would refrain from attempting to kill herself. After performing another suicide risk assessment, I determined that she needed to see the psychiatric resident on call in order to be hospitalized. But as soon as the psychiatrist arrived, to my chagrin, Cheryl denied feeling suicidal at all. Feeling quite embarrassed, I thanked the doctor for his attention and told him that I would handle things from here on. Yet as soon as he left and I pushed to end the session, she claimed once again to be suicidal. Annoyed yet composed, I told her that if she continued to manipulate me in such a fashion we would not be able to work with one another any longer. I acknowledged her pain and desperation, but I equally needed to institute a firm frame delineating the boundaries of treatment. Because of our positive work together and her (albeit tenuous) attachment to me, this intervention was successful, but the parameters of therapy were never to be the same.

We resumed our biweekly schedule, but in a stormy fashion. She was enraged with me for ending the crisis session and not making her a priority over my other patients. My once coveted idealized presence rapidly devolved into a detested and worthless obstacle to her happiness. Torn from the pedestal, I was reduced to rubbish and seen as a cold, unavailable, invalidating, and withholding dependency figure not unlike Jonathan or her family members. No longer the apotheosis of warmth and concern, I, like Jonathan, was intrapsychically recast through a prolonged devaluation period. The transference not only became negative, but it was toxic and nihilistic. For months I became of the object of intense hate, disparagement, and ridicule. She treated me in the abusive ways she herself was treated by the significant figures from her past, yet this time the shoe was on the other foot. Her constant barrage of criticism, deprecation, and unremitting verbal maltreatment seemed unconsciously designed to seek revenge toward all those who had wronged her through her displaced discord onto me. The weeks of being assigned the role of the emotional whipping boy took a toll on me and mobilized intense countertransference feelings of rage, hate, helplessness, and inadequacy—as well as revenge fantasies of my own that I wanted to act out. I loathed getting up in the morning and going to work on days that I had to see Cheryl, knowing only too well that I would be verbally accosted as the bad object and recipient of her projected abhorrence and destruction. At times, the containment of affect (hers and mine) was so difficult that I literally would be riding out the chair (white knuckles and all) as though I were being plummeted into the eye of a hurricane, writhing the whole way. Verbal tirades and yelling monologues were common, and one time she was screaming at me so loudly that two staff members opened the door to my office, fearing that someone was being beaten.

The following dialogue comes from a tape recording of one of our sessions approximately a year and a half into the treatment. This episode depicts the heart of the devaluation period characterized by extreme splitting, omnipotent evacuation, and projective identification. I chose this particular interchange because it illustrates how I was drawn into a countertransference enactment under the pressure of feeling threatened, persecuted, and assailed—a possible scenario I believe any clinician can potentially identify with. Yet I feel I was able to recover from the assault within a timely enough manner to respond in a more optimal therapeutic fashion. This dialogue begins with volatility as I suggest the value of examining interpersonal connections between her current hostility toward me and conflicts with others she repeatedly encounters outside of therapy. In order not to the disrupt the natural flow of the dialogue, which is punctuated by the patient's loud voice accentuated by her intense and explosive affect, I will present the exchange in unedited form and then offer my analysis of the intervention.

Therapist: Cheryl, understanding what's going on between us will help you understand what's going on and feel better about your life in general.

Patient: No! How about when I come in and I was loving and good and responded to you? You still didn't do any good, so what's the difference? It wasn't manipulation.[5] It was like, you know, like the parts of me that are healthy, that are happy, that connect, that are very intellectual, that are very intuitive, that are very sharp, multi-eclectic, able to deal with people on different psychological levels—No! I don't feel I'm backed up by you.

Therapist: You don't feel I've appreciated that in you?

Patient: *No!* Not at all! You've never said it, how would I know? I can't read minds. How the fuck would I know?

Therapist: Because I recall several times saying . . .

Patient: Yeah, but it's so low, and it's such a pip-squeak voice, it has no strength to it.

Therapist: So it must mean that I don't believe it?

Patient: Right.

Therapist: It must mean . . .

Patient: It's weak, ineffectual, half-assed, half-meaty. I've got to bully it out of you 'cause you couldn't just give me something naturally like you promised to give me, so naturally I'm *bullying* it out of you—*aggressing* it out of you!—instead of it being something loving and nice, like I go to reach out to people.

[*a moment of silence*]

Therapist: Cheryl, there's so many parallels between you and your relationship with Jonathan and with me . . .

Patient: *No* there isn't! Because you weren't there when I did all the loving good things. And you won't read the evidence about what a good woman I was through it. You're goin' to try to switch it like I demanded and pressured Jonathan beyond—yeah maybe I wanted Jonathan to love me like the way I wanted him to love me, but it was the way he had professed. And when I'm dealing with—I was dealing with lies and broken promises, and fuckin' intimacy distancing, and fuckin' drunken asshole, selfish jag-off behavior! That was fuckin' Jonathan's fault. It doesn't matter who the fuck he was with—let's get that straight right now. Now we can go into blaming me for whatever you want to blame me for, but that's Jonathan's shit, period. Jonathan had his shit long before me, and that's why I've tried to show you evidence of how he treated others or who came before me, or his journals. But that's his shit—OK. He was onto something loving, honest, and good. What's really funny is when I'm not abused, like when I was with the Redpath's, I'm able to heal, I'm less angry, I'm treated better, because there's a little support or validation there, which is the normal fuckin' support that every human being needs as according to Maslow—OK, just normal shit. When I get normal shit without people criticizing me, judging me, or throwing their shit on me—and Jonathan was trying to make me codependent—that's the shit that was going on, that's the dynamic. And my esteem was fighting that crap. I wasn't goin' be another person so I could have my husband whomp me—that was the fuckin' dynamic.

Therapist: I guess because I don't always comment and respond and verify what you say that you do feel that I'm not on your side, that I must think that it's your fault, you're to blame, and I want to throw things right back onto . . .

Patient: Absolutely!! [*breaks down sobbing*]

In the initial part of this segment, the patient was complaining that I was not available to her as a responsive and validating agent in the way that she wanted and needed for me to be, and therefore she interpreted my comments and actual presence as frustrating, withholding, and depriving. Initially I tried to appeal to the healthy part of her ego by introducing some reality testing around the fact that I had on several occasions in the past demonstrated my support and appreciation of her, but no sooner had I begun to call her attention to this than she met it with a steadfast disavowal of its importance and sincerity. Unable to acknowledge my previous treatment toward her due to her splitting and affective coloration, she continued to disparage my past supportive comments toward her as being vapid, hence lacking vigor or conviction; they were now tainted by her disappointment, condemnation, and rage directed at me for not giving her what she felt entitled to receive in that instant. She then projected her fantasy that I had "promised" to give her some form of unconditional acceptance, which was probably fueled by the previous idealized transference but now was contaminated by my perceived withholding comportment, which only mobilized more rage as she continued to intimidate and "bully" me into providing her with the selfobject functions she so demandingly craved.

By this time, I was sufficiently feeling attacked and under the influence of my own countertransference, which I enacted through a transference interpretation. Tracking my own defenses over the years, I recognize that I will sometimes resort to premature interpretations as a way to diffuse my own anxiety related to tensions in the clinical moment. But my transference interpretation, while perhaps accurate, fell flat and only provoked more negation, rage, and effusive indignation. With the further onslaught from her devaluations and need to destroy me for my transgressions and empathic failures, her emotional diatribe slowly precipitated my awareness that I was responding to her projective identification. In other words, I became self-conscious enough in the exchange to realize that I was identifying with the projected attributes and behavioral fantasies she was evacuating into me. Although I was feeling besieged, defensive, and emotionally pummeled, I could recognize that this was how she was experiencing me in that moment: like Jonathan and her family, I was ganging up on her, negating her—aggressing against her to the point that she needed to attack me in order to combat the affect dysregulation and dread associated with the negative introjects and internal objects imperiling her psychic integrity. It is here that I was able to use my countertransference to her projective identification (viz., through vicarious introspection) by acknowledging her affective pain about feeling invalidated, blamed, and rejected by me. By recovering my therapeutic leverage through empathic attunement to her perception of my unavailability and lack of recognition and support, I was able to defuse her rage in the emotional clash of our intersecting subjectivities, which then allowed us to explore throughout the remainder of the session how this felt like a reenactment and recapitulation of her whole volatile interpersonal history with her family.

Throughout the course of this tempestuous period in therapy, Cheryl was able to see her repetition of setting up interpersonal relationships to fail by orchestrating conflict and hence bringing about the very thing she did not want to happen; in the end, people distanced, repudiated, devalued, and ultimately rejected her. When Jonathan hit her—only to end their relationship—she was transported back to her first divorce (which ended bitterly) and ultimately to feeling abused by her father, forsaken by her mother, and ganged up on by her brothers.

As with so many borderlines with aggressive self-structures, the imminent threat of her encroaching abandonment depression signaled rage that was mobilized as a self-preservative defense to ward off disabling depletion, concomitant with a concurrent impulse derived from a deep narcissistic injury to destroy the bad object who had transgressed and aggressed upon her self-integrity. Jonathan went from idealized prince to detested batterer, which paralleled the negative transference and radical splitting that transpired in the treatment.

There was a malignant narcissism to Cheryl's need to avenge her damaged self. It turned out that during the alleged beating from her husband, the patient initiated physical aggression toward Jonathan during a mutual drunken stupor, whereby he slapped her in return. After he made it perfectly clear that he did not want anything to do with her again, she wanted to vindictively hurt and deeply humiliate him for his callous rejection. Apparently the couple had leased a new apartment for the fall and put their belongings into storage before traveling for the summer in order to save expenses on rent. Because the altercation and subsequent breakup of the relationship took place while they were visiting his family, she returned to the city without him. Upon arriving home, she immediately opened the storage unit that they had rented together and sold many of his personal belongings to pawnshops, including several vintage guitars for which she received only a fraction of what they were worth. After this, she stood on a busy sidewalk corner and gave away crates of his jazz albums to strangers who were passing by on the street. Furthermore, she sent a letter to Jonathan's place of employment stating that he was an abusive alcoholic and should be fired for moral turpitude, and then she wrote another letter to the Internal Revenue Service charging Jonathan with income tax evasion and fraud for failing to claim his extra earnings from his weekend music gigs. As if this weren't enough, she stalked him outside his new apartment and threw a brick through his car window, resulting in her having a peace bond placed on her under an order of protection.

After we sufficiently worked through this stormy period in therapy, I was reinstated as a supportive and validating selfobject but in a less idealized (hence more healthy) light. Cheryl was more capable of seeing me (albeit imperfectly) in a more integrative and holistic fashion as someone who was fallible yet well intentioned, with both positive and negative qualities. In essence, she "forgave" me for my limitations and was more able to bear frustrations she had once found simply intolerable.

Our work together was unavoidably and prematurely ended because I had accepted another job that required me to move to another city. We had approximately three months of dealing with our termination that predictably brought up old wounds around rejection, abandonment, loss, and emptiness surrounding failed relationships and her lack of receiving parental love. An erotic transference began to emerge during our termination period, which rekindled old patterns of acting out. She began hanging out at nightclubs, began doing heavy drugs, was sexually promiscuous, and engaged in risky behavior, such as riding the subway late at night in dangerous parts of the city. As a turning point, what was a most fortunate denouement was that she was eventually able to acknowledge that she was acting so desperately as a means of warding off the depletion associated with mourning my loss. This shift allowed us to return to looking at our relationship and the positive feelings she had experienced from my valued presence and responsiveness. The treatment ended with mutual recognition of each other, and Cheryl surprised me with a gift that had certain personal significance to her, namely, a small decorative harp that symbolized the therapy that allowed her "soul to sing."

I consider my treatment of this case to be both successful (within the limited context of the established therapeutic milieu) yet ultimately delinquent, for it failed to produce the type of structural shifts that only long-term intensive analytic treatment could bring about. At the time, Cheryl rejected the idea of being referred to another therapist to continue with the work that we had initiated, instead wanting to preserve the positive ambiance we had eventually achieved together. Years later I was told by my old boss that the patient had called the clinic and demanded to know my exact whereabouts in order to contact me, only to verbally threaten the director when she did not release such information. While this points to the unabated aggressivity that saturates her psychic structure, it may also suggest that I was at least partially internalized as a positive presence within her representational world.

NOTES

1. The term *analytic instrument* is an unfortunate one because it evokes a mechanistic, antiseptic technical metaphor akin to a medical procedure, when Lasky arguably has in mind the signification of the analyst's professional, clinical sensibility informed by his entire subjective agency.

2. The term *transcendence* has a long history of meanings in theology and philosophy. It often implies overcoming or surpassing something to the point that one achieves a beatific, sublime, divine, or ineffable relation to the past. Here I wish to emphasize a more ordinary transcendence (also see Grotstein 2000; Gargiulo 2004) of sublating previous dynamics within a higher order of understanding as the comprehension of such previous dynamics, rather than the religious-spiritual definitions that are often associated with this word. Here countertransference is never totally dissolved or left behind but rather incorporated into higher organizations of meaning and personal-intersubjective awareness.

3. In *The Ontology of Prejudice* (1997), Janusz Polanowski and I argue that human subjectivity is ontologically conditioned to be prejudiced a priori by virtue of the fact that consciousness is the elemental expression of value preferences and judgments that are necessarily self-referential. Prejudice is a universal expression of our narcissistic facticity with positive and negative valences derived from the unconscious disclosure and expression of value preferences. Preference is prejudicial, for it signifies discriminatory value judgments that are self-referential and typifies the priority of determinate valuation. Because valuation is a particular form of self-expression, and all judgments are imbued with value, valuation is prejudicial because it stands in relation to our self-preferences. Therefore, all judgments presuppose self-valuation that is by definition prejudicial. This is why, at bottom, every human being by nature is prejudiced; only the degree and forms of prejudice vary from person to person.

4. I submitted a previous, shorter version of this chapter to an esteemed, peer-reviewed psychoanalytic journal for consideration of its publication. The manuscript was rejected. In the feedback provided to me from the editor, one anonymous reviewer wrote, "This . . . paper . . . begins with a presentation of the analyst's countertransference reaction to a patient that seems rather extreme. . . . And his personal antagonism to authority [is] so apparent (he states that instructors, supervisors, and training analysts are pretentious, deny and encourage students to lie about their true feelings about patients), that his ideas are hard to appreciate." This is a perfect example of the disingenuous attitudes and bias that I am speaking about that sustain the politicalization and ideological oppression of ideas that deviate from mainstream orthodoxy.

5. In "Negation," Freud (1925) tells us how spontaneous denial (*Verneinung*) is often in the service of repression.

8

@

Reaching the Affect

There is often a tacit assumption that when patients prefer to stay on the level of intellectual processing or logical analysis, they do so in the service of a rationalized defense; namely, cognitive investigation and rational discourse keep patients from exploring more vulnerable emotions that are part and parcel of their pathologies. I am not so sure that this is entirely the case since intellectualization and rationalization are sublimated intrapsychic dynamics that help people achieve and sustain healthy adjustment and adaptation, as well as protect the self from chaos, fragmentation, internal division, and regression to more primitive processes. I am reminded of a philosopher who became incensed when told he was too rational and not in touch with his feelings; he insisted that his very sense of being was being invalidated. Undoubtedly, rational integration and insight are paramount for a successful analysis, and as Freud (1914a) reminds us, this requires working through conflicted inner experience in order to transcend psychic pain. The work of working through is indeed about bringing affect to bear on our conceptual understanding of ourselves in the world, which undergoes adventures of change and transformation that are necessary in order to make mutative shifts in self-structure possible.

The question of affect in psychoanalysis has garnered increasing theoretical attention and technical priority within the past decade. Whether the therapeutic locus is situated in uncovering strangulated affect (e.g., see Breuer and Freud 1893–1895), repressed or disavowed unconscious feelings, somatically organized trauma, dissociated or split-off emotional reactions, compartmentalized or unformulated affect, or conscious emotional resonance states, the role of emotionality in governing human motivation and conflict is generally an uncontested fact. While distinctions can be made between affect (as sentient, psychophysiological manifestations of mental events) versus emotions (as more qualitatively organized threads of experiential feeling), for the sake of parsimony, here I will refer to each synonymously.[1] Affect has an ontological and logical priority in psychic functioning for the simple fact that it developmentally precedes linguistic acquisition and the higher-order faculties of cognition, while still influencing perception, information processing, motivation, and conceptual thought. It may furthermore carry the seed of psychogenic disturbances that inform the nucleus of psychopathology. The unconscious life of emotions has a ubiquitous presence in mental functioning, as does the more readily accessible phenomenon of conscious feelings or qualia; and it is precisely in the domain of affect where conflict acquires malignant organizations in need of more direct expression in order for such conflict to abate.

Within the consulting room, affect is disclosed somatically (through physical permutations) and emotively, yet it is subjected to ongoing linguistically mediated events and verbal expression. Reaching the affect often signals forays into unformulated inner experience and rupture, surprise and pain, disclosedness followed by reconcealment, exposure and vulnerability (typically associated with loss of control), as well as cleansing and healing, just to name a few. Many clinicians believe that working through difficult emotions is the heart of therapeutic efficacy, to the degree that emotion-focused interventions become core technical aims. Indeed, psychoanalysis is not merely about achieving insight through unearthing and understanding unconscious processes but, rather, is more appropriately a metamorphosis through affective expression and articulation, intersubjective dialogue, and self-reflective meditation achieved through personally derived meaning. Unraveling sequestered emotions becomes a cardinal task of treatment on the way toward working through psychic pain via affective transmogrification subjected to ongoing meaning construction. Taken together, psychoanalysis becomes a proper holistic totality of experiencing and understanding one's entire sense of selfhood.

In this chapter I will focus on the role of affect in the treatment of attachment disorders by examining a few select case studies. I will be specifically interested in exploring the relation between affect, trauma, and attachment, the emotional bond with the analyst, emotional reservation in the therapeutic encounter, abreactive vulnerabilities, and the process of working through. Reaching deep affect requires breaching certain functional and fortified defenses within a holding environment marked by sufficient trust, empathic attunement, containment, and supportive engagement. Depending upon the patient's personality structure and unique disposition toward emotional expression within the particular contingencies of the therapeutic hour, patients with attachment deficits show a wide gambit of emotions that mirror the attachment styles considered in our previous chapters. Here I will be more focused on addressing the apprehension, vulnerability, shame, horror, and the overcontrolled comportment of affect in the analytic process rather than more extreme polarities of negativity—such as the aggressive volatility, rage, and hate we typically encounter with borderline and psychopathic attachment disorders. Because unresolved developmental trauma is often the germ of attachment pathology of the self, it becomes important to understand how emotional vulnerability, dysregulation, and affective paralysis are related to developmental trauma and subsequent deficits in self-structure that continue to negatively color affective experience. Emotional discoveries and disclosures require the emotional presence of the analyst and the capacity to solicit, encourage, and tolerate anxiety and sensitivity in the moment, a process that mutually strengthens the therapeutic alliance and attachment bonds within the analytic dyad.

AFFECT AND PSYCHOANALYSIS

Psychoanalysis is ultimately about process over anything else—perhaps even above technical principles, theory, and interventions—for it relies on the indeterminate unfolding of inner experience within intersubjective space. In our training we learn to cultivate an analytic attitude of clinical composure, optimal listening, data gathering, hypothesis testing, critical reflection, clarification, and reevaluation—all of which conceptually and behaviorally guide the analytic process. Process is everything, and attunement to process will determine whether you can take the patient where he needs to go. Observation becomes a way of being that requires listening on multiple levels of experiential complexity, from manifest to latent content; detecting unconscious communications; recognizing resistance, defense, drive derivatives, transference manifestations, and differential elements of each compromise; tracking the dialectical tensions between competing wishes, fantasies, and conflicts with close attention to their affective reverberations; listening at different levels of abstraction; ferreting out one's countertransference from ordinary subjective peculiarities; and tracing the multifarious interpersonal components of therapeutic exchange.

Analytic space and the process of therapy is (metaphorically) tantamount to architectural retransformation; it is characterized by the language of complexity and chaos, phase transitions, and continuous evolution flowering labyrinthine forms of discontinuities allowing for supple reconstitutions in shape and appearance, thus leading to more structural stability and processential invariances. Begetting new complex surfaces and expansive depths, psychic transmogrification appropriates fresh composites garnered from the analytic process with creative advances in novelty and self-definition, thereby giving rise to further concrete strength and vitality—all unfolding as temporal phenomena mediated by the analyst within intersubjective territory.

The analyst has the challenging task of attending to the patient's associations within particular contexts of content and form, perpetuity versus discontinuity, sequence and coherence, thus noting repetitions of themes and patterns, and the convergence of such themes within a teleological dynamic trajectory of conceptual meaning. The clinician has to be vigilant for competing, overlapping, and/or parallel processes that are potentially operative at once, thus requiring shifts in focal attention and process. There are always realities encroaching on other realities, and affect plays a crucial part. What adds to this challenge is that affect may not always be transparent. In fact, it may appear amorphous or formless, unarticulate and intangible, namely, ineffable—hence foreclosed from conceptual thought, linguistic specificity, or qualitative description, banished to the realm of soma. Sometimes affect escapes linguistically mediated events and takes on a body organization and language all to itself—such as in the case of felt somatic trauma (despite the absence of memory or conceptual elucidation). When patients genuinely struggle to identify feelings, only to arrive at empty reconstructions or superimposed interpretations that attempt to give them voice and form, I sometimes wonder whether this is because, for some patients, certain conflictual mental events transpired before the subject actually acquired language; and that is partially why labeling abstruse affect is such a slippery enterprise subjected to social construction. Equally, when meaningful constructions of latent affective reverberations appear successful, we may speculate that there is an unconscious transformation of affective impasse through the expressed medium of language. Under these circumstances, one reason why a construction is so meaningful is that it unconsciously resonates within the core of one's being, namely, the feeling soul.

The philosophy of emotions is a current philosophical preoccupation (Borch-Jacobsen 1992; Corradi 1991; Plutchik 2003), a topic that has been largely eclipsed by the emphasis on reason in the history of Western ideas. But many systematic philosophers, from Hegel to Sartre, Whitehead, and those in contemporary continental circles, have attempted to find a place for the emotions in the ontology of consciousness. Psychoanalysis, on the other hand, has always been immersed in the phenomenology of feeling and the subsequent theoretical conundrums it has created for both theory and practice. Psychoanalysis has generally shied away from providing a coherent theory of affect, and, in fact, there is no systematic or unified agreement among psychoanalysts today. This is undoubtedly due in part to how difficult it is to explain the role of affect in mental economy; its purpose and function in relation to unconscious structure and consciousness; and its role in the constitution of drive, defense, conflict, ego development, self-identity, and relational motivation. Furthermore, competing theoretical schools that privilege various theoretical principles over others understand emotions differently—thus leading to a great deal of ambivalence and ambiguity over the characterization of feeling. This ambivalence was prepared by Freud (1930), who warned us, "It is not easy to deal scientifically with feelings" (65), despite the fact that Freud had always placed a premium on emotions—catharsis, abreaction, and working through all entail intense emotional work, literally a voyage through psychic *labor* (*durcharbeiten*). For decades, a psychoanalytic theory of affect was largely omitted, remained "unfocused" (Knapp 1987), or was dismissed altogether because it was seen as "impossible" to provide (Rapaport 1953), which led Leo Rangell (1967) to conclude that it was "the forgotten man."

In psychoanalysis, affects are generally seen as complex psychophysiological phenomena encompassing cognitive, physical, and qualitative subjective, experiential elements. Moore and Fine (1990) distinguish between affects, emotions, and feelings, although we are accustomed to view them as interchangeable constructs. *Feelings* refer to subjective experiential states that may or may not be accessible to consciousness, while *emotions* are viewed as outwardly observable manifestations of feelings. *Affects*, on the other hand, are broad and enveloping, comprising all qualitative and quantitative instantiations, from the most primordial to the most cognitively differentiated, complex psychic state under the direction of both conscious and unconscious forces. In contrast, *moods* may be viewed as prolonged and enduring affect states dominated by unconscious fantasy.

From the analytic literature, we may observe that affect is theorized on three main levels of conceptualization: (1) as clinically reported experiential feeling states that lie on a pleasure–unpleasure qualitative gradient; (2) as neurobiological manifestations ranging from genetically endowed, fixed physiological response patterns to somatic, hormonal, and chemical-secretory processes; and (3) as a metapsychological construct or organizing principle. Affects may be characterized as multiply determined; imbued with motivational qualities linked to developmentally acquired ideational representations and fantasies, perceptual information processing and transmission, and unconscious associations and communication; and related to mnemonically imprinted cognitive organizations and anticipated behavioral adaptations, what Bucci (2003) refers to as a multiple code system of emotional schemas, thus giving rise to specific affective responses and symptom profiles that are enacted on linguistic, nonverbal symbolic, and subsymbolic information-processing levels.

Classical interpretations tend to view affects as unconscious derivatives and as expressions or signals, hence as psychophysical transformations of drive activity that can be both in the service of tension reduction and expressive of conflict typically known through the process of representation, compromise formations, and conversion symptoms. Ego psychologists generally tend to conceive of affects as being within mutative ego structures operative during defense and psychic regulation aimed toward adaptation. Object relations theorists emphasize the qualitative aspects of affect attached to internal and external objects and self/object representations. Self psychologists view affects within the realm of self-structure, as selfobject functions and experiential self-states; while relational analysts focus on the quality of relational motivation, attachment, and intersubjectively negotiated space.

Freud's theory of affects went through many modifications in his lifetime, leading many early commentators to conclude that a coherent theory of affect was not possible. Charles Spezzano (1993) offers a brilliant defense and exegetical critique of Freud's theoretical transformations, showing how affect is the ontological foundation of psychic life. He specifically traces Freud's early views of affect as innate drive-discharge channels, which Freud later conceived as safety valves for tension buildup, then as signals of unconscious expression and danger. He eventually viewed affective structures as patterns of readiness, thus following a trajectory toward feeling states elaborated in presymbolic enactments and action, then to ideational representations (such as in the realm of the symbolic and signification, wish, and fantasy), and eventually to verbal communications, linguistic articulation, and intersubjective dialogue. This leads Lear (1990) to conclude that "emotions are, by their nature, attempts at rational orientation toward the world" (51). And for Spezzano (1993), "This struggle of affect to shape all psychic activity (both subjective and intersubjective) and even the physical world in its own image is, at its heart, Freud's story and the object of his science" (63). We may further see this sentiment echoed in Sartre (1965), who tells us, "An emotion is a transformation of the world" (76). Affect is transformative as it transforms, thus producing permutations in psychic structure and meaning as the self feels its Self. And since the advent of ego psychology and the object relations movement, the notion of unconscious affect—emphasizing the nature of anxiety, hate, pre-Oedipal guilt, envy, reparation and gratitude, ego orientation, self-identity, and adaptive functioning, just to name a few—has become a mainstream of psychoanalytic doctrine.

In one of the most comprehensive assessments of affect in the psychoanalytic literature, Spezzano (1993) cogently argues for an integrative model of affect within a descriptive, developmental, and technical synthesis. He shows that affect theory is the logical candidate to bridge the gap between a clinical theory of treatment and a general psychological theory because what we talk about more than anything else with our patients is their affective lives. While I cannot do justice to his comprehensive integration here, nor explore the philosophy of emotion with much precision, Spezzano outlines the multidimensional nature of the way in which analysts of all persuasions talk about affect, including (1) how affective experience comes to be represented in the mind; (2) how understanding and confusion over inner emotional states transcend first-person, epistemologically privileged access to such inner experiences and may be objectively observed by others; (3) how difficult affect manifests within the transference and countertransference; (4) how it may be disclosed as part of the analyst's subjectivity even when not verbally expressed by the analyst directly; (5) how psychopathology is an extension of affect regulation; (6) how the dialectic of desire (such as wish and defense, fear and satisfaction, the need for power and affiliation, etc.) suffuses our emotional states; (7) how the intersubjective nature of therapy can produce contradictory or congruent feelings in the analytic dyad that are in need of mutual clarification; (8) how affects press for action but need to come under the dominion of contemplation and understanding before action is taken; and (9) how affects transpire on parallel streams of other competing processes in mental life. This leads Spezzano to conclude that despite our lack of unified consensus in theory, from a practical standpoint of utility and technical orientation, the role of affect is elevated to a superordinate position in psychoanalytic thought.

ATTACHMENT AFFECT STYLES AND THE EMOTIONAL TIE

I have repeatedly emphasized that the process of attachment is much more than the mere evolutionary pressures that instinctively drive the organism toward ethologically oriented dynamics; rather, it further requires an emotional connection to love objects that regulates the behavioral attachment system. As with the internalization of attachment figures, so do patients internalize their therapists in distinct emotive ways, and this is conditioned on the unique attachment style each party brings to the clinical encounter. It obviously takes time for patients to genuinely develop an emotional bond with their analyst (for if it were to occur precipitously, it would surely be transferentially based or abnormally driven), as it does for the analyst to truly appreciate and care for his patients in authentic ways coupled with endearing feelings. When this happens naturally, it becomes an aesthetic supplement to analytic work, work that is mutually enhanced and potentially beatific. But when it is manipulated, forced, or manufactured, only dubious or pseudoemotional ties transpire, the purpose and motives of which are undoubtedly tinged with ambivalence, suspicion, and pathological currents.

Here I am reminded of a patient who was shocked when I said that I could not feel for her situation because she acted as if she were entitled to

receive my sympathy rather than earn it genuinely. And during appropriate times when I do disclose tenderness or compassion, I will encounter some patients who are astonished that I really care for them, for
they see me only as a catalyst for symptom relief—and that's all. It is
equally surprising for them when they report having positive and affectional feelings for me based on my manner of attunement and relatedness,
which often awakens fear and doubt, guilt and shame, pain and lack, and
the anticipation that I will only disappoint, hurt, or judge them as do all
others. In many respects, some attachment disordered patients have no
desire nor inclination to form a relationship with the therapist at all, and
this becomes a daunting realization that brings into question the whole
theoretical edifice of relational psychoanalysis. In fact, many traumatized
attachment deficit patients do not wish to know anything about the subjectivity of the analyst at all because of their prolonged experience with
boundary violations at the hands of significant dependency figures, such
as being inappropriately exposed to personal disclosures, affective revelations, confessions that should have remained private, and behaviors
that threaten attachment security. These types of patients are often terrified of knowing about their analysts' self-states or the subjective contents
of their minds based on the simple fear of retraumatization, which furthermore underscores the notion that self-disclosure should be tempered
and thoughtfully weighed for risk management. And when the interpersonal spontaneity of therapeutic exchange leads to mutual intimate feelings, this may usher in new expectations for relationality that go far beyond the goal of self-analysis or symptom relief. As one patient once told
me, "Do you mean that I pay you all this money so we can be close
friends?" While therapy is not friendship due to its asymmetry (see
Buirski and Haglund 2001), it certainly broaches intimacies that even the
best of friends are leery to disclose without certain stipulations.[2]

As with the many disordered attachment styles we have already considered in our previous chapters, emotional disposition, mood, temperament, and capacities for affective regulation and expression correspond to
how feelings are experienced, consciously understood, and explored in
the analytic process. Bollas (1987) speaks of how certain patients live and
express their self-experiences through certain moods that reflect particular states of being. Patients with attachment disorders have difficulty living through moods, that is, tolerating enduring emotional patterns maintained by unconscious fantasy; and when they do, these moods are often
circumscribed, repetitive, and austere. Let us look more directly at the role
of affect in a few attachment styles.

Avoidant-dismissive patients can't seem to tolerate the intrusion of negative affect, which they attempt to skirt through defended comportments,
such as resistance, disavowal, avoidance, or Pollyannaish denial, thus re-
buking the thrust and import of certain emotional reverberations they

find unbearable, especially shame (also see Morrison 1989). These patients want to flee from affect associated with certain internal objects that elicit disruption in experiential self-states vis-à-vis attachment-related vulnerabilities. Emotional descriptions of self and others associated with conflict are typically minimized, deemed unimportant, or claimed to have been forgotten, thus leaving no lasting impact or impression. Dismissive styles rely on denial and repression, fantasy and daydreaming, evacuation, and/or simply tuning out interpersonal intrusion or developmental trauma when it occurs, thus attempting to render it meaningless or irrelevant to psychic integrity. There may be a tendency to focus on the positive, and selective memory helps serve this aim to preserve and protect good internal objects. Patients ensconce feelings toward others in blanket terms rather than focusing on minute details of content or relatedness, or else they portray them in simplistic generalizations and concrete idioms. Such patients avoid conflict and negativity, as well as attempts to confront themselves with their more authentic feeling states in relation to others.

The *preoccupied patient* can become more obsessional, angry, resentful, labile, and controlling and can repetitively dwell on psychic injury, deprivation, and real or perceived trauma. Such patients tend to experience an ongoing and unremitting assault on their self-structures by internal objects, which they feel the need to continuously denigrate and devalue as a means of self-protection and retribution for their suffering. Bad self-representations and feeling states are intolerable and must be quickly aborted before contamination sets in. Because of the internalization and acute absorption of negativity, primitive aggression, projection, blame, projective identification and introjection, and annihilation fantasies are mobilized to ward off structural depletion, anxiety, and destructive inversion. This type of attachment style has difficulty in regulating extreme emotions, which must be evacuated in order to safeguard against inner corrosion and contagion, but, like a vortex, these patients can never sustain distance from their pain; negativity is always reinternalized and recycled. Polarities of emotions mirror the splitting phenomena of idealization and devaluation based on a simple economy of good and bad. The integration of ambivalent emotive states is difficult to sustain, and these experiences typically fall under the beleaguering peril of agonizing self-reproach. When these self-states are realized, they must be converted into their opposite form and violently eliminated. These types of patients are stalked and haunted by negative self and object representations that are nihilistic, hateful, destructive, and persecutory. Mistrustful and paranoid associations are mnemonically linked to objects distorted by extreme presentations in affect coloration, for the self anticipates being exploited and used. These patients particularly struggle with the aftermath of unresolved developmental trauma.

Angry-dismissive patients show a hybrid between the dismissive and preoccupied attachment affect styles. They tend to be less intense than the preoccupied type, but they can be just as caustic, hostile, and devaluing toward others. They tend to harbor grudges and acrimony, dwelling on how others have hurt or abused them in some way. There are often narcissistic components to these patients, who are enraged and aggrieved by various injuries to their egos or disappointments from attachment figures. The hostile dismissal of objects may appear as a defensive identification with being rejected and abandoned by those with whom they had experienced or wished to have experienced an emotional tie. In essence, by disregarding the bad object, they also disregard their bad self, which the other was perceived to have abnegated and devalued.

Disorganized patients rely more on dissociation, compartmentalization of affect, and schizoid mechanisms to regulate psychic structure and ward off disabling feelings of emptiness and fragmentation. Feelings are divided, partitioned, and split off, thus denied an existence to conscious assimilations in the ego. False self presentations are common, and emotions are often experienced as foreign and segregated from ego-syntonic organizations. These patients may appear very disoriented when asked to focus upon their affective states, become confused, experience emotional blockage or suppression, and persist in the realm of experiential absence, thus claiming not to be able to locate or verbally describe their inner experiences. There are presumably attacks on linking; it is as if affect is not allowed to attach to the original object or internally mediated events and is instead kept sequestered and unformulated. Getting in touch with dissociated feelings is often eruptive and discombobulating, which only intensifies defensive needs to distance or evade them, or return to more grounded modes of experiential being through dissociative strategies.

Detached patients typically appear as expressionless androids with little awareness of their feelings, which can readily appear as pronounced depressive and schizoid symptomatology. The more functionally detached person prefers problem solving, intellectualization, reason, abstraction, and behavioral interventions over process-oriented exploration. These patients may appear stoic, impassive, imperturbable, stolid, and aloof. The more regressed or ingrained the patient's detachment, the more traumatized, morose, empty, bovine, torpid, and vacuous he appears, as if he were devoid of self-reflective awareness of any feelings at all. These patients appear alexithymic: they possess marked difficulty in identifying feelings (Troisi et al. 2001), have a diminished fantasy life, and have an externally oriented cognitive style (Bagby and Taylor 1997). Emotions are so segregated, lulled, and overcontrolled that they appear as if they had been killed off and never allowed to bloom or flourish. Emotional life may seem to be completely shut down or nonexistent; extremities in affect, such as hate or joy, are unidentifiable. Clinically, one gets the feeling that such patients are dead inside but they don't realize it. These patients appear to have never formed an attachment or have been so traumatized that internal objects have been depersonalized. Deficits in self-structure are so salient that they appear to have the affective life of a zombie. It becomes excruciatingly difficult to encourage and foster spontaneous affective expression when patients of this caliber seem incapable of forming an emotional tie with anyone.

How do you get patients with attachment pathology to form an emotional bond with you? How do you get patients to value affective meaning when their ability to experience close interpersonal intimacy is severely curtailed to begin with? You as therapist inevitably have to prove to them that you are safe, trusting, and secure enough to weather the myriad tests they will inevitably put you through in order for them to feel reasonably convinced that it is worth taking a risk in disclosing their innermost affective world without the infectious worry that you will immediately challenge, invalidate, or tear them to pieces. This is no easy task and must be laboriously nurtured. At first you are a stranger and they are in a foreign land. Both of you must navigate the domain of forming a therapeutic alliance before the risk of affect exploration seems warranted, and even after that is reasonably secured, the internal resistance to such a process sabotages the potential gains and rewards the patient may likely attain. Attachment affect styles are associated with specific kinds of deficits in self-structure; those who are more preoccupied or angry-dismissive are likely to have variations of structural depletion or aggressivity, while disorganized and detached patients tend to have borne structural trauma, fragmentation, and vacuity.[3] Patients with little capacity for affect regulation, or those who are easily contaminated by affect coloration, such as character disorders, easily fall within these various categories. Their problem is not so much being resistant to experiencing deep affect, but it becomes more of a challenge of containment because they are so easily overwhelmed.

When those patients who are more resistant or experientially removed from their emotional life have breakthroughs in affect, therapy is often taken to a deeper and more meaningful level of processing and emotional elaboration. Hammer (1990) stresses the point that getting patients in touch with their feelings is really a matter of style, namely, the manner of communication one assumes rather than the content one conveys. This leaves the therapist in the experimental position of discerning what manner or style of communication will likely puncture the membrane of defense and touch the affective interior the patient is so sensitive about concealing and careful to protect. Infant research tells us that there is more affective tracking between a child and his mother when the child is insecurely attached (Beebe and Lachmann 2003; Beebe, Jafee, and Lachmann 1992; Fonagy et al. 2002); therefore, it is incumbent on the therapist to be highly attuned to the shifting affective states of the patient in response to the analyst's comportment. While working with attachment disordered patients, I have noticed time and again how unanticipated and spontaneous breaches in affect have increased cathartic value and more personally significant meaning.

Irene, for example, was a very angry-preoccupied woman who had suffered from many traumas throughout her life, including being beaten on a regular basis as a child by her mother, being kicked in the stomach by her alcoholic husband during the third trimester of her pregnancy and losing the baby, and having a second baby die during a complicated delivery. When her parents were killed in a car accident, she never shed a tear. In fact, she refused to cry and had not for many years. Because her occupation was in the helping profession, she frequently made home visits to people's houses. One day she was greeted at the door by a very hungry little girl who pleaded with her to make her some food. After she fed the little girl, the child reached out in gratitude and gave her a big embrace with profuse thanks. When the patient was describing this experience, I could not help but envision her own deprivation and neglect she incurred as a child. I asked how she felt when the girl gave her such an appreciative hug; she said that it felt nice. I then asked the patient whether the girl reminded her of anyone, but she said she did not think so. When I interpreted, "The girl is you," she was immediately brought into touch with her own pain associated with her split-off self-states and began to sob. This was the first time in two years that she had shown any vulnerable emotions in my presence, which opened a space for us to affectively explore more directly her childhood trauma.

Moments like these are transformative for patients and advance the emotional tie with the analyst. Christine was another trauma victim of insidious and multiple forms of physical abuse by a tyrannical father who would hit her "just for fun." She had been estranged from him for many years but still felt he was the reason for her current suffering. When her father was on his deathbed, he asked if she would come to visit him, but she refused. His request and impending death brought forth contradictory feelings of sadistic pleasure and persecutory guilt. During a session following this event, the patient was rattling off a litany of reasons why her father did not deserve to see her nor to receive her forgiveness for his abuse. Then, after providing a coherent, articulate argument with some resolve, she asked me abruptly, "Why should he matter?" "Because he's your father," I replied. Cascades of tears couldn't begin to wash away the pain.

Charlie is another patient who comes to mind. He was as detached as a log, unable to give or receive tender feelings from his wife or children. His father, now dead, was a cold, distant, unaffectionate man who never had a nice thing to say about the patient or the world at large. Charlie shut down his emotional world and became an automaton as a means to survive; but he paid the steep price of not living. After chipping away week after week at his impenetrable emotional walls with long, excruciating moments of silence, we finally struck oil. Sitting in shame, holding his hand over his face, his mouth quivering, he could no longer bear the weight of his world-weariness. "It's okay to go there; I'll be there too," I told him. And the tears welled up in us both. We can only keep misery at a distance for so long. And, as Freud (1933a) reminds us, "We can understand how it is that so often we cannot suppress a cry: 'Life is not easy!'" (78).

THE MAN WHO WOULDN'T CRY

Butch was on his third wife when he came to see me for "anger problems." His wife was asking for a separation because he was verbally abusive and devaluing toward her for no apparent reason, and she couldn't take it anymore. Butch readily admitted that he had had a bad temper ever since he could remember, was easily frustrated, and was prone to frequent outbursts of uncontrollable rage, but he could not tell me why. His previous wives left him due to his tantrums and verbal tirades, and his four children rarely spoke to him. He had managed to alienate everyone he had ever felt close to and was too stubborn, selfish, and proud to apologize for his transgressions. As a result, he was alone, angry, and depressed.

From the initial interview, it was apparent that Butch was enslaved by a repetition compulsion: his mother died when he was twelve, thus abandoning him and his father, who was an abusive drunk with whom he identified, and he successfully kept others from loving him because deep down he did not feel worthy of love or devotion from a woman. In his unconscious mind, convinced that any woman would leave him as did his mother, he ensured that he would drive them away first before they got the chance. Except that this time, he was genuinely distraught and regretful, for he could no longer run away from the truth that he was to blame. He knew that he was wrong and felt ashamed for his cruel actions, but he could not bring himself to say that he was sorry.

Butch was a stereotypical "man's man" who spoke crudely and unreservedly and always attempted to turn an uncomfortable moment into a joke, only to produce a loud nervous laugh. Freud (1905) talks about how jokes bind psychic injury; the laugh is a way of achieving a transcendence (albeit illusory) over pain, while a festering wound still rumbles inside. How does that wound heal? How does it rise above its misery? When his wife moved out, Butch became sad but despondent. He couldn't cry because he did not know what he was feeling. In fact, he *wouldn't* cry—he refused to allow it—because it was not manly. In his attempt to show her that he could change, hoping to win back her trust so she would return to him, Butch wanted to understand the source of his aggression. With a simple, innocuous question, he revealed to me that when he was ten years old, an older man fondled his penis while he drove the man's truck during a visit to his grandparents in the country. This went on for the duration of a summer. He had never spoken of it since and was deeply ashamed that he had allowed it to continue.

Butch was terrified of his emotions and preferred to run away. After our second session, he called to say that he would not be returning to see me. "This is your chance to understand why you are so angry, to deal with your pain—to heal," I replied. He came back and we continued. We focused on the abuse, his mother's death, his father's aloofness and emotional unavailability, the aloneness he felt as a child and the subsequent bitterness it produced. "I think you need a good cry," I said, but he refused, only to deny the need or the cathartic value. He was afraid to break down: the vulnerability, shame, and helplessness were too horrific to confront. His impenetrable wall of stone would not allow the affect to break. We discussed his fear of being vulnerable and out of control, and what an abreaction would mean for him. He was convinced his wife would never come back because he was a totally worthless and unlovable person who, like his father, pushed his family and children away. He was afraid to reach out to them for fear of further hurt and rejection and instead was hostile and withdrew his affections. He knew what to do and what he needed to say in order to seek forgiveness and repair his relationships, but he confessed that he found it too difficult to give them love and validation. He simply found it too painful *to give*.

As the weeks turned into months, the sadness over the loss of his wife turned into a profound mourning concomitant with self-reproach and self-loathing. His defenses of angry stoicism, self-protective detachment, and feigned laughter were breached by the remorse for driving another woman away, which only precipitated the resurfacing of his early childhood pain. He realized he needed to face the echo of his inner truth rather than run from it; after all these years, regret had found him. He felt guilty for abandoning his own children, as he was abandoned, and realized that his inability to tell his children that he loved them was in part due to not feeling or being told that he was loved by his parents. "It's never too late to show them your love," I said. He felt he deserved to be punished for his verbal and emotional abuse toward women, which he came to believe was displaced rage for being forsaken and deserted by his mother, and for enjoying the attention of an older man who was a surrogate for his own unavailable father. I encouraged him to reach out to his wife and children, and despite being terrified of their ambivalence and rejection, he did. After visiting his youngest son, he told him for the first time that he loved him and gave him a firm hug. "I love you too, Dad," he said, starving for his father's recognition. Butch told his wife about the abuse, communicated to her his genuine desire for change, and asked for her forgiveness, which she reciprocated. In telling me these events, he got teary. Soon the tears turned into an emotive torrent of relief when he said, "She's comin' back." Then this 210-pound man curled up in a fetal position on my couch and sobbed like a baby.

HOMICIDAL INVERSION

Faye and her husband, Bill, had chronic marital problems. He had been clinically depressed for years following the death of his father, was apathetic toward his wife and children, withdrew from his familial responsibilities, was completely nonsexual, and didn't seem to care. Faye was determined to stick by her husband, persevered to get him help, and relied on her faith as a practicing Christian and her duty to the sanctity of marriage in order to get through years of strain, acute frustration, and exhausted discontent. Then Faye impulsively took a bottle of pills after her husband attempted to sodomize her daughter. After more than twenty years of trying to hold together her tenuous union, the marriage was over, her daughter was traumatized, and her husband was facing criminal charges.

Faye was in a coma for several days before she came out of it. Her children were furious with her for "being selfish," and she was left to pick up the pieces. She came to see me about six months after her suicide attempt since medication had proved to be of little use. She reported being in a surreal state of not feeling alive, as if time had been suspended, for she was depersonalized from her own sense of existence. She did not understand the nature of her impetuousness, nor what motivated her behavior, only that she wanted the nightmare to end. She reported that after her daughter's disclosure that her father had tried to molest her, Faye was emotionally distraught although rational and called both the police and paramedics to her home, where Bill was retained and then arrested for attempted rape. No one detected or suspected that Faye was suicidal, nor did she have a conscious inclination, intention, or fantasy of overdosing; but later that night she did. She described the event as if she were in a dissociative fugue ruled by an ego-dystonic impulse to act without choice or refutation.

Throughout her therapy, Faye was very conservative and reserved about her personal disclosures concerning anything that was socially inappropriate. Upholding good and respectable Christian values, she was embarrassed over acknowledging anything remotely "sinful," and she was guilt ridden if she did. Early in treatment she gave me a book by L. B. Cowman, *Streams in the Desert: 366 Daily Devotional Readings*, and told me that this book would explain who she was all about. She wrote an inscription inside that read, "'Emancipation through, not from sorrow' is probably the strongest sense of spiritual support I've gleaned from this book." I thanked her for the present and then asked her if she had chosen extra suffering, a question she had wondered herself. Her psychiatrist had told her it was best to make a marriage work no matter what, which her faith had previously instilled.

Three years after her suicide attempt, Faye casually asked me if I had noticed the high waves on Lake Ontario billowing against the shoal just outside my office. I told her I had not noticed but asked her if she had been down to the lake. Apparently this query upset her because during our next session, she told me she thought I was inferring from her comment that she must be suicidal again (despite having recovered marvelously since that time). She went on to say how people in the community still treated her gingerly because of her overdose, which made her feel even more embarrassed, exposed, and angry when reminded of the incident. I asked her whether she had yet to fully understand why she tried to take her own life and whether there was more to learn from it. Sufficiently describing what we had already discussed on many occasions before, I asked her whether her attempt was more because of her inability to accept her own rage. "Well, you can't just go about killing people, now can you?" she asked. "Homicidal fantasies are healthy," I replied, "as long as they remain fantasies." Upon this comment, she confessed with emotional effusion, yet with great relief, that she had wanted to kill Bill for years, but her impulses were too unacceptable to admit. As I asked her to tell me about what she had been thinking, the suppressed fantasies came pouring out profusely: she wanted to tie him to the clothesline, take a strip off his back with a carving knife, and then subject him to the extreme torture that one would expect from a horror movie. Then, like a lightning flash, she made the connection: there was a gun in the house that frightened her—she wanted Bill to get rid of it for years, fearing an accident would happen. The wish to kill Bill was so transparent, yet she could not see nor accept it at the time. When her daughter disclosed the assault, the years of his apathy, withdrawal, isolation, and sexual rejection mobilized such intense hatred in that instant that the festering fantasies she had been unconsciously harboring were clamoring for eruption. The impulse, guilt, and wish to murder was so reprehensible and in danger of being actualized that she had no choice but to end the urge. Realizing the end of what she had built her whole life to be—the life of a devoted wife and mother, only to be destroyed in a flickering moment—she could no longer take the assault on her self-integrity. She was living a falsehood, a lie—a sham: her values and mores evaporated before her very eyes. In the face of her homicidal impulse and the loss of her life as she knew it, she was left with an empty rage with no meaning.

Her only defense was to kill it; her projected death wish was reincorporated and inverted onto herself.

EMOTIONAL YO-YO

Al was a business manager in his midthirties who had been married to his wife, Debbie, for twelve years when he came to see me in crisis after entering into an extramarital affair with his wife's friend. Debbie had been his high school sweetheart for some six years before they got married, yet on their honeymoon night she refused to consummate the marriage despite their having been sexual with one another on a few occasions beforehand. For the first year of the marriage, Debbie refused to have sex with Al, and when they finally did, she would lie on the bed motionless while instructing him to hurry up and finish. These episodes led to persistent patterns of dissociation on the part of Debbie, followed by protest and crying spells during intercourse, and she would be upset and hostile afterward toward Al for days. For years the couple lived a strained marriage, whereby Al retreated into work and endurance sports, while Debbie secluded herself and became more and more dysfunctional. Finally, after three years of marriage, Debbie began to recover repressed memories of being chronically sexually molested by her grandfather from the ages of two through seven. This realization brought on a severe regression accompanied by dissociative shifts in self-states, suicidal depression, and acute posttraumatic shock.

Al had adopted the role of Debbie's therapist and was her main source of comfort. He ministered to her emotional needs for support during her frequent crises, crying spells, and desperate moods, yet the psychological devastation she had incurred was too horrendous for her to bear, thus leading her into regression, decompensation, and subsequent hospitalization. After being diagnosed with dissociative identity disorder, she was not able to work, so the brunt of all financial responsibilities (as well as continuing to be her comforter) fell on Al's shoulders. Al considered leaving the marriage many times but stayed out of obligation, guilt, and fear that she would commit suicide if he abandoned her. As a result, he developed a fine false self through the denial of his own needs, which he subjected to continual avoidance, disavowal, and self-sacrifice.

In an attempt to salvage the union, the couple had two children, who were ages six and four when Al sought out therapy. While his kids provided him with a sense of love and satisfaction, he struggled with his wife's ongoing dysfunction, despite the fact that she had entered into long-term psychotherapy with a skilled clinician. Al could not be physical with Debbie or show affection or warmth because she would interpret this as a sexual advance, which she abhorred with great protest. When she rarely performed her "womanly duties," about twice a year, sex was mechanical and unfulfilling for both partners, and sometimes Debbie would have flashbacks of her sexual molestation, thereby enlisting Al to reassure her that it was only him and not her abuser.

The couple drifted aimlessly, while focusing on their children as a common means of connection, until Al could not take his emotional solitude and sexual abstinence any longer. Amy was a neighborhood friend of Debbie's who was disenchanted with her marriage. When Al and Amy became morning jogging partners, it didn't take long for a fling to flourish. Amy was a good listener and Al opened up; she was emotionally available and supportive and he felt genuinely close to her. Their affair led to mutual feelings of love, and soon Al was confronted with his emotional longings for intimacy and mutual recognition he had sequestered for years. Amy had made plans to leave her husband, and Al was forced to make up his mind about what he wanted to do about his marriage. Claiming to love each woman, he was authentically ambivalent and torn about what he should do, which produced an affective crisis.

Al had a very dissociative presence to his interpersonal style and manner of relatedness. He seemed internally preoccupied and distracted yet had a constant smile affixed to his face with eyes that conveyed anxious trepidation. He rarely looked at me during session or sought out eye contact or facial recognition. As a result, he had little trouble in freely associating. During our initial consultation, he told me he was molested as a child on two occasions; in one of these episodes he voluntarily performed fellatio on an older neighbor boy. He also confessed that he had experimented with homosexuality during adolescence with his best friend, but he was dismissive of my suggestion that these events may have had some impact on his adult personality. Not only did he feel a sense of connection and mutual understanding with Debbie because of their shared childhood abuse, but he also confided that Amy had told him that she was raped as a teenager. His unconscious attraction to victims of sexual abuse and the identificatory power of needing to mollify their pain and feelings of helplessness made it that much more difficult for him to live with the divided feelings he had for both Debbie and Amy. When I asked him whether he thought his attraction to abused women and his need to rescue them from their anguish might also reflect his own unresolved conflicts of being abused, he was more receptive yet worried that these possible motivations might be clouding his judgment even further about what decision to make regarding his marriage.

Al was not certain whether he wanted to leave his marriage or attempt to make it work as he had always done before; but Amy was gently pressuring him to leave in order to start a proper relationship with her. When he told me that he was still sleeping with Amy and at the same time expressed the genuine desire to examine his feelings for his wife, I told him

I was worried that his desire to maintain a sexual liaison with Amy would surely cloud his judgment even further. I did not, however, admonish him to stop seeing Amy; this was a matter for him to decide.

In the weeks that followed, Al became more and more detached and emotionally removed from his feelings, preferring to dissect his situation into a puzzle that needed to be solved rather than experienced. He was deeply troubled and confused over his life and his motives, so much so that he simply wanted to return to some modicum of predictability and expressed grave second thoughts about leaving his wife. One week he complained that he was no longer able to locate his feelings. When I interpreted that he had turned himself into an emotional android in order not to experience his own internal needs and feelings, he said it was easier that way. He wanted to flee from having to make a decision, from his own trauma, from the anticipated disparagement from family, and escape into the illusion that Amy would heal him and provide a sense of connection he did not have with Debbie.

Al then started withdrawing from his wife and moved into a separate bedroom in the house. Sensing Al's distance and emotional reserve, Debbie accused him of having an affair and then started to make uncharacteristic sexual advances on him, which he reciprocated, only to have Debbie enter into transitional states of dissociation and multiplicity that he had to talk her through during intercourse, leaving them both feeling disjointed and abused. Al maintained his sexual relationship with Amy, which only exacerbated his ambivalence and guilt until he could no longer juggle his dual role, and thus he ended the union after repeatedly going back and forth between afternoon sexual excursions followed by distancing. But he started plummeting. In an attempt to patch the lacunae, he bought a motorcycle and would disappear on long day trips, reportedly at times driving recklessly as he found himself slipping into prolonged daydreaming and fantasy.

After staving off the inevitable for so long, Al had an affective breakdown. He came to session visibly distraught, claiming that he felt like an "emotional yo-yo," descending in and out of despair, trepidation, and sorrow. All week he had been flooded with the fear of loss, pain, guilt, and melancholia over losing his family, his years of companionship with Debbie, and the emotional significance of what their relationship meant to him despite their tumultuous history and her pathology. In describing how they first met in high school, he recalled how he rescued her from a verbally abusive boyfriend in the hallway by the lockers, which led her to idealize him as her prince. Now he was on the brink of leaving his princess and his children. He was the product of an unwanted pregnancy and had always felt that this was the reason why he did not feel love from his father. Debbie had given him a sense of worthiness, desirability, and joy, and he loved his children and received their love, an experience he had lacked in his own upbringing. As he was telling me this poignant story, he was smiling mechanically, yet his face was white. "You're smiling," I said, "but behind it I see nothing but pain and trauma." "I just want my life back," he replied torpidly. "You can't have it." There was a massive unearthing in that moment, and a torrent of tears and intense moaning came pouring out—his mouth was wide open, and he was looking directly into my eyes, seeking relief, recognition, compassion. This was the transition to mourning the loss of what he had hoped his life would be.

STAND BY YOUR MAN

Farrah came to see me after having an acute onset of panic attacks, tremors, profuse sweating, difficulty sleeping, persistent nausea, crying spells, decreased energy and appetite, and depressed mood following her separation from her husband of three years, Jimmy, who was identified as a cocaine addict, sociopath, and abuser. Farrah reportedly had a history of bulimia as a teenager and was married for the first time by the age of seventeen to a man ten years her senior in order to get away from her dysfunctional home environment. Her mother was a depressive, chronic drunk and her father was a caustic, detached, and devaluing individual who showed her no warmth or acceptance. She described her family as "secretive" and "codependent," characterized by constant negativity, shame, and critical rejection. Her mother would often sit in the living room at night in the dark listening to country music and drink herself into oblivion while her father sat there and bitched her out, only to tote her gin bottles out to the garbage in the middle of the night so the neighbors wouldn't see the amount of booze she consumed. Farrah learned from her mother that she was expected to "Stand by Your Man" no matter what, a song by Tammy Wynette, which her mother played over and over again ad nauseam while she sat in her chair "drunk as a skunk" in the living room and balled her eyes out night after night.

But after three kids, Farrah's first marriage dissolved after her husband disclosed he was bisexual and was having multiple affairs with men on the side. She could not stand by her man any longer, and because of her family dynamics, she did not confide in her parents nor explain the reason why she sought a divorce, which only invited more condemnation and reproach. This was why it was so difficult for Farrah at first to decide to divorce her second husband; it was another failed marriage, a blemish on her self-concept, and another element of shame to heap on the family pile of humiliations. Despite her strong gut feelings to end the marriage, she felt guilt over her desire to abandon Jimmy and feared being alone for the second time. She had already supported him through one rehabilitation program for his drug addiction, and despite his relapse and continual verbal abuse, she was contemplating staying in the marriage for the sake of her kids if he agreed to get help. Because she was never told she was loved by her parents and never received their affection or warmth, the ideal of family was important to her, and she did not want to give up so easily.

It was clear that Farrah was entrenched in an insidious repetition of picking unavailable, rejecting, and abusive men like her parents who could not show her proper recognition or love. Although she continued to remain separated from her husband, she began to see him frequently to discuss the possibility of reconciliation, only to be plagued by an onslaught of fresh symptoms. She began having panic attacks while driving her car, and on a few occasions she developed hysterical conversion symptoms of paralysis in her legs, hips, and lower back and torso area that lasted for hours. She feared she may have multiple sclerosis, but all medical tests came back inconclusive. We came to interpret her paralysis as her inability to mobilize the action necessary to leave her marriage as a result of her shame, guilt, and masochistic need to fix Jimmy as a means to procure the love and acceptance she never received from her parents, especially her mother. She dreaded being plummeted into an abyss of aloneness, which dredged up her feelings of unlovability and disconnection from others, her regret over not tolerating her first husband's bisexuality, and fears over not remarrying.

Then Farrah called me in a suicidal crisis. Jimmy had been using cocaine heavily, had been verbally harassing her at home and at work, and was threatening her over the financial division of assets. She felt helpless, endangered, and out of control; however, she had no choice but to move ahead with legal action, which precipitated suicidal urges due to the inevitable loss of her marriage. In a truly hysterical fashion, Farrah's suicidality vanished the minute she was able to link Jimmy's threats and intimidation to her childhood helplessness and lack in relation to her parents. Her childhood was devoid of interpersonal connection and affect: her mother was a cold, rejecting lush who favored her brother to Farrah, while her father discounted everything she said or stood for as a woman. When Jimmy started to deteriorate from his addiction, this mobilized inner strength in Farrah that allowed her to distance herself from her own pathology, which was merely a repetition of what she had always known from her parents. Her ambivalence and guilt began to wane into a more objective realization that she did indeed deserve a better man who would love her and her children rather than abuse her as did her parents.

As Farrah began to acquire more emotional distance and resolve in ending the marriage, Jimmy's sociopathy became more transparent: he began harassing her on the phone, alluding to violent threats, then to suicide. He was desperate for money to support his drug habit and attempted to tap into their joint bank accounts. When she cut off his ability to get at their financial assets, he began stalking her outside her home and at work, which led Farrah to legally pursue a restraining order for her protection. During this time, Farrah brought into session a dream she had had the night before about her husband, who had overdosed. She was standing by his graveside, and then she threw her wedding ring into the casket. I interpreted this dream as a disguised death wish toward Jimmy for causing her so much misery, but she would only concede to the wish to see him "gone." When Jimmy continued his unabated harassment, I convinced her to have him charged. He was unpredictable, vengeful, and had a criminal history of battery, and I was concerned for her safety. After he was arrested, all harassment and threatening behavior subsequently stopped.

Farrah began to settle into a "letting-go" process with regard to her marriage and was keen on exploring the dynamics of why she had chosen men in her past who had perpetuated her childhood experiences of invalidation, devaluation, and neglect, a dynamic she did not desire to repeat. During this time, she had been approached by several older men who wanted to date her, yet she resisted. But it was not very long after that Farrah had two brief sexual excursions, one with a man she had met on a week's vacation, and another with a total stranger she slept with on New Year's Eve under the influence of alcohol. In both instances, she was dumped. The man from her holidays (who lived in another city) never called her again after they returned, while the one-night stand was only interested in sex and nothing more. In the end, she felt "used," "stupid," and "cheap." She could not tolerate being alone yet was compelled to repeat her masochism by picking bad objects. During this time in the therapy, I had simultaneously noticed that Farrah was beginning to wear more provocative clothing to her sessions. She would often come to therapy wearing low-cut blouses and miniskirts, spreading her legs slightly while sitting down, thus exposing her crotch, rather than crossing her legs or demurely turning them to one side. I tracked the sexualized transference for weeks but did not want to prematurely comment upon her dress and body comportment for fear that it would be taken as a shaming value judgment—something she was acutely sensitive to—despite feeling as though she was trying to seduce me as she had done with the others. Instead, we focused on the sexual objectification she felt from men and the role she played in soliciting such objectification, her conflicted needs for attachment that she confounded with sex, and the self-destructive pattern she unconsciously felt compelled to repeat out of the belief that a man would not want to have her for anything else. This was all preparatory work for exploring the transference when, out of the blue, the patient disclosed that she had been anally raped by her husband on a few occasions, but she was too mortified and traumatized to want to discuss it with me. Andrew Morrison (1989) speaks of shame as the underside of a narcissistically vulnerable and deficit self. Farrah was so humiliated, disgraced, and guilt ridden over feeling that she may have invited the abuse that she, as in her early home life, learned to keep it as a dirty little secret.

Farrah harbored such profound shame around the rapes that the sexualized transference abruptly altered into projections that I was judging her austerely; she further feared my condemnation and rejection. Talking about her feelings about being sodomized was fiercely humiliating for her, which elicited more feelings of mistrust and betrayal, and thus she relapsed into self-blame for staying in such an abusive relationship. Speaking up about the trauma was initially unfathomable; disavowal and dissociative compartmentalization of affect was easier, a skill she had honed during childhood, where it was selfish to have her own needs—better to be a false self. During this period of treatment, it became more palpable that her unexplained paralysis in her legs, hips, and lower torso was a compromise formation and reenactment of the rape trauma. This further led her to speculations that she was sexually abused as a young child; she recalled that from the ages of five to six she had unexplained vocal and physical tics, but she could not remember any direct events that would substantiate this conjecture, only the internal affective, somatic resonance that something had happened to her.

After a few weeks had passed since the disclosure of the abuse, the patient grew more angry and impassioned about seeking revenge and justice. Once she received consultation and encouragement from a local sexual assault clinic, she was even more determined to pursue criminal charges against her husband. Farrah was examined by the rape-team doctor, who detected severe scarring from the sodomy. This mobilized a great deal of rage, which further helped her find courage and self-conviction to confront her perpetrator in court, although she vacillated between the desire to seek justice versus the need to "move on" with her life. She was afraid that the legal process and scrutiny around the details of the assaults would lead to overwhelming feelings of shame and demoralization. Because Farrah had largely dissociated through the actual rapes, she was worried that the Crown would not find her sufficiently credible because of the paucity of details she was able to provide, which would only prove to be more retraumatizing. She was also terrified that her husband would retaliate, and therefore she feared for her life. Because of the shame, self-exposure, and uncertainty a trial would entail, her decision to press criminal charges was conscientious and arduous. Yet she steadfastly showed courage and conviction. Her decision to pursue legal action was motivated out of genuine self-respect, which she felt was needed for her own healing; he had to pay for his cruelty, injustice, and defilement, and she felt obligated to prevent him from doing such an atrocious act to other women in the future.

The following, rather long therapy segment, taken verbatim from an audio recording, comes from our immediate session after Farrah's visit to the sexual assault clinic where she was examined by the physician. Here we explore the fragile and vulnerable elements of her self-shame in disclosing her traumatic experience to me as therapist—as the Other. She is poignantly aware of her desire to want to avoid her humiliating emotions, but with the recognition that she must face them directly in order to work through her ordeal. It is difficult for these written words alone to capture the emotional tone and intersubjective immediacy of the moment, as well as the apprehension and awkwardness that resonate in the wake of self-consciousness in the presence of another bearing witness to private confessions that are met with affective repudiation.

Patient: It brought back a lot of memories; it was a lot more emotional than I thought it would be.

Therapist: What did it bring back?

Patient: Memories of different situations; just felt like one more humiliation I had to go through, one more degradation.

Therapist: Was he sensitive to this?

Patient: Yeah, he was really nice, just brought back a lot of things; but the good news is that I am healing all by myself and I don't need to have any surgery, so that worked out.

Therapist: Well, good, I'm glad to hear that, must be a relief.

Patient: Yeah, that was really nice to hear, that everything was OK.

Therapist: But I imagine just being in that situation and having to sit with that type of humiliation, as you put it—being reminded of it—is truly difficult.

Patient: Yeah, it's very difficult; I just kept thinking, "My God, one more thing" . . . I even tried to write about it, tried to write about my feelings, and I still have a lot of difficulty with that.

Therapist: In what way?

Patient: I just notice that I find myself . . . I can say that it happened, but I can't let myself go back there.

Therapist: You don't want to focus on the memory.

Patient: Right. And I thought maybe if I did some writing, I thought maybe that if I just forced myself to just go back there . . . and deal with how I felt, that . . . I could maybe just put all this stuff away. Meanwhile I'm just so concerned that I don't want this to be following me forever . . . and some way of not wanting to give Jimmy the satisfaction that he's had that much of an effect on me that he can . . . these experiences will have an effect on my future.

Therapist: And that would be another shaming experience I imagine.

Patient: Mmm-hmm.

Therapist: But there's a real anxiety for you about going back and rehashing, rethinking about what happened.

Patient: Mmm-hmm.

Therapist: Are you afraid it's going to precipitate you crumbling to pieces?

Patient: [sighs] I don't know, it's like it's a mental block—I don't know, I don't even, I don't know what it is that I'm afraid of . . . I just have a feeling that I need to . . . I just want to get rid of this—I want to get rid of this, I want to get rid of the last few years and I just want to move on with the rest of my life, and this is just a bad chapter. I don't want it to be haunting me forever, and I don't want to get into another relationship eventually and have this . . . interfere. So I guess I realized yesterday when I was having that exam done that . . . that I'm not as over it as I thought I was. I just started crying [*laughs nervously*], just started crying, and I really didn't anticipate that I would do that. When I first went I was just more uncomfortable about the procedure and about possible results. I didn't expect that the actual procedure would bring out those feelings.

Therapist: I'm sure it must have felt like another intrusion.

Patient: Yes, that's how it felt like—one more humiliation.

Therapist: Maybe it would be helpful to talk more about feeling humiliated.

Patient: I guess because I try to be so logical about everything, that I'm somehow trying to make myself logically think that I can just not feel humiliated. And then I tell myself, "Don't be stupid, he should be the one who's humiliated." But I am. And I had to discuss little bits of it with the doctor yesterday, and that was uncomfortable. I think the court case is going to be a lot more difficult than I thought. Deep down I know I did the right thing, but there is a part of me that thinks that maybe I shouldn't have, maybe I just should have just let it go . . . I just want him so badly to know that what he did was wrong.

Therapist: So your ambivalence about wanting to revisit those memories is also connected with wanting to move on and not deal with it.

Patient: Mmm-hmm.

Therapist: And on some level you know that you are an intelligent woman and you've got it figured out in your head; it's just the residual emotions that are not so easy to let go of.

Patient: I thought of it yesterday kind of like a posttraumatic event, you know, that I think that I'm OK, then go for this exam thinking that not in a million years that those issues would come up and they just came out of nowhere.

Therapist: It *was* traumatic.

Patient: That's why I'm afraid that if I don't deal with this, I can't begin to
. . . [*Patient starts crying. A minute passes in silence.*]

Therapist: What do you need right now?

Patient: I don't know. I don't know what . . . why it's so difficult, just even
sitting by myself with a piece of paper, I have a hard time. I'll think of fifteen
other things to do, even though I don't have the time to do it. And yesterday
I tried to force myself to write a little bit, and I just can't seem to talk about
the experiences—period. [*silence*] Then I get angry. I was angry yesterday after I left the doctor's . . . and thought, "He should be castrated" [*laughs*] . . .
which should be obvious. He abused his first wife, and abused me worse.
The next woman he's involved with will bear the brunt of his first relationship and our relationship, and she will probably be abused worse than I was.
And he feels that he didn't do anything wrong. Especially if he walks away
and is not convicted; he'll really feel he didn't do anything wrong. You know,
just carry on.

Therapist: Do you have to have a conviction to know that some form of justice is happening?

Patient: [*long pause*] It's hard to say because with the type of personality that
he is, even with a conviction . . . he's just not a remorseful person.

Therapist: You're never going to get that from him.

Patient: Never, never . . . I have to go into court on the twenty-fourth to settle with Family Law, and that's going to be really tough, really tough. [*sighs*]
That's going to be the first time I've seen him in a really long time and I'm
goin' try, just try not to look at him.

Therapist: What do you fear might happen?

Patient: I don't know, I don't know anymore. I'll be prepared either which
way. And if the judge rules more in his favor, then I'll pick up the pieces.

Therapist: But from what you told me last week, it seems very unlikely.

Patient: I would think so, I would think, I don't know for sure.

Therapist: There's a couple thoughts I have—of not wanting to focus on the
humiliation; thinking what he has done, however, has mobilized your anger,
and he deserves to be punished for what he's done.

Patient: I still think that deep down, I still feel responsible. . . [*silence*]

Therapist: Why is that?

Patient: Because I didn't do anything sooner.

Therapist: Such as what?

Patient: Leave. [*laughs nervously*]

Therapist: So because you didn't leave, you're responsible that he assaulted
you?

Patient: I guess in a sense I feel I allowed it to continue by keeping myself in that situation.

Therapist: Is that you talking or is that your mom?

Patient: [*smiles dejectedly*] I think it's me, I think . . . deep down I still have some shame that I didn't leave earlier. That's why it took me so long to even talk about what happened. I've had so many humiliating experiences—and it happened more than once.

Therapist: So you blame yourself.

Patient: Mmm-hmm . . . I think so. I know he's an asshole, OK. I was such a different person—oh God, I was such a different person. I became a person in that marriage that I didn't even recognize. I just didn't have the strength to get out of it . . . but I did, I guess, eventually. [*large audible sigh*]

Therapist: I notice that when you get in touch with these very vulnerable feelings, that gets turned into anger—and rage to some degree, then it gets thought out logically . . .

Patient: Mmm-hmm.

Therapist: . . . but then it comes back to self-blame. So it starts with shame and ends up with shame.

Patient: 'Cause I really haven't worked through the shame. [*laughs nervously*]

Therapist: What's it like for you to even talk through it with me?

Patient: Uncomfortable, uncomfortable even with my two close friends who know, who basically know what you know. I've sat down but haven't gone into it too deeply. I can't even find the words.

Therapist: What keeps you from going that next step?

Patient: [*very long pause*] Because it's goin' be how I'm going to feel, 'cause I already feel humiliated enough as it is. But unlike before, I do realize I do have to deal with this. Hopefully, I have a long life ahead of me and this is a very short period of my life in the grand scheme of things, and I don't want this haunting me.

Therapist: You're aware that you need to talk about it, yet you don't want to go there, but you don't want it to follow you like some ghost the rest of your life.

Patient: Yep. [*laughs*]

Therapist: Well, let's give it a shot, and we'll take it as it comes, and we'll see how it feels.

[*a minute of silence*]

Patient: It's totally hard to go there. I can't even remember the first time, I can't remember, I don't know what that's all about, but I can't remember, I can't remember the first time. I should be able to remember that, that should've been the worst, but I can't. [*begins sobbing*]

What I was attempting to do during this exchange was allow the patient to be in control of guiding her own process of emotional exploration and elaboration of her multiple fears, affective disruptions, and the extreme helplessness associated with the assaults in the hopes that her shame would be bound to the actual events rather than generalize to her perceived sense of responsibility stemming from irrational self-blame. What is often an unspoken yet extremely poignant aspect of dealing with shame in the clinical encounter is the exposure the patient feels in eyes of the other, for transference apprehensions of how the therapist will respond to the patient's vulnerability in the moment magnify the patient's perceived sense of shameful intolerability. This session continued along a path of unraveling her emotional elaborations of shame, to the invalidation and anguish she felt over the fact that her husband was never bothered about how he had crudely violated her as a sexual object, nor did he care that he had caused her immense suffering. This experiential self-state of being treated as merely an object rather than a feeling subject with her own needs, moral rights, and sense of dignity was then converted into indignation over his cruelty, thus mobilizing harsh superego judgments of condemnation and the need for justice.

Farrah came to realize that there was nothing intrinsically wrong with her or her actions, and that her affective sense of responsibility connected to the assaults was motivated from genetic deposits stemming from her dynamic past, where she had come to unconsciously believe that she should stay in unhealthy relationships as did her parents. Seeing more objectively that her dissociation during the rapes, ensuing compartmentalized affect, and her gaps in memory (representing punctuated attempts at repression) were defensive in nature, she could now see that these were adaptive efforts enlisted to help her survive her trauma. By transforming her vulnerabilities around shame, guilt, self-indictment, and personal accountability for the assaults into the conviction that her actions were functional strengths at adaptation in the face of horrific abuse from a psychopath, she was able to maintain resolve in her pursuit of justice. In the end she handled herself with courage and dignity, sufficiently worked through her trauma and residual feelings of humiliation, and testified in court against her husband's nefarious actions, whereby he was subsequently convicted for criminal sexual assault.

TERMINATION, EGO INTEGRATION, AND INTIMACY

There is no set protocol to determine when a therapy is ready for termination, given that analysis is an ongoing endeavor that is in effect interminable, as Freud (1937) would tell us. In my experience, the process of termination is usually initiated by the patient rather than the therapist when a sufficient amount of symptom relief, behavioral change, and/or personal goals has been achieved, if termination is not mediated by other life circumstances, such as financial constraints, relocation, or illness. When the processes of resistance, transference enactments, repetition, acting out, and working through developmental traumas by transforming deep affect are satisfactorily resolved, we may only hope that the analytic task has imparted a generalized skill set of self-examination, affect regulation, functional adjustment, personal insight, and meaning construction in such a way that the patient will carry forth the analytic work without relying on the therapist or without experiencing further symptomatic emergence. This often entails relinquishing the transference neurosis, including dependency on and idealization of the therapist, for more realistic appraisals of what relationships are truly like in the "real world." With attachment disordered populations, there is the further hope that we succeed in attaining unconscious shifts in personality structure concomitant with ego integration and the fortification of functional defenses that aid in patients' psychosocial adjustment and enrich the quality of their interpersonal relationships.

Initiating the termination phase often engages very early issues around attachment and the quality of object relationships, separation, autonomy, individuation, abandonment, and loss. Patients may become very reluctant to give up their attachment to their therapists when a posture of dependency and/or idealization has been established; their reluctance thus signifies unresolved transference manifestations. Alternatively, the need to separate and distance from the therapist as an autonomous agent may be more prevalent when secure feelings of independence and individuation have been adequately achieved. Depending upon the unique personality constellation of the patient, anticipating and planning for termination may excavate vulnerabilities around separateness, privation, abandonment, and absence, which can further influence a regression to previous developmental phases and primitive defenses, lead to symptomatic reemergence—often as a failure of working through or as a need to preserve unconscious fantasies associated with anxiety about separation (Miller 1965)—and bring about the recapitulation of individuation experiences commensurate with early life. Patients with character pathology often find a need to be angry, resentful, and devaluing of the therapist (Levy 1984), may unconsciously wish to spoil or diminish the importance of the clinician or the analytic work, and may resort to acting out rather than discussing their vulnerable feelings or expressing their tenderness and appreciation toward the therapist for his availability during times of struggle and personal growth. It is very difficult to say good-bye because of the realization of permanence and the interpersonal demands for acknowledgment and mutual recognition that such experiences stimulate.

Attachment disordered patients are especially intimidated by the call to embrace the challenges of intimacy, so they often attempt to sabotage the significance of the relationship with the therapist in order to gain critical distance (e.g., by adopting a dismissive, rejecting, or withdrawing detachment) as a way of letting go of the value that person had on them. In this way, their narcissism and vulnerability around intimacy continue to interfere with their personal happiness, which is indicative that treatment is far from complete. When these experiences transpire in the therapy, analysts may also find themselves enveloped by their own countertransference as a means of protection against their own vulnerabilities around attachment, intimacy, and rejection.

Singer (1965) tells us that the ultimate criterion for the termination of therapy is the willingness of the patient to engage in a genuine search and weather its hardships alone. Freud (1937) informs us, as does Basch (1980), that happiness is never a touchstone for therapeutic success, for this only leads to interminable and frustrating expectations that place extra burden on the course of treatment. While the pursuit of happiness is an ideal aim, it is neither a necessary nor sufficient condition for analytic success. As Freud once said in the early years of psychoanalysis, much can be achieved by turning "hysterical misery into common unhappiness" (Breuer and Freud 1893–1895, 305). The most we can hope for is that the pursuit or process of self-knowledge will lead to inner liberation, personal meaning, and the fulfillment of possibilities—even if they only make our suffering more tolerable. Schafer (1973) advises us to explore with the patient what has been accomplished in the therapy as well as to place into perspective what has been left undone. I find it useful to reflect upon the patient's originally expressed therapeutic goals, establish whether they have been adequately met (in part or in whole), and propose the need to cultivate an ongoing attitude of self-reflection. Termination will inevitably dredge up evocative memories of the dynamic past, including earlier separations and painful affect—from rage to devaluation, grief, and mourning—associated with earlier attachment figures and developmental traumas (Strupp and Binder 1984), therefore necessitating more affective work around mourning and loss. Kohut (1977) further notes that the terminal phase of treatment will signal a return to structural conflicts that had been a major part of the working-through process, whereby the patient must confront "the ultimate relinquishment of the objects of his childhood love and hate" (15). This often excavates unconscious fantasies for insatiable gratification and intolerable frustration over transference wishes that are besieged from never being fulfilled, thus intensifying a negative transference (Dewald 1964). The disparagement or expressed disappointment that nothing significant has come from the therapy is often an attempt to avoid feeling the loss of an important attachment and thereby skirt the anguish of grief.

I recall from my early days of training being told that I shouldn't get too attached to patients because this will only produce ambivalent and complicated emotions that will detract from appropriate therapeutic work. How often are we advised not to let our needs get in the way of what is best for the patient? I feel this is an unspoken rule that still governs most formal education and clinical supervision: you should be satisfied with the beauty of knowing you serve a valuable purpose for patients' psychic economies, even if you are not acknowledged or appreciated by them for your impact. Perhaps this is a rationalized defense against knowing that we as analysts will not receive what we hope to from our patients, and we must safeguard from such anticipated disappointments. Contemporary relational approaches to treatment seem to be combating this bias, thus elevating the nature of the analyst's subjectivity (including his own needs, wishes, and feelings) as an adjunct to the therapeutic matrix. Exploring one's sense of self-in-relation to another's in the consulting room seems to me to be an appropriate forum for the patient to begin to appreciate the transmuting nature of relationships he will encounter in the real world.

The patient's acquisition of autonomous capacities to analyze life experiences and seek his own resolutions in adaptive ways may be the most optimal benchmark for judging when therapy is nearing an end. This requires an appropriate degree of ego integration characterized by the patient's ability to achieve a margin of synthetic appreciation of the overdetermined complexifications of one's self and intrapsychic subjective life in relation to others and the world at large, to develop capacities for empathy for others, to recognize and be sensitive to others' needs and pain, and to seek some form of intersubjective negotiation and mutual understanding of competing desires and defenses that govern psychosocial reality. Here Fonagy's admonition to foster and strengthen skills at mentalization is well taken. It is in this way that the self comes to recognize its self-in-relation to its ontological facticity as a dynamic self-articulated complex holism. The pursuit of wholeness is an unfolding dialectical process that is never complete but only approximated through ongoing immersion in self-discovery, creativity, ethical consideration, intersubjective exchange, and mutual recognition. Heidegger (1927) would refer to this as the call of conscience, the subject's obligation to seize upon one's being-in-the-world as care. And as Erwin Singer (1965) aptly states, "It would be a folly to believe that psychotherapy will activate the patient's total capacity to love and care and to use his powers fully and productively. All that one may hope for is that he will become engaged in a never-ending effort to love, to care, and to use his abilities fully and creatively" (353). The puissance of therapy is the indoctrination into a lifelong process of becoming.

Is there truly an appropriate ending to therapy? Are there certain things that should be said, secrets confessed, emotions conveyed? During the termination period of an analysis, I tell patients honestly what they have meant to me, what I have learned from them, what strengths and gains I perceive they have acquired, and what areas of further exploration and growth I feel are needed. If tender emotions naturally arise in me, I do not bother to hide or suppress them, because I have come to believe that expressing intimacy spontaneously is what health is all about. I genuinely wish all my patients well in the hopes that they achieve the love and wisdom that makes life so beautiful. When I am recognized for my efforts in their process, I am grateful for their gift. And if the patient initiates some display of affection, all the better. Harry Guntrip (1975) once spoke of his termination session after completing his analysis with Fairbairn in a very endearing way:

> As I was finally leaving Fairbairn after the last session, I suddenly realized that in all that long period we had never once shaken hands, and he was letting me leave without that friendly gesture. I put out my hand and at once he took it, and I suddenly saw a few tears trickle down his face. *I saw the warm heart of this man with a fine mind and a shy nature.* (149)

This sentiment conveys nicely the mutual recognition, appreciation, and gratitude of how both the patient and the therapist are moved by the emotional bond that ensues from feeling a loving attachment to another. Shared intimacy, no matter how subtle or robust, enriches the yolk of our being. What better place to be authentic?

NOTES

1. In *The Unconscious Abyss* (2002a), I meticulously outline the developmental unfolding of the unconscious soul as a corporeal, sentient physiological embodiment, to the life of feeling as a desirous, pre-reflective unconscious self-consciousness, to the actual ego of perceptual consciousness, sensuous cognition, and reflective, rational self-conscious life.

2. Aristotle (1962) tells us of three forms of friendship, based on mutual pleasure, utility or commerce, and selfless love, the latter being the most exalted form of the soul's union with the subjectivity of the other. Therapy could be easily viewed as a form of monetary exchange for services rendered that provide utility, and sometimes bring mutual pleasure, but it could hardly be classified as the true form of friendship Aristotle envisions (see bks. 8–10).

3. See our previous discussion of structuralization in chapter 3.

III

EXTENDED CASE STUDIES

9

℗

Engaging Alexithymia in a Depressed, Eating Disordered, Body Dysmorphic Adolescent Female

the following three chapters, I will focus on the application of attachment-related strategies to the analytic process in the treatment of severely troubled, structurally deficient, attachment disordered patients. These extended case studies show the deleterious effects of developmental trauma and abuse on attachment security, psychic structuralization, the process of representation, ego integrity, affect regulation, and defensive repetitions, leading to unremitting clinical symptomatology and dysfunctional adjustment patterns. All three of these patients have suffered differential degrees of trauma that inform their disorganized attachments, and they serve as intended prototypes for conceptualizing the challenges inherent in the treatment process. Relational strategies augur well for providing a secure base while working with patients with entrenched structural deficits and polysymptomatic profiles. Through these case analyses, it is my intention to offer further empirical support for relational sensibilities to treatment lead to reparative shifts in self-structure that bolster attachment capacities.

Andrea was seventeen years old when she first entered into treatment with me because she was suffering from recurrent suicidal ideation after a breakup with her boyfriend. She had been hospitalized the previous year following a severe overdose and had an unabated history of depression; anxiety and panic symptoms; anorexic food restriction followed by binge eating, compulsive exercise, and active bulimia; affect dysregulation; mood instability; and chronic self-mutilation through cutting behaviors. She had dropped out of regular high school due to her depressive symptoms, intense feelings of inadequacy, distorted self-perceptions of ugliness, and social rejection by her peers and was attempting to complete

her courses through correspondence school with little success. She complained of being depressed, withdrawn, and periodically suicidal since the age of eleven, reported a brief psychotic episode at the age of thirteen, was excluded and ridiculed by her peer group, struggled with her racial identity as a mixed African-Caucasian girl, and was profoundly sensitive to feelings of interpersonal dejection, abandonment, and an intolerable sense of internal aloneness. She had been placed on two different antidepressant medications (Effexor and Celexa) after her overdose and had seen two previous therapists within the previous year with no changes in her symptomatology.

Andrea had been dating her first serious boyfriend for four months—a white male from the same high school—when he had unexpectedly ended the relationship after he had sex with her. While she could identify feelings of being hurt and injured by him, she denied any anger and ultimately felt she was to blame because she thought she was inherently ugly and unlovable despite having substantial evidence to conclude that the boy was a racist with sociopathic tendencies. It became quite obvious to me within the first few sessions that Andrea was alexithymic: she explained that at times she could not locate, discern, describe, nor articulate internal feelings, emotional resonance states, affective schemas, or somatic representations with any precision and frequently vacillated between an avoidant and angry-dismissive attachment style dominated by interpersonal resistance, passive-aggressive withdrawal, and conflict evasion. She primarily has an externally oriented cognitive style, yet, unlike many alexithymic patients who have a paucity of fantasies, Andrea is profoundly affected by mood invariance dominated by unconscious fantasy systems. A schism exists between her internal affective life and her ability to cognitively mediate such internal events. She struggles with being able to linguistically label internal phenomena, has a negative affect style (e.g., a preoccupation with criticism, intrusiveness, and guilt induction), is susceptible to affective coloration, self-blame, and self-vilification, and acts out impulsively, including binge eating and cutting her arms with sharp objects such as scissors, razors, or glass, thus requiring medical attention in the past.

The patient comes from a mixed racial background, which serves as an ongoing source of identity diffusion. Her parents are South African immigrants who escaped apartheid and established themselves in Canada. By Andrea's reports, her mother was physically beaten as a child by her parents, who demanded strict discipline and obedience and subjected her to a rigorous religious upbringing under the auspices of the Catholic faith. Andrea's paternal grandfather was an African tradesman who did not share the same language as his Irish bride, and the two of them parted ways when Andrea's father was quite young. Andrea described how her parents have ongoing marital problems and rarely talk to each other, and

when they do it is often critically focused on their three children as a displacement for their own interpersonal frustrations. There is no display of warmth or love in the family, and Andrea, who is the middle child, having a brother three years older and a sister five years her junior, is often the object of negative attention because of her identified symptoms and inability to complete school.

Throughout the course of the therapy, it soon became apparent that Andrea's parents themselves had disturbed intergenerational parental attachments and negative affect styles and struggled with their own inner burdens stemming from early conflicted internalized representations, which they enacted and projected onto their children. The transgenerational transmission of attachment disruptions had unequivocally disposed Andrea to developing insecure attachments toward her parents marked by prolonged separation anxiety, pervasive fears and childhood phobias, and a fundamental submissiveness to the threat of parental authority and abandonment, which became organized on a borderline level of functioning. For example, Andrea was terrified by her mother's threats of rejection and punishment, and her mother frequently used intimidation and fear tactics to discipline or control Andrea's behavior. Andrea reports that her mother would threaten to leave her with her maternal grandfather to be abused as she was if Andrea did not mind her instructions or behave as expected. Her mother would also make pronouncements that Andrea would "be the death of her," and that God would punish her for behaving in sinful ways. As a result, Andrea developed intense fears of "the devil," "evil," and "sin," and cultivated rituals to keep her safe in her room at night while she slept (i.e., she had seven Bibles, prayer books, and several crucifixes positioned in her room, and she prayed in a certain rote fashion). While her relationship to her mother was marked by fear, her relationship to her father was virtually nonexistent. He showed her no warmth or attention when she was a child and acted as if she and her other siblings were a burden to him because he would often complain there were "too many mouths to feed." Not only did Andrea not feel wanted, but she never felt loved.

Andrea characterized her early childhood as an incessant pursuit of trying to be perfect in order to please her mother. She excelled in choir, gave piano recitals, attended church regularly, and was a top student until approximately fifth grade, when the onset of puberty, negative treatment from her social peer group, and increased pressures from her parents ushered in increased self-perceptions of being ugly, feelings of suicidal depression, and the onset of anorexia. By the time the patient entered into high school, she had begun binging and purging to regulate her weight, and she still has episodes of binging followed by periods of restriction or compulsive exercise to undo her gorges. Many professionals would in all likelihood diagnose her with body dysmorphic disorder

due to her distorted perceptions of being physically deformed, whereby she claims she has asymmetrical facial morphology and skin pigmentation that accentuates her ugliness, despite being an objectively attractive girl. Her preoccupation with self-loathing based on skin color further reflects her conflicted racial identity, her lack of identification with black culture, and a negatively internalized anti-ethnocentrism characterized by the belief that "black people are ugly," a statement expressed by her white counterparts whom she wished to be accepted by.

Andrea's personality structure began to acquire more borderline levels of organization in response to repeated developmental trauma surrounding fear, guilt induction, and abandonment anxiety, resulting in mood instability with affect dysregulation, thus leading to problems in emotional lability, impulse control, and self-harm under the influence of dissociative strategies. Her attachment disruptions further led to a primary developmental failure in the formation of holding introjects, internal soothing functions, and relational continuity, marked by ambivalence toward dependency figures and resulting in negative self and object representations, which stirred up annihilation threats and paranoid ruminations (e.g., about evil, fear of becoming possessed) associated with a fundamental inner emptiness. Her increased preoccupation with her identity confusion, perceived homely appearance, and distorted body image further reinforced an uncohesive sense of self and a deficiency in developing an observing ego. These structural conditions continue to inform her lack of self-reflectivity and incapacity to think about mental states in herself and others.

I had to assume a very active level of engagement from the very beginning of treatment, which has not changed after two years. The patient's demeanor is naturally quiet, timorous, guarded, and readily resistant to spontaneous associations or initiations of discussions unless in response to being engaged in a more direct manner. She has always displayed the same pattern of interaction upon initiating each session: she tends to sit in silence like a clam for long periods of time, does not offer associations until prompted, and mainly responds to explicit questioning. Getting her to talk is like pulling taffy. Even a dentist would find it excruciating. She prefers to sit in the middle of the couch with her legs crossed, head and shoulders down, with her hands between her legs. She usually avoids direct eye contact except for when she is addressed or when she becomes more unreserved and animated in response to my questions or comments. I have to take a very active therapeutic role of engagement or we would simply sit there in silence the whole time.

During the second session, Andrea told me that she often daydreams for hours and will lose track of time, as if she enters into a dissociative trance. Her fantasies are typically grandiose and immersed in an aura of perfection: she imagines herself as a beautiful, popular movie star, such as Jen-

fer Lopez, and she envisions herself looking aesthetically flawless in unning, sexy clothing and speaking facilely in several languages, thus ooing a crowd with her intelligence and wit as she is the center of atten-on and the object of men's amorous affection. As a compensatory defense ;ainst profound feelings of inadequacy, this is in sharp contrast to her real e, which is dominated by a fear of rejection and devaluation from others. ie has such a needy plea for social acceptance that she will grovel and de-.ean herself in order to be liked, will continually allow herself to be taken dvantage of by others who use her for various selfobject functions, such ; being a mirror, coach, or source of support, without reciprocity or mu-.al recognition in return, and plays the "role" she thinks others want her play in order to get their approval. Her false self presentation with her eers is in contrast to the way she presents in therapy, as demure, resistant, nd devoid of self-reflection, especially when the emotional immediacy of xamining her life mobilizes defensive fortifications.

Andrea's suicidality in response to "being fucked then dumped" by er boyfriend brought on an abandonment depression that triggered her arly developmental pathognomonic vulnerabilities of fear of separation, ejection, and not feeling loved by her parents. She was furthermore en-enched in a pattern of self-defeat that she perpetuated by failing to go o her classes or complete her schoolwork, which inevitably led her to rop out of high school and pick up her subjects through a correspon-ence program. Andrea was quite depressed at this point, had very dis-orted views of her self-worth and current capabilities, and felt hopeless bout the perceived unalterability of her future, despite having been on ntidepressant medication for some time. In my experience, patients who ave attachment-based characterological deficits are typically resistant to rug intervention because it does not penetrate the deep structural con-igurations of how developmental trauma is unconsciously organized round psychic pain that is affectively and somatically sustained inde-endent of linguistic mediatory processes. I often tell patients that while sychotropic medication may "take the edge off," it does nothing to ame-iorate the unarticulated emotional resonance states that clamor for re-olve, let alone "take the memories away." What Andrea needed to do vas talk about her inner experiences more directly and give them an al-ernative voice rather than keep them bottled up in surreptitious fash-ons. Because of her immense mistrust of being exploited or invalidated, he learned years ago to be obsequious and stifle her true feelings and uthentic expressions to ensure psychic survival.

Initially Andrea focused on her symptoms, rapidly changing mood, iegative self-representations, personal inadequacies, and conflict over her dentity disturbance. She is a light-skinned black girl who looks more In-lian than African and reportedly identifies more with whites than with he black culture in her community. For example, she does not identify

with "rappers" or "hip-hop" culture, the fashion, or the purported openly defiant attitudes she uses to characterize black youth. As she puts it, she is intimidated and turned off by black males her age because they "are rude and all they want to do is have sex." She has experienced racial prejudice from both white and black culture for either being identified as "ethnic" by whites or "washed" by blacks due to her mixed racial heritage. She did not socialize with black groups at her school, which were very segregated from their white counterparts, did not sit in the black section of the cafeteria, which she called "Cafrica," and had mainly white friends, which sometimes made her feel as if she was the "token black girl" of the group. Discussing her ambivalence and ambiguity over her identity initially made her feel "more lost" because she confessed that she had never thought about her own needs or desires before, independent of how she was told she should be. While she is still in the process of negotiating and reconciling her divided and multifarious identifications, she is less inclined than before to think in terms of color and race, and she is more likely to think about what she values in juxtaposition to what others say she should.

Andrea's parents had a crippling effect on her personality formation and continue to be a source of negation and pain. She described the traumatic effects of fear that her mother would "go away," and she recalls being told on several occasions that she would be the "death of" her mother for being "bad" or oppositional. Andrea's mother would frequently threaten to abandon her as a form of discipline and on at least two occasions said, "Don't cry at my funeral," when Andrea was thought to be misbehaving. When Andrea complained, "It's not fair," in response to her mother's contradictory and hypocritical attitudes, her mother would respond by saying, "Then why don't you go to the hospital and see all the dying children, and then come home and tell me what's not fair." Andrea's mother used fear, guilt, and shame as an instrument of control and domination, often appealing to religious authority, which led to the tyrannical colonization of Andrea's personality, hence giving rise to persecutory feelings that Satan was after her soul.

When I first met Andrea I asked her how she felt inside; she said that she didn't feel anything. By our fourth session, she told me, "I feel dead inside," and claimed to be indifferent to almost everything. Having her examine her inner world more directly vis-à-vis her parents precipitated a series of suicidal fantasies that began to become more passively manifest in her daydreams. She reported fantasizing that she was killed in some tragic or ghastly fashion, such as being hit by a car or struck by a stray bullet in a drive-by shooting. Furthermore, she envisioned that her family members would feel sorrow over her death. She then associated to how she had always had fantasies like these since she was a little girl and remembered having nightmares and generalized worry that her parents

ould be hurt in an accident while driving home from work, or that her
other would be hit by a car and killed. Andrea further noted that these
aranoid obsessions shifted to feelings that she would go to hell or that
e would be possessed by incarnate evil. When I suggested that perhaps
e was angry at her family for the way they had always treated her, she
egan to enter into a period of becoming more attuned to her own inner
ge. She was particularly hateful toward her mother for her continual
arrage of critical judgments, lack of warmth, and guilt-inducing com-
ents that made her always feel that she was to blame for everything. She
called how her father had referred to her suicide attempt as "tomfool-
ry," while her mother was angry that she had tarnished the family's im-
ge in the eyes of others. Her brother would tend to use the episode as a
eans of hurting her when he was angry and frequently called her "psy-
ho" at the dinner table without any intervention from her parents, who,
their silence, condoned such treatment. Their ongoing shame, cruelty,
nd lack of support was simply deplorable, and I appeared to be the only
ne who had validated her suffering; even her friends saw her as troubled
nd were anxious about bringing up such an uncomfortable topic because
ndrea never discussed it.

As Andrea began to more directly address her feelings toward her fam-
ly, she also started to become more withdrawn, obstinate, and verbally
ppositional toward her parents, who became increasingly threatened by
er change in behavior and out of desperation even attempted to sabotage
he therapy by taking her to another psychiatrist who simply wanted to
ut her on another medication due to the "chemical imbalance in my
rain." Yet Andrea continued with me in weekly therapy, only to reveal
ore childhood pathogenic events that appeared to have left much traumatic residue on her burgeoning psyche. She disclosed that at the age of
hree she was left unattended in her parents' apartment, became terrified
vhen she realized she was alone, and then opened the door and ran down
he hall screaming. Her mother had apparently just popped out to visit a
eighbor, and she became frantic when she returned to find Andrea miss-
ng. Andrea had made her way into an open elevator and was found cry-
ng in the hallway on another floor. When Andrea was four, she remem-
ered going to South Africa because her maternal grandmother had died.
She distinctly identifies this time period as the beginning of her preoccupations about evil and paranoia over death, later augmented by her
mother's comments about death, which she internalized as *parasitic introjects*. Here I refer to parasitic introjects as emotionally heightened elements of subjective experience that are negatively incorporated into the
ego and feed off their own toxicity. Andrea also identifies age four as a
time when she was persuaded to touch the genitals of another girl her age
by a thirteen-year-old neighbor girl who lived down the street. She furthermore acted out such sex play with her brother by grabbing his penis

and once walked out of the bathtub naked, only to be reproached by her mother. While these events were reportedly not bothersome to her at the time, Andrea began to increasingly identify them as sources of conflict and guilt that were associated with her lifelong visions of sin and death.

Along with her attachment insecurities, these pathognomonic occurrences have heavily contributed to her fluid structuralization processes and have informed her disposition toward abandonment anxiety, melancholia, affect dysregulation, and a pervasive internal aloneness due to the inability to internalize positive holding-soothing introjects from parental imagoes. Furthermore, Andrea's self-disparagement and negative view of herself as ugly, bad, and sinful disposes her toward further guilt over her more recent actions, such as lying, doing drugs, drinking, and having sex with her boyfriend, which she identified as being primarily motivated out of fear of losing him. Her symptoms at times seem to be motivated, in part, by an unconscious need for self-punishment, while her destructive trends are a means of acting out her rage toward her parents by deliberately not living up to their expectations for a dutiful daughter. Whereas her self-defeating behaviors have multiple, overdetermined motivations and meanings, one of which is to hurt her parents via hurting herself by failing everything she endeavors, Andrea came to understand that she really just wanted her parents' attention and approval.

Forming a working alliance with Andrea was unnaturally slow. Authority figures have always been a source of invalidation, misunderstanding, and neglect, and she has been forthcoming only in response to my pointed questioning and gentle confrontations within a supportive and empathic therapeutic frame. Despite her trepidation, she has imbued me with positive significance, which at one time took on certain erotic currents. She began dressing seductively in skimpy clothing such as halter tops and miniskirts, thus exposing her legs and cleavage, and once made a point of telling me that her parents had insisted that she cover herself when coming to see me for sessions. Upon hearing this I asked her whether this was one way she felt as if she could get some attention, and she acknowledged that this was the case. In fact, by wearing "sleazy clothing" she ensured she would both get noticed and be admonished. In addition, this was one of the "roles" she played with her girlfriends. Andrea explained that she was the first to have sex out of her group of friends, and her seductive clothing and appearance earned her the reputation of being the group "slut." When she got attention from boys or from her friends based upon her appearance, it tended to counteract her own intense conviction that she was ugly. But because her friends were very superficial, self-centered, and incapable of sustaining a genuine reciprocal friendship, Andrea always felt excluded and angry that they really did not seem to care about her needs or feelings, which reinforced her own sense of inadequacy that she had nothing to offer others.

The following segment comes from a therapy session about eight months into the treatment and depicts the typical awkwardness of beginning the session and engaging Andrea in self-reflective dialogue. The main themes addressed in the previous session were the patient's disclosures that her ex-boyfriend had started dating a new girl and that consequently she had been binge eating, had been engaging in mildly active bulimia, and was having passive suicidal fantasies mainly involving daydreams of being killed with concomitant associations of imagining how people would feel sorry for her.

Therapist: How you doing?

Patient: OK.

Therapist: How's your week been?

Patient: Same as always.

Therapist: What's that mean?

Patient: I wake up, eat, then go to sleep.

Therapist: You've been feeling depressed, huh?

Patient: [*she nods*]

Therapist: Is that a yeah?

Patient: I don't know, I guess so.

Therapist: This has been coming on for a couple of weeks now. Have you been feeling worse since the last time we spoke?

Patient: Um-hmm.

Therapist: What's happened since then?

Patient: Nothing.

Therapist: Then what do you seem to be bothered by?

Patient: Nothing in particular.

Therapist: Well, last time I can recall a lot of things that were bothering you. Have you been thinking about them?

Patient: I haven't been thinking of anything.

Therapist: Well, what stands out for me is Jason having a new girlfriend.

Patient: Well I . . . it doesn't matter, I haven't seen him. [*long period of silence*]

Therapist: So what do you think you have been down about then?

Patient: [*gives facial expression of uncertainty*] I can't think of anything in particular. [*one minute of silence*]

Therapist: Have you still been having those thoughts of something happening to you?

Patient: Not so much, no. Not in these past few days.

Therapist: But prior to that?

Patient: I can't really remember what I did last week, so yeah, probably.

Therapist: Have you been purging?

Patient: No.

Therapist: Binging?

Patient: Yeah.

Therapist: Have you been hurting yourself?

Patient: [*shakes head*] Nu-uh.

Therapist: Have you been thinking about it?

Patient: Sort of, nothing serious or anything.

Therapist: So what do you think all that is connected to?

Patient: I don't know.

Therapist: Last time you were telling me that you recognized the pattern that when you feel others don't care about you, you find yourself withdrawing and not caring about them; and when they come around and start to involve you again in their lives, you end up feeling worse. Then you feel like eating and have fantasies of hurting yourself or dying, where people end up feeling sorry for you if something bad were to happen. Maybe we can make more sense out of that together.

Patient: [*remains silent*]

Therapist: Are you still feeling really disconnected to people?

Patient: Yeah.

Therapist: Well, how about, let's say, with your friend Tina. Where do you stand with her this week?

Patient: I don't know; I went to the mall with Tina on Saturday, and she just pisses me off. She's just, like, I don't know, she's all depressed and everything. We came home from the mall and she's like [*in an animated voice*], "Well, that was a total waste of the day," and blah blah blah. The only good thing was that she saw Rick, and da da da da. And she's calling up all these people and saying, "I'm so bored, you want to do something?" blah blah blah, 'cause she wanted to go to a club. So it's like everything else sucks except going to a club, like it's the only thing that would have been acceptable. But even if we had to drive to a club, which we didn't, she wouldn't have gone anyways 'cause her mom doesn't let her go to clubs; so she'd have to lie and say she's sleeping over at someone's house—but she's not allowed to sleep over at anyone's house—so where? She's never asked to sleep over at my house, so she doesn't know if she'd be allowed; and even if we did that, I mean even if we had a way there and back, we wouldn't have been able to go anyways.

Therapist: So this is another time when all she did was complain about herself and her life . . .

Patient: Yeah.

Therapist: . . . and really wasn't concerned about you.

Patient: I don't really care that she wasn't concerned about me, I just didn't have, I mean after a while I was getting tired of her and wasn't having a good time because all she was doing was complaining. And even if circumstances were different, she still wouldn't have done what she wanted to do anyways, so she's complaining about nothing.

Therapist: But this is how she typically treats you: she uses you as a sounding board. You are the one who listens to her but she doesn't think about your needs. And doesn't that bother you every time you're together?

Patient: It really didn't bother me that much, I was just, like, umm . . .

Therapist: So how did that bring you down then?

Patient: It didn't. I don't care. [*silence*]

Therapist: See, I think you do. You care that she's so selfish. But I guess it's hard for you to address that head on.

Patient: [*sits in silence for one minute*]

Therapist: How do you feel right now?

Patient: I don't know.

Therapist: What's your understanding of the times when you come here and find it hard to talk to me?

Patient: [*gives ambiguous facial expression*]

Therapist: Do you know why?

Patient: [*shakes head no*]

Therapist: I recall you telling me one time that your parents often say something like, "Oh, quit whining," or, "You're only wanting to get attention."

Patient: Umm-hum, well, that's more like my dad than my mom.

Therapist: Your mom would say?

Patient: I don't know, sometimes she would act like that too, but it was mostly my dad.

Therapist: So do you think something like that is going on in here at times?

Patient: [*dubiously*] Hum, I guess.

Therapist: That you feel that if you were to really tell me how you feel, it would almost be like hearing, "Quit whining about it."

Patient: I guess, I don't know. I guess like . . . [*silence*]

Therapist: Like what?

Patient: [*silence*]

Therapist: I guess I can't help but notice that you act the same way in here like you do with Tina, for instance. I do all the talking and you do all the listening, and you don't say anything back.

Patient: I do talk.

Therapist: [*I chuckle*.] Don't you feel that sometimes, though, you're more comfortable not disclosing certain things, instead keeping them inside, then being dissatisfied later on?

Patient: Yeah.

Therapist: Maybe this is now an opportunity for you to try a different role. I'm not Tina, I'm not your dad. You can be yourself . . . and tell me whatever.

This interchange shows how I, apart from getting her to talk, attempted to engage her resistance, alexithymia, and repetitious patterns of passivity within the transference relationship while opening an invited space for her to act more authentically in relation to me. The following week she came in and uncharacteristically started speaking the minute she took her seat and told me that my confrontation about her not speaking in session made her realize that she was defeating the purpose of coming to therapy. She wanted to open up more and had written down some thoughts she had been having the previous week. She pulled a piece of paper from her pocket and started reading off a list including her body dysmorphic preoccupations, her fear of being possessed by the devil, her inability to modulate her mood and affect, and her intensifying hopelessness. The patient had also superficially cut her forearm the previous day as a means of containing her destructive rage in response to a verbal exchange with her mother. Her cutting behaviors are primitive attempts at affect regulation that she reports make her "feel more calm." Because Andrea has not sufficiently developed an individuated sense of self nor attained an appropriate degree of emotional object constancy, the real threat of abandonment and rejection from her mother produces fragmentation anxiety and projected rage that comes back as haunting reintrojections. While Andrea can express her anger toward her father with little repercussion, she is afraid that in her mind her rage will destroy her mother. Unable to directly express her rage toward her mother due to an undifferentiated archaic merger, which mobilizes unconscious fears that she will be annihilated because she cannot individuate her autonomous sense of self from their symbiotic union, she instead redirects her destructive impulses onto herself. This serves many motives of self-regulation and self-punishment as well as projecting her own internalized bad self onto her mother as an identificatory means to induce guilt and shame for her threatening atti-

ides. Andrea learned long ago to be complacent and not speak up or be heard in more genuine ways out of her inability to value herself as a separate agent independent of her mother's approval. During times of intense affect dysregulation, rage is mobilized to ward off her abandonment depression but then is inverted onto her self in calamitous and self-deprecatory ways. When binging on food does not satiate her hole in being, she tarries in agitated-depleted moods domineered by destructive unconscious fantasies and self-loathing that at times appear as isomorphic beliefs that others see her flaws in the same way as she experiences them, thereby exacerbating her preoccupations of worthlessness and conviction that she is ugly.

Andrea's symptoms improved once she began getting in touch with her anger and expressing herself more assertively in safeguarded ways without the fear that she would be contaminated by persecutory internal objects, annihilation impulses, or abandonment anxieties. Part of her ability to distance herself from these threats was due to realizing that her family was emotionally limited and uninterested in changing, thus dominated by their own vulnerabilities and conflicts, and that this did not necessarily reflect upon her. Allowing herself to be legitimately angry at their lack of concern or responsiveness was both cathartic and alienating. But she was dialectically torn between her desire to be loved and accepted by them and her self-debasement and fury that she was needy and dependent. The following segment captures her increased feelings of anger, disillusionment, and ambivalence about her need for recognition and the dependency she both fosters and resents.

Therapist: How are things going with your parents?

Patient: Umm, they bug me. So, I guess, nothin' new.

Therapist: Weren't you getting along better with them?

Patient: Yeah, but I guess they're just bugging me. My dad, he has always done this thing where if I am watching TV, he comes and he just starts changing the channels whether I'm in the middle of watching a show; and yesterday I got mad and I started yelling at him; and he said I was rude, and blah blah blah—whatever, and I said, "No, you're rude!" And, I don't know, he didn't like it. And they always do this thing where I can't say anything 'cause if I do I'm rude, and then they'll be like, "Oh yeah, and you expect us to drive you everywhere, and you expect us to give you money," and blah blah blah.

Therapist: So, if you stick up for yourself you're punished.

Patient: Yeah. Then yesterday I went to Tina's house and came home at one. And, yeah, my mom asked me to be home early, but honestly, this is summertime, I'm nineteen years old, and she wants me to be home by eleven o'clock. Like who does that? And she says [*in a lugubrious voice*], "Oh, she can't go to sleep unless I'm home, and she can't fall asleep, she lies awake worrying about

me, and she can't lock the door unless I'm home." OK, fine, that's true, I can take the garage door opener, I can get in through the garage if I have to, you know? And they always act like I'm doing something wrong if I stay out. Yesterday my mom and my dad's like [*in a deep voice*], "Oh, this has got to stop, this has got to come to an end," and blah blah blah, 'cause they locked the door on me; so I had to ring the doorbell so they could come and open the door. And then he was already in bed, and he had to get out of bed. They're so retarded. If you know someone's coming home, then why would you lock the door on them?

Therapist: I sense that at times when you stick up for yourself, either you're made to feel you've done something wrong, like, "You've been a bad girl," or they induce guilt, like your mother "can't go to sleep." But it seems like for you that no matter what you do—when you stick up for yourself or try to communicate like an adult—they want to keep you as a kid.

Patient: Yeah! And then they expect me to have responsibilities—they want me to act like an adult, then they do that. I don't get it. [*period of silence*]

Therapist: Do you see how the patterns of communication and relatedness with your folks also spill over into how you relate with your friends?

Patient: [*shakes head no*]

Therapist: You've often complained how your friends really don't think about your needs—all they do is focus on themselves. And when you do speak up, either they brush you off or don't attend to you in the way that you would like, which is very similar to how your parents act. Then you end up being all pissed off about it, and kind of withdraw, and maybe sulk a little bit, and distance yourself, while they keep disparaging you.

Patient: Well, I'm *not* pissed off. I'm pissed off because I have to depend on everyone else for everything.

Therapist: Tell me more about that?

Patient: I mean I have to, I have to depend on everyone; like I have to depend on my parents for money, like for a drive, and even if I worked, I'm still going to need them to drive me to work or to give me money for bus fare, or whatever.

Therapist: And they resent you for having to give to you in that way. They keep bringing it up, right?

Patient: Well, yeah.

Therapist: But a part of you likes to be dependent, or you wouldn't be delaying finishing your school or getting a job.

Patient: I don't know, I just don't see a point.

Therapist: So a part of you can't stand being dependent on your family, particularly your father it sounds like, but at the same time, you don't know how you'll do it. But you *do* know how to do it. You and I both know you're

pable of completing school, yet you don't want to. So what do you think ᴇ motive behind that is?

ᴘatient: I don't know. [*silence*]

ᴛherapist: Well, often these things have multiple causes. I know you're anx- ᴜs about a number of things, but do you feel that it might be possible that ᴛ remaining dependent on your family you are also hoping that they are go- ᴦ to give you the things that you have wanted from them all along, like ᴇir recognition and respect?

ᴘatient: Don't know.

ᴛherapist: What I mean is, I sometimes wonder that what you might be say- ᴦ to them in indirect ways is: "I want you to pay attention to me. I want ᴏu to notice me for a change."

ᴘatient: Um-hum. [*nods head affirmatively*]

ᴛherapist: Is that true?

ᴘatient: Yeah.

ᴛherapist: But what they end up doing is noticing you in a very negative ᴀy, like, "You're a burden, you've got problems," or, "Something's wrong ith you," so you don't seem to be getting what you really want.

ᴘatient: [*long period of silence*]

ᴛherapist: I'm curious how they would treat you if you finished school, got job, got your license and could drive yourself.

ᴘatient: I don't know, I don't think they would . . . [*silence*]

ᴛherapist: You don't think they'd what?

ᴘatient: [*affected*] I don't think they'd really care. It's something that ᴏu're suppose to do anyways; it's not something special, like they're go- ᴦg to notice.

ᴛherapist: This must be very emotionally painful for you. "Here you are," ᴜt nobody pays attention.

ᴘatient: [*long period of silence*]

ᴛherapist: If you had it your way, what would you like to see happen?

ᴘatient: I don't know. I don't think about these things, "if I ever had it my ᴡn way," because I'm never going to have it my own way.

ᴛherapist: Why do you think that?

ᴘatient: When have I ever had it my own way? Please.

ᴛherapist: So, just because you have never had it your way means that you ᴇver will in the future?

ᴘatient: Yeah.

Therapist: I'm curious why you would think that's not possible.

Patient: Why? What's going to change that I'm going to have what I want in the future when I didn't have what I wanted in the past?

Therapist: It could be entirely different circumstances.

Patient: [*long period of silence*]

Therapist: I guess it's hard for you to imagine there ever being a better life for yourself.

Patient: [*silence*]

Therapist: But you fantasize about that all the time, don't you? Having—

Patient: A better life, yeah, well, doesn't everyone? [*one minute of silence*]

Therapist: Andrea, why do you think it seems to be so helpless for you to make any changes?

Patient: [*long silence*] I've never done anything by myself.

Therapist: So it's scary?

Patient: No, it's not that it's scary, it's just, I don't feel I can do it.

Therapist: And why is that?

Patient: 'Cause if I could do it, I would have done it already.

Therapist: Not necessarily, not if something is holding you back inside.

Patient: Well, what's holding me back?

Therapist: I don't fully know yet; what do you think?

Patient: I don't know.

Therapist: Part of you wants to be dependent on your family and part of you doesn't. If you weren't dependent on your family then what kind of connection would you have?

Patient: I guess we wouldn't have a connection.

Therapist: You wouldn't have one?

Patient: Na.

Therapist: So what does that tell you?

Patient: Don't know.

Therapist: If you were to succeed at these things, maybe they wouldn't have any need for you anymore.

Patient: But they already don't have a need for me.

Therapist: Oh, I think they do. They must have some need. You must serve some type of purpose for them. It sounds more and more like you're afraid

not having anything, so you'd rather be in this kind of subordinated role where you're looked down upon, yet tolerated, yet pitied.

Patient: Hmm. [*long silence*]

Therapist: You think it would make a difference if your parents were more warm toward you?

Patient: I don't want them to be warm towards me. They irritate me.

Therapist: I suppose it would hurt if they were to show you some genuine feelings of care, or concern, or love, since you're not very accustomed to that.

Patient: I guess. [*laughs nervously*]

Therapist: At times I wonder what it must be like for you having to think about who you are, coming from the family that you come from, what your identity is all about. It seems like you're very overidentified with being flawed in some way, like something's wrong with you. Is that how you look at yourself?

Patient: Yeah.

Therapist: Rather than you're just struggling with stuff and it's hard to figure out all at once because it's a confusing time?

Patient: Yeah.

Therapist: So tell me, why do you see yourself in such a negative light?

Patient: I don't know, I always have, ever since I was little.

Therapist: Aren't you sick of feeling that way?

Patient: Yeah, but I don't know, I feel like the only way that I'm going to be able to do anything is if I move out of my house. I've been thinking about that, but then I won't have a reason and my mom will feel, "Oh, why don't you want to live with us?" and it'll be a whole big thing. I don't know, and I wouldn't have enough money, like if I lived with my aunt, it would not be fun. I wouldn't even have enough money to buy food for myself, and things like that, 'cause she can't shop, and she's not exactly a fun person to live with because, I don't know, she's like a wreck herself.

Therapist: So it wouldn't be much better, huh?

Patient: No. And I don't have any other option.

Therapist: Sounds like you got a life sentence or something.

Patient: [*smiles*]

Therapist: So a part of you is aware that it could be different for you if you were on your own?

Patient: Yeah.

Therapist: You may feel much better about yourself if you were away from the way your family makes you feel.

Patient: Yeah. I think I would like them better too.

Therapist: My thought is that there's something that's keeping you from wanting to get better; and until we fully understand what it is in yourself that's contributing to that, I think you'll always feel stuck like you do now. Part of it seems to me to be that you're really hoping to get your parents' recognition. "When are they going to pay attention, when are they going to give to me?" And as long as you're struggling with school, with your depression—with life—then you still maintain some kind of connection with them. But I guess I'm wondering if in the back of your mind is that little wish or that hope that someday they're going to straighten up and be more kind to you.

Patient: Well, I don't know. They've kind of just, I don't know—I've totally given up on people. They're not going to change, that's just the way they are. So, why bother?

Therapist: So, Andrea, that means you're going to have to change. You're the one who's the author of your own life—you have control over that. You may not have any control over how other people relate to you, but until you value yourself enough to go after what you really want without sabotaging it, then I think you're just going to be unhappy.

At the beginning of this segment, Andrea was in touch with her anger over being treated rudely by her father and being made to feel guilty by her mother, and then she experienced intense frustration over being so dependent, and hence being unable to do anything about it. This led to my confrontations about her ambivalence about wanting to be treated like an adult but sabotaging her bid for independence by acting so helpless and reliant due to the underlying wish of gaining her parents' acceptance and not losing what little connection she feels she has toward them. But this strategy, albeit largely unconsciously motivated, only leads to impasse and reproach from her family, who resents her lassitude and passive-aggressive self-expression that betrays her previous pattern of complacency. Here we began to engage the question of her future as broaching the possibility for a different way of being. This session created a clearing for how she increasingly began to feel more in control over her life by seizing her responsibilities to act differently for her own sake via making better choices in the service of actualizing her freedom. But she did not achieve this without first going through a few more crises.

At my encouragement, Andrea decided that she needed to have closure over her past relationship with her ex-boyfriend, Jason, so she therefore wrote him a letter expressing her thoughts and feelings in a mature way. This led to his apology, followed by mutual flirtation resulting in a date overshadowed by heavy petting, which was only to end with her feeling further rejected. While she was proud of herself for being assertive and showing self-conviction, this brief encounter rekindled her feelings of loss,

ıptiness, and abandonment by someone who once professed his love.
ıe became more angry at her friends for their selfishness and lack of
ıvailability and began feeling depressed again, resumed binge eating, and
ıs unable to sleep at night, and when she finally did fall asleep, all she
ɪanted to do was sleep all day. She had maintained a masochistic attach-
ıent to Jason, who more than a year after their breakup had rejected her a
ɪcond time; as a result, Andrea preferred to isolate herself from her fam-
⁊ by staying in her room, nor did she make any effort to complete her cor-
ɪspondence courses. Avoiding discussing her feelings of sadness, mourn-
ɪg, and anger, she instead entered into a withdrawn period in the therapy
ɪhere she would sit in silence for long stretches and say very little in re-
ɪonse to any of my questions. When I told her that I felt she was shutting
ɪe out rather than entrusting me with her pain, she said that she had to
ɪut could not tell me why. Her suicidal impulses had returned and she was
ɪtting herself again. Here we had entered into therapeutic impasse.

During this time, Andrea once came twenty minutes late to a session
ɪnd sat practically the whole time and said nothing. She explained that
ɪr father had forgotten that he was supposed to drive her to her ap-
ɪointment, so she had to walk. Upon arrival, she was visibly sweaty and
ɪppeared pissed off, and then she became detached in a dissociative man-
ɪer and was unable to speak about or articulate her inner experience nor
ɪrocess the interpersonal dimensions of our relationship or the transfer-
ɪnce. All attempts at engaging her were met with silence, eye aversion,
ɪnd an ensuing distant gaze.

The next week Andrea came on time to session and immediately gave
ɪne this letter, which I read in her presence:

Dr. Mills,
  I know I don't usually harass you after hours, however I am writing this
down because if I don't I will come to see you every week for the next however long talking shit around the things that are really bothering me.
  I know you thought it was kinda funny how I got upset about something
as trivial as having to walk for twenty minutes, but the truth is that I have the
tendancy to ignore a spark until the bomb goes off and everything's on fire.
I wasn't upset about my dad forgetting about me again. (Okay, maybe a little.) I was pissed because I had to walk through the neighborhood looking
like an ass. The whole time I was thinking of how I would excuse my disgusting appearance if I happened to run into anyone I know. I was thinking
that I'd just pull a white rabbit and be all, "Sorry, no time, I'm late!!" and run
away. That always works.
  I stopped going to school because I'm ugly. I'm also an airhead and I've no
personality. I hate leaving my room. I spend ALL MY TIME imagining. I take
forever to fall asleep because I can't stop thinking and imagining. I prolong
staying in bed. Sometimes I don't brush my hair or shower for days (I know
that's attractive).

I don't have anyone to talk to. You are literally the only person I talk to. I lost all my friends and I don't know why. In fact, I don't know why I have always felt it so important to gain the approval of everyone else. But I have. I have been working my ass off since I was 3 fucking years old for people to like me and who does?

I have no interest in anything, least of all being alive. I don't want to go outside. I don't want to have a job. I don't want to go to fucking university and deal with all this shit again. I have to say that grades 5–11 were the worst of my life (not that anything prior to that was a party). I am scared of boys. Isn't that wonderful? I am scared of black people. In fact, I am scared of people in general. Me no people, I guess. I told you I feel like a child? I feel like that same nasty loser kid that no one likes and everyone makes fun of. I know other people have had it way worse, and when I think that, I can't imagine being able to deal with it. I feel so ashamed of everything. I always have.

I never told you yet that a couple of weeks ago I started having dreams about all these people that I know. They weren't nightmares in the typical "Ooo, I'm so scared, I wanna wake up" sense, but more like a revisitation of previous feelings, and it wasn't pleasant.

I have been planning my suicide for a few weeks (two maybe?). I feel totally disconnected from everyone. I have been eating cookies and ice cream by the package. I feel like I am walking around but I am not even alive. Nothing matters. I'm like a stick figure like kids draw, with a happy face head with X's for eyes. It's been like this for so long, what if it never changes? I don't think I can talk about this stuff in person.

    Andrea

After reading the letter silently, I looked up and said, "It sounds like you want to be real with me, so tell me in your own way what you really want to say." Andrea discussed more openly how she felt her ugliness was one reason why she perceived that other people did not like her. Her distorted self-perceptions about her appearance have both developmental and cultural precursors of being conditioned to think that beauty is proportional to social desirability and acceptance. As a child, she was told she had a round face and looked like a boy. Later she was teased by family members about her weight and told she had chubby fingers. Her teenage friends are shallow and doltish, and she is too easily swayed by their idealization of physical appearance due to her unabated pining for peer popularity. Her tendency toward splitting and the inability to critically analyze her assumptions (let alone integrate competing experiences into a meaningful whole) further colored her judgment, which devolved into loathing and self-hate. When I told her that there was nothing about her appearance that objectively warranted the conclusion that she was ugly but that instead this belief was based on her identity diffusion and inner feelings of ugliness she conceals from herself, she began to confide more about how her female friends define worthiness, desirability, and success based on

hysical aesthetics, money, and material possession, which she finds su-
erficial and which in fact betrays the values she espouses. Here we made
ome substantial gains in her understanding that her disconnectedness to
er friends is because of her poor choices in friendship rather than her ap-
earance or personality.

In the sessions that followed, Andrea's depressed mood and suicidality
iminished and she began to talk more openly about her feelings and con-
icts in generally less resistant ways. Revisiting a familiar theme, Andrea
epeated that she felt like a little child who was helpless and could not do
nything for herself. When I suggested that she liked being a little child
ecause she got some attention from being the sick one in the family, she
greed. She furthermore disclosed that she was jealous and resentful of
er little sister, who received special treatment and got her father's
varmth and affection and her mother's overprotection, while she was
'starving" for such emotional sustenance. Andrea was also furious at her
)arents for forcing her to play the sick role because they had a "fucked-
ıp relationship" and were unable to provide her with proper guidance or
.tructure. Food became symbolic for her deprived relational needs, which
.he craved but lacked, and binge eating became an immediate way to
emporarily regulate her emotional discomfort when she became upset.

Andrea began focusing more on the notion of not feeling loved by her
)arents and how her need to be "the best" in whatever she undertook
.was connected to the fantasy that the accomplishment of perfection
would win over her parents' acceptance and admiration. She was also
aware that her dissociative proclivity to daydream of grandiose visions
of personal success, beauty, and fame was a compensatory defense
against feelings of profound inadequacy motivated by the archaic wish
to be mirrored by unadulterated love objects. Although her fantasy life
was a source of refuge and pleasure, she would tend to regress in mood
to depleted feelings of inferiority and sadness when the realization that
it was fantasy became transparent, leaving her once again feeling forlorn,
empty, and alone.

I avoided addressing the erotic transference for several months, despite
the fact that she was increasingly wearing seductive clothing, thus exposing more sensual areas of her body, and frequently spoke of her nineteen-
year-old friend who was having sex with a thirty-five-year-old married
man with two kids who was cheating on his wife. One such attempt to engage the developing transference was when she wore a miniskirt to session and sat with her legs spread slightly apart; but she became embarrassed, quickly crossed her legs, and then skirted the issue when I asked
whether she felt more attractive about herself when she dressed up. But
another opportunity emerged that was less seductively tinged and more
naturally comfortable: the patient had come dressed nicely yet non-
provocatively, and her hair was fully styled. I commented that she looked

nice and asked her whether she had made herself up for me. Despite not having any function to attend that evening or any other special reason, she merely claimed that she just felt like dressing up. Here I said that I had been noticing at times her sexy clothing and wondered whether she had wanted me to "check her out." "Dr. Mills," she replied demurely. I then asked her whether she thought that by dressing up she was really wanting me to notice her in a positive way that her family does not, which she conceded was the case. I acknowledged, "I can understand why you would want me to find you attractive, but I think that you really just want me to like you, which I do." Her face immediately lit up in response to my affirmation, and she thanked me for validating her. We discussed how it was perfectly natural that she would have some affectionate feelings for me, and I invited her to simply say how she felt rather than having to show it in other ways. With appreciation, she had reciprocated my recognition of her, and for the first time I felt we had entered into a space where she could be herself without the fear of exploitation, guilt induction, or shame. This unfolding exchange led me to tell her that I found her vulnerability most attractive because I felt more emotionally connected to her. This was a transformative session in the therapy, for we had advanced our mutual sense of attachment; by engaging her wish for recognition that was behind the erotic veil without inducing shame or further impasse, we had strengthened our relational bond.

From that point on in the therapy, Andrea has steadily shown an improvement in her symptomatology, affect regulation, and psychosocial functioning, despite her structural deficits and attachment disorganization. Although food has become a primary form of self-regulation, she has ceased all purging and cutting behaviors and is able to relate to me more directly about her thoughts, feeling states, and internal experiences without the level of resistance, alexithymic confusion, or dissociative reactions that occupied our first two years of treatment. She has internalized my presence as a calming-soothing introject, keeps a regular journal where she processes her thoughts throughout the week, which allows her to bring in her reflections to session, and makes frequent reference to me, for example, commenting that I make her feel good about herself due to my nonjudgmental comportment, and that she appreciates the fact that I make an effort to listen to and understand her. While Andrea will in all likelihood remain in therapy with me for quite some time, her structural deficits are transmuting in relation to her increased self-worth, capacity for more genuine relatedness, and symptomatic improvement.

The proportional success of Andrea's treatment, in my opinion, demonstrates the value of an insight-oriented approach to raising the patient's level of personal awareness into her dynamic motivations and unconscious repetitious patterns through the medium of forming a relational bond. It was only after she developed a sense of security and trust with

me that she could form certain identifications with me as someone who authentically cared about her and had faith in her abilities to induce self-change. There is no doubt that we as analysts profoundly influence the course of treatment and the burgeoning personal identity our patients come to have about themselves through identification and the process of incorporating the analyst's values and inferred expectancies. The more I interpreted her ambivalent need for autonomous self-expression and fear of failure, validated her inner wish for more genuine relatedness, combated by the anticipation of abandonment, and recognized her need to individuate from her family yet still remain attached, she began making her own connections to the dynamic motives governing her behavior and affective life and hence started making better choices.

Andrea came to realize that part of the reason she was dependent on her parents was that they were just as dependent on her in order to diffuse the tensions in their lack of marital intimacy, whereby she served the function of being a displaced scapegoat for their frustrations. By seeing that her father was a sexist who devalued his wife and by extension Andrea, a dynamic that informed her brother's rudeness and entitlement as well, and that she was further drawn to friends who were neglectful and debasing, and who simply wanted her to be a mirror for their egos as her mother did, Andrea was more empowered to adopt different roles and boundaries as well as establish new parameters for relatedness. As a result, Andrea started sticking up for herself more at home, decided to change the personae she assumed with others, and confronted two friends directly on their devaluation of her as being "washed," another for being a "moocher," and another for being so totally self-absorbed that Andrea felt like she no longer desired to remain her friend.

Equally important was her change of attitude toward her little sister, who was given no responsibilities in the house and was still allowed to sleep in her parents' bed. Whereas in the past Andrea would harbor great resentment toward her and displace her rage via rejection of her, as did Andrea's mother to her, Andrea decided to be nice to her sister in a way she wished her older brother would have been to her when she was a kid. Andrea realized that her previous antipathy was mainly because her little sister tried to emulate her, when all Andrea could feel was self-loathing. Accepting her sister's need to look up to her as an older sibling, Andrea was able to bracket her negative identifications with her own self-hatred and allowed for the development of a warmer connection.

Andrea abandoned her need to hurt herself in order to hurt her parents. She realized she needed to learn to accept their limitations and receive what they could affirmatively offer her, while finding emotional strategies to distance herself from their negativity. Like many older adolescents, she is in the process of developing her own separate identity and values independent of her parents and their wishes, is negotiating her own racial

identifications without feeling she has to conform to the rigid demands of stereotypical popular culture, and is more wed to the notion that self-value is contingent upon the cultivation of a personal aesthetic rather than on the superficiality, appearance, and materialism that predominately preoccupies the attitudes of many youth today. Andrea has been most successful in taking new risks in self-assertion and conveying her own opinions to her family and friends without the fear of social rejection, avoids dysfunctional fights with her parents and brother, and continues to relate to her sister in more affectionate ways. Whereas before she thought that the reason why people mistreated her was that she had an unappealing personality and physical appearance, she now knows she was picking bad objects who invalidated, used, and neglected her, as symptomatic of her masochistic repetitions.

Andrea completed her high school through correspondence studies, earned her driver's license so she would no longer be reliant on her father, and acquired a full-time job. She is beginning to enjoy her life for the first time, is meeting new friends, has returned to playing piano and singing for her own self-satisfaction, is exercising in moderation, and is exploring her talents as a creative writer. While structural anxieties, self-doubt, sensitivity to social acceptance, and mood fluctuations will likely persist, she strikes me as better equipped to weather the throes of adulthood.

10

☙

Feeling Closeted: *Der Todestrieb*, Guilt, and Self-Punishment in a Bipolar Gay Man

A t this point I wish to turn our attention to an extended case study of a four-year treatment with a forty-two-year-old, epileptic gay man who has had a twenty-year history of chronic, unremitting rapid-cycling bipolar disorder, a case I initially introduced in chapter 3. Cliff may be said to primarily tarry in a state of structural fragmentation organized on a borderline level of attachment pathology due to repeated developmental traumas. Cliff has been the most difficult and clinically challenging person I have ever treated on an outpatient basis, and my countertransference with him cycled just as rapidly as did his fluctuations in mood, suicidality, psychosis, and behavioral unpredictability. Over the course of my work with Cliff, I have violated many therapeutic caveats that in some circles would be considered sacrosanct, such as encouraging the permeability of the treatment frame, offering unsolicited self-disclosure, visiting his house, running personal errands, taking him to the hospital, giving him a gift, precipitously accepting and returning phone calls, engaging in lengthy, ongoing e-mail discussions, and letting the patient run up a large debt. On the face of things, these actions may look palpably incompetent, which you may indeed conclude in the end. It is for these reasons that it becomes instructive to consider just how far one should go in the name of therapy.

It may prove useful to give a terse overview of the patient's psychiatric history before delving into the course of treatment. Cliff was raised in a strict religious, Protestant household; affection was never displayed, yet hard work was expected. He describes his early childhood life as replete with material necessities but bereft of interpersonal warmth and love. His mother was a controlling, depriving woman who demanded strict conformity and would administer physical discipline by pinching and twisting his biceps or the skin under his arms until they turned black and blue. His father was a devaluing and volatile man who would deliver stern whippings with a belt strap during Cliff's early childhood that eventually turned into regular beatings with his fists from the time Cliff was twelve through his university years. Despite the ongoing physical abuse and emotional torment that Cliff had to endure, his parents attempted to portray themselves as the pillars of their community. He learned to passively accept an imposed obsequious role out of fear, while stifling his inner rage through dissociative strategies and inversion, the reversal of destructiveness turned onto himself.

Church was a regular event in order to keep up social appearances, so Cliff was brought up to observe his faith. As a result, he became a very religious teenager; but this was juxtaposed with his increasing realization that he was homosexual, thus causing immense psychic torment, depression, and suicidality associated with feeling that his sexual impulses were unnatural, immoral, and sinful. Cliff became sexually active in his early university years and then lived with a partner for the remainder of his academic studies. During this time he was battered on a regular basis and was thrown from a two-story balcony—thereby fracturing his hip and pelvis—by his lover, who was a volatile alcoholic. Shortly after that he began having sporadic twitching fits followed by passing out and would periodically wake up to discover himself in a cold bath. This pattern got progressively worse and developed into grand mal seizures. He simultaneously began to undergo significant changes in his mood and temperament characterized by extreme fluctuations in affect ranging from intense suicidal depression to disjointed feelings of euphoria. He was diagnosed with epilepsy and manic depression during his early twenties and had several subsequent hospitalizations due to his illness. Cliff had attempted suicide on numerous occasions and was once in a coma for six days following a heavy overdose during an alcoholic bender. On another occasion, he was found unconscious in a closet in his apartment, barely alive. Despite these moments of crisis, he was able to work effectively for more than ten years after graduating from college, but his illness became so insidious that he had to go on medical disability, which he has remained on ever since. For more than twenty years he has been taking myriad medications for his seizures, mood, and anxiety symptoms to help stabilize his condition, but he has largely been treatment resistant. He even had a series of right unilateral ECT (electroconvulsive therapy) treatments, but with minimal success.

I first met Cliff in one of my therapy groups when he was on the inpatient psychiatric unit of a general hospital following an overdose. I agreed to take him on as an outpatient when he was well enough to leave the hospital because at the time I recall thinking that if he did not get the appropriate form of long-term individual therapy he needed, he would in all likelihood succeed in killing himself. In retrospect, this was my first identifiable countertransference reaction—I was going to be his savior. Most patients where I worked in inpatient psychiatry were the chronically mentally ill who came in and out of the hospital as if through a revolving door. As soon as they were stabilized and doped up on meds, they were discharged with little follow-up care. Most never sought individual therapy simply because it was not encouraged by their psychiatrists, was not available, and was not financially feasible unless one had the means to seek it out on one's own. I distinctly remember thinking that I would probably have profound regret if I were to hear down the road that Cliff committed suicide and I had done nothing at the time to try to help him. Waiess (2000) tells us of the propensity to have countertransference reactions of protectiveness while working with homosexual patients. Not only did my savior fantasy correspond to his acute state of need and helplessness, which I witnessed during his vulnerability in the hospital, but it ironically echoed his religious preoccupation with sin that I felt was doubly condemning. The fact that I have been an ardent atheist for many years did not help the countertransference. Cliff had a right to be saved not only from God but from himself.

Cliff has been actively yet intermittently manic, psychotic, suicidal, and medically unstable since I began seeing him in therapy. Simply put, it's been a hell of a ride for both of us. Our first session was fraught with crisis. Less than three days after his discharge from the psychiatric unit he was informed that his uncle had died and that his then current partner of three years was seeing another man while Cliff was in the hospital. Cliff was already feeling suicidal over being devalued by estranged family members at his uncle's funeral for being gay, only to have a bomb dropped that he was likely to be abandoned by his partner, who he sensed was planning to leave him in just a matter of time. Cliff contracted for safety, and we initially began a three-day-a-week treatment until his suicidality had sufficiently become more tractable. During this time, the majority of our treatment had centered on symptom management, affect regulation, the furtive aftereffects of his previous abuse, and exploration into his long-seated developmental traumas. Cliff told me the details of his very traumatic history of chronic childhood neglect, physical battery, and emotional devaluation by his parents, which at this time in therapy manifested as an experientially depleted, empty-core self-structure. His bipolarity only exacerbated his shifting self-states from depleted to more manic and fragmentary organizations.

Cliff shows a pattern of unconsciously seeking out people in his adult life who use, hurt, and abuse him, which involves a compulsion to repeat his early traumatic experiences. Moreover, because he has profound dependency longings and needs for acceptance, interpersonal affiliation, and succor, he would often submit to personally demeaning and exploitive acts by those who would take advantage of him. This became readily apparent with his then recent partner, who had been using him for money, lodging, and sex, as well as other so-called friends who had apparently manipulated him into buying them expensive gifts he could not afford. As Cliff began observing these patterns more directly, this mobilized more feelings of rejection, worthlessness, and unlovability that plummeted him into deep emotional pain and deprivation from never being touched, hugged, or held by his parents as a child. Because of the abuse and lack of affection and interpersonal warmth he experienced growing up, he felt he did not know how to love or connect to people. He had an intense aversion to nonsexual physical touch, which spoke to his inner void and extreme anaclitic anguish informing his attachment pathology. His depression and feelings of worthlessness were magnified by the intense shame and cowardliness he experienced in not being able to confront those who had used and hurt him, which he masked as silent (disquieted) rage, apathy, passive-aggressiveness, and the hostile inversion of destructive impulses turned on himself.

When his partner dumped him, he became suicidal and vacillated between dysphoric states of profound sadness, despair, rage, and hate directed toward all those who had ever hurt him. Cliff began noticing rapid-cycling changes and was becoming more manic as the sessions progressed. Partly as a defensive need to flee and escape from his unabated pain, and partly as a felt attack on his psychic integrity, his mania was both liberating yet enslaving, eventually opening up into an abyss of fragmentation. Cliff was in constant crisis. He called me incessantly in suicidal panic, or in order to seek my reassurance and mollification. He moved in with his widowed mother but could not stand her devaluations, invalidation of his illness, and the associations to memories of his bereft and abusive childhood years, so he moved into his own apartment, only to feel even more alone, empty, and tormented.

We spent months attempting to work through the pain and vulnerability over his loss and dejection, attempting to shore up the devastation from losing the only person he loved. Sessions were filled with intense sobbing and regression. Then he started missing appointments, got confused about the days and times, and became physically ill. The only thing that purportedly gave him any sense of pleasure or comfort was his dogs. He had four Scottish terriers, and one was a show dog. One day he phoned in a suicidal crisis and I insisted that he come to my office. When he arrived, he looked and smelled as if he had not bathed for days. He informed me that he had taken all his dogs to the Humane Society and was preparing to go to his family's isolated cottage in order to kill himself. Apparently his former partner had just called and told Cliff that he had never loved him.

There were several incidents where I was feeling that I was constantly having to put out fires. Countertransferential reactions ran rampant. I relied on basic cognitive-behavioral interventions in order to manage the crises, and then I wanted to refer the patient to a cognitive therapist, thinking I was not adept at such strategies. I even tried a trial of EMDR (eye movement desensitization and reprocessing), which provided some temporary relief, but that proved equally ineffectual. I consulted with colleagues and was convinced to hang in there despite feeling helpless and frazzled, introprojective emotive states I absorbed from Cliff like a sponge. I not only allowed but encouraged the permeability of the treatment frame. I invited Cliff to call me when he was feeling impulsive or unpredictable so I could pacify or talk him down, and these mini phone sessions, or "windows," as Hoffman would say, were increasingly used for containing purposes. I spoke to his mother and his previous partner in order to appeal to their sensibilities and empathy for Cliff's fragile state. But nothing was working.

Cliff had gone off all his medication because he was cognitively disheveled and convinced that nothing was helping, and this just precipitated his decompensation. He began having several seizures a day and was growing increasingly more confused, disoriented, and out of control. He told me that he had woken up at three in the morning to find himself standing on a pier overlooking Lake Ontario in his pajamas in the snow with no shoes or socks on. If he wasn't going to kill himself, his unconscious certainly was. The holidays were approaching, and I was scheduled to take my annual vacation and would not be back until after the new year. I was encouraging Cliff to make contingency plans to leave his dogs with friends or relatives so he could return to the hospital during my absence, but he refused. Then he called stating that his mother had allegedly told him that she had hated him for the past twenty years (since he had come out of the closet), and his ex-partner had just phoned to tell him to kill himself. Cliff wished he was dead so he didn't have to feel the pain. I told Cliff I was coming to get him to take him to the hospital, and I was not going to take "no" for an answer.

I drove to Cliff's apartment and helped him pack for his stay. We then loaded the dogs into my minivan and drove to a kennel to have them properly cared for, and then we went to the store to get him some personal toiletries before taking him to the inpatient unit. Cliff disclosed more about his past and his inner conflicts during that hour-long drive than he had in more than thirty hours of therapy. There was a bond developing between us during these poignant moments. Despite his regression and decompensation, I began to feel he was truly letting me into his inner world and was hopeful that a trusting and secure attachment was possible. Before I went on my holidays, I decided to give Cliff a Christmas gift, hoping it would serve as a sort of transitional object during my absence. It was a small hourglass that a former patient had once given me as token of appreciation. "It takes time," I said. "Healing is a process."

After Cliff's stabilization and discharge from the hospital, we began the arduous process of working through his traumas and affective devastation over losing his partner. Cliff had a pathological dependency and masochistic attachment to this man, an obsessional need to cling to an abusive internal object. His ex-partner was calling four to five times a day only to debase, reject, and harass, but Cliff continued to receive his calls. As in his relationship with his father, mother, and past partner who battered him, Cliff could not give up his dysfunctional connection to abuse. During a session, Cliff confessed that he had recently slept with his former partner after a seductive phone conversation, only to be discarded once again the next morning. Cliff would speak frankly about how "I will kill myself, it's just a matter of when."

A turning point in the therapy emerged when Cliff's pain over abandonment and loss was converted to anger. He began to distance himself emotionally from his ex-partner after he was able to consider how manipulative, sadistic, and exploitive his partner had been, for example, using him for money, lodging, and support under the guise of love. Once he was able to view more realistically how disturbed his former partner was, this realization mobilized rage as a primary defense against his suffering, which turned into a need for revenge. Cliff purportedly reported his ex-partner to the police and to creditors for fraud, which provided some relief and satisfaction to him as he kept me informed of the criminal investigation. The times of intense therapeutic impasse and psychological upheaval leading to psychotic depression, suicidal uncertainty, and a tenuous grasp of reality that had once punctuated the treatment were beginning to remit and level off into pockets of functional adaptation. During this time, the patient was able to trust and open up to me more about his traumatic past and the affective aftermath it left on his psychic structure. After being on disability for more than ten years, he told me that he had secured a stress-free part-time job and moved into Toronto in order to be connected to the gay community for support and social interaction. I convinced him to consult another psychiatrist and a neurologist for a second opinion about his medication regime, and modifications were made, including adjustments in his lithium levels. I felt we were making some progress: his symptoms were stabilized, he was not suicidal, he was working and living autonomously, and he was socially involved with others. Furthermore, I felt he was slowly internalizing me as an empathic, soothing selfobject; he called my answering machine to hear my voice when he was upset rather than needing to speak to me directly, was less inhibited in his disclosures during the session, was able to address our developing relationship, was more tolerant of examining his defenses and the emergent transference, and was reporting more experiential qualities of daily living. On the face of things, he was getting better, so it seemed.

Then Cliff started getting high again. He was going on uninhibited spending sprees, engaging in foolish business ventures, and acting out sexually. He was indulging in unprotected sex with many strangers, was frequenting gay bathhouses, was participating in orgies, and had one ephemeral fling after another, including with a man named "John." His mania served as a feeble attempt to flee from the anguish of mourning the loss of his former relationship and dealing with his past trauma; but his one-night stands and destructive hypersexuality only triggered more internal upheaval and feelings of worthlessness, loss, and inner emptiness.

Then I discovered that Cliff had been lying to me. Certain aspects of his narratives were contradictory, so I confronted the discrepancies. He had no job, nor did he move to the city. I now had reason to question his entire story, not knowing what was fiction or fact. A breach in trust and in honesty was orchestrated by the patient, but why? Cliff confessed that since I had been so available to him throughout all his crises, he felt beholden to show me that he was doing better in my eyes. He felt a sense of guilt and obligation to be more functional than he really was, and pretending to live a life through such fantasized achievements provided him some temporary escape into satisfaction. I have no doubt that my countertransference was fueling this dynamic, a sort of reverse projective identification where the patient felt compelled to internalize my fantasies and adopt a role responsiveness in order to fulfill my wishes that he get better and hence pacify my anxieties. Examining the transference and our "real relationship" only created more feelings of shame and self-reproach in him for disappointing me, which in retrospect signaled the beginning of his downhill plunge.

Cliff started acting out more impulsively and became more reckless. He was spending money he did not have and was giving it away to friends. Refusing to turn his finances over to his mother, he claimed that his apartment was burglarized (which I later found out was a lie) and that he was in danger of being evicted for violated boarding codes for harboring too many dogs. His seizures were more frequent and he had two minor car accidents, thus necessitating my having to encourage his physician to report him to the provincial department of transportation for endangering other people's lives. When his license was revoked he was furious. He was angry with me and the world and temporarily refused to continue treatment. Consequently, he rapidly decompensated.

Cliff became paranoid and actively psychotic. One day he came to session palpably agitated with florid hallucinations, stating that "they" did not want him to speak to me any longer. "Who are they?" I asked. "Bill and Fred; they are sitting right beside you." Bill and Fred were incarnations of previous lovers, one protective and one abusive. Each was dialectically at war with the other; they were projections of Cliff's divided self. Bill wanted him to fight, while Fred wanted him to die. Cliff was internally splintered and disoriented and was fragmenting more by the day. His hallucinations and delusions persisted despite a change in his medication regime. I got his mother involved with some success. Then Cliff's psychosis gave way to unremitting paranoia and delusional persecution: people were watching him, following him, trying to poison his food, so he stayed cooped up for days, didn't eat or bathe, and neglected his dogs. Friends of his were on a suicide watch; they took turns staying with him in order to get him through his plight. Then one afternoon, Cliff called to tell me good-bye. I couldn't talk him down and couldn't get him to agree to come to see me or to go to the ER. His hallucinations and feelings of persecution were simply unbearable. When he hung up the phone and would not answer when I attempted to return his call, I had no other choice than to call the police to have him hospitalized.

While coming off of his manic psychosis, Cliff was criminally charged with theft and fraud. He claimed that he had no recollection of his activity and pursued criminal diversion under the mental health code rather than face a trial. During this time, his psychosis leveled into generalized paranoia and fear, and he preferred to seclude himself and avoid the world as a protective refuge. He dissociated through much of our sessions and was internally preoccupied with his hallucinatory experiences, refusing to accept them as delusional psychotic projections. He had constructed in his mind the presence of more benevolent protective figures to get him through the uncertainty of his impending court case. He reported having increased seizures and had several serious falls. I was concerned that he had incurred a concussion given that his psychosis entailed synonymous symptoms. Then, bizarrely, the patient came to session in an angry demeanor, talking in a different voice and under a different name. He appeared crazed and tough, while his more typical comportment was passive, meek, and helpless. Claiming to be another person named Hal (his alter ego he wished he could be), the patient explained that Cliff could not cope, so *he* was taking charge of things before Cliff killed himself. Hal told me that Cliff was charged with another count of defrauding a merchant and had to give a deposition to the police the next day. By the end of the session, Cliff had reconstituted and Hal had disappeared. Cliff began to sob but managed to gather his defenses enough to examine the practical tasks that were needed in order for him to cooperate with his lawyer and prepare for the criminal investigation that lay ahead.

Cliff managed to evade prosecution of his charges, and over the next two years we explored more directly his self-destructive path, his passive-aggressiveness and failure to take personal responsibility for his life choices, his death wish and sadomasochistic need to suffer, his incessant complaints toward family members and the self-sabotaging role he plays, his fixation with loss and lack as a failure to mourn, his physical abuse and anaclitic deprivation during childhood, and his persistent oscillation between apathy and self-pity, associated with unresolved trauma. Treatment with Cliff could be characterized as a protracted carnival ride—intense, turbulent, and abrupt, punctuated by moments of calm before the scream. Over this time period, Cliff was profoundly depressed, was intermittently hypomanic, manic, and psychotic, was unpredictably suicidal, had disrupted his medication schedule several times, became detached, and grew increasingly more fragmented. His alter ego returned, this time as another part-self, and confessed again that Cliff had been lying to me. Unable to speak about it directly in the first person, he was afraid of losing me, and hence he sheltered me from many things to protect the specialness of our relationship, afraid I would abandon him if he were to be completely honest. Although there was clearly an erotic component to the transference, this was never directly acknowledged due to the competing array of associations pressing for attention. A new delusional system had taken seed in these split-off ego organizations as he assumed the role of the fantasized defender—his self-ideal—what he would like to be (via identification with me). In my attempt to understand his deliberate deception and dishonesty, he had been moving away from me in order to protect me from his bad self, as well as protect himself from his erotic and affectional feelings toward me.

As Cliff became more religiously preoccupied, he could not escape the affective self-certainty that he was evil and living in sin for being gay, a sin so sordid that he believed he could only be forgiven by God through death. Doing everything he could to destroy himself, he was brought up once again on more fraud charges and spent a week in jail. When I met with him after his release, the temporary incarceration paradoxically had helped mobilize self-preservation strategies for survival and partly satisfied his punitive superego injunctions. I was concerned that Cliff was not getting the quality of legal representation he needed. His attorney was a fresh graduate with no experience handling mental health cases and had contacted me with his own anxieties about my patient. I gave Cliff a referral to a respected specialist in the region and he got better legal council.

During the months before the trial, Cliff's symptoms had stabilized. He took some time away at his family's cottage with his dogs for an interim reprieve, where he reportedly experienced periods of solitude, contentment, and quiet reflection. During this time, I was available through e-mail and provided him with ongoing support. The Internet in many ways is an impersonal phenomenon despite being highly intimate: Cliff was able to communicate more openly and uninhibitedly—in a manner akin to free association—without the social pressure of having to censor or modify his self-conscious thoughts. His e-mail communications were always unedited and often full of run-on, tangential, spontaneous thoughts or confessions, which were more or less coherent amalgamations of fused inner experiences. There was a progression in his correspondences from gratitude to more panicky, agitated, disoriented, suicidal, and psychotic associations, eventually leading to helplessness, dread, and ominous fragmentation as his trial date approached. My responses were always laconic yet encouraging and optimistic. I offer below just a few sentences of Cliff's unedited communications:

E-mail 1:   I just wanted to say thank-you for your support. I do not feel that I am really worth anyones time and effort, it always amazes me how much you seem to care.

E-mail 3:   Things are just starting to push their way back into my mind. I really do not think that I am going to be able to withstand court and going to jail. I have pretty much decided that I am going to disappear before then. I think you know what I mean by that without me saying anymore. I do promise that I will attend my next appointment with you first, but I am just tired of my life and I think you have known that for quite some time.

E-mail 4:   It is too bad that my other illnesses have gotten in the way, I think you and I could have had some great sessions. There is so much that I want to tell you, but have always been afraid. I am always afraid of losing someone that I care for. You have been good for me and have tried to show that I am worth something. I thank you for that, I really am not worth anything, I wish that I had the courage to kill myself.

E-mail 6:   I am holding together, but I am not doing very well. I don't even admit to my mother when I am getting confused, I don't understand anything on the television. I have never wanted to admit it, but I will tell you, I hear strange messages from the television, I cannot stand music, because I get too many messages from there. I cannot believe I am telling you this, I do not want this discussed in court, this is between you and I. I also have some friends, you would call them imaginary, I wouldn't. Please don't hold this against me, I was never going to tell you this. I keep it under control most of the time, I am finding it more and more difficult living with my mother, I am sure she is going to figure it out sooner or later. Please do not pass this on, I want this to be our secret. I am very good at keeping it under c!!ontrol.

E-mail 9:   I am sorry to dump all of this on you. I really respect you as a doctor, but I feel like I can trust you as a friend. I told you once of my secrets, there are many more for us to break through. Once again thank-you for caring.

E-mail 14:   I always counted on my faith in God and I have totally lost that, I realize that I am to blame for all of this and that I need to be punished. You try so hard to help me, which I do appreciate, I think you and my mother are the only ones that care what happens to me. I honestly don't. I wish they would give the death sentence for what I have done. I never lied to you, I honestly do not remember a ting. I just want to plead guilty, even if that is the worst thing to do. Once again thank-you from the bottom of my heart.

E-mail 16:   My voices and paranoia are getting stronger all of the time, I do not want that discussed with anyone but you and I.

E-mail 20:   All I can think about is running or killing myself. I think that I am at the most critical point that you have ever known me. I am not afraid of death and I am very well prepared. I worry about my mother, and dogs of course, luckily she has become very attached to them. I will not go to jail for something I did not do. How is that going to look for the other charges, I will be just digging my own grave, I might as well get it over quickly.

E-mail 23:   You have been the most patient and kind doctor I have ever known. You I think know that you have been the only one that I have ever trusted into the iner circle of my thoughts and you were just starting to get there. In many ways we are alike surprisiling [*notice the twinship transference*], except I do not like to let people into what is really happening in my life. Belief me I have done a lot of analzing of myself, the problem is none of it makes sense to me. I came from your typical upper middle class family and we had everything. The only thing that I can figure is that I consider love to be something that you must give to someone in the forn [*as in fornication*] of something material. I hate to touche even to shake hands but it does not bother me during sex [*now the transference has become erotic*]. I don't know why I am telling you all of this now, I have probably told you before. Maybe it can help you close the chapter on me. I think I have been a waste of your time. I think that I have been a waste of all the wonderful people that have tried to help me. Fine they may have found a physical problem, but I can promise you there is a hell of a lot more.

Cliff and I prepared for his testimony in our final session. This is an e-mail he sent just prior to his court date:

E-mail 25:   I want to thank you for being such a kind and understanding man, sometimes, most of the time I consider you my only real friend. I promise this will not be happening tonight, Wednesday, Thursday, I cannot promise about Friday morning. Please do not call hospitals, that would make matters worse, I would look more guilty, and it would just delay matters and the outcome would be the same anyway, this has just come sooner, do you actually think I was going to go through an entire court scene. I am embarassed to look in the mirror. How can I stand in court while they read charges against me, even the ones that

I deserve. I believe I am getting the final punishment in life that God has put on me and that is death.

I helped the best I could in Cliff's defense. I wrote letters and reports for the Crown and testified in court on his behalf. Cliff had a total of five felony charges, including fraud over $5,000, perjury, and obstruction of justice. My expert testimony was the deciding factor. The judge was acerbic during sentencing but agreed that Cliff needed to maintain his established psychological and medical treatment regimes, which prison would not afford. Cliff was sentenced to eighteen months of home incarceration with many stipulations, including continuing his treatment with me. But Cliff's death drive (*Todestrieb*), need for punishment, and self-destruction were too cosmic. He violated the conditions of his home incarceration within twenty-four hours of leaving the courthouse, was subsequently re-arrested, and was then placed in a minimum-security prison for the remainder of his sentence. At the time of his incarceration, he had an outstanding therapy debt of over $1,000. When Cliff did not show up for his scheduled appointment after his sentencing, I sent him an e-mail asking him to give me a call to reschedule. This was Cliff's last correspondence to me before his rearrest:

E-mail 26:   Hello, I do not know whether I will ever be able to speak to any analyst again in my life. That judge opened up an entire new perspective of the way I look at myself, and it is not a good one. When he stood there and told everyone especially me that I was a con artist and a thief, that I do things that are only for me, he basically killed what was left of my soul, so I do not see any reason in trying. I unfortunately pointed out to the probation officer that they cannot force me to go to a doctor and she almost had a fit. Unfortunately she is applying to the courts to have that changed, she pointed out that if they force me to see you that they have to pay. My mother has your money ready. She is not aware that I am no longer seeing any doctors, at first I thought that I would go without pills as well, and I realize that the doctors will only renew [prescriptions] for so long. Right now I don't trust any doctor, I believe that you helped to get my ass out of a jam but were you right?, after listening to that judge I am even more convinced that Hell is my future. I cannot call right now, I need all of the quiet I can get otherwise I will explode.

He always signed his name in the following way:

all the best
Cliff
☺

What do you do when the treatment frame has been broken? How do you go back to reinstituting limits and boundaries when the therapist has dissolved traditional parameters for treatment and even encouraged permeability in the frame? Some clinicians would say this therapy was doomed from the start, and some may even say that the patient is not capable of treatment in any conventional way. If there was a mismanagement of this case, it may be due to the general criticism that I allowed the patient to violate all established boundaries. Was this because of my own countertransference, of being sucked into destructive borderline manipulations and needy-dependent projective identifications to rescue Cliff from his own internal hell? Was my desire to be his savior through therapeutic availability too much for the patient to bear? I wonder whether the patient would have continued treatment if I had not been flexible and malleable in the frame. Would he have succeeded in suicide? Would the classical or Langsian analyst have had much success with such a patient if strict observance of the frame were a stringent requirement? How far would other clinicians go? Would you have been able to do better; and if so, what would make the difference?

I am quite certain that this type of attachment disordered patient needed my availability in order to feel some modicum of trust and attachment, but whether it was too much or too little I have no way of knowing. My impression is that he hated himself so much and hurt too deeply when given my gift of availability, one he could not receive—and in fact needed to repudiate in order to reinforce his own destructive convictions, so much so that his compulsion toward death overrode his wish to cultivate and sustain the emotional closeness he had always been deprived of yet yearned to have fulfilled. The motivations of his criminal actions are undoubtedly overdetermined: he stole because he felt entitled to receive that which he was always denied (viz., the symbolic surrogate of love through material possession, an echo of his childhood). But such entitlement is poisonous and caustic; in the end, he punishes himself for the need to be loved.

This persistent impulse to abrogate and sabotage interpersonal warmth and happiness in the service of destructive repetition substantiates the concept of the death drive through circuitous interventions: he unconsciously orchestrates his death by having others (society) continue to oppress him through a return of his own actions, punishment from the law. For Lacan (1977), the Name-of-the-Father is law of signification—a signification of the phallus as lost or negated, hence castrated: *jouissance.* Cliff's father was a tormenting, violent brute who hated his son for being gay. He gave no love, only negation. Cliff did not form an attachment to his parents, and sexuality is perceived to be his only positive way of engaging with people. But Cliff's own sexuality is what he must negate, as did his father. Cliff perennially castrates himself. Could Cliff have unconsciously equated his father with the Christian metaphor of God as the ultimate Law, the law of negation, of lack—death? Would an analysis of this possibility do anything to repair his deficient psychic structure? Would it ameliorate his self-loathing, anaclitic depression, and emotional pain? Would it help him to accept his facticity and form more authentic relationships with others?

When I have consulted other colleagues on this case, most say that they would not have taken this patient on. My fantasy is that anyone treating Cliff would hope that he would drop out of treatment in order to assuage the therapist's own discomfort and responsibility to act. I am guilty of this. Although Cliff had been out of the closet since his university days, I felt closeted, trapped, sentenced—bootstrapped to this man for the rest of my life, as if it were out of my hands. But it is a duty I freely choose, an obligation to care. Despite the personal taxation this case has had on my emotional life, I maintained my commitment to Cliff when he was released from jail. After being sufficiently punished for his transgressions, he is now "reborn" and "no longer of the gay persuasion," at least for now. Some may say I'm a fool, that my countertransference has consumed and infected the treatment, and that I would do best to refuse to see him any further and instead refer him elsewhere. I would view this as a cop out. More auspiciously, perhaps some may say I am virtuous to continue to be so dedicated, a virtue I could do without. But perhaps this commitment is what he truly needs in order to surmount his pathology, a therapist who will not reject him no matter how chronically ill he is or how egregious his actions, a fantasy we may all harbor. Either we accept our responsibilities to care for others no matter what the personal cost may potentially be, or we accept less of a standard; but regardless of one's own human limitations or moral principles, we at least need to be honest with ourselves.

11

❂

Homo Homini Lupus: Treating a Case of Systemic Ritualistic Abuse

There are some acts that are so immoral, so beastly—so horrific—that they create a metapsychological aftermath of psychic ruin. Among these atrocities are prolonged physical and emotional trauma, chronic sexual abuse, child prostitution, and murder. When we encounter these anomalies in the human race we are confronted with the disturbing and unremitting question—Why? What could possibly lead one human being to treat others in such a ghastly fashion, to treat them as objects of perverse and sadistic pleasure, to destroy their minds and spirits—to commit psychic genocide? Given Freud's (1933b) ontological treatise on the structure of the psyche, "there is no use in trying to get rid of men's aggressive inclinations" (211). They are as natural as breathing; for we can never escape from the fact that our minds are primitive. *Homo homini lupus*—"Man is a wolf to man."[1]

Patrick was eighteen years old when I first saw him in treatment after he tumultuously experienced the delayed onset of an acute, full-blown posttraumatic stress disorder. The patient reported that he was repeatedly sexually molested and physically tortured by both of his paternal grandparents, his uncle, his aunt, and several unidentified strangers from approximately three to eight years of age, including occult ritualistic group molestation, childhood prostitution, and isolated acts of sexual violence. He described vivid, detailed memories of sordid abuse that he had managed to dissociate, compartmentalize, and repress for more than ten years until a recent disclosure from his younger brother triggered an onslaught of recollections that paralyzed his ability to function in all major areas of his life. Patrick's younger brother William had apparently been diagnosed with an atypical eating disorder since childhood: he would only eat bread and potatoes. One evening over family dinner, William recalled an incident from early childhood when his grandfather had violently stuffed his mouth full of pancakes at the breakfast table because he had refused to eat. William recalled how Patrick, yelling in protest, had jumped on his grandfather's back in order to protect him. Patrick was then thrown onto the floor and beaten by his grandfather while William was able to run away and hide in another portion of the house. As William continued with his narrative, Patrick became besieged with panic and dread and began to sob profusely as he retrieved from the recesses of his mind events he had managed to block out since they occurred. Unbeknownst to William, who was hiding, their grandfather had then taken Patrick into another room, thrown him over a table, and sodomized him as Patrick depersonalized throughout the rape.

Patrick's symptoms mushroomed into chronic and unremitting flashbacks of the abuse, night terrors, generalized anxiety, paranoia, and panic attacks with a pervasive sense of helplessness, rage, and suicidal depression. When he came to see me he was in acute crisis, simply tormented by the memories of the multiple traumas, as if they had just experientially occurred. Agitated yet affectively detached, he recounted four distinct episodes of being molested; in addition to his grandfather's assault, he told me that when he was about age five his grandmother forced him to perform cunnilingus on her in the shower. More horrifically, he recounted in moderate detail how he was the focus of at least two occult rituals that he called "satanic": his grandparents, aunt, and several other people dressed in black robes had tied him up while repeating synchronous chants, beaten him, and then begun to sexually grope his body. He recalled feeling as though he was drugged, seemingly awakened from sleep during these nightly rituals at his grandparents' home during overnight visitations. While the specifics of these two incidents were not very clear and were perhaps screen memories, Patrick speculated that he must have been around three years old at the time because his grandparents moved to another house when he was about five.

Patrick's grandparents were Dutch immigrants and practicing Christian fundamentalists who raised four children of their own. Patrick's father left home at the age of sixteen and entered into active missionary work for several years. When he returned he married a woman from his congregation and they had three children. As the middle child among three siblings, a sister two years his senior and a brother three years younger, Patrick was raised in the same fundamentalist environment as were his parents, what many people would say is equivalent to a cult. Patrick's religious upbringing was marked by strict obedience to authority and the literal belief in the dogma and concrete writings of scripture that were not to be questioned but simply accepted as unadulterated truth. Alcohol, dancing, gambling, the use of psychoactive stimulants such as caffeine, and premarital sexual relations were strictly prohibited. Part of the teachings of his religion is the mandatory practice of active evangelism that involves preaching the imminent approach of the millennium, thus prioritizing the need for active recruitment and conversion of the masses before the arrival of Armageddon. For Patrick and others in whom such beliefs and practices are inculcated, followers are literally indoctrinated to think from day one that their way of being is directly ordered from the word of God and that only they will be chosen to enter the kingdom of heaven for their piety and active faith. This religion is strongly opposed to the authority of organized government in matters of conscience or morality and has a deep distrust of outsiders with competing religious doctrines, who are seen as prospectively dangerous and sinful, thus potentially corrupting the youth.

When alleged transgressions and intermember conflicts arise among followers, including concerns regarding social justice, they are encouraged to keep matters within the church without seeking external mediation or outside assistance. And when disputes or allegations of misconduct arise—no matter how criminal or egregious—the accuser must publicly face his or her accused in the presence of a counsel of elders from the community, all of whom are men, where the accused is interrogated about the minutiae of the accusations brought against one of his brothers who stands accused. If the accused denies the charges brought before him and there are no collaborative witnesses to substantiate the allegations, it is merely seen as one person's word against another's, and the matter is considered closed. The accuser has no recourse to legal reprisal without running the risk of being excommunicated from the congregation. In other words, this is arguably a practice based on ongoing fear, oppression, colonization, and submission to the dominance of patriarchy. In fact, there is such a climate of secrecy and duplicity that the victimization of members is often whitewashed under the hubris that only God has the right to judge and punish. These disturbing attitudes and customs have led many concerned social advocacy groups and law enforcement agencies to charge that even the observatory disciplinary organization that presides over the actions of its membership is merely a haven for pedophiles.[2]

Patrick confessed to being tormented his whole life but was unable to comprehend or remember the specifics of his traumatic experiences until now. In retrospect, he had shown palpable forms of sexual victimization since early childhood, including multiple food allergies, continuous somatic complaints and stomach cramps, constipation, rectal bleeding, chronic insomnia, paranoia, separation anxiety, fear of being left alone or sleeping alone, dissociative fugue states, accident proneness resulting in multiple injuries to his body, uncontrollable episodes of rage, violence, destruction of objects, bullying and physically hurting other children, intermittent suicidal impulses resulting in self-harm that only became more pervasive throughout high school, sexual preoccupation and masturbation since the age of five, voluntary homosexual activity during adolescence including oral and anal sex, repeated violation of church precepts, drug and alcohol abuse, and chronic bed-wetting that still persists today. Patrick reported always feeling sad, agitated, and high-strung as a kid, had exaggerated startle responses, was unable to tolerate being touched or held, was mistrustful toward everyone, and was hateful of others whom he viewed as being happy. He reported that as a child he had no warm or loving feelings toward his parents, who were strictly authoritative, disciplinary, emotionally unavailable, and constantly critical of his misbehavior, to which they responded with continuous blame and punishment. The sheer magnitude of such abuse, deprivation, and unremitting developmental trauma would surely dispose anyone toward forming an entrenched attachment pathology.

In the very beginning of treatment, which has been ongoing for more than four years, Patrick was attempting to cope with the acute phase of his posttraumatic symptoms, which were exacerbated as more memories of abuse surfaced in his consciousness. At first I adopted a very supportive, holding, and containing role of empathic validation and safety, and despite his trepidation and paranoia, he expressed his desire to trust me and subsequently felt comforted by my presence and reassurance that the process of therapy would eventually lead to some degree of healing. I encouraged him to freely associate to whatever came to his mind, but such free association proved to be both cathartic and anxiety provoking. He had several abreactions in the first few sessions that allowed various somatic and unarticulated affective experiences to undergo transformation through linguistic expression, but they did so at the expense of precipitating more regression to insulated traumatic resonance states by puncturing through fortified defenses that had once allowed him to function more adaptively. Resistance to speaking about the abuse directly out of fear of being revisited by the traumatic images only led to more feelings of panic, fragmentation, and retraumatization that were combated by profound dissociation during our sessions. The onslaught of terror brought on by ceaseless flashbacks and nightmares only fueled his fragmentary anxieties, paranoia, and dysphoric states. I referred the patient to a psychiatrist for psychotropic medication in order to take the edge off the acute nature of his symptoms, and this allowed for some containment and relief for us to continue to reprocess and work through the trauma. With the aid of his acquiring more functional defenses, his symptoms began to sufficiently remit within a couple of months, and he was able to productively return to work. Over the course of our biweekly treatment, Patrick gradually weaned himself off the medication within a year.

Patrick was initially enraged with his grandparents—particularly his grandfather—as well as his own father and mother for not protecting him from the abuse. While his mother was characterized as a moody, anxious hysteric who was herself sexually molested as a child, his father was described as a cold, overcontrolled, emotionally detached man. But to his parents' credit, they were a source of grave support for the first time in his life. His father confronted his own parents on the allegations and threatened to approach church elders on the matter, only to be lambasted with complete categorical denial marked by rage, verbal abuse, legal threats, and unsophisticated blame foisted back onto Patrick as his grandparents claimed that his accusations were egregious lies. Patrick's parents unquestioningly believed that he was being truthful and as a result broke complete ties with the grandparents and all extended family members who did not believe in the veracity of Patrick's allegations. The family virtually became outcasts, except in the view of one uncle who supported Patrick's courage.

Patrick was preoccupied with seeking revenge for his abuse, had increasingly aggressive and homicidal fantasies directed toward his grandfather, and was generally irritable and hostile toward all of his family members. His hostility sometimes escalated into enraged fits and yelling matches marked by interpersonal volatility, which on one occasion provoked him to put his fist through drywall. With his level of aggressivity also came free-floating anxiety, panic episodes, and persecutory fears that his grandfather would have him killed for his disclosures. He recalled how multiple times during and after the abuse he was threatened with death if he ever told anyone about the physical beatings or sexual violations. His recollections were so strong that it would turn his stomach or precipitate a panic attack if he thought about taking action against his perpetrators. Although Patrick had leaned toward criminally charging his grandparents since the onset of his posttraumatic symptoms, he is still fundamentally afraid of the possible repercussions. We may speculate that since Patrick was a child when the abuse and verbal death threats first occurred, he would have only had a very naive cognitive grasp of such events, which were concretely encoded through preoperational modes of thought under the influence of dissociative strategies and deposited as rigid unconscious fantasy systems. Unable to reflexively discern the threat or fear of death from the actual occurrence of death, he was impotent over the emotional representations and core affective organizing principles that were associated with his agonizing feelings of terror. Throughout the treatment, he became consistently more able to subject his gut-level affective and somatic experiences organized around the aftermath of the traumas to a more logically and critically derived appreciation of how he would have processed such events as a latency-age child.

Within the first three months of analysis, more memories of abuse came to the fore with frightening clarity, which only fueled his symptoms. But he also began suspecting that his father may have been involved or played some role in the abuse, despite his father's current support. He holds his father responsible for not protecting him, for repeatedly taking him to his grandparents' house, and for leaving him in their care unsupervised, where he was abused. The patient reports that recollections of early life are fraught with large gaps of memory, suspended temporality, and dissociative void. The ages from seven through eight are virtually nonexistent in his mind, for he has little recall of his life outside of school.

Patrick became increasingly more dissociative in session: he was prone to thought blocking, internal preoccupation, and losing his train of thought when describing difficult affective matter. He reported that during the ages of six to eight he would frequently be found in fugue trances, walked in his sleep, lost track of time, and would wake to find himself in places without knowing how he got there. During one incident he remembered being led into the basement by a male figure, and another time he woke up in a cold bath shivering. He could not remember any details of these events, only the impression that he was drugged and molested. He had reported a sequence of events where he was awakened at night in his home and taken for a ride in a car by his grandparents, but when he asked his mother about such occurrences, she reported that they must have only been a dream. Patrick began to question the validity of his memories due to his confusion over what was real and what was fantasy or merely reconstructions of events that never took place. But despite the fact that there were admittedly dubious constructions, omissions, historical inconsistencies, and narratives under the influence of fantasy, he was indubitably certain about specific abuse episodes that revisited him regularly through vivid imagery and the emotional and corporeal reactions they elicited.

A word here is in order about the question and controversy over false memories and the etiology of abuse. Ian Hacking (1995) insists that the mnemonic reconstruction of abuse is epistemologically illegitimate and urges us instead to focus our attention on how one "finds or sees the cause of her condition in what she comes to remember about her childhood," which "is passed off as a specific etiology" (94). For Hacking, the question of etiology is not anchored to the past but rather to the present and how the individual "redescribes," "rethinks," and "refeels" her past. As a result, the past becomes rewritten in memory, with new words, descriptions, and feelings that fall under the general canon of child abuse. This new vocabulary and the accompanying affects, conceptualizations, and memories are produced rather than reproduced. Hacking continues to argue that the false causal connection is forged through the intervening semantic models that offer an explanation of how we come to be the way we are. In effect, the way we interpret our past through current semantic labels determines who we are in the present.

According to Hacking, not only do one's own past thoughts, feelings, and events undergo transformation, redescription, and reinterpretation, but so do others' actions and intentional states attributed to them. Retroactive redescriptions may be either correct or incorrect (hence an empirical issue), but at the very least, Hacking asserts, we rewrite the past because we present old actions under new descriptions, many of which are derived from political rhetoric and the social conditioning of our day, and thus we create psychological states that were never there in the first place. We do not reproduce unadulterated memories of actual events, Hacking insists; "instead we rearrange and modify elements that we remember into something that makes sense"; thus, "we touch up, supplement, delete, combine, interpret, [and] shade" the past (247).

Despite his concise inquiry into the nature of dissociation, multiplicity, and memory, Hacking virtually ignores the ontology of the unconscious and its primordial direction over conscious manifestations. What Hacking fails fully to appreciate is the role of the unconscious and its dynamic influence on the vicissitudes of the self, memory, and personal identity.[3] In the spirit of Foucault and Wittgenstein, Hacking assumes that semantics and language practices solely structure reality, hence inner reality, but he neglects to consider how the multifarious and overdetermined matrices of developmental, interpersonal, and intrapsychic forces may influence the formation and expression of multiple self-states independently of conscious cognitive-linguistic processes.[4] Furthermore, he fails to appreciate, let alone privilege, first-person epistemic access to one's own mind and the subjective organizations that inform the phenomenological qualities of lived experience, which he believes is merely the product of social construction, determined by our linguistic, cultural facticity. This position has several palpable philosophical limitations, including the demise of the self, freedom, subjectivity, and the qualia of personal agency, not to mention the abnegation of universals and objective science, which are displaced by semantic reduction informed by postmodern idolatry. While Patrick certainly was and is confused over many past events of abuse, the details of which remain elusive, vague, and uncanny, this certainly does not negate the fact that he can with clear and indubitable certainty remember some of the horrors that plague him, horrors that are anchored in the compulsory repetition of historically traumatic events that were previously maintained as dissociated ego states under the constant press of anxiety, persecution, and inner rupture mediated by unconscious fantasy systems. And even if we were to grant Hacking's propositions to be epistemologically superior, this would not negate the fact that Patrick's lived subjective experience is his phenomenological world, hence his psychic reality. In the case of Patrick, the conscious organization of traumas is largely foreclosed from linguistic articulation because it is somatically and affectively maintained as unformulated, prereflective unconscious experience. Therefore, Hacking's claim that the relationship between dissociation and the causal inference of trauma is illegitimate is for all practical purposes worthless; the clinical evidence is overwhelming. The archaic primacy (Mills 2005), or what Whitehead (1927) calls causal efficacy, of the past is traumatically and restlessly imprinted on the deep structural configurations of his psyche, clamoring for retransformation and reprieve.

Patrick's mobilization of rage devolved into a sublimated need to seek social justice by reporting the abuse to the counsel of church elders that governed his congregation. The confrontation of the grandparents in the presence of a committee of elders was brutally tempestuous and ended in a verbal tirade marked by devaluation, intimidation, and the threat of legal action against Patrick and his family. Because of his grandparents' chaotic and aggressive behavior, Patrick was reasonably assured that the counsel would view this display as an indication of their transgressions and was relieved that he had faced his perpetrators with grit and dignity and had not succumbed to his own impulse to initiate violence on the man who sullied his innocence and youth. While the confrontation was both difficult and promising, the aftermath was horrendously stressful, demoralizing, and ultimately revictimizing. The grandparents mobilized support from their other children to harass and alienate Patrick and his parents from the rest of the extended family, including those in Europe, created friction between intermember loyalties within their congregation, and continually threatened a civil lawsuit if Patrick did not retract his accusations. To make matters more dehumanizing, the counsel of elders not only did not follow up with an appropriate investigation of the alleged perpetrators but instead punished Patrick for confessing to participating in sexual relations, which was strictly forbidden. Despite the fact that Patrick's brother testified in front of the counsel that he was physically abused by the grandfather, there were no forthcoming witnesses to substantiate the allegations of sexual assault, so the matter was dropped, resulting in Patrick losing his congregational privileges for a specified period of time. With no tangible evidence to substantiate the charges of molestation, Patrick's motives for bringing allegations against his grandparents were chalked up to his history of mischief, oppositional defiance to religious authority, and past drug and alcohol use.

These events plummeted Patrick into a morose abyss of despair with dejected feelings of being damaged beyond repair. Unable to regulate his intense and disruptive affect, concomitant with pronounced periods of dissociation, he began initiating verbal arguments with his family and others at work who were perceived as hostile and belittling, which only escalated into outbursts and fits of rage. He began to openly defy the tenets of his religion, which led to ongoing conflict with his parents over his feeling brainwashed and abused by the perversions of their faith, ultimately leading him to question the existence of God. Anxiety symptoms, flashbacks, night terrors, insomnia, and depressive features worsened as more memories of the assaults resurfaced.

Patrick began to tell me in more detail about various past events and preoccupations, but he was still somewhat guarded and secretive. By this time we had established a stable working alliance, and he viewed me as an empathic and validating presence. I felt he had formed a preliminary attachment to me (albeit tenuous) and I to him, and he was quite grateful for my availability, recognition, and support, which he frequently verbalized. Because of his developmental and cumulative traumas, Patrick could not trust anyone, let alone a stranger. He was profoundly suspicious of others' motives, and this equally applied to me. By virtue of the fact that he had to describe to me the tenets of his religion, he knew that I did not observe his particular faith; but, conversely, this proved to be more reason why he could increasingly open up and take more risks in his disclosures. I could sense that, in part due to the intense magnitude of his experiences of shame, emotional exposure, and fear of further humiliation, he was not being totally revealing about his associations. He openly acknowledged his reticence and I respected his need to maintain control. At one point, I asked him to continue to elaborate on his thoughts rather than avoid or dismiss them, and he told me that it was "none of your business." This was the first time in the treatment that I could directly detect the presence of negative transference acting as a resistance to remembering and working through the trauma. I commented on how he must perceive me at times to be too intrusive and unworthy of his trust, which must bring forth certain feelings of dread, exploitation, and shame he wished to keep to himself. Patrick was petrified over finding out the depths of his suffering, things he desired to know nothing about whatsoever. He told me that at times he had to fight the urge not to come to therapy, but he knew that he had to, and in fact he has never missed a session. Furthermore, he confessed that he was fighting the conditioned impulse not to "tell" because it was stirring up frightening panic associated with the death threats he internalized from his perpetrators. Talking more directly about his vulnerabilities and fear of reexperiencing emotional pain in my presence (rather than focusing on the details), as well as his perception of my responsiveness, allowed us to strengthen our therapeutic bond.

Patrick confided that his memories around the occult practices were murky at best because he was so young, but he could recall that the participants in the rituals were all dressed in dark clothes and that his grandmother used hypnotic gestures while in a formal gown in a room surrounded by candlelight. He claimed he was often the focus of the meetings, with people staring at him and engaged in some form of prayer that he equated as "devil worship." Although he could not remember the words that they used, he thought the chants were in some foreign language, perhaps Latin. His family was given an unusual clock by his grandparents that was from Holland, a gift that was given to each of the grandparents' children within their extended family. Patrick described it as having a Gothic design with occult symbolism and feared that it was some form of a hypnotic that mesmerized him and induced him to fall into a trance. He avoided it all his life, preferring to run by it as a child in order to evade its penetrating effects. Patrick claimed that he had uncanny, haunting associations to its visibility and chime, and he referred to it as "pure evil." The clock sat as a mantle piece in his home. Because it was a constant reminder of his grandparents' ritualistic abuse, he insisted that his parents get rid of it. Even after the object had been removed from the house for more than two years, he would still find himself abruptly awakened at night and even heard it during the day as he audibly hallucinated its chime.[5]

Patrick increasingly speculated that his grandparents had drugged him during visitations to their home by giving him a special candy or fruit punch drink that he said "tasted funny." This description was also substantiated by his younger brother, and both of them had recurrent food allergies. As Patrick attempted to piece together the fragments of his past in order to conceive of a plausible story that would lend more conceptual coherence to his reported traumas, he sought out other extended family members from home and abroad for confirmation. Most of his extended family were enraged with his accusations toward his grandparents, but some had acted with reservation and trepidation about his intrusive questioning. A cousin in the Netherlands wrote him to verify that he also did not like going to visit his grandparents, let alone being left in their care, but he did not elaborate on any reasons why other than that he felt very uncomfortable. But one of Patrick's uncles—his father's brother—refused to talk to the grandparents again because of the sexual assault accusations. This was Patrick's first real sense of validation that others too were victims of insidious abuse. Yet when he tried to openly discuss this with his uncle, wondering whether he had experienced similar violations, his uncle refused to talk about it, only saying that he was upset. It became reasonable to conclude that there was an aura of secrecy, anxiety, and fear that permeated the family, but no one would confirm that he or she was also sexually molested.

At least one episode of abuse reportedly occurred in Patrick's parents' home. This fueled more abstruseness and hatred toward his parents for their lack of security and prevention, as well as their culpability for not knowing about the assaults, or perhaps, even worse, for not wanting to know by turning a blind eye. Patrick's ambiguity surrounding their potential indirect involvement stimulated fantasies that they were also part of the grandparents' rituals and trauma, thus leaving agonizing uncertainty and unabated rage. Because I speak in the language of my patients, at one point in Patrick's pine for recognition, I said, "They should have fuckin' known." This attunement to Patrick opened in him a flow of associations about his desire not to know what really occurred out of fear of betrayal and complete psychic fragmentation. Although he felt less confused about his life history of unremitting dissociative symptoms, chronic suicidality, disorganized inner self-states, and inexplicable emotional pain now that he had some explanation for his past, he was still left with profound feelings of helplessness and shame over being defiled.

Patrick had somatized his whole life, including having vague food allergies, spontaneous vomiting, and persistent ulcers. He recalled holding his stomach in pain in the emergency room of a general hospital while attempting to speak about the abuse to his father, but then he "forgot" what he wanted to say. As he started to describe this particular event, he began visibly shaking. When he was a child, he would act out defiantly and get the belt from his father. When he was older he would prefer to stand in contempt and take the belt strap across his face rather than show deference or subject himself to the humiliation of bending over to be spanked. Rather than suspecting that Patrick was acting out his various traumas through misbehavior and self-victimization, his parents thought he was a disobedient kid who simply needed strict punishment and firm restraint. What was "almost worse" was their unavailability to safeguard him from systematic abuse; as he put it, he was unable to forgive them for "what did not happen rather than what did." Although Patrick had made many advances in affect regulation, modulating disruptive inner states, and forming accurate perceptual judgments in the moment, he was emotionally devastated by the realization that he had always been fundamentally alone, abandoned, and defenseless. Tormented by the anguish of repeated, reinforced episodes of verbal devaluation punctuated by screaming from his grandfather, he could not rid himself of that atrocious hole in his being. Struggling in himself with what he might have done differently to have prevented the assaults, Patrick could only envision was his grandfather's menacing facial expressions as he yelled ferociously just inches away from his own face, repeatedly branding the toxic introjects of being "worthless, dirty, and stupid" in his mind. As he sat in tears with a sunken head on my office sofa, I told Patrick, "I wish I was there to protect you." During reparative moments of recognition and responsiveness like these, Patrick became more alert and appreciatively cognizant of me, no longer avoiding eye contact or completely averting his face, which was his usual custom. In a subsequent session, he was moved when I told him, "I wish I could take your pain away," and this was followed by an awkward moment at the end of the hour when I thought he was initiating a hug, but he pulled away.

Patrick always dreaded speaking in public out of fear of being humiliated because he struggles with putting words to internal feeling states that gnawingly reverberate but offer little clarity. When besieged by mood swings oscillating from anger to sadness, he often reports being overwhelmed by an unarticulate emotional upheaval associated with the resurfacing of trauma. During these times he becomes quite alexithymic, for he can't seem to locate, discern, or linguistically label his fleeting amorphous affect or split-off ego states afflicted with melancholic contagion. For example, he attended a friend's wedding and became very distraught seeing everyone happy, so much so that he had to remove himself from the festivities because he started to cry uncontrollably but could not understand why at the time. At times obsessive fantasies of rage, hate, homicidal violence, and intrusive homosexual impulses would saturate his consciousness. He was sexually attracted to girls but was terrified of approaching them out of fear that they would see him as a little boy who was "not strong, inadequate, [and] impotent," hence not desirable. He saw himself as irreparably deformed and not worthy of being loved or nurtured; he viewed the thought of sexual contact with anyone as potentially retraumatizing and indicative of further sexual abuse. Speaking to me about these matters was a cathartic relief to him; he told me he had never been able to speak so frankly with another human being without running the risk of incurring judgment and possible retaliation.

Patrick described events of being offered to other people as a sexual fetish, which he flatly referred to as "child prostitution"; he was passively forced to pleasure one of his uncles and perform fellatio on strange men. Later confused about his sexual identity, thus experimenting with homosexuality in adolescence, he described the sensation of "not being there," not only in a dissociative manner, but in a very Winnicottian sense of *not* "going on being." His description left the distinct impression that at those times he was psychically dead.

Ferenczi (1933) was one of the first analysts to emphasize how trauma inflicted by adults in external reality is internalized and thereby disfigures the psyche of the child; not only did Patrick identify with the aggressor, but he also introjected the projected guilt and perverse desire of his abusers that they disavowed in themselves. During episodes of abuse, Patrick was repeatedly made to believe that his victimization was due to an unforgivable and punishable offense by God for being worthless and bad, thus leaving an aftermath of self-hatred and obsessive shame.

Patrick suffered extreme forms of persecutory guilt; at one point in session he was brought to tears out of remorse for how he used to ridicule, pick on, and physically abuse his younger brother (in part due to resentment he felt for protecting him from his grandfather's battery only to be anally raped as a consequence), and how he beat on other kids with the deliberate sadistic intention of hurting them for the simple reason that they seemed happy. Through hurting others he could gain some sense of mastery via the illusory dislocation that he was now the one in charge, hence the internalized abuser who had serendipitous power over his own pain, which mobilized in a very Kleinian way an insidious envy and desire to spoil and poison the other through his destructive will to deracinate the other's perceived experience of pleasure, which he would never know.

There has been a recent upsurge of attention in contemporary psychoanalysis on dissociation and on the question of multiplicity of the self (Bromberg 1996b; Davies 1996; Harris 1996; Joseph 1989; Loewenstein and Ross 1992; Stern 1997). In a series of works, Philip Bromberg (1994, 1995, 1996a, 1996b) has advocated for a nonunitary, nonlinear conceptualization of the self that accounts for a discontinuity of being in both normative and clinical populations. Bromberg, as do others (Hermans, Kempen, and van Loon 1992; Mitchell 1991), argues for a fluid, discontinuous, and dissociative interplay of self-states that vacillate between experiences of unity and cohesion on the one hand, and separateness and fragmentation on the other, thus making multiplicity a normative construct.[6] The oscillation between relatively unlinked yet internally congruent self-states and the experiential coherency of a singular unitary self, Bromberg argues, is an illusory adaptive means of maintaining cohesive integrity and personal continuity through the vicissitudes of multiple self-experiences. Like Lacan (1936), who argued that the unified self is an imaginary construction based on the identificatory *méconnaissances* with the imago that provide an illusory sense of autonomy, mastery, and self-cohesion, Bromberg (1993, 1996b) urges us to conceptualize multiplicity as constituting the amalgamation of segregated and disparate domains of mental reality while being able to "stand in the spaces" between feelings of unity and disunity, where disjointed self-states may be contained under the semblance of integration. Unlike Hacking, who believes that the self is ultimately constructed through linguistic and symbolic interactions imposed by language and sociopolitical structures, Bromberg highlights the intersubjective space of the ongoing relational encounters that forge the contours of dissociative and multiply instantiated realms of selfhood.

My attempt to "stand in the spaces" was at times more like floating in the fog. Dissociative patients have a very seductive yet toxic ability to induce various countertransference reactions including the therapist's (unconsciously) mimicking (via projective identification) various defensive constellations that shelter patients from emotional pain in order to help them survive. During Patrick's moments of recounting various horrific events, I encountered my own felt resistance to wanting to hear the descriptive details of his abuse, thinking that this could not be possible—not in terms of questioning the veracity of his narrative, but in terms of experiencing a refusal to believe that people could be so perverse and evil to other human beings. Fighting my own tendency toward self-retreat into dissociative fantasy, I felt a vacillation between both wanting to soothe and comfort Patrick as well as wanting to flee from the associations of helplessness that were being elicited in me. It was easy for me to identify and empathize with Patrick but at the same time fall prey to my own countertransference. I was the object of years of bullying and physical abuse by peers beginning in elementary school and ending in early high school. I was easily intimidated and fearful and felt agitated and helpless because I had no one to turn to for protection. My father was only irritated when I attempted to approach him about my anxieties, and my mother at one time called me a "wimp" when I complained of being picked on, chastised, and ridiculed by my circle of peers. During Patrick's disclosures of vulnerability and abuse, I would often find myself preoccupied with my own emotional pain as I was transported back to my past. It was at those times that I felt the need to be more active in session rather than listen as a means to mobilize reassurances that we both survived.

During a particularly poignant session, Patrick described remembering two ceremonies where he was sitting in a circle surrounded by others who were staring directly at him in the eyes as they all listened to the chimes of a clock. As the details of the recollection became more vivid, he started to dissociate throughout his narrative. He recalled being groped by a forest of limbs as these menacing figures continued to stare without speaking; then he reported the vile smell of body odor as a penis was placed in his mouth. At this moment in the session he became nauseated, as if he were going to throw up, and then he suddenly stopped speaking and looked as though he had entered into an autistic void. I called his name twice before he returned, saying he had forgotten what he was talking about. I reminded him of what he had just said, and he continued to associate to how scared he felt thinking about everyone's eyes during the rituals—evil eyes, kids at school, in crowds, eyes that judge, the eyes of God. He thought this was the main reason why he couldn't stand to look at people in the eye, preferring instead to avert his gaze, as though it would shelter him from being put "under a spell" or in a "trance." Patrick then recalled how he would sit up at night in his bed with his night-light on while he drew pictures of people on separate pieces of paper and then would surround himself in a circle with the figures he drew. At this point, I took out some paper from my desk and asked him to draw what he could remember, only to have him turn his head away shamefully. He replied that they were stick figures of both men and women with different body parts accentuated by their genitalia. Here I offered an interpretation: "You were attempting to master what had been done to you by doing the same thing to them." Whether or not this interpretation was accurate, he became immediately relieved and animated and then declared that he was elated that he now knew the reason why he did such things. In offering a retrospective meaning construction, Patrick felt he was attempting to control what had happened to him; rather than feeling like a "useless thing," he had turned them into benign puppets as a means to "cope" with the abuse. This must be why, Patrick averred, he drew his perpetrators as part objects with no faces; during the ceremonies he reportedly only saw a sea of eyes rather than the faces of family members who were molesting him. We may speculate that his tendency toward gaze and facial aversion is in part a conditioned defense against knowing the pathognomonic details surrounding his discrete episodes of trauma. Patrick was glowing as he left from this session with the professed feeling that he had more power over the past through his newfound insight rather than being enslaved by the fear of emotional breakdown.

In the next session Patrick said he felt as though he was on a "natural high—never felt so happy in my whole life." He felt invigorated unlike any time in his past, and he referred to this feeling as "the real me without the crap." He realized that he had dominion over how to think about his past and that he had survived. In his words, "If I could get through that, then I can get through this; there is a reason to live."

About this time, Patrick had started dating his first girlfriend. Nadine sparked fantasies of love but at the same time paranoia over being used and rejected. His fear of trusting her and being exploited was diametrically opposed to his wish for the love and tenderness he had never known. But when she told him that he was kind and a good listener, it unearthed several toxic introjects that plummeted him into a depressogenic state of self-loathing for not feeling worthy of love. As the relationship progressed, his guardedness and melancholia transformed into genuine feelings of care and warmth he had never felt before, and they fell in love. With the development of closeness and affection came Patrick's fear that their impending sexual intimacies would trigger a regression or intensification of his flashbacks. We discussed the need to move slowly. Over the months that followed, he relayed to me his difficulty in initiating physical intimacy; for example, he would freeze when being touched, which produced an urge for flight, and then he would get depressed. He reported having some dissociative experiences during genital touching, followed by intrusive homosexual impulses that were reawakened. Patrick came to understand his homosexual fantasies and past enactments as the residual deposits of abuse, which further activated repetitious compulsions due to confusion over his sexual identity precipitated by early sexual stimulation by males. For example, during latency age Patrick used to dress up in his sister's clothing and put on his mother's cosmetics in the bathroom mirror, but he did not know why. Now he attributes his sexual incongruities to his victimization; pretending to be a girl was the only way he knew how to make sense out of why men would violate him sexually.

Patrick's relationship with Nadine proved to be mutually tender, empathic, and healing and over a year progressed into plans for marriage. He increasingly took more risks in being genuinely open and honest despite his fears of exploitation, judgment, and rejection, and he was emotionally relieved when she was unconditionally supportive in response to his disclosures about his years of sexual molestation. She helped bind much of his psychic pain through acceptance and love. During this time, he also developed more positive feelings for his family, who was supportive of his relationship, and thus he shifted his role from that of a child to that of an adult in relation to his more mature communication patterns with his parents and newly required work responsibilities. Whereas in the past he would experience intense affect dysregulation, leading at times to the inability to de-escalate his rage or dysphoria, he could now talk calmly with family members and even assertively stand up to coworkers who he felt were derisive and verbally abusive. During this time I noticed that he would increasingly greet me with facial recognition and look me in the eye while talking, and that he generally looked less dissociative or disorganized. He was confident and less worried about how other people would perceive him or how he thought he was expected to act. In fact, Patrick performed so well at work that he was promoted from his apprenticeship as a toolmaker to a program and design engineer.

When Patrick discontinued his psychotropics, he went through a period of feeling more buoyant and less inhibited, acted giddy and spontaneous, and was in awe over how he felt he was allowing his true self to breathe and roam freely. As he put it, "I never thought I would know how to feel like me." But Patrick still ruminated about his past and experienced "body memories" of the abuse. He particularly had the uncanny feeling of being "dirty," as though he was wearing something on his skin. Patrick still struggled between his desire to confront his abusers versus "letting it go." He was furious that the congregation elders would not push for an investigation due to the refusal of his extended family members to cooperate as well as the elders' worry about a lawsuit from the grandparents. He once again started questioning his faith, the hypocritical nature of the church elders, and the level of pathology condoned by the religion itself, to the degree that he finally left his church for another congregation. His gut reaction was to want to press criminal charges against his grandparents, but he was very anxious that the stress of such an ordeal would precipitate a breakdown, nor did he feel he had enough strength or guts to stand up to the scrutiny of a legal process.

The thought of publicly exposing his grandparents mobilized a great deal of annihilation anxiety. He wanted to seek justice as a means of self-healing as well as to vindicate himself and potentially protect possible future victims, but despite my encouragement of this instrumental move toward recovery, he became more frightened and paranoid. It soon became more clear as to why. Patrick told me about a particular series of events he had been mnemonically recycling as if they were "preprogrammed tapes" he could not erase from his mind, events he had refused to directly tell me about earlier because they were so ghastly, events that were inbred in him not to reveal. Patrick claims that he witnessed his uncle murder a girl-friend by slitting her throat with a knife in the kitchen of his apartment. Patrick recalls vividly how when he was about six or seven years old his uncle's girlfriend attempted to get him out of the apartment to safety, when the uncle in a fit of rage grabbed a blade from a wooden block in the kitchen and slashed open her throat, only to immediately turn to him wielding the knife to his face, threatening to kill him and his family if he ever said a word. Patrick stated that he was so petrified that he froze and then collapsed to the floor in catatonic shock. The next thing he remembered was his grandparents storming into the apartment yelling at him and his uncle. He was then removed to his grandparents' car while the girlfriend's body was placed in the trunk. Patrick reports then being driven to his grandparents' farm, where he watched as the body was placed in potato sacks and then buried in a location on the farm. Patrick recalls being blamed for causing the murder and repeatedly threatened with death if he ever spoke about the killing to anyone.

Patrick was under great distress over reliving the events in his mind, which precipitated more flashbacks and nightmares about the episode—dreams where he was awakened just as his uncle killed him. He further associated to feeling drugged all the time when he was around his uncle and specifically recalled being given a substance in powdered form and then being used for sex by men. Patrick surmises that his uncle prosti-tuted him in order to supply enough money for his uncle's drug habit. De-scribing these events allowed him to make inferential causal connections between his repeated abuse experiences and why he had had enuresis most of his life, multiple food allergies, blood in his stool, and episodes of childhood sleepwalking, and why he would often urinate all over his room and furniture during the night without remembering doing so.

While the uncle has been dead for a few years, Patrick is still terrified that his grandfather will have him killed if he makes any public allega-tions about his abusive past. Patrick reportedly does not know the girl-friend's name who disappeared, and his grandparents moved from their farm to another community years ago, so he is unsure whether he could relocate the burial ground, yet he suspects that the evidence would have been removed or destroyed even if he could. When his uncle died of undisclosed health complications, Patrick described being detached dur-ing the whole funeral service as if he was emotionless and in a dissocia-tive fugue. But what he recalls is his grandmother's voice saying, "He's a good boy," the same words she used to calm down the uncle after he al-legedly committed murder.

Whether the events surrounding the homicide are reproductions of ac-tual historical occurrences or whether they are fantasized productions in-formed by the diffuse cacophony of dissociated experiences imbued within functionally discrete self-states, these empirical considerations have little to do with the affective phenomenology of Patrick's psychic reality.[7] From a therapeutic standpoint, discussing these events with me was a cathartic relief that allowed for further integration of what Bucci (1997, 2003) refers to as "emotion schemas," which are specific types of memory schemas that operate on "subsymbolic" levels of sensory, affective, and somatic representations. According to Bromberg (2003), dissociation is enlisted as a defense against the recurrence of trauma that helps maintain a "hypnoid separateness of incompatible self-states, so that each can continue to play its own role, unimpeded by awareness of the others" (561). Following current work in cognitive neuroscience, it is plausible to conclude that during extreme forms of traumatic dissociation, the higher-order rational capacities for self-reflectivity would be hindered from forming conceptual, hence linguistically mediated links, and would thereby be unable to integrate the split-off or compartmentalized affective reverberations typical of dissociative hyperarousal and the bodily representations that are operative on distributed parallel or connectionist processing systems of the brain (see McClelland et al. 1989). Following Bucci and others, I suggest that Patrick's attempt at adaptive cognitive integration through conceptual reorganization and reconstruction would be sufficiently impeded because the affective-somatic representations of trauma override the higher-order functions of reflective self-consciousness that facilitate such consolidating functions. If a danger situation arises, the ego will be immediately alerted by "signal anxiety" (Freud 1926), or what Bromberg (2003) calls an "early warning system," that leads to a hyper state of arousal, to the degree that "the individual is *unable to acknowledge the source of danger*" (Bucci 2003, 548) due to dissociative strategies aimed at survival. What Patrick persistently reexperiences is a recapitulation of the original traumatic episodes that are imprisoned within the affective core of his distributed yet segregated sensory-affective-somatic information-processing systems. Because of such functionally segregated mechanisms of information processing, it is no surprise that Patrick remains epistemologically confused about the conceptual links between the traumatic events, his emotional arousal, and the unformulated, prereflective somatic resonance states that abide unrecognized because such links were probably never forged to begin with. Furthermore, Patrick's cognitive development at the ages he reportedly was abused would be at the naive preoperational to concrete operations phase at best (see Pulaski 1980); therefore, he would not have the abstract capacities for deduction and reflexivity that occur in later development under normative conditions, let alone under the press of trauma.

In the immediate sessions that followed the homicide disclosure, Patrick reported having much symptom relief due to the confession of his secret. He conveyed that the awkwardness he had always had speaking in front of groups of people throughout his life was connected to the threat of speaking about the molestation and the murder out of paranoia that his unidentified and unarticulated embodied terror would lead to annihilation. With this liberation in speaking the unspeakable also came a shift from the subsymbolic to the symbolic mediation of experiencing and talking about his feelings, not just reacting to them. This connection led Patrick for the first time into a realm of experiencing profound sadness over being treated all those years as a perverse object of sleazy gratification by his own family. Memories of putting on his mother's makeup as an effort to make sense of the discordant contradiction of sexual activity perpetrated against him by men—only to be laughed at and ridiculed by his family, which created more shame and humiliation—plunged him further into despair over not being protected or treated with love.

His rage over his parents' failures to recognize his behavioral signs and symptoms as cries for help succumbed to the helplessness of accepting the brute facticity that he was a senseless victim of deranged psychopathy he could not control or undo. The "worst part" was accepting that the abuse really did happen. Images he attempted to avoid through dissociative withdrawal or through secondary defenses at threat reduction were now being allowed to passively enter his consciousness, and he had no recourse but to acknowledge, sympathize with, and then let them slowly evaporate. Self-representations of repeatedly being physically and sexually desecrated with no one to mollify his anguish as he cried unabatedly—only to be further mocked and sadistically laughed at by his assailants—were unbearably poignant to relive. The most tormenting imagoes that were burned into his memory were the visual facial expressions of delight during his humiliation when he cried or showed tears or vulnerability. As Patrick put it, "I always hated other people because they looked happy." Not only was he bludgeoned by the unshakable residue of being spoiled and damaged, but his remorse, lament, and shame over hurting other children for pleasure justified his own self-flagellation. But he came to accept that his senseless bullying of other kids was his way to displace the affects of his trauma in an effort to take away his pain; and if only momentarily, it served as an omnipotent evacuation by making the other the bad object rather than having to sit with the pathos of his sordid self-representations. Sitting in tears throughout a session, he realized that because he had been unable to fight his own bullies (viz., internal objects), this had been his adaptive way to cope, even though it had made him remorseful because it caused others unnecessary woe.

Reaching the affect and working through the emotional pain associated with his tainted self-image eventually led to the valuable processes of finding meaning in his suffering and mourning the loss of his childhood. The importance of finding meaning in suffering is a personal enterprise only each of us can define, but I believe for Patrick it was in recognizing the positive significance of the negative. If he had not suffered, he surely would have entered into a schizoid void of psychic decay and would not have prevailed. As he puts it, "I'm a strong person to have survived, and no one can take that away." Despite having undergone horrific acts of inhumanity, Patrick can now look back at his life and feel that something good has come of it. Patrick developed the virtuous yet tragic gift of empathy forged through the identifications with his own suffering. Unlike most men his age, he is attuned to the inner experiences of others and genuinely feels for people's pain. His relationship with Nadine is a testament of this, as is his consanguinity for children. Patrick reports having a special connection with children, one marked by mutual play, caring, warmth, and recognition; now married, as he plans for a life of fatherhood, there is no doubt, as Freud (1914c) tells us, that he will live as a child through his own children. In a particularly touching session, after we celebrated the triumph of all his accomplishments since coming into treatment, I asked Patrick somberly, "Have you mourned the loss of your self?"

"I sometimes still cry for him," he replied as the tears began to well up in his eyes. When I saw his desolate gaze, I felt my body freeze up from my legs to the nape of my neck, and my eyes got teary. In a beautiful moment of mutual recognition, we both looked into each other's eyes and knew that the connection we felt between us in that instant was more real than ever before.

"Now he can rest so you can live," I continued. "But you'll always remember him and keep him close to your heart." Upon hearing this, he started to weep.

While Patrick still continues on his sojourn of recovery, he is no longer enslaved by the atrocious repetitions of his past trauma that once contaminated his present being as well as imperiled his future with the inane pointlessness of existential absurdity. Although he has for the most part thrown away the shackles of the past, the past still lives in him, but it does not define who he is now. While he had no control over his traumatic history, he now feels he has a choice over the way he wishes to view his facticity through the empowerment of his own subjective agency. Among the tempestuous sea of psychic debris, Patrick is invigorated with the prospects of his new life and is immensely happy to have found love.

More than ever before, Patrick is focused on his current existence, along with the challenges, banalities, and successes he has at work; but more importantly, he is focused on cultivating a quality relationship with the one whom he believes will be his partner for life. Once unable to regulate his mood or affective tensions, he is now able to show self-control, can defuse and transmute internal disruptions when they occur, is proactive and assertive rather than reactive and explosive, has more calming-evoking capacities to elicit soothing introjects, and employs positive cognitions for adaptive functioning rather than descending into the morose pit of his past. He is less likely to personalize conflict from coworkers and his family and is more aware of his self-alienating patterns that only serve to fuel interpersonal difficulties. No longer wanting to test or punish his parents with his rage, thus abnegating his need to set up fights so he can reject them only to be rejected in turn, he now is earning their respect in his own right as an adult. While Patrick still contemplates the possibility of pursuing criminal and civil action against his abusers, he is still in the process of weighing the risks to his mental economy against the need for revenge, justice, and retribution. For the time being he is content with moving forward with his own needs for individuation-within-relation, is separating more from his family and church, and is enveloped in the dialectical process of creative self-discovery, thus showing more intrapsychic fortitude, courage, and resolve. For someone who once told me, "I can't imagine life without hate or with happiness," he is now in marvel over "feeling so much love and trust."

What I particularly feel was most therapeutic for Patrick, as with other traumatized patients, was his ability to form an attachment to me in an authentic, mutually affirming manner within an intersubjective milieu of safety, acceptance, and honest reflection on psychic pain. Here we witnessed the transformative power of revamping previously inaccessible and unarticulated emotional resonance states through meaningful dialogue and extralinguistic mediation in a holding environment marked by empathic responsiveness, validation, and bona fide care. In what small part I played, I was granted the privilege of seeing Patrick emerge from the rubble of his inner hell to transcend the chronicity of his trauma and attachment disorganization through the providence and compassion that only genuine human relatedness can afford, what might not be inappropriately called the true spirit of *agape*. Seeing this damaged and demure adolescent boy turn into a fine young man has truly been one of the most satisfying experiences of my life.

NOTES

1. Derived from Plautus, *Asinaria* II, iv, 88; see Freud 1930, 111.
2. According to a recent national news program, *The Fifth Estate*, aired on September 4, 2003, by the Canadian Broadcasting Corporation (CBC), the watchtower organization that oversees and investigates allegations of sexual abuse perpetrated by its members has more than 20,000 documented cases on record of sexual molestation that it is not willing to properly investigate or discipline.
3. While the self is in constant flux, a state of unfolding possibility, there are also immutable structures or invariances that foster evolution and change within the nocturnal abyss of the mind. Without such unifying structural *processes*, the self would have no cohesion, no organizing functions at all, hence, no ground. The self would be too chaotic and amorphous, continuously on the verge of nonbeing. While memory, identity, and self-representations of the past are fleeting, Hacking never questions whether there is

uniformity and persistence in the unconscious regions of the mind, those of the inner self, whether multiple or unitary. While Hacking cogently demonstrates that certain aspects of identity and memory come under the spell of semantic construction, this is certainly not a complete account of the self or multiplicity. Hacking's nominalism assumes that personhood, what he refers to as the "soul," is not determined by one's biography but rather determined by the way in which we conceive of our biography. Hence, a person is composed of consciousness and memory, nothing more. While the agency of consciousness gives definition to self-identity, the unconscious is the core of our very being, the primal self that holds the secrets to the soul.

4. This is particularly germane for Lacan (1977), who sees the unconscious as being structured like a language. While the theory of self-as-process has been addressed by contemporary thinkers (Joseph 1989; Kristeva 1986), there seems to be an implicit theoretical assumption that process or change automatically nullifies the concept of essentialism. With homage to Heraclitus, the fundamental notion of the self-as-process originates with Hegel. In the *Phenomenology of Spirit*, Hegel (1807) compellingly demonstrates that the structures of the psyche are not opposed to essentialism at all; rather, the appearances of consciousness are made possible through the essential, dialectical unfolding of subjectivity. This is further echoed in the *Science of Logic* (1812), where reason is shown to be the coming to presence of self-consciousness. Elsewhere I have argued that the dialectic of process is the essential structural foundation of the unconscious (see Mills 1996; 2002a).

Like many contemporary psychoanalytic theorists, I view the self as process, but I maintain that the polarity that bifurcates the self into *either* a unitary, singular, and cohesive matrix *or* a multiple, nonlinear, and dissociative mosaic is a false dichotomy. The question that needs to be posed is whether multiplicity can exist within continuity and whether process and flux can exist within a stable unifying psychic structure. Opponents of essentialism argue that theories of human nature that espouse universal structures of the mind ignore the individual, gendered, social, ethnocentric, and cultural forces that govern subjectivity, thereby conceptualizing the human being as a rigid, fixed, static, and immutable entity. As an alternative paradigm, the decentered, nonunitary, and dissociative characterization of multiplicity augurs well for a heterogeneous conception of selfhood that accounts for the discrepancies of human existence, thus valorizing psychic diversity without running the risk of ontological reductionism. The problem with this dichotomy, including the view Hacking professes, is the fallacious belief that *process* automatically rules out *essence*.

It is important to define what we mean by *essence*. Originating with Aristotle, the term usually refers to that which necessarily makes a thing what it is, without which it would not and could not exist. Unlike certain views of essentialism within the Anglo-American analytic philosophical tradition that maintain that certain definitions describe or reveal the true or exact essence of a thing in itself, following Hegel (1807, 1812), the essential nature of *Geist* as *aufgehoben* necessarily involves its dialectical movement that constitutes its structural ontology. From this account, essence does not suggest a fixed or static immutable property belonging to a substance or a thing; rather, it is dynamic, relational, and transformative. As a result, Hegel underscores the notion that *essence is process*. Thus, what is essential is change constituted through temporal-spatial relations and the dialectical positionality toward similarity and difference that comprise its very nature, without which existence would not be possible.

The process of fragmentation, separateness, discontinuity, and multiplicity is uncritically thought to be in fundamental contradiction with the concept of a singular, unifying, and integrative agent, when this assumption is simply unwarranted. What is *essential*, hence a necessary and universal condition of subjectivity, is the ontological process of the dialectic, insofar as if it were to be removed, consciousness and the unconscious would evaporate. From this standpoint, the ontology of the self is a complex holism that allows for multiply dissociated (hence alienated) shapes of subjectivity to phenomenally *appear* as distinct, punctuated, and discontinuous self-states within an integrative dialectical process. The ontology of the dialectical unfolding of subjectivity not only allows for multiplicity, but it makes multiplicity possible.

5. In "The 'Uncanny,'" Freud (1919) tells us how a haunting object represents a return of the repressed.

6. Although the dissociability of the psyche was originally addressed by Jung (1946), and many before him, including Morton Prince, Charcot, and Janet, the question of normative multiplicity has divided many thinkers within the psychoanalytic community. Pizer (1996) underscores the ability of the self to endure and manage paradox as distributed forms of self-experience and challenges the dissociative hypothesis that favors disunity over unity. While dissociative paradigms account for myriad dimensions of shifting self-states experienced as "splits and fissures in subjectivity" (Harris 1996, 548), this does not mean that there is no unified or unifying process to psychic structure. Lachmann (1996), and Lichtenberg, Lachmann, and Fosshage (1992), have argued for a unitary process model of the self that allows for change and multiplicity within an integrative network of psychic unification. Rather than conceiving of the human being as possessing several "selves," each with its own unique ontology, Lachmann assumes the existence of a singular self that strives for self-integration while sustaining the capacity for disparate self-state experiences to live and flourish. This is precisely my position. To envision multiple "selves" is philosophically problematic on ontological grounds, introduces a plurality of contradictory essences, obfuscates the nature of agency, and undermines the notion of freedom.

7. Here a comment about the professional responsibility to act is warranted. When this case was initially referred to me, the local child and family protection agency had already been alerted by the mental health worker who initiated the referral because of the direct disclosure of alleged abuse and the possibility that other children in the extended family may have been involved. With regard to the allegations of murder, I am not certain whether these events actually took place in this fashion, nor could I ever be without direct evidence, but I do believe that the detailed linguistic descriptions, images, eschewed emotional schemas, and the patient's somatic hyperarousal speak to the level of symptom repetition and psychic reconstruction organized around unmitigated trauma.

Postscript from
the Unconscious

After Freud's discovery of his new science, he always maintained that "the unconscious is the true psychical reality" (1900, 613). Throughout his clinical investigations and theoretical evolution of unconscious explanation, he further emphasized the notion that "every psychical act begins as an unconscious one" (1912c, 264), and that "even when it is unconscious it can produce effects, even including some which finally reach consciousness" (1915c, 166). For Freud (1940), unconscious drives (*Triebe*) are the "ultimate cause of all activity" of the mind, and they inevitably take the mother as their most original form of attachment "established unalterably for a whole lifetime as the first and strongest love-object and as the prototype of all later love-relations—for both sexes" (188). It is here that Freud unequivocally places object relations with the mother at the pinnacle of unconscious motivation as the aim and transformation of libidinal life, which is the foundation for the attachment system to materialize and thrive. Furthermore, identification with the mother "is a very important form of attachment" (Freud 1933a, 63), which developmentally prepares the child for functional adaptation, interpersonal social relatedness, and the fulfillment of primary needs and wishes, including the capacity for love and intimacy throughout the lifespan.

Throughout this book, I have attempted to show that the rudimentary yet fundamental nature of attachment underlies unconscious structure, health and pathology, and the overall formation of personality and adjustment. It becomes important to reiterate that the process of attachment is a general ontological configuration that broadly conditions human psychology and social development. As I have endeavored to demonstrate throughout my theoretical and clinical investigations presented in this project, attachment theory may be viewed as an ecumenical psychological paradigm explaining both mental health and illness that can complement psychoanalytic doctrine and help guide treatment interventions. Because attachment processes heavily inform the most basic ontological levels of psychic organization, including unconscious morphology, the process of internalization, representation, and fantasy, the institution of defense, self-structure, and relational desires and motivations toward others, attachment pathology may be seen as constituting a disorder of the self realized on a continuum of competing mental phenomena. Having examined the domain and range of attachment pathology in multiple clinical and diagnostic groups, I hope this contribution aids in our understanding of personality formation and its relation to developmental trauma, and in the conceptualization of psychopathology as due in part to developmental deficits in attachment.

Stephen Miller (2003) tells us that "the greatest fears of our lives are based on our childhood anxieties, underscored by childhood disappointments and traumas, embellished by our own rage and desires" (15). This is a fitting characterization of how psychic pain dates back to early experiences with others; and nowhere do we encounter this more forcefully than with our parents. Even with the healthiest of individuals, there is never a pristine world of inner bliss. Just as pathology stems from the germ of conflict *in-relation* to others, health and normalcy are forged through suffering, with qualitative differences in scope and magnitude. To live is to want, and to want is to suffer—a dialectical tension between the inner and outer, self and other. For those of us who have been fortunate enough to have acquired adequately secure attachments, and who were raised in loving homes with interpersonal warmth and availability from our parents, we can still never completely elude the fact that infantile and archaic experiences belonging to our developmental histories still unconsciously moan for fulfillment and resolve. Whether this involves having to mourn the loss of childhood wishes for love, recognition, validation, acceptance, and idealization, or having to relinquish our most cherished or unsavory desires, we are still left with the deposits and derivatives of unconscious experience—for a wish never dies.

Psychoanalysis teaches us that there is so much more to existence than this mere surface, for the ontological processes of unconscious experience largely determine the variegated paths and possibilities of lived subjective reality, including our suffering as well as actualizing our personal potential. This ultimately makes psychoanalysis an existential enterprise concerned with the ground, scope, and limits to human freedom. The unconscious abyss becomes the foundational stone from which all experience arises—from the intrapsychic to the intersubjective. We can never escape the truth of our brute facticity, the beauty and horror of the life within. As Theodor Reik (1949) reminds us, "Dere's No Hidin' Place

Down Dere." There are things that terrify us down there—in the nether regions, to which we want to flee—things that endanger our securities, that imperil our self-integrity, even to the point that anyone could conceivably take one's own life if the rupture of inner truth became too unbearable to accept. Conflictual impulses, tormenting emotions, repressed content, forbidden fantasies, traumas, deprivation, lack, desire and its objects—they always exist vis-à-vis others, including our most coveted attachments, transpiring in the depths of the underworld; for the unconscious is the house of Being.

References

Adler, G. 1985. *Borderline Psychopathology and Its Treatment*. Hillsdale, NJ: Aronson.

Ainsworth, M. D. S. 1963. The Development of Infant-Mother Interaction among the Ganda. In *Determinants of Infant Behavior*, vol. 2, ed. B. M. Foss, 57–112. London: Methuen.

———. 1967. *Infancy in Uganda: Infant Care and the Growth of Love*. Baltimore: Johns Hopkins University Press.

Ainsworth, M. D. S., M. Blehar, E. Waters, and S. Wall. 1978. *Patterns of Attachment*. Hillsdale, NJ: Erlbaum.

Alexander, F. 1948. *Fundamentals of Psychoanalysis*. New York: Norton.

Alexander, F., and T. French. 1946. *Psychoanalytic Therapy*. New York: Ronald.

Allen, J. P., S. T. Hauser, and E. Borman-Spurrell. 1996. Attachment Theory as a Framework for Understanding Sequelae of Severe Adolescent Psychopathology: An 11-Year Follow-up Study. *Journal of Consulting and Clinical Psychology* 64:254–63.

Allen, J. P., and D. Land. 1999. Attachment in Adolescence. In *Handbook of Attachment: Theory, Research, and Clinical Applications*, ed. J. Cassidy and P. R. Shaver, 319–35. New York: Guilford.

American Psychiatric Association. 2000. *Diagnostic and Statistical Manual of Mental Disorders*. 4th ed., text revision (DSM-IV-TR). Washington, DC: American Psychiatric Association.

Ammaniti, M., C. Candelori, N. Dazzi, et al. 1990. Intervista sull'attaccamento nella latenza. Unpublished manuscript.

Aristotle. 1958. *Metaphysics*. Bk. 1. In *The Pocket Aristotle*, trans. W. D. Ross. New York: Washington Square Books.

———. 1962. *Nicomachean Ethics*. Trans. M. Ostwald. Englewood Cliffs, NJ: Prentice Hall.

Armsden, G. C., and M. T. Greenberg. 1987. The Inventory of Parent and Peer Attachment: Individual Differences and Their Relationship to Psychological Well-Being in Adolescence. *Journal of Youth and Adolescence* 16:427–54.

Aron, L. 1991. The Patient's Experience of the Analyst's Subjectivity. In *Relational Psychoanalysis: The Emergence of a Tradition*, ed. S. Mitchell and L. Aron, 243–68. Hillsdale, NJ: Analytic Press, 1999.

———. 1996. *A Meeting of Minds*. Hillsdale, NJ: Analytic Press.

Atkinson, L., and K. J. Zucker, eds. 1997. *Attachment and Psychopathology*. New York: Guilford.

Bacal, H. A. 1985. Optimal Responsiveness and the Therapeutic Process. In *Progress in Self Psychology*, vol. 1, ed. A. Goldberg, 202–26. New York: Guilford.

———, ed. 1998. *How Therapists Heal Their Patients: Optimal Responsiveness*. Northvale, NJ: Aronson.

Bagby, R. M., and G. J. Taylor. 1997. Measurement and Validation of the Alexithymia Construct. In *Disorders of Affect Regulation: Alexithymia in Medical and Psychiatric Illness*, ed. G. J. Taylor, R. M. Bagby, and J. D. Parker, 46–66. Cambridge: Cambridge University Press.

Balint, M. 1950. Changing Therapeutic Aims and Techniques in Psycho-Analysis. *International Journal of Psychoanalysis* 31:117–24.

———. 1968. *The Basic Fault: Therapeutic Aspects of Regression*. New York: Brunner/Mazel.

Barnett, D., K. H. Hunt, C. M. Butler, J. W. McCaskill, M. Kaplan-Estrin, and S. Pipp-Siegel. 1999. Indices of Attachment Disorganization among Toddlers with Neurological and Non-neurological Problems. In *Attachment Disorganization*, ed. J. Solomon and C. George, 189–212. New York: Guilford.

Basch, M. F. 1980. *Doing Psychotherapy*. New York: Basic Books.

———. 1983. Empathic Understanding: A Review of the Concept and Some Theoretical Considerations. *Journal of the American Psychoanalytic Association* 31:101–25.

Beckwith, L., S. E. Cohen, and C. E. Hamilton. 1999. Maternal Sensitivity during Infancy and Subsequent Life Events Related to Attachment Representation at Early Adulthood. *Developmental Psychology* 3:693–700.

Beebe, B., J. Jafee, and F. Lachmann. 1992. A Dyadic Systems View of Communication. In *Relational Perspectives in Psychoanalysis*, ed. N. Skolnick and S. Warchaw, 61–82. Hillsdale, NJ: Analytic Press.

Beebe, B., and F. Lachmann. 2003. The Relational Turn in Psychoanalysis: A Dyadic Systems View from Infant Research. *Contemporary Psychoanalysis* 39 (3): 379–409.

Bellak, L., and P. Faithorn. 1981. *Crises and Special Problems in Psychoanalysis and Psychotherapy*. New York: Brunner/Mazel.

Belsky, J. 1999. Modern Evolutionary Theory and Patterns of Attachment. In *Handbook of Attachment: Theory, Research, and Clinical Applications*, ed. J. Cassidy and P. R. Shaver, 141–61. New York: Guilford.

Benjamin, J. 1988. *The Bonds of Love*. New York: Pantheon Books.

———. 1992. Recognition and Destruction: An Outline of Intersubjectivity. In *Relational Perspectives in Psychoanalysis*, ed. N. Skolnick and S. Warchaw, 43–60. Hillsdale, NJ: Analytic Press.

———. 1995. *Like Subjects, Love Objects: Essays on Recognition and Sexual Difference*. New Haven, CT: Yale University Press.

———. 1999. *Shadow of the Other: Intersubjectivity and Gender in Psychoanalysis*. New York: Routledge.

Beres, D., and J. A. Arlow. 1974. Fantasy and Identification in Empathy. *Psychoanalytic Quarterly* 43:26–50.

Berger, D. M. 1987. *Clinical Empathy*. Northvale, NJ: Aronson.

Binswanger, L. 1962. *Ausgewählte Werke Band 2: Grundformen und Erkenntnis menschlichen Daseins*. Ed. M. Herog and Has-Jürgen Braun. Repr., Heidelberg: Asanger, 1993.

Bion, W. R. 1954. Notes on the Theory of Schizophrenia. *International Journal of Psycho-Analysis* 35:113–18.

———. 1957. Differentiation of the Psychotic from the Non-psychotic Personalities. In *Melanie Klein Today: Developments in Theory and Practice*, vol. 1, *Mainly Theory*, ed. E. B. Spillius, 61–78. London: Routledge, 1988.

———. 1959. Attacks on Linking. In *Melanie Klein Today: Developments in Theory and Practice*, vol. 1, *Mainly Theory*, ed. E. B. Spillius, 87–101. London: Routledge, 1988.

———. 1962a. A Theory of Thinking. In *Melanie Klein Today: Developments in Theory and Practice*, vol. 1, *Mainly Theory*, ed. E. B. Spillius, 178–86. London: Routledge, 1988.

———. 1962b. *Learning from Experience*. London: Heinemann.

Blanck, G., and R. Blanck. 1974. *Ego Psychology: Theory and Practice*. New York: Columbia University Press.

Blatt, S. J., and S. A. Bers. 1993. The Sense of Self in Depression: A Psychodynamic Perspective. In *Self Representation and Emotional Disorders: Cognitive and Psychodynamic Perspectives*, ed. Z. V. Seagl and S. J. Blatt, 171–210. New York: Guilford.

Bleiberg, E. 1994. Borderline Disorders in Children and Adolescents: The Concept, the Diagnosis, and the Controversies. *Bulletin of the Menninger Clinic* 58 (2): 169–96.

Blos, P. 1962. *On Adolescence: A Psychoanalytic Interpretation*. New York: Free Press.

Bollas, C. 1987. *The Shadow of the Object: Psychoanalysis of the Unthought Known*. New York: Columbia University Press.

Borch-Jacobsen, M. 1992. *The Emotional Tie: Psychoanalysis, Mimesis, and Affect*. Trans. D. Brick. Stanford: Stanford University Press.

Bowie, M. 1991. *Lacan*. Cambridge, MA: Harvard University Press.

Bowlby, J. 1969. *Attachment and Loss*. Vol. 1, *Attachment*. Repr., New York: Basic Books, 1982.

———. 1973. *Attachment and Loss*. Vol. 2, *Separation*. New York: Basic Books.

———. 1980. *Attachment and Loss*. Vol. 3, *Loss*. New York: Basic Books.

———. 1988. *A Secure Base*. New York: Basic Books.

Bradie, M. 1986. Assessing Evolutionary Epistemology. *Biology and Philosophy* 1:401–59.

Brandchaft, B. 1994. Structures of Pathologic Accommodation and Change in Analysis. Unpublished manuscript.

Breier, A., J. R. Kelsoe, P. D. Kirwin, S. A. Beller, O. M. Wolkowitz, and D. Pickar. 1988. Early Parental Loss and Development of Adult Psychopathology. *Archives of General Psychiatry* 45:987–93.

Brenner, C. 1982. *The Mind in Conflict*. Madison, CT: International Universities Press.

———. 2002. Conflict, Compromise Formation, and Structural Theory. *Psychoanalytic Quarterly* 71 (3): 397–417.

Breuer, J., and S. Freud. 1893–1895. *Studies on Hysteria*. Reprinted in Freud 1966–1995, vol. 2.

Brisch, K. H. 2000. *Treating Attachment Disorders*. New York: Guilford.

Bromberg, P. M. 1993. Shadow and Substance: A Relational Perspective on Clinical Process. *Psychoanalytic Psychology* 10:147–68.

———. 1994. "Speak!, That I May See You": Some Reflections on Dissociation, Reality, and Psychoanalytic Listening. *Psychoanalytic Dialogues* 4:517–47.

———. 1995. Psychoanalysis, Dissociation, and Personality Organization. *Psychoanalytic Dialogues* 5:511–28.

———. 1996a. Hysteria, Dissociation, and Cure: Emmy von N Revisited. *Psychoanalytic Dialogues* 5:55–71.

———. 1996b. Standing in the Spaces: The Multiplicity of Self and the Psychoanalytic Relationship. *Contemporary Psychoanalysis* 32:509–35.

———. 2003. Something Wicked This Way Comes: Trauma, Dissociation, and Conflict; The Space Where Psychoanalysis, Cognitive Science, and Neuroscience Overlap. *Psychoanalytic Psychology* 20 (3): 558–74.

Bucci, W. 1997. *Psychoanalysis and Cognitive Science: A Multiple Code Theory*. New York: Guildford.

———. 2003. Varieties of Dissociative Experiences: A Multiple Code Account and a Discussion of Bromberg's Case of "William." *Psychoanalytic Psychology* 20 (3): 542–57.

Buirski, P., and P. Haglund. 2001. *Making Sense Together: The Intersubjective Approach to Psychotherapy*. Northvale, NJ: Jason Aronson.

Carlson, E. A., and L. A. Sroufe. 1995. Contributions of Attachment Theory to Developmental Psychopathology. In *Developmental Psychopathology*, vol. 1, ed. D. Cicchetti and D. J. Cohen, 581–617. New York: Wiley.

Carveth, D. L. 1994. Selfobject and Intersubjective Theory: A Dialectical Critique. Pt. I, Monism, Dualism, Dialectic. *Canadian Journal of Psychoanalysis/Revue Canadienne de Psychanalyse* 2 (2): 151–68.

Cashdan, S. 1988. *Object Relations Therapy*. New York: Norton.

Cassidy, J., and R. S. Marvin. 1992. Attachment in Preschool Children: Coding Guidelines. Seattle: MacArthur Working Group on Attachment. Unpublished coding manual.

Cassidy, J., R. S. Marvin, and the Working Group of the John D. and Catherine T. MacArthur Foundation on the Transition from Infancy to Early Childhood. 1987. *Attachment Organization in Three- and Four-Year-Olds: Coding Guidelines*. Unpublished manuscript, University of Virginia, Charlottesville. (Revised 1990, 1991, 1992.)

Cassidy, J., and P. R. Shaver, eds. 1999. *Handbook of Attachment: Theory, Research, and Clinical Applications*. New York: Guilford.

Cohen, M. B. 1952. Countertransference and Anxiety. *Psychiatry* 15:231–43.

Corradi, G. F. 1991. *The Mind's Affective Life: A Psychoanalytic and Philosophical Inquiry*. London: Brunner-Routledge.

Crittenden, P. M. 1992. Quality of Attachment in the Preschool Years. *Development and Psychopathology* 4:209–41.

———. 1995. *Coding Manual: Classification of Quality of Attachment for Preschool-Aged Children*. Miami, FL: Family Relations Institute.

Crowell, J. A., R. C. Fraley, and P. R. Shaver. 1999. Measurement of Individual Differences in Adolescent and Adult Attachment. In *Handbook of Attachment: Theory, Research, and Clinical Applications*, ed. J. Cassidy and P. R. Shaver, 434–65. New York: Guilford.

Davies, J. M. 1996. Dissociation, Repression and Reality Testing in the Countertransference: The Controversy over Memory and False Memory in the Psychoanalytic Treatment of Adult Survivors of Childhood Sexual Abuse. *Psychoanalytic Dialogues* 6:189–218.

Deutsch, H. 1926. Occult Processes Occurring during Psychoanalysis. In *Psychoanalysis and the Occult*, ed. G. Devereaux. Repr., New York: International Universities Press, 1970.

Dewald, P. 1964. *Psychotherapy: A Dynamic Approach*. New York: Basic Books.

Diamond, D., and J. A. Doane. 1994. Disturbed Attachment and Negative Affective Style. *British Journal of Psychiatry* 164:770–81.

Donnelly, C. 1979. The Observing Self and the Development of Cohesiveness. *British Journal of Medical Psychology* 52:277–79.

Eagle, M. 1996. Attachment Research and Psychoanalytic Theory. In *Psychoanalytic Perspectives on Developmental Psychology*, ed. J. M. Masling and R. F. Bornstein, 105–49. Washington, DC: American Psychological Association.

———. 1999. Attachment Research and Theory and Psychoanalysis. Paper presented to the Psychoanalytic Association of New York, November 15.

———. 2000. A Critical Evaluation of Current Conceptions of Transference and Countertransference. *Psychoanalytic Psychology* 17:24–37.

Eagle, M., D. L. Wolitzky, and J. C. Wakefield. 2001. The Analyst's Knowledge and Authority: A Critique of the "New View" in Psychoanalysis. *Journal of the American Psychoanalytic Association* 49:457–88.

Ehrenberg, D. 1993. *The Intimate Edge*. New York: Norton.

Ekstein, R., and J. Wallerstein. 1954. Observations on the Psychology of Borderline and Psychotic Children. *Psychoanalytic Study of the Child* 9:344–69.

Emde, R. 1988. Development Terminable and Interminable. Pt. I, Innate and Motivational Factors from Infancy. *International Journal of Psycho-Analysis* 69:23–42.

Engelman, E. 1998. *Sigmund Freud: Vienna IX. Berggasse 19*. New York: Universe Publishing.

Erikson, E. H. 1950. *Childhood and Society*. New York: Norton.

———. 1964. *Insight and Responsibility*. New York: W. W. Norton.

Erreich, A. 2003. A Modest Proposal: (Re)Defining Unconscious Fantasy. *Psychoanalytic Quarterly* 72 (3): 541–74.

Fairbairn, W. R. D. 1941. A Revised Psychopathology of the Psychoses and Psychoneuroses. *International Journal of Psycho-Analysis* 22:250–79.

———. 1943. The Repression and the Return of Bad Objects. *British Journal of Medical Psychology* 19:327–41.

———. 1952. *Psychoanalytic Studies of the Personality.* London: Tavistock, Routledge & Kegan Paul.

———. 1958. On the Nature and Aims of Psycho-Analytical Treatment. *International Journal of Psycho-Analysis* 39 (5): 374–85.

Ferenczi, S. 1933. Confusion of Tongues between Adults and the Child. In *Final Contributions to the Problem and Methods of Psycho-Analysis,* ed. M. Balint, trans. E. Mosbacher et al., 156–67. New York: Brunner/Mazel, 1980. (First published in English in 1949 in *International Journal of Psycho-Analysis* 30:225.)

———. 1950. *Further Contributions to the Theory and Technique of Psycho-Analysis.* London: Hogarth Press.

Ferenczi, S., and G. Groddeck. 1982. *Briefwechsel 1921–1933.* Ed. Pierre Sabourin et al. Repr., Frankfurt: Fischer, 1986.

Fichte, J. G. 1794. *The Science of Knowledge.* Trans. and ed. P. Heath and J. Lachs. Repr., Cambridge: Cambridge University Press, 1993.

Fink, B. 1997. *A Clinical Introduction to Lacanian Psychoanalysis.* Cambridge, MA: Harvard University Press.

Fliess, R. 1942. The Metapsychology of the Analyst. *Psychoanalytic Quarterly* 11:211–27.

Fonagy, P. 2000. Attachment and Borderline Personality Disorder. *Journal of the American Psychoanalytic Association* 48 (4): 1129–46.

———. 2001. *Attachment Theory and Psychoanalysis.* New York: Other Press.

Fonagy, P., G. Gergely, E. L. Jurist, and M. Target. 2002. *Affect Regulation, Mentalization, and the Development of the Self.* New York: Other Press.

Fonagy, P., T. Leigh, M. Steele, H. Steele, R. Kennedy, G. Mattoon, M. Target, and A. Gerber. 1996. The Relation of Attachment Status, Psychiatric Classification, and Response to Psychotherapy. *Journal of Consulting and Clinical Psychology* 64:22–31.

Fonagy, P., H. Steele, G. Morgan, M. Steele, and A. Higgitt. 1991. The Capacity for Understanding Mental States: The Reflective Self in Parent and Child and Its Significance for Security of Attachment. *Infant Mental Health Journal* 13:200–217.

Fonagy, P., M. Steele, H. Steele, T. Leigh, R. Kennedy, G. Mattoon, and M. Target. 1995. Attachment, the Reflective Self, and Borderline States: The Predictive Specificity of the Adult Attachment Interview and Pathological Emotional Development. In *Attachment Theory: Social, Developmental, and Clinical Perspectives,* ed. S. Goldberg, R. Muir, and J. Kerr, 233–78. New York: Analytic Press.

Fosshage, J. L. 1994. Toward Reconceptualizing Transference: Theoretical and Clinical Considerations. *International Journal of Psycho-Analysis* 75:265–80.

Foucault, M. 1965. *Madness and Civilization.* Trans. R. Howard. New York: Random House.

Fox, N. A., and J. A. Card. 1999. Psychophysiological Measures in the Study of Attachment. In *Handbook of Attachment: Theory, Research, and Clinical Applications,* ed. J. Cassidy and P. R. Shaver, 226–45. New York: Guilford.

Fraley, R. C., P. R. Shaver, and M. T. Greenberg. 1999. Loss and Bereavement: Attachment Theory and Recent Controversies Concerning "Grief Work" and the Nature of Detachment. In *Handbook of Attachment: Theory, Research, and Clinical Applications,* ed. J. Cassidy and P. R. Shaver, 735–59. New York: Guilford.

Freud, S. 1900. *The Interpretation of Dreams.* Reprinted in Freud 1966–1995, vols. 4–5.

———. 1905. *Jokes and Their Relation to the Unconscious.* Reprinted in Freud 1966–1995, vol. 8.

———. 1910. The Future Prospects of Psycho-Analytic Therapy. Reprinted in Freud 1966–1995, vol. 11.

———. 1912a. The Dynamics of Transference. Reprinted in Freud 1966–1995, vol. 12.

———. 1912b. Recommendations to Physicians Practicing Psycho-Analysis. Reprinted in Freud 1966–1995, vol. 12.

———. 1912c. A Note on the Unconscious in Psycho-Analysis. Reprinted in Freud 1966–1995, vol. 12.

———. 1913. On Beginning the Treatment. Reprinted in Freud 1966–1995, vol. 12.

———. 1914a. Remembering, Repeating, and Working-Through. Reprinted in Freud 1966–1995, vol. 12.

———. 1914b. On the History of the Psycho-Analytic Movement. Reprinted in Freud 1966–1995, vol. 14.

———. 1914c. On Narcissism: An Introduction. Reprinted in Freud 1966–1995, vol. 14.

———. 1915a. Observations on Transference-Love. Reprinted in Freud 1966–1995, vol. 12.

———. 1915b. Instincts and Their Vicissitudes. Reprinted in Freud 1966–1995, vol. 14.

———. 1915c. Repression. Reprinted in Freud 1966–1995, vol. 14.

———. 1915d. The Unconscious. Reprinted in Freud 1966–1995, vol. 14.

———. 1916–1917. *Introductory Lectures on Psycho-Analysis.* Reprinted in Freud 1966–1995, vols. 15–16. (Lectures delivered in 1915–1917.)

———. 1919. The "Uncanny." Reprinted in Freud 1966–1995, vol. 17.

———. 1920. *Beyond the Pleasure Principle.* Reprinted in Freud 1966–1995, vol. 18.

———. 1921. *Group Psychology and the Analysis of the Ego.* Reprinted in Freud 1966–1995, vol. 18.

———. 1923. *The Ego and the Id.* Reprinted in Freud 1966–1995, vol. 19.

———. 1925. Negation. Reprinted in Freud 1966–1995, vol. 19.

———. 1926. *Inhibitions, Symptoms and Anxiety.* Reprinted in Freud 1966–1995, vol. 20.

———. 1927. *Future of an Illusion.* Reprinted in Freud 1966–1995, vol. 21.

———. 1930. *Civilization and Its Discontents.* Reprinted in Freud 1966–1995, vol. 21.

———. 1931. Female Sexuality. Reprinted in Freud 1966–1995, vol. 21.

———. 1933a. *New Introductory Lectures on Psycho-Analysis.* Reprinted in Freud 1966–1995, vol. 22. (Lectures delivered in 1932.)

———. 1933b. Why War? (Freud's letter to Einstein.) Reprinted in Freud 1966–1995, vol. 22. (Letter written in 1932.)

———. 1937. Analysis Terminable and Interminable. Reprinted in Freud 1966–1995, vol. 23.

———. 1940. *An Outline of Psycho-Analysis.* Reprinted in Freud 1966–1995, vol. 23. (Written in 1938.)

———. 1940–1952. *Gesammelte Werke, Chronologisch Geordnet.* Ed. Anna Freud, Edward Bibring, Willi Hoffer, Ernst Kris, and Otto Isakower, in colloboration with Marie Bonaparte. 18 vols. London: Imago Publishing Co.

———. 1966–1995. *The Standard Edition of the Complete Psychological Works of Sigmund Freud.* Trans. and ed. James Strachey in collaboration with Anna Freud, assisted by Alix Strachey and Alan Tyson. 24 vols. London: Hogarth Press.

Frie, R. 1997. *Subjectivity and Intersubjectivity in Modern Philosophy and Psychoanalysis.* Lanham, MD: Rowman & Littlefield.

Fromm-Reichmann, F. 1950. *Principles of Intensive Psychotherapy.* Chicago: University of Chicago Press.

Furer, M. 1967. Some Developmental Aspects of the Superego. *International Journal of Psycho-Analysis* 48:277–80.

Gabbard, G. 1994. *Psychodynamic Psychiatry in Clinical Practice: The DSM-IV Edition.* Washington, DC: American Psychiatric Press.

Gargiulo, G. J. 2004. Aloneness in Psychoanalysis and Spirituality. *Journal for Applied Psychoanalytic Studies* 1 (1): 36–46.

Gedo, J. E. 1996. *The Languages of Psychoanalysis.* Hillsdale, NJ: Analytic Press.

Geleerd, E. R. 1958. Borderline States in Childhood and Adolescence. *Psychoanalytic Study of the Child* 13:279–95.

George, C., N. Kaplan, and M. Main. 1996. Adult Attachment Interview. 3rd revision. Unpublished manuscript, Department of Psychology, University of California, Berkeley. Originally produced in 1984 and 1985.

Gill, M. M. 1954. Psychoanalysis and Exploratory Psychotherapy. *Journal of the American Psychoanalytic Association* 2:771–97.

———. 1982. *Analysis of the Transference.* Vol. 1, *Theory and Technique.* New York: International Universities Press.

———. 1983. The Interpersonal Paradigm and the Degree of the Therapist's Involvement. *Contemporary Psychoanalysis* 19:200–237.

———. 1984. Psychoanalysis and Psychotherapy: A Revision. *International Review of Psychoanalysis* 11:161–179.

Giovacchini, P. L. 1972. The Treatment of Characterological Disorders. In *Tactics and Techniques in Psychoanalytic Therapy*, ed. P. L. Giovacchini, 236–53. New York: Science House.

Gitelson, M. 1952. The Emotional Position of the Analyst in the Psychoanalytic Situation. *International Journal of Psycho-Analysis* 33:1–10.

Goldberg, S. 1997. Attachment and Childhood Behavior Problems in Normal, At-Risk, and Clinical Samples. In *Attachment and Psychopathology*, ed. L. Atkinson and K. J. Zucker. New York: Guilford.

Goldberg, S., A. Gotowiec, and R. J. Simmons. 1995. Infant-Mother Attachment and Behavior Problems in Healthy and Chronically Ill Pre-Schoolers. *Development and Psychopathology* 7:267–82.

Goodwin, J. M., K. Cheeves, and V. Connell. 1990. Borderline and Other Severe Symptoms in Adult Survivors of Incestuous Abuse. *Psychiatric Annals* 20:22–32.

Greenberg, J., and S. Mitchell. 1983. *Theories of Object Relations*. Cambridge, MA: Harvard University Press.

Greenberg, M. T. 1999. Attachment and Psychopathology in Childhood. In *Handbook of Attachment: Theory, Research, and Clinical Applications*, ed. J. Cassidy and P. R. Shaver, 469–96. New York: Guilford.

Grinberg, L. 1962. On a Specific Aspect of Countertransference Due to the Patient's Projective Identification. In *Classics in Psychoanalytic Technique*, ed. R. Langs, 201–6. Northvale, NJ: Aronson, 1990.

Grosskurth, P. 1991. *The Secret Ring: Freud's Inner Circle and the Politics of Psychoanalysis*. Toronto: MacFarlane, Walter & Ross.

Grotstein, J. 2000. *Who Is the Dreamer Who Dreams the Dream?* Hillsdale, NJ: Analytic Press.

Grünbaum, A. 1984. *The Foundations of Psychoanalysis*. Berkeley: University of California Press.

———. 1999. The Hermeneutic versus the Scientific Conception of Psychoanalysis: An Unsuccessful Effort to Chart a *Via Media* for the Human Sciences. In *The White Book of Einstein Meets Magritte*, ed. D. Aerts et al., 219–39. Dordrecht, Netherlands: Kluwer Academic Publishers.

Gunderson, J. G. 1996. The Borderline Patient's Intolerance of Aloneness: Insecure Attachments and Therapist Availability. *American Journal of Psychiatry* 153 (6): 752–58.

Gunderson, J. G., and M. T. Singer. 1975. Defining Borderline Patients: An Overview. *American Journal of Psychiatry* 132 (1): 1–10.

Guntrip, H. 1975. My Experience of Analysis with Fairbairn and Winnicott. *International Review of Psychoanalysis* 2:145–56.

Hacking, I. 1995. *Rewriting the Soul: Multiple Personality and the Sciences of Memory*. Princeton, NJ: Princeton University Press.

Hammer, E. 1990. *Reaching the Affect: Style in the Psychodynamic Therapies*. Northvale, NJ: Aronson.

Harris, A. 1996. The Conceptual Power of Multiplicity. *Contemporary Psychoanalysis* 32:537–52.

Harris, T., G. W. Brown, and A. Bifulco. 1986. Loss of Parent in Childhood and Adult Psychiatric Disorder: The Role of Lack of Adequate Parental Care. *Psychological Medicine* 16:641–59.

Hartocollis, P. 2003. Time and the Psychoanalytic Situation. *Psychoanalytic Quarterly* 72 (4): 939–57.

Hazan, C., and P. Shaver. 1990. Love and Work: An Attachment Theoretical Perspective. *Journal of Personality and Social Psychology* 59:270–80.

Hegel, G. F. W. 1807. *Phenomenology of Spirit*. Trans. A. V. Miller. Repr., Oxford: Oxford University Press, 1977.

———. 1812. *Science of Logic*. Trans. A. V. Miller. Repr., London: George Allen & Unwin, 1969. (Revised 1831.)

———. 1817. *Philosophy of Mind*. Vol. 3 of *Encyclopaedia of the Philosophical Sciences*. Trans. William Wallace and A. V. Miller. Repr., Oxford: Clarendon Press, 1971. (Revised 1827, 1830).

———. 1978. *Hegels Philosophie des subjektiven Geistes* [Hegel's Philosophy of Subjective Spirit]. Vol. 1, *Introductions*; vol. 2, *Anthropology*; vol. 3, *Phenomenology and Psychology*. Ed. M. J. Petry. Dordrecht, Netherlands: D. Reidel Publishing Company. (Written in 1817, 1827, 1830.)

Heidegger, M. 1927. *Being and Time*. Trans. J. Macquarrie and E. Robinson. Repr., San Francisco: Harper Collins, 1962.

Heimann, P. 1949. On Counter-transference. In *Classics in Psychoanalytic Technique.*, ed. R. Langs, 139–42. Northvale, NJ: Aronson, 1990.

Heinicke, C., and I. Westheimer. 1966. *Brief Separations*. New York: International Universities Press.

Herman, J. L. 1992. *Trauma and Recovery*. New York: Basic Books.

Herman, J. L., J. C. Perry, and B. A. van der Kolk. 1989. Childhood Trauma in Borderline Personality Disorder. *American Journal of Psychiatry* 146:490–95.

Hermans, H. J. M., H. J. G. Kempen, and R. J. P. van Loon. 1992. The Dialogical Self: Beyond Individualism and Rationalism. *American Psychologist* 47:23–33.

Hesse, E. 1999. The Adult Attachment Interview: Historical and Current Perspectives. In *Handbook of Attachment: Theory, Research, and Clinical Applications*, ed. J. Cassidy and P. R. Shaver, 395–433. New York: Guilford Press.

Hesse, E., and M. Main. 2000. Disorganized Infant, Child, and Adult Attachment: Collapse in Behavioral and Attentional Strategies. *Journal of the American Psychoanalytic Association* 48 (4): 1097–1127.

Hinshelwood, R. D. 1991. *A Dictionary of Kleinian Thought*. 2nd ed. Northvale, NJ: Jason Aronson.

Hoffman, I. Z. 1983. The Patient as the Interpreter of the Analyst's Experience. In *Relational Psychoanalysis: The Emergence of a Tradition*, ed. S. Mitchell and L. Aron. Hillsdale, NJ: Analytic Press, 1999.

———. 1998. *Ritual and Spontaneity in the Psychoanalytic Process*. Hillsdale, NJ: Analytic Press.

Holmes, J. 1995. Something Is There That Does Not Love a Wall: John Bowlby, Attachment Theory and Psychoanalysis. In *Attachment Theory: Social, Developmental, and Clinical Perspectives*, ed. S. Goldberg, R. Muir, and J. Kerr, 19–45. New York: Analytic Press.

———. 1996. *Attachment, Intimacy, Autonomy*. Northvale, NJ: Aronson.

Hughes, D. A. 1997. *Facilitating Developmental Attachment*. Northvale, NJ: Aronson.

Husserl, E. 1950. *Cartesian Meditations: An Introduction to Phenomenology*. Trans. D. Cairns. Dordrecht, Netherlands: Kluwer.

Jacobson, E. 1971. *Depression*. New York: International Universities Press.

Jacobvitz, D., and N. Hazen. 1999. Developmental Pathways from Infant Disorganization to Childhood Peer Relationships. In *Attachment Disorganization*, ed. J. Solomon and C. George, 127–59. New York: Guilford.

Jaspers, K. 1974. Causal and "Meaningful" Connexions between Life History and Psychosis. In *Themes and Variations in European Psychiatry*, ed. S. Hirsch and M. Shepard. Charlottesville: University of Virginia Press.

Jones, E. 1955. *The Life and Work of Sigmund Freud*. 3 vols. New York: Basic Books.

Joseph, B. 1989. *Psychic Equilibrium and Psychic Change*. London: Tavistock Routledge.

Jung, C. G. 1946. Der Geist der Psychologie. Trans. R. F. C. Hull. In *The Basic Writings of C.G. Jung*, ed. V. S. de Laszlo, 37–104. New York: Modern Library/Random House, 1959.

Kant, I. 1781. *Critique of Pure Reason*. Trans. N. K. Smith. Repr., New York: St. Martin's Press, 1965.

Kernberg, O. 1965. Countertransference. In *Classics in Psychoanalytic Technique*, ed. R. Langs, 207–16. Northvale, NJ: Aronson, 1990.

———. 1975. *Borderline Conditions and Pathological Narcissism.* New York: Jason Aronson.

———. 1982. The Theory of Psychoanalytic Psychotherapy. In *Curative Factors in Dynamic Psychotherapy,* ed. S. Slipp, 21–43. New York: McGraw-Hill.

———. 1984. *Severe Personality Disorders.* New Haven, CT: Yale University Press.

Klein, M. 1930. The Importance of Symbol Formation in the Development of the Ego. In *Love, Guilt and Reparation and Other Works, 1921–1945.* London: Hogarth Press, 1981.

———. 1946. Notes on Some Schizoid Mechanisms. *International Journal of Psycho-Analysis* 27:99–110. Reprinted in *Envy and Gratitude and Other Works, 1946–1963,* 1–24. London: Virago Press, 1988.

———. 1952. *Developments in Psycho-Analysis.* London: Hogarth Press.

———. 1957. Envy and Gratitude. In *Envy and Gratitude and Other Works, 1946–1963,* 176–235. London: Virago Press, 1988.

Knapp, P. 1987. Some Contemporary Contributions to the Study of Emotions. *Contemporary Psychoanalysis* 36:205–48.

Kobak, R. 1999. The Emotional Dynamics of Disruptions in Attachment Relationships: Implications for Theory, Research, and Clinical Intervention. In *Handbook of Attachment: Theory, Research, and Clinical Applications,* ed. J. Cassidy and P. R. Shaver, 21–43. New York: Guilford.

Kohut, H. 1966. Forms and Transformations of Narcissism. *Journal of the American Psychoanalytic Association* 14:243–72. Reprinted in *Self Psychology and the Humanities,* ed. C. S. Strozier. New York: Norton, 1985.

———. 1971. *The Analysis of the Self.* New York: International Universities Press.

———. 1977. *The Restoration of the Self.* New York: International Universities Press.

———. 1984. *How Does Analysis Cure?* Ed. A. Goldberg and P. Stepansky. Chicago: University of Chicago Press.

Kriegman, D. 1998. Interpretation, the Unconscious, and Analytic Authority: Toward an Evolutionary, Biological Integration of the Empirical-Scientific Method with the Field-Defining, Empathic Stance. In *Empirical Perspectives on the Psychoanalytic Unconscious,* ed. R. F. Bornstein and J. M. Masling, 187–272. Washington, DC: American Psychological Association.

Kris, E. 1956. The Recovery of Childhood Memories in Psychoanalysis. *Psychoanalytic Study of the Child* 11:54–88.

Kristeva, J. 1986. Woman's Time. In *The Kristeva Reader,* ed. Tori Moi. Oxford: Blackwell.

Lacan, J. 1936. The Mirror Stage as Formative of the Function of the I. In *Écrits: A Selection,* trans. Alan Sheridan. New York: Norton, 1977.

———. 1953–1954. The See-Saw of Desire. In *The Seminar of Jacques Lacan,* bk. 1, *Freud's Papers on Technique, 1953–1954,* ed. Jacques-Alain Miller, trans. John Forrester. Cambridge: Cambridge University Press, 1988.

———. 1955–1956a. Introduction to the Question of Psychoses. In *The Seminar of Jacques Lacan,* bk 3, *The Psychoses, 1955–1956,* ed. Jacques-Alain Miller, trans. Russell Grigg. New York: Norton, 1993.

———. 1955–1956b. The Other and Psychoses. In *The Seminar of Jacques Lacan,* bk. 3, *The Psychoses, 1955–1956,* ed. Jacques-Alain Miller, trans. Russell Grigg. New York: Norton, 1993.

———. 1955–1956c. *The Seminar of Jacques Lacan,* bk. 3, *The Psychoses, 1955–1956,* ed. Jacques-Alain Miller, trans. Russell Grigg. New York: Norton, 1993.

———. 1972–1973. On the Baroque. In *The Seminar of Jacques Lacan,* bk. 20, *Encore, 1972–1973,* ed. Jacques-Alain Miller, trans. Bruce Fink. New York: Norton, 1998.

———. 1973. *Le Seminaire,* vol. 11. Paris: Seuil. Reprinted in *The Four Fundamental Concepts of Psycho-Analysis,* ed. J. A. Miller, trans. A. Sheridan. New York, Norton, 1978.

———. 1977. *Écrits: A Selection.* Trans. Alan Sheridan. New York: Norton.

Lachmann, F. M. 1996. How Many Selves Make a Person? *Contemporary Psychoanalysis* 32:595–614.

Langs, R. 1988. *A Primer of Psychotherapy.* New York: Gardner Press.

———, ed. 1990. *Classics in Psychoanalytic Technique.* Northvale, NJ: Aronson.

———. 1992. *A Clinical Workbook for Psychotherapists.* London: Karnac Books.

———. 1993. *Empowered Psychotherapy.* London: Karnac Books.

Lasky, R. 2002. Countertransference and the Analytic Instrument. *Psychoanalytic Psychology* 19 (1): 65–94.

Lear, J. 1990. *Love and Its Place in Nature: A Philosophical Interpretation of Freudian Psychoanalysis.* New York: Noonday Press.

Levin, J. D. 1992. *Theories of the Self.* Washington, DC: Hemisphere.

Levy, S. T. 1984. *Principle of Interpretation.* Northvale, NJ: Aronson.

Lichtenberg, J. 1989. *Psychoanalysis and Motivation.* Hillsdale, NJ: Analytic Press.

Lichtenberg, J. D., F. M. Lachmann, and J. Fosshage. 1992. *Self and Motivational Systems.* Hillsdale, NJ: Analytic Press.

Linehan, M. M. 1993. *Cognitive-Behavioral Treatment of Borderline Personality Disorder.* New York: Guilford Press.

Lipton, S. 1977. The Advantages of Freud's Technique as Shown in His Analysis of the Rat Man. *International Journal of Psycho-Analysis* 58:225–74.

Litman, R. 1970. Suicide as Acting Out. In *The Psychology of Suicide,* ed. E. Shneidman, N. Farberow, and R. Litman, 293–306. New York: Jason Aronson.

Litman, R., and N. Farberow. 1970. Emergency Evaluation of Suicide Potential. In *The Psychology of Suicide,* ed. E. Shneidman, N. Farberow, and R. Litman, 259–72. New York: Jason Aronson.

Little, M. 1951. Counter-transference and the Patient's Response to It. In *Classics in Psychoanalytic Technique,* ed. R. Langs, 143–51. Northvale, NJ: Aronson, 1990.

Loewenstein, R. J., and D. R. Ross. 1992. Multiple Personality and Psychoanalysis: An Introduction. *Psychoanalytic Inquiry* 12:3–48.

Lohser, B., and P. Newton. 1996. *Unorthodox Freud: A View from the Couch.* New York: Guilford.

Lyons-Ruth, K., E. Bronfman, and G. Atwood. 1999. A Relational Diathesis Model of Hostile-Helpless States of Mind: Expressions in Mother-Infant Interaction. In *Attachment Disorganization,* ed. J. Solomon and C. George, 33–70. New York: Guilford.

Lyons-Ruth, K., A. Easterbrooks, and C. Cibelli. 1997. Infant Attachment Strategies, Infant Mental Lag, and Maternal Depressive Symptoms: Predictors of Internalizing and Externalizing Problems at Age 7. *Developmental Psychology* 33:681–92.

Mahler, M. S., F. Pine, and A. Bergman. 1975. *The Psychological Birth of the Human Infant.* New York: Basic Books.

Mahler, M. S., J. R. Ross Jr., and Z. DeFries. 1949. Clinical Studies in Benign and Malignant Cases of Childhood Psychosis (Schizophrenic-like). *American Journal of Orthopsychiatry* 19:295–305.

Main, M. 1981. Avoidance in the Service of Attachment: A Working Paper. In *Behavioral Development: The Bielefield Interdisciplinary Project,* ed. K. Immelman, G. Barlow, L. Petrinovich, and M. Main, 651–93. New York: Cambridge University Press.

———. 1999. Attachment Theory: Eighteen Points with Suggestions for Future Studies. In *Handbook of Attachment Theory: Theory, Research, and Clinical Applications,* ed. J. Cassidy and P. R. Shaver, 845–88. New York: Guilford Press.

———. 2000. The Organized Categories of Infant, Child, and Adult Attachment: Flexible vs. Inflexible Attention under Attachment-Related Stress. *Journal of the American Psychoanalytic Association* 48 (4): 1055–96.

Main, M., and E. Hesse. 1990. Parents' Unresolved Traumatic Experiences Are Related to Infant Disorganized Attachment Status: Is Frightened and/or Frightening Parental Behavior the Linking Mechanism? In *Attachment in the Preschool Years,* ed. M. T. Greenberg, D. Cicchetti, and E. M. Cummings, 161–82. Chicago: University of Chicago Press.

Main, M., and J. Solomon. 1990. Procedures for Identifying Infants as Disorganized/Disoriented during the Ainsworth Strange Situation. In *Attachment in the Preschool Years,* ed. M. T. Greenberg, D. Cicchetti, and E. M. Cummings, 121–60. Chicago: University of Chicago Press.

Malan, D. 1979. *Individual Psychotherapy and the Science of Psychodynamics*. London: Butterworths.

Malin, A., and J. S. Grotstein. 1966. Projective Identification in the Therapeutic Process. *International Journal of Psycho-Analysis* 42:26–31.

Marcus, J. 1963. Borderline States in Childhood. *Journal of Child Psychoanalytic Psychiatry* 4:208–18.

Masterson, J. F. 1981. *The Narcissistic and Borderline Disorders*. New York: Brunner/Mazel.

———. 1983. *Countertransference and Psychotherapeutic Technique*. New York: Brunner/Mazel.

McClelland, J. L., D. E. Rumelhart, and the PDP Research Group, eds. 1989. *Parallel Distributed Processing: Explorations in the Microstructure of Cognition*. Vol. 2, *Psychological and Biological Models*. Cambridge, MA: MIT Press.

McLaughlin, J. T. 1981. Transference, Psychic Reality, and Countertransference. *Psychoanalytic Quarterly* 50:639–64.

Menninger, K. A. 1958. *Theory of Psychoanalytic Technique*. New York: Basic Books.

Merleau-Ponty, M. 1962. *Phenomenology of Perception*. Trans. C. Smith. New York/London: Routledge.

Miller, I. 1965. On the Return of Symptoms in the Terminal Phase of Psychoanalysis. *International Journal of Psycho-Analysis* 46:487–501.

Miller, S. J. 2003. Analytic Gains and Anxiety Tolerance: Punishment Fantasies and the Analysis of Superego Resistance Revisited. *Psychoanalytic Psychology* 20 (1): 4–17.

Mills, J. 1996. Hegel on the Unconscious Abyss: Implications for Psychoanalysis. *The Owl of Minerva* 28 (1): 59–75.

———. 1997. The False Dasein: From Heidegger to Sartre and Psychoanalysis. *Journal of Phenomenological Psychology* 28 (1): 42–65.

———. 1999. Unconscious Subjectivity. *Contemporary Psychoanalysis* 35 (2): 342–47.

———. 2000a. Hegel on Projective Identification: Implications for Klein, Bion, and Beyond. *The Psychoanalytic Review* 87 (6): 841–74.

———. 2000b. Dialectical Psychoanalysis: Toward Process Psychology. *Psychoanalysis and Contemporary Thought* 23 (3): 20–54.

———. 2002a. *The Unconscious Abyss: Hegel's Anticipation of Psychoanalysis*. Albany: SUNY Press.

———. 2002b. Five Dangers of Materialism. *Genetic, Social, and General Psychology Monographs* 128 (1): 5–27.

———. 2002c. Deciphering the "Genesis Problem": On the Dialectical Origins of Psychic Reality. *Psychoanalytic Review* 89 (6): 763–809.

———. 2003a. A Phenomenology of Becoming: Reflections on Authenticity. In *Understanding Experience: Psychotherapy and Postmodernism*, ed. R. Frie. London: Routledge.

———. 2003b. Lacan on Paranoiac Knowledge. *Psychoanalytic Psychology* 20 (1): 30–51.

———. 2004a. *Rereading Freud: Psychoanalysis through Philosophy*. Albany: SUNY Press.

———. 2004b. *Psychoanalysis at the Limit: Epistemology, Mind, and the Question of Science*. Albany: SUNY Press.

———. 2005. *Relational and Intersubjective Perspectives in Psychoanalysis: A Critique*. Lanham, MD: Rowman & Littlefield.

———. In press. A Critique of Relational Psychoanalysis. *Psychoanalytic Psychology*, forthcoming.

Mills, J., and J. A. Polanowski. 1997. *The Ontology of Prejudice*. Amsterdam: Rodopi.

Mitchell, S. A. 1988. *Relational Concepts in Psychoanalysis: An Integration*. Cambridge, MA: Harvard University Press.

———. 1991. Contemporary Perspectives on Self: Toward an Integration. *Psychoanalytic Dialogues* 1:121–47.

———. 1992. True Selves, False Selves, and the Ambiguity of Authenticity. In *Relational Perspectives in Psychoanalysis*, ed. N. J. Skolnick and S. C. Warshaw, 1–20. Hillsdale, NJ: Analytic Press.

——. 2000. *Relationality*. Hillsdale, NJ: Analytic Press.

Mitchell, S., and L. Aron, eds. 1999. *Relational Psychoanalysis: The Emergence of a Tradition*. Hillsdale, NJ: Analytic Press.

Moore, B. E., and B. D. Fine, eds. 1990. *Psychoanalytic Terms and Concepts*. New Haven: American Psychoanalytic Association/Yale University Press.

Morrison, A. 1989. *Shame: The Underside of Narcissism*. Hillsdale, NJ: Analytic Press.

Moss, E., D. St-Laurent, and S. Parent. 1999. Disorganized Attachment and Developmental Risk at School Age. In *Attachment Disorganization*, ed. J. Solomon and C. George, 160–86. New York: Guilford.

Muller, J. P., and W. J. Richardson. 1982. *Lacan and Language*. New York: International Universities Press.

Natterson, J. 1991. *Beyond Countertransference*. Northvale, NJ: Aronson.

Ogawa, J. R., L. A. Sroufe, N. S. Weinfield, E. A. Carlson, and B. Egeland. 1997. Development and the Fragmented Self: Longitudinal Study of Dissociative Symptomatology in a Nonclinical Sample. *Development and Psychopathology* 9:855–79.

Ogden, T. H. 1982. *Projective Identification and Psychotherapeutic Technique*. New York: Jason Aronson.

——. 1986. *The Matrix of the Mind*. Northvale, NJ: Aronson.

——. 1989. *The Primitive Edge of Experience*. Northvale, NJ: Aronson.

——. 1994a. *Subjects of Analysis*. Northvale, NJ: Aronson.

——. 1994b. The Analytic Third: Working with Intersubjective Clinical Facts. *International Journal of Psycho-Analysis* 75:3–19.

Ogdon, D. P. 1988. *Psychodiagnostics and Personality Assessment: A Handbook*. Los Angeles: Western Psychological Services.

Orange, D. M., R. D. Stolorow, and G. Atwood. 1997. *Working Intersubjectively: Contextualism in Psychoanalytic Practice*. Hillsdale, NJ: Analytic Press.

Owen, M. T., and M. J. Cox. 1997. Marital Conflict and the Development of Infant-Parent Attachment Relationships. *Journal of Family Psychology* 11:152–64.

Pao, P-N. 1979. *Schizophrenic Disorders: Theory and Treatment from a Psychodynamic Point of View*. New York: International Universities Press.

Pine, F. 1983. Borderline Syndromes in Childhood: A Working Nosology and Its Therapeutic Implications. In *The Borderline Child: Approaches to Etiology, Diagnosis, and Treatment*, ed. K. S. Robson, 83–100. New York: McGraw-Hill.

Pizer, S. A. 1996. The Distributed Self. Introduction to the symposium "The Multiplicity of Self and Analytic Technique." *Contemporary Psychoanalysis* 32:499–507.

——. 1998. *Building Bridges: The Negotiation of Paradox in Psychoanalysis*. Hillsdale, NJ: Analytic Press.

Plato. 1981. *Meno*. Trans. G. M. A. Grube. Indianapolis: Hackett.

Plotkin, M. B. 2001. *Freud in the Pampas*. Stanford: Stanford University Press.

Plutchik, R. 2003. *Emotions and Life: Perspectives from Psychology, Biology, and Evolution*. Washington, DC: American Psychological Association.

Posada, G., Y. Gao, F. Wu, et al. 1995. The Secure Based Phenomenon across Cultures: Children's Behavior, Mothers' Preferences and Experts' Concepts. *Monographs of the Society for Research in Child Development* 60:27–48.

Pulaski, M. A. S. 1980. *Understanding Piaget*. New York: Harper & Row.

Racker, H. 1968. *Transference and Countertransference*. Madison: International Universities Press.

——. 1972. The Meanings and Uses of Countertransference. In *Classics in Psychoanalytic Technique*, ed. R. Langs, 177–200. Northvale, NJ: Aronson, 1990.

Ragland, E. 1995. *Essays on the Pleasures of Death: From Freud to Lacan*. New York: Routledge.

Rangell, L. 1967. Psychoanalysis, Affects, and the Human Core. *Psychoanalytic Quarterly* 36:172–202.

Rapaport, D. 1953. On the Psychoanalytic Theory of Affects. *International Journal of Psycho-Analysis* 34:177–98.

Reich, A. 1951. On Counter-transference. In *Classics in Psychoanalytic Technique*, ed. R. Langs, 153–59. Northvale, NJ: Aronson, 1990.

Reik, T. 1949. *Listening with the Third Ear*. New York: Farrar, Straus.

Reisner, S. 1992. Eros Reclaimed: Recovering Freud's Relational Theory. In *Relational Perspectives in Psychoanalysis*, ed. N. J. Skolnick and S. C. Warshaw, 281–312. Hillsdale, NJ: Analytic Press.

Ricoeur, P. 1970. *Freud and Philosophy*. New Haven, CT: Yale University Press.

Roazen, P. 1995. *How Freud Worked*. Hillsdale, NJ: Aronson.

Robertson, J., and J. Bowlby. 1952. Responses of Young Children to Separation from Their Mothers. *Courrier Centre Internationale Enfance* 2:131–42.

Robertson, J., and J. Robertson. 1989. *Separation and the Very Young Child*. London: Free Association Books.

Rogers, C. 1980. *A Way of Being*. Boston: Houghton Mifflin.

Rosenfeld, S., and M. P. Sprince. 1963. An Attempt to Formulate the Meaning of the Concept of "Borderline." *Psychoanalytic Study of the Child* 18:603–35.

Rosenstein, D. S., and H. A. Horowitz. 1996. Adolescent Attachment and Psychopathology. *Journal of Consulting and Clinical Psychology* 64 (2): 244–53.

Ross, S. 1987. *Psychotherapy: The Art of Wooing Nature*. Northvale, NJ: Aronson.

Rowe, C. E., and D. S. Mac Isaac. 1991. *Empathic Attunement*. Northvale, NJ: Aronson.

Rudnytsky, P. L. 2002. *Reading Psychoanalysis*. Ithaca, NY: Cornell University Press.

Ruse, M. 1986. *Taking Darwin Seriously*. Oxford: Blackwell.

Sandler, J. 1967. Trauma, Strain, and Development. In *From Safety to Superego: Selected Papers of Joseph Sandler*, 127–41. New York: Guilford Press, 1987.

———. 1976. Countertransference and Role-Responsiveness. *International Review of Psycho-Analysis* 3:43–47.

———. 1989. *Dimensions of Psychoanalysis*. Madison, CT: International Universities Press.

Sartre, J. P. 1943. *Being and Nothingness*. Trans. H. E. Barnes. New York: Washington Square Press, 1956.

———. 1965. *The Philosophy of Jean-Paul Sartre*. Ed. R. D. Cumming. New York: Vintage Books.

Schafer, R. 1959. Generative Empathy in the Treatment Situation. *Psychoanalytic Quarterly* 28:342–73.

———. 1973. The Termination of Brief Psychoanalytic Psychotherapy. *International Journal of Psychoanalytic Psychotherapy* 2:135–48.

———. 1983. *The Analytic Attitude*. New York: Basic Books.

Schelling, F. W. J. 1800. *System des transzendentalen Idealismus* [System of Transcendental Idealism]. Trans. Peter Heath. Repr., Charlottesville: University Press of Virginia, 1978.

Schore, A. N. 2001. The Effects of Early Relational Trauma on Right Brain Development, Affect Regulation, and Infant Mental Health. *Infant Mental Health Journal* 22:201–69.

Segal, H. 1957. Notes on Symbol Formation. *International Journal of Psycho-Analysis* 38:391–97.

———. 1964. Phantasy and Other Mental Processes. *International Journal of Psycho-Analysis* 45:191–94.

Semrad, E. 1980. *Semrad: The Heart of a Therapist*. Ed. S. Rako and H. Mazer. New York: Aronson.

Shaw, D. S., E. B. Owens, J. I. Vondra, K. Keenan, and E. B. Winslow. 1996. Early Risk Factors and Pathways in the Development of Early Disruptive Behavior Problems. *Development and Psychopathology* 8:679–700.

Siegel, D. J. 1999. *The Developing Mind*. New York: Guilford.

Simpson, J. A. 1999. Attachment Theory in Modern Evolutionary Perspective. In *Handbook of Attachment: Theory, Research, and Clinical Applications*, ed. J. Cassidy and P. R. Shaver, 115–40. New York: Guilford.

Simpson, J. A., and W. S. Rholes, eds. 1998. *Attachment Theory and Close Relationships*. New York: Guilford.

Singer, E. 1965. *Key Concepts in Psychotherapy*. New York: Basic Books.

Smith, D. 1991. *Hidden Conversations: An Introduction to Communicative Psychoanalysis.* London: Routledge.

———. 1998. The Communicative Approach. In *Current Theories of Psychoanalysis*, ed. R. Langs. Madison, CT: International Universities Press.

Solomon, J., and C. George, eds. 1999. *Attachment Disorganization.* New York: Guilford.

Spangler, G., and K. E. Grossmann. 1993. Biobehavioral Organization in Securely and Insecurely Attached Infants. *Child Development* 64:1439–50.

Sperling, M. B., and W. H. Berman, eds. 1994. *Attachment in Adults.* New York: Guilford.

Spezzano, C. 1993. *Affect in Psychoanalysis: A Clinical Synthesis.* Hillsdale, NJ: Analytic Press.

———. 1997. The Emergence of an American Middle School of Psychoanalysis. *Psychoanalytic Dialogues* 7:603–18.

Spillius, E. B., ed. 1988. *Melanie Klein Today: Developments in Theory and Practice.* Vol. 1, *Mainly Theory.* London: Routledge.

Sroufe, L. A. 1983. Infant-Caregiver Attachment and Patterns of Adaptation in Preschool: The Roots of Maladaptation and Competence. In *Minnesota Symposia on Child Psychology*, vol. 16, *Development and Policy Concerning Children with Special Needs*, ed. M. Perlmutter, 41–83. Hillsdale, NJ: Erlbaum.

Sroufe, L. A., N. Fox, V. Pancak, and E. Waters. 1977. Heart Rate as a Convergent Measure in Clinical and Developmental Research. *Merrill Palmer Quarterly* 23:3–27.

Stern, D. B. 1997. *Unformulated Experience: From Dissociation to Imagination in Psychoanalysis.* Hillsdale, NJ: Analytic Press.

Stern, D. N. 1985. *The Interpersonal World of the Infant.* New York: Basic Books.

Stolorow, R. D., and G. Atwood. 1992. *Contexts of Being: The Intersubjective Foundations of Psychological Life.* Hillsdale, NJ: Analytic Press.

Stolorow, R., D. Orange, and G. Atwood. 2001. World Horizons: A Post-Cartesian Alternative to the Freudian Unconscious. *Contemporary Psychoanalysis* 37 (1): 43–61.

Strupp, H., and J. Binder. 1984. *Psychotherapy in a New Key—A Guide to Time-Limited Psychotherapy.* New York: Basic Books.

Sullivan, H. S. 1949. The Theory of Anxiety and the Nature of Psychotherapy. *Psychiatry* 12:3–12.

———. 1953. *Conceptions of Modern Psychiatry.* New York: Norton.

Szasz, T. 1960. The Myth of Mental Illness. *American Psychologist* 15:113–18.

Tansey, M. J., and W. F. Burke. 1989. *Understanding Countertransference: From Projective Identification to Empathy.* Hillsdale, NJ: Analytic Press.

Taylor, G. J., R. M. Bagby, and J. D. Parker, eds. 1997. *Disorders of Affect Regulation: Alexithymia in Medical and Psychiatric Illness.* Cambridge: Cambridge University Press.

Teicholz, J. 2003. Some Further Thoughts on Empathy and Authenticity: Their Dialectical Tension and Common Ground in the Analyst's Affect. Paper presented to the Toronto Society for Contemporary Psychoanalysis, October 1.

Teti, D. M. 1999. Conceptualizations of Disorganization in the Preschool Years: An Integration. In *Attachment Disorganization*, ed. J. Solomon and C. George, 213–42. New York: Guilford.

Thomä, H., and H. Kächele. 1987. *Psychoanalytic Practice.* Vol. 1, *Principles.* Trans. M. Wilson and D. Roseveare. New York: Springer-Verlag.

Thompson, M. G. 1996. The Rule of Neutrality. *Psychoanalysis and Contemporary Thought* 19 (1): 57–84.

———. 2004. *The Ethic of Honesty: The Fundamental Rule of Psychoanalysis.* Amsterdam: Rodopi.

Tower, L. E. 1955. Countertransference. In *Classics in Psychoanalytic Technique*, ed. R. Langs, 161–75. Northvale, NJ: Aronson, 1990.

Troisi, A., A. D'Argenio, F. Peracchio, and P. Petti. 2001. Insecure Attachment and Alexithymia in Young Men with Mood Symptoms. *Journal of Nervous and Mental Disease* 189 (5): 311–16.

Tyson, P. 2000. Psychoanalysis, Development, and the Life Cycle. *Journal of the American Psychoanalytic Association* 48 (4): 1045–49.

Urban, W. H. 1963. *The Draw-a-Person Catalogue for Interpretive Analysis.* Los Angeles: Western Psychological Services.

van Ijzendoorn, M. H., and A. Sagi. 1999. Cross-Cultural Patterns of Attachment: Universal and Contextual Dimensions. In *Handbook of Attachment: Theory, Research, and Clinical Applications,* ed. J. Cassidy and P. R. Shaver, 713–34. New York: Guilford.

Waelder, R. 1936. The Principle of Multiple Function: Observations on Over Determination. *Psychoanalytic Quarterly* 5:45–62.

Waiess, E. A. 2000. The Countertransference Reaction of Protectiveness in Working with Homosexual Patients. *Psychoanalytic Psychology* 17 (2): 366–70.

Warren, S. L., L. Huston, B. Egeland, and L. A. Sroufe. 1997. Child and Adolescent Anxiety Disorders and Early Attachment. *Journal of the American Academy of Child and Adolescent Psychiatry* 36:637–44.

Waters, E. 1995. The Attachment Q-Set. *Monographs of the Society for Research in Child Development* 60:247–54.

Waters, E., and K. E. Deane. 1985. Defining and Assessing Individual Differences in Attachment Relationships: Q-Methodology and Organization of Behavior in Infancy and Early Childhood. *Monographs of the Society for Research in Child Development* 50:41–65.

Waters, E., C. E. Hamilton, and N. S. Weinfield. 2000. The Stability of Attachment Security from Infancy to Adolescence: General Introduction. *Child Development* 71:678–83.

Weil, A. P. 1953. Certain Severe Disturbances of Ego Development in Childhood. *Psychoanalytic Study of the Child* 8:271–87.

Weinfield, N. S., L. A. Sroufe, B. Egeland, and A. E. Carlson. 1999. The Nature of Individual Differences in Infant-Caregiver Attachment. In *Handbook of Attachment: Theory, Research, and Clinical Applications,* ed. J. Cassidy and P. R. Shaver, 68–88. New York: Guilford.

Whitehead, A. N. 1927. *Symbolism.* New York: Free Press.

Wilson, T. D. 2002. *Strangers to Ourselves: Discovering the Adaptive Unconscious.* Cambridge, MA: Harvard University Press.

Winnicott, D. W. 1949. Hate in the Counter-transference. *International Journal of Psycho-Analysis* 30:69–74.

———. 1958. *D. W. Winnicott: Collected Papers.* London: Tavistock.

———. 1960. Ego Distortions in Terms of True and False Self. In *The Maturational Processes and the Facilitating Environment.* New York: International Universities Press, 1965.

———. 1965. *The Maturational Processes and the Facilitating Environment.* London: Hogarth Press.

———. 1971. *Playing and Reality.* London: Tavistock.

Wuketits, F. M. 1990. *Evolutionary Epistemology.* New York: SUNY Press.

Zetzel, E. R. 1958. The Therapeutic Alliance. In *The Capacity for Emotional Growth,* 182–96. New York: International Universities Press, 1970.

Žižek, S. 1992. *Enjoy Your Symptoms! Jacques Lacan in Hollywood and Out.* New York: Routledge.

Index

About the Author

Jon Mills, Psy.D., Ph.D., ABPP, is a psychologist, philosopher, and psychoanalyst in private practice in Ajax, Ontario, Canada. He is a diplomate in psychoanalysis and clinical psychology with the American Board of Professional Psychology and is currently president of the Section on Psychoanalysis of the Canadian Psychological Association. He received his Ph.D. in philosophy from Vanderbilt University, his Psy.D. in clinical psychology from the Illinois School of Professional Psychology, Chicago, was a Fulbright scholar at the University of Toronto and York University, and is a member of the Toronto Society for Contemporary Psychoanalysis. He is also editor of an international book series, Contemporary Psychoanalytic Studies, and is on the editorial board of *Psychoanalytic Psychology*. He is the author and/or editor of eight other books, including *The Unconscious Abyss: Hegel's Anticipation of Psychoanalysis* and an existential novel, *When God Wept*.